THE
APOCRYPHA

THE APOCRYPHAL/DEUTEROCANONICAL BOOKS
OF THE OLD TESTAMENT

NEW REVISED STANDARD VERSION
UPDATED EDITION

CAMBRIDGE
UNIVERSITY PRESS

University Printing House, Cambridge CB2 8BS, United Kingdom

Cambridge University Press is part of the University of Cambridge.

It furthers the University's mission by disseminating knowledge in the pursuit of education, learning and research at the highest international levels of excellence.

www.cambridge.org

This edition first published 2023

Typeset by Scribe Inc. in 9.5/10.5pt Minion Pro

Scripture text proofed by Peachtree Publishing Services (www.PeachtreeEditorial.com)

ISBN 978-1-009-370325 Hardback

Printed and bound in Italy by L.E.G.O. S.p.A., Vicenza

TABLE OF CONTENTS

THE NAMES AND ORDER OF THE APOCRYPHAL/DEUTEROCANONICAL BOOKS

*The Apocryphal/Deuterocanonical Books are listed here
in four groupings, as follows:*

TO THE READER

From the National Council of the Churches of Christ in the USA

Motivated by love and respect for Scripture, the National Council of the Churches of Christ in the USA (NCC) hopes that you will find this *New Revised Standard Version Updated Edition* (*NRSVue*) suitable to inspire, inform, and guide daily living. The goal of the *NRSVue* is to offer a readable and accurate version of the Holy Bible to the global English-speaking community for public worship and personal study, for scholarship and study in classrooms, and for informing faith and action in response to God.

Together with religious leaders from diverse communities of faith, we join in the conviction that the Scriptures offer good news of God's love—wisdom to guide, hope to sustain, truth to empower, forgiveness to change, and peace to bless all of creation.

The *NRSVue* extends the *New Revised Standard Version's* (*NRSV*) purpose to deliver an accurate, readable, up-to-date, and inclusive version of the Bible. It also continues the work of offering a version as free as possible from the gender bias inherent in the English language, which can obscure earlier oral and written renditions. The *NRSVue*, like the *NRSV*, follows "in the tradition of the *King James Bible*, [introducing] such changes as are warranted on the basis of accuracy, clarity, euphony, and current English usage, . . . as literal as possible, as free as necessary" (*NRSV's* preface "To the Reader"). As also stated in the *NRSV* preface, the Bible's message "must not be disguised in phrases that are no longer clear or hidden under words that have changed or lost their meaning; it must be presented in language that is direct and plain and meaningful to people today."

Why an Update?

The *NRSV* has been called the most accurate of English-language translations, based on the available manuscript evidence, textual analysis, and philological understanding. In the more than thirty years since its first publication, hundreds of ancient manuscripts have been studied in exacting detail. The *NRSVue* is informed by the results of this research. Laboring through this material has deepened scholarly insight into Jewish and Christian sacred texts and advanced understanding of ancient languages. With new textual evidence, historical insights, and philological understandings (which include exploring the meanings of ancient texts in light of the cultures that produced them), the *NRSVue* brings greater precision in interpreting Scripture today. The goal of these practices has been to translate the ancient texts as accurately as possible while reflecting the cultural differences across time and conditions. Such a translation approach permitted the Editorial Committee to present the text as literally as possible and as freely as necessary.

The Update Process

The current updating process involves scores of scholars and leaders from multiple faith communities, inclusive of gender and ethnic identities, with the unwavering goal to render an accurate version of original source texts into the most current understandings of contemporary language and culture.

It is for this reason, too, that the NCC commissioned the Society of Biblical Literature (SBL), the leading international association of biblical scholars, to review and update the *NRSV*. The SBL's mandate and process were single-mindedly intended to ensure the currency and integrity of the *NRSVue* as the most up-to-date and reliable Bible for use and study in English-language religious communities and educational institutions.

A Final Word

Since its beginnings in the early 1950s, the NCC has supported the work of scholars who dedicate their lives to the study of the Hebrew and Christian Scriptures. Likewise, the NCC's steadfast aim has been to encourage readers to study the Scriptures so they will be inspired and informed in their faithful action to love God with their hearts, souls, minds, and strength and to love each other as God loves.

The communions of the National Council of the Churches of Christ in the USA have undertaken this work as a sacred trust.

PREFACE TO THE
APOCRYPHAL/DEUTEROCANONICAL BOOKS
OF THE *NRSV UPDATED EDITION*

From the Society of Biblical Literature

PURPOSE OF THE REVISION

First published in 1611, the *King James Version* slowly but steadily attained a well-deserved stature as the English language's "Authorized Version" of the Scriptures. At the same time, the scholarly foundation that produced the *King James Version* shifted as new manuscripts came to light and philological understandings improved. As a result of these scholarly advances, the *Revised Standard Version* was authorized to improve the translation, based on more evidence of the original texts and early translations of the Bible, the meanings of its original languages (Hebrew, Aramaic, and Greek, as well as ancient translations into Arabic, Armenian, Coptic, Ethiopic, Georgian Greek, Syriac, and Latin), and changes to the English language itself. The forty years between the *Revised Standard Version* and the *New Revised Standard Version* likewise witnessed many developments in biblical scholarship, textual criticism, linguistics, and philology. The same has occurred over the last thirty years, including the publication of all the biblical texts discovered near the Dead Sea, and these developments warrant this update. As with its predecessors, the *NRSVue* can claim a well-known line from the 1611 preface to the *King James Version*: "We never thought from the beginning that we should need to make a new translation . . . but to make a good one better."

The National Council of Churches, which holds the copyright of the *New Revised Standard Version*, commissioned the Society of Biblical Literature to direct the *NRSVue* revision project thirty years after its original publication. The editors of this edition encourage readers to read the excellent prefaces to both the *Revised Standard Version* (1952) and the *New Revised Standard Version* (1989); some elements of the latter have been incorporated herein. This preface also outlines the process of the update and the mandate under which it was conducted.

PROCESS OF THE REVISION

The review managed by the Society of Biblical Literature included seven general editors and fifty-six book editors, with several general editors serving also as book editors. The general editors were divided into three teams: Old Testament (also known as the Hebrew Scriptures), Apocrypha (also known as the Deuterocanon), and the New Testament. In addition to the seven general editors, the National Council of Churches appointed two members of its Bible Translation and Utilization Advisory Committee to serve as liaisons to the committee of general editors appointed by the Society of Biblical Literature. Three members of the Society's staff participated in and managed the project.

Beginning in 2017, each book of the Bible was assigned to one or more book editors. Over the course of two years (2018–2019), the book editors submitted their proposed updates to the general editors. Each of the three teams of general editors met at least once a month for two years (2019–2020) to review and discuss the proposed updates submitted by the book editors. The accepted updates were submitted to the National Council of Churches in 2021 for its final review and approval of what is now the *NRSVue*.

The *NRSVue* presents approximately 12,000 substantive edits and 20,000 total changes, which include alterations in grammar and punctuation.

Like its predecessors, this *NRSVue* has relied on the best results of modern discovery and scholarship. The mandate primarily focused on two types of revisions: text-critical and philological. The

New Revised Standard Version Updated Edition (*NRSVue*) is not a new translation. While some stylistic improvements have been made, these were reserved for instances where the translation was awkward, unclear, or inaccurate. Other changes involve matters of consistency, grammar and punctuation, and general improvements that render the translation and notes more consistent and uniform.

TEXT-CRITICAL REVISIONS

The role of text criticism in Bible translation is to establish a base text from which to translate, a text reconstructed from the earliest versions in the original languages (Hebrew, Aramaic, and Greek), as well as in ancient translations of the books of the Old Testament, Apocrypha, and New Testament. Translators rely on scholarly critical editions of the Bible for their work. A typical text-critical resource establishes a text based on scholarly judgment of the preferred reading among the readings available, with important alternative readings provided in a detailed apparatus. Scholars follow well-established rules in their effort to determine one preferred or superior reading from among others, though this remains both art and science.

The goal of the text-critical review was to evaluate whether or not to modify the textual basis for the revision. To this end, the text underlying the *New Revised Standard Version* was examined in the light of all available evidence, making use of new data, perspectives, and scholarly resources. The review occasionally resulted in a change to the translation itself or to the textual notes that have been an integral feature of the *New Revised Standard Version*.

The *Revised Standard Version of the Bible* containing both the Old and New Testaments was published in 1952; a translation of the Apocrypha in the Old Testament followed in 1957. In 1977, this collection was issued in an expanded edition containing three additional texts considered canonical by Eastern Orthodox communions (3 and 4 Maccabees and Psalm 151). Thereafter the *Revised Standard Version* gained the distinction of being officially authorized for use by all major Christian churches: Protestant, Anglican, Roman Catholic, and Eastern Orthodox. The translation of the Apocrypha, therefore, is not peripheral but of equal import as the translation of the Old Testament and the New Testament. Indeed, some of the deuterocanonical books were originally written in Hebrew or Aramaic and were considered sacred texts by the early Jewish communities who first transmitted them and the later Christians who preserved them.

The *NRSVue* includes a considerable number of changes to the Apocrypha. Because there is no single critical edition for the books in this collection, the team made use of a number of texts. For most books the basic Greek text used was the edition of the Septuagint prepared by Alfred Rahlfs (Stuttgart, 1935). For several books the more recent volumes of the Göttingen Septuagint project were utilized. *A New English Translation of the Septuagint* (Oxford, 2009) also served as a resource to compare translations and evaluate critical texts for individual books.

For the book of Tobit, the *New Revised Standard Version* relied on the shorter Greek manuscript tradition; the *NRSVue* translated the longer Greek tradition (preserved in Codex Sinaiticus), while taking the Qumran manuscripts and other ancient witnesses into account. For the three Additions to Daniel, the Committee continued to use the Greek version attributed to Theodotion. Ecclesiasticus has an especially challenging textual history. The team generally followed the Greek text of Joseph Ziegler (and the versification in the Prologue), while giving particular consideration to the earliest Hebrew manuscripts from the Dead Sea region, with occasional recourse to the Syriac. The versification of 1 Esdras now follows Robert Hanhart's edition (Göttingen, 1974), which also brings the book into conformity with its usage in the Eastern Orthodox tradition. The basic text adopted in rendering 2 Esdras is the Latin version given in Robert Weber's *Biblia Sacra* (Stuttgart, 1971), with consultation of the Latin texts of R. L. Bensly (1895) and Bruno Violet (1910), as well as by taking into account the Syriac, Ethiopic, Arabic, Armenian, and Georgian versions. Since the Additions to the Book of Esther are disjointed and unintelligible as they stand in most editions of the Apocrypha, we provide them with their original context by translating the entirety of Greek Esther from Hanhart's edition (Göttingen, 1983). The versification of the Letter of Jeremiah now conforms to Ziegler's edition (Göttingen, 1957, 1976). The Septuagint's Psalm 151 is an abbreviated version of the Hebrew composition found in the 11QPsalms[a] scroll. While the Greek remains the basis for the translation, the team also consulted that scroll.

Textual criticism continues to evolve. Not only have additional manuscripts become available, but some of the goals and methodology have changed over the last several decades. In the *NRSVue*, care was taken not to push too far ahead of the existing critical editions or to turn the translation itself and its notes into a critical edition. Nevertheless, a careful reader will notice in general a more generous use of the notes for alternative readings. The editors hope that this work will serve translators in the future.

PHILOLOGICAL REVISIONS

Deciphering the meanings of the Bible's ancient languages involves a host of efforts: the study of the languages themselves, the comparative study of cognate languages from the ancient Near East and the Greco-Roman world, the disciplines of philology and linguistics, and the historical study of the social, cultural, and economic contexts in which the Bible was written. The *NRSVue* took special care not to use terms in ways that are historically or theologically anachronistic, though, as in every translation, anachronism is unavoidable.

The *NRSVue* continues and improves the effort to eliminate masculine-oriented language when it can be done without altering passages that reflect the historical situation of ancient patriarchal culture. This goal is to provide a historically accurate and acceptable rendering without using contrived English. Only occasionally has the pronoun "he" or "him" or other gendered language been retained in passages where the reference may have been to a woman as well as to a man, for example, in several legal texts in Leviticus and Deuteronomy. In such instances of formal, legal language, the options of either putting the passage in the plural or of introducing additional nouns to avoid masculine pronouns in English could easily obscure the historical background to and literary character of the original. In the vast majority of cases, however, inclusiveness has been attained by simple rephrasing or by introducing plural forms when this does not distort meaning.

THE FUTURE OF REVISIONS AND A VIRTUE OF THIS TRANSLATION

The *NRSVue* represents a base text that was produced from a variety of textual witnesses, a text that was not used by any one community but combines readings from several of them. This, however, may well be a model and a reminder to us today: it results in a text that can be used across both Jewish and Christian traditions and in all their diverse communities. Indeed, this model stretches back to 1611, the origin of this edition. The translators of the *King James Version* took into account all of the preceding English versions and owed something to each of them. In 1977 the *Revised Standard Version* incorporated books that permitted it to become officially authorized by all the major Christian churches, and the use of the Masoretic Text of the Hebrew Scriptures reflects the use of that text in synagogues. Beginning with the Revised Standard Version Bible Committee, the translation teams became both ecumenical and interfaith. The process that produced this translation of the Bible represents an ideal and a virtue. It is a Bible produced by consensus that can be used among and across pluralistic communities in contexts both academic and religious.

In the future, new text-critical resources will become available, the methodology and goals of textual criticism may change, translation theory may evolve, and the need to reflect contemporary language will be constant. In short, efforts to update the translation of the Bible will continue. As they do, it is the hope of the Society of Biblical Literature that this translation will continue to be produced by a diverse team and for diverse readers.

THE
APOCRYPHA

**THE APOCRYPHAL/DEUTEROCANONICAL BOOKS
OF THE OLD TESTAMENT**

**NEW REVISED STANDARD VERSION
UPDATED EDITION**

TOBIT

1 The book of the words of Tobit son of Tobiel son of Hananiel son of Aduel son of Gabael son of Raphael son of Raguel of the descendants*ᵃ* of Asiel, of the tribe of Naphtali, ²who in the days of King Shalmaneser*ᵇ* of the Assyrians was taken into captivity from Thisbe, which is to the south of Kedesh Naphtali in Upper Galilee, above Asher toward the west, and north of Phogor.

Tobit's Youth and Virtuous Life

3 I, Tobit, walked in the ways of truth and righteousness all the days of my life. I performed many acts of charity for my kindred and my nation who had gone with me in exile to Nineveh in the land of the Assyrians. ⁴When I was in my own country, in the land of Israel, while I was still a young man, the whole tribe of my ancestor Naphtali deserted the house of David and Jerusalem. This city had been chosen from among all the tribes of Israel, where all the tribes of Israel should offer sacrifice and where the temple, the dwelling of God, had been consecrated and established for all generations forever.

5 All my kindred and my ancestral house of Naphtali sacrificed upon all the mountains of Galilee to the calf that King Jeroboam of Israel had erected in Dan and on all the mountains of Galilee. ⁶But I alone went often to Jerusalem for the festivals, as it is prescribed for all Israel by an everlasting decree. I would hurry off to Jerusalem with the first fruits of the crops and the firstlings of the flock, the tithes of the cattle, and the first shearings of the sheep. ⁷I would give these to the priests, the sons of Aaron, at the altar, likewise the tenth of the grain, wine, olive oil, pomegranates, figs, and the rest of the fruits to the sons of Levi who

ministered at Jerusalem. Also every six years I would save up a second tenth in money and go and distribute it each year in Jerusalem, ⁸giving it to the orphans and widows and to the converts who had attached themselves to the Israelites. In the third year I would bring it and give it to them, and we would eat it according to the ordinance decreed concerning it in the law of Moses and according to the instructions of Deborah, the mother of my father Tobiel,*ᶜ* for my father had died and left me an orphan. ⁹When I became a man I married a woman,*ᵈ* a member of our own family, and by her I became the father of a son whom I named Tobias.

Taken Captive to Nineveh

10 After I was carried away captive to Assyria and came as a captive to Nineveh, everyone of my kindred and my people ate the food of the nations, ¹¹but I kept myself from eating the food of the nations. ¹²Because I was mindful of God with all my heart, ¹³the Most High gave me favor and good standing with Shalmaneser,*ᵉ* and I used to buy everything he needed. ¹⁴Until his death I used to go into Media to buy for him there, and I left in trust bags holding ten talents of silver with Gabael, the brother of Gabri, in the country of Media. ¹⁵But when Shalmaneser*ᶠ* died and his son Sennacherib reigned in his place, Median roads became lawless, and I could no longer travel to Media.

Courage in Burying the Dead

16 In the days of Shalmaneser*ᵍ* I performed many acts of charity to my kindred, those of my

---

a 1.1 Other ancient authorities lack *of Raphael son of Raguel of the descendants*
b 1.2 OL: Gk *Enemessaros*
c 1.8 OL: Gk *Hananiel*
d 1.9 Other ancient authorities add *Anna*
e 1.13 OL: Gk *Enemessaros*
f 1.15 OL: Gk *Enemessaros*
g 1.16 OL: Gk *Enemessaros*

people. [17] I would give my food to the hungry and my clothing to the naked, and if I saw the dead body of any of my nation thrown out behind the wall of Nineveh, I would bury it. [18] I also buried any whom King Sennacherib put to death when he came fleeing from Judea in those days of judgment that the King of heaven executed upon him because of his blasphemies. For in his anger he put to death many Israelites, but I would secretly remove the bodies and bury them. So when Sennacherib looked for them he could not find them. [19] Then one of the Ninevites went and informed the king about me, that I was burying them, so I hid myself. But when I realized that the king knew about me and that I was being searched for to be put to death, I was afraid and ran away. [20] Then all my property was confiscated; nothing was left to me that was not taken into the royal treasury except my wife Anna and my son Tobias.

[21] But not forty days passed before two of Sennacherib's[h] sons killed him, and when they fled to the mountains of Ararat, his son Esar-haddon[i] reigned after him. He appointed Ahikar, the son of my brother Hanael,[j] over all the accounts of his kingdom, and he had authority over the entire administration. [22] Ahikar interceded for me, and I returned to Nineveh. Now Ahikar was chief cupbearer, keeper of the signet, and in charge of administration and accounts under King Sennacherib of Assyria, so Esar-haddon[k] appointed him as second-in-command. He was my nephew[l] and so a close relative.

2 In the days of[m] Esar-haddon[n] I returned home, and my wife Anna and my son Tobias were restored to me. At our Festival of Pentecost, which is the sacred Festival of Weeks, a good dinner was prepared for me, and I reclined to eat. [2] When the table had been set for me and an abundance of food placed before me, I said to my son Tobias, "Go, my son, and bring whatever poor person you may find of our kindred among the exiles in Nineveh who is wholeheartedly mindful of God,[o] and he shall eat together with me. I will wait for you, my son, until you come back." [3] So Tobias went to look for some poor person of our kindred. When he had returned he said, "Father!" And I replied, "Here I am, my son." Then he went on to say, "Look, father, one of our own nation has been killed and thrown into the marketplace, and now he lies there strangled." [4] Then I sprang up, left the dinner before even tasting it, and removed him from the square and laid him in one of the outbuildings at my home until sunset, when I might bury him. [5] When I returned, I washed myself and ate my food in sorrow. [6] Then I remembered the prophecy of Amos, how he said against Bethel,

"Your festivals shall be turned into
      mourning
   and all your songs[p] into lamentation."
And I wept.

Tobit Becomes Blind

[7] When the sun had set, I went and dug a grave and buried him. [8] And my neighbors laughed and said, "Is he still not afraid? He has already been hunted down to be put to death for doing this, and he ran away, yet here he is again burying the dead!" [9] That same night I washed myself and went into my courtyard and lay down by the wall of the courtyard; my face was uncovered because of the heat. [10] I did not know that there were sparrows on the wall; their fresh droppings fell into my eyes and produced white films. I went to physicians to be healed, but the more they treated me with ointments, the more my vision was obscured by the white films, until I became completely blind. For four years I remained unable to see. All my kindred were sorry for me, and Ahikar took care of me for two years before he went to Elymais.

Tobit's Wife Earns Their Livelihood

[11] At that time my wife Anna earned money at women's work. [12] She used to send what she made to the owners, and they would pay wages to her. One day, the seventh of Dystrus, when she cut off a piece she had woven and sent it to the owners, they paid her full wages and also gave her a young goat for a meal. [13] When it came toward me, the goat began to bleat, so I called her and said, "Where did you get this goat? It is surely not stolen, is it? Return it to the owners, for we have no right to eat anything stolen." [14] But she said to me, "It was given to

---

h 1.21 Gk *his*
i 1.21 Gk *Sacherdonos*
j 1.21 Other authorities read *Hananael*
k 1.22 Gk *Sacherdonos*
l 1.22 Q ms adds *a member of my father's household*
m 2.1 Q ms: S *Then under*
n 2.1 Gk *Sacherdonos*
o 2.2 OL: S lacks *of God*

---

p 2.6 OL mss: S reads *ways*

me as a gift in addition to my wages." But I did not believe her and told her to return it to the owners. I became flushed with anger against her over this. Then she replied to me, "Where are your acts of charity? Where are your righteous deeds? These things are known about you!"^q

Tobit's Prayer

3 Then with much grief and anguish of heart I wept, and with groaning I began to pray:

2 "You are righteous, O Lord,
and all your deeds are just;
all your ways are mercy and truth;
you judge the world.^r

3 And now, O Lord, may you be mindful
of me
and look favorably upon me.
Do not punish me for my sins
or for my unwitting offenses
or for those of my ancestors.
They sinned against you

4 and disobeyed your commandments.
So you gave us over to plunder, exile, and
death,
to become the talk, the byword, and an
object of reproach
among all the nations among whom you
have dispersed us.

5 And now your many judgments are true
in dealing with me according to my
sins.
For we have not kept your commandments
and have not walked in accordance with
truth before you.

6 So now deal with me as you will;
command my spirit to be taken from me,
so that I may be released from the face of
the earth and become dust.
For it is better for me to die than to live,
because I have had to listen to undeserved
insults,
and great is the sorrow that attends me.
Command, O Lord, that I be released from
this distress;
release me to go to the place of eternity,
and do not, O Lord, turn your face away
from me.
For it is better for me to die
than to see so much distress in my life
and better not to listen to insults."

Sarah Falsely Accused

7 On the same day, at Ecbatana in Media, it also happened that Sarah, the daughter of Raguel, was reproached by one of her father's female slaves. 8 For she had been married to seven husbands, and the wicked demon Asmodeus had killed each of them before they had been with her as is customary for wives. So the female slave said to her, "You are the one who kills^s your husbands! See, you have already been married to seven husbands and have not borne the name of^t a single one of them. 9 Why do you beat us? Because your husbands are dead? Go with them! May we never see a son or daughter of yours!"

Sarah's Prayer for Death

10 Overcome with emotion at that time, she wept and went up to her father's upper room, intending to hang herself. But she thought it over and said, "Let no one ever reproach my father, saying to him, 'You had only one beloved daughter, and she hanged herself out of distress!'^u I would bring my father in his old age down in sorrow to Hades. It is better for me not to hang myself but to beg the Lord that I may die, so that I will not have to listen to these reproaches for the rest of my life." 11 At that same time, with hands outstretched toward the window, she prayed and said,

"Blessed are you, merciful God!
Blessed is your name^v forever;
let all your works bless you forever.

12 And now,^w my face is toward you,
and I have raised my eyes.

13 Command that I be released from the earth
and not listen to such reproaches any more.

14 You know, O Master, that I am innocent^x
of any defilement with a man

15 and that I have not disgraced my name
or the name of my father in the land of
my exile.
I am my father's only child;
he has no other child to be his heir,
and he has no close relative or other kindred
for whom I should keep myself as wife.

---

q **2.14** Or *to you*; Gk *with you*
r **3.2** Other ancient authorities read *you render true and righteous judgment forever*
s **3.8** Other ancient authorities read *strangles*
t **3.8** Other ancient authorities read *have had no benefit from*
u **3.10** Other ancient authorities lack *out of distress*
v **3.11** Other ancient authorities add *holy and honorable*
w **3.12** Other ancient authorities add *Lord*
x **3.14** Q ms adds *in my bones*

Already seven husbands of mine have died.
    Why should I still live?
But if it is not pleasing to you, O Lord, to
    take my life,
    hear me in my disgrace."

An Answer to Prayer

16 At that very moment, the prayers of both of them were heard in the glorious presence of God. 17 So Raphael was sent to heal both of them: Tobit by removing the white films from his eyes, so that he might see God's light with his eyes,[y] and Sarah, daughter of Raguel, by giving her in marriage to Tobias son of Tobit, and by setting her free from the wicked demon Asmodeus. For Tobias was entitled to have her before all others who had desired to marry her. At the same time that Tobit returned from the courtyard into his house, Sarah daughter of Raguel came down from her upper room.

Tobit Gives Instructions to His Son

4 That same day Tobit remembered the money that he had left in trust with Gabael at Rages in Media, 2 and he said to himself, "Now that I have asked for death, why do I not call my son Tobias and explain to him about this money before I die?" 3 Then he called his son Tobias, and when he came to him he said, "Give[z] me a proper burial. Honor your mother and do not abandon her all the days of her life. Do whatever pleases her, and do nothing that makes her unhappy. 4 Remember her, my son, because she faced many dangers for you[a] while you were in her womb. And when she dies, bury her beside me in the same grave.

5 "Be mindful of the Lord all your days, my son, and refuse to sin or to transgress his commandments. Do what is right all the days of your life, and do not walk in the ways of wrongdoing, 6 for those who act honestly will prosper in all their activities. To all those who practice righteousness,[b] 7 give alms according to your circumstances, my son, and do not turn your face away from anyone who is poor. Then the face of God will not be turned away from you. 8 Act according to what you have, my son. If you have much, give alms from it; if you have little, give alms in accordance with what you have. Do not be afraid, my son, to give alms. 9 You will be laying up a good treasure for yourself against a day of need. 10 For almsgiving delivers from death and keeps you from going into the darkness. 11 Indeed, almsgiving, for all who practice it, is an excellent offering in the presence of the Most High.

12 "Beware, my son, of every kind of sexual immorality. First of all, marry a woman from among the descendants of your ancestors; do not marry a foreign woman, who is not of your father's tribe, for we are the descendants of prophets and true-born sons of prophets. The first prophet was[c] Abraham, then Isaac and Jacob, our ancestors of old. Remember, my son, that these all took wives from among their kindred. They were blessed in their children, and their posterity will inherit the land. 13 So now, my son, love your kindred, and in your heart do not be so arrogant against the daughters of the members of your people as to refuse to take one of them as a wife. For in arrogance there is ruin and great confusion, and in idleness there is loss and dire poverty, because idleness is the mother of famine.

14 "Do not keep over until the next day the wages of those who work for you, but pay them their wages the same day, and let not the pay of those among you be delayed overnight. Your pay will not be kept over if you serve God faithfully. Watch yourself, my son, in everything you do, and discipline yourself in all your conduct. 15 And what you hate, do not do to anyone. May[d] no evil go with you on any of your way. 16 Give some of your food to the hungry and some of your clothing to the naked. Give all your surplus as alms, my son, and do not let your eye begrudge your giving of alms. 17 Pour out your food and your wine on the grave of the righteous, but do not give it to sinners. 18 Seek advice from every wise person, and do not be disdainful, since any counsel is useful. 19 At all times bless God and ask him that your ways may be made straight and that all your paths and plans may prosper. For no nation has good counsel, but the Lord himself gives it. Whom he wants to, he exalts, and whom he wants to, he casts down to Hades below. So now, my son,

---

y 3.17 Other ancient authorities lack *with his eyes*
z 4.3 Other ancient authorities read *My son, when I die, give*
a 4.4 Q ms adds *and carried you*
b 4.6 S lacks 4.6–19, reading *To those who practice righteousness* [19]*the Lord will give good counsel*; 4.7–18 supplied here from another Gk ms

---

c 4.12 Other ancient authorities add *Noah, then*
d 4.15 Other ancient authorities read *Do not drink wine to excess, and may*

remember these commandments of mine, and do not let them be erased from your heart.

Money Left in Trust with Gabael

20 "And now, my son, let me explain to you that I left ten talents of silver in trust with Gabael son of Gabrias, at Rages in Media. 21 Do not be afraid, my son, because we have become poor. You have great wealth if you fear God and flee from every sin and do what is good in the sight of the Lord your God."

The Angel Raphael

5 Then Tobias answered his father Tobit, "I will do everything that you have commanded me, father, 2 but how can I obtain the money*e* from him, since he does not know me and I do not know him? What evidence*f* am I to give him so that he will recognize and trust me and give me the money? Also, I do not know the roads to Media or how to get there." 3 Then Tobit answered his son Tobias, "He gave me his bond, and I gave him my bond. I*g* divided his in two; we each took one part, and I put one with the money. And now twenty years have passed since I left this money in trust. So now, my son, find yourself a trustworthy man to go with you, and we will pay him wages until you return. But get back the money from Gabael."*h*

4 So Tobias went out to look for a man to go with him to Media, someone who was acquainted with the way. He went out and found the angel Raphael standing in front of him, but he did not perceive that he was an angel of God. 5 Tobias*i* said to him, "Where do you come from, young man?" "From the Israelites, your kindred," he replied, "and I have come here to work." Then Tobias*j* said to him, "Do you know the way to go to Media?" 6 "Yes," he replied, "I have been there many times; I am acquainted with it and know all the roads. I have often traveled to Media and would stay with our kinsman Gabael who lives in Rages of Media. It is a journey of two days from Ecbatana to Rages, for it lies in a mountainous area, while Ecbatana is in the middle of the plain." 7 Then Tobias said to him, "Wait for me, young man, until I go in and tell my father, for I do need you to travel with

me, and I will pay you your wages." 8 He replied, "All right, I will wait, but do not take too long."

9 So Tobias went in to tell his father Tobit and said to him, "I have just found a man who is one of our own Israelite kindred!" He replied, "Call the man in so that I may learn about his people and to what tribe he belongs and whether he is trustworthy enough to go with you, my son."

10 Then Tobias went out and called him and said, "Young man, my father is calling for you." So he went in to him, and Tobit greeted him first. He replied, "Many greetings to you!" But Tobit retorted, "What is left for me to greet any more? I am a man without eyesight; I cannot see the light of heaven, but I lie in darkness like the dead who no longer see the light. Although still alive, I am among the dead. I hear people's voices, but I cannot see them." But the young man*k* said, "Take courage; the time is near for God to heal you; take courage." Then Tobit said to him, "My son Tobias wishes to go to Media. Can you accompany him and guide him? I will pay your wages, brother." He answered, "I can go with him, and I know all the roads. I have often gone to Media, have crossed all its plains, and am familiar with its mountains and all of its roads."

11 Then Tobit*l* said to him, "Brother, of what family are you and from what tribe? Tell me, brother." 12 He replied, "Why do you need to know my tribe and lineage? Are you seeking an employee or a tribe and lineage?"*m* But Tobit*n* said, "I want to be sure, brother, whose son you are and what your name is." 13 He replied, "I am Azariah, the son of the elder Hananiah, one of your relatives." 14 Then Tobit*o* said to him, "You are very welcome, brother. Do not feel bitter toward me, brother, because I wanted to be sure about your family. It turns out that you are a kinsman and of good and noble lineage. For I knew Hananiah and Nathan, the two sons of the elder Shemeliah,*p* and they used to go with me to Jerusalem and worship with me there; they were not led astray. Your kindred are good people; you are of good stock. Welcome!"

15 Then he added, "I will pay you a drachma a day as wages, as well as expenses for yourself

---

e 5.2 Gk *it*
f 5.2 Gk *sign*
g 5.3 Other authorities read *He*
h 5.3 Gk *from him*
i 5.5 Gk *He*
j 5.5 Gk *he*

k 5.10 Gk *he*
l 5.11 Gk *he*
m 5.12 OL: S lacks *and lineage? Are you seeking an employee or a tribe and lineage?*
n 5.12 Gk *he*
o 5.14 Gk *he*
p 5.14 Other ancient authorities read *Shemaiah*

and my son. So go with my son, [16]and I will add something to your wages." Raphael[q] answered, "I will go with him, so do not fear. We shall leave in good health and return to you in good health because the way is safe." [17]So Tobit[r] said to him, "Blessings be upon you, brother."

Then he called his son and said to him, "Make preparations for the journey, my son, and set out with your brother. May God in heaven bring you safely there and return you in good health to me, and may his angel, my son, accompany you both for your safety."

Before he[s] went out to start his journey, he kissed his father and mother. Tobit then said to him, "Have a safe journey."

[18]But his mother began to weep and said to Tobit, "Why is it that you have sent my son away? Is he not the staff of our hand as he goes in and out before us? [19]Do not heap money upon money, but let it be a ransom for our son. [20]The life that is given to us by the Lord is enough for us." [21]Tobit[t] said to her, "Do not worry; our son will leave in good health and return to us in good health. Your eyes will see him on the day when he returns to you in good health. Say no more! Do not fear for them, my sister, [22]for a good angel will accompany him; his journey will be successful, and he will come back in good health." [1]So she stopped weeping.

Journey to Rages

The young man went out, and the angel went with him, [2]and the dog came out with him and went along with them. So they both journeyed along, and when the first night overtook them they camped by the Tigris River. [3]Then the young man went down to wash his feet in the Tigris River, and a large fish leaped up from the water and tried to swallow the young man's foot, and he cried out. [4]But the angel said to the young man, "Catch hold of the fish and hang on to it!" So the young man grasped the fish and drew it up on the land. [5]Then the angel said to him, "Cut open the fish and take out its gall, heart, and liver. Keep them with you, but throw away the intestines. For its gall, heart, and liver are useful as medicine." [6]So after cutting open the fish the young man gathered together the gall, heart, and liver; then he roasted and ate some of the fish and kept some to be salted for the journey.[u]

The two continued on their way together until they were near Media. [7]Then the young man questioned the angel and said to him, "Azariah, my brother, what medicinal value is there in the fish's heart and liver and in the gall?" [8]He replied, "As for the fish's heart and liver, you must burn them to make a smoke in the presence of a man or woman afflicted by a demon or evil spirit, and every affliction will flee away and never remain with that person any longer. [9]And as for the gall, anoint a person's eyes where white films have appeared on them; blow upon them, upon the white films, and the eyes[v] will be healed."

Raphael's Instructions

[10]When they entered Media and were already approaching Ecbatana, [11]Raphael said to the young man, "Tobias, my brother." "Here I am," he answered. Then Raphael[w] said to him, "We must stay this night in the home of Raguel. That man is your relative, and he has a daughter named Sarah. [12]He has no male heir and no daughter except Sarah only, and you, as next of kin to her, have before all other men a hereditary claim on her. Also, it is right for you to inherit her father's possessions. Moreover, the young woman is intelligent, brave, and very beautiful, and her father is a good man." [13]He continued, "You have every right to take her in marriage. So listen to me, brother; tonight I will speak to her father about the young woman, so that we may take her to be your bride. When we return from Rages[x] we will celebrate her marriage. For I know that Raguel can by no means keep her from you or promise her to another man without incurring the penalty of death according to the decree of the book of Moses. Indeed, he knows that you, rather than any other man, are entitled to marry his daughter. So now listen to me, brother, and tonight we shall speak concerning the young woman and arrange her engagement to you. And when we return from Rages, we will take her and bring her back with us to your house."

[14]Then Tobias said in answer to Raphael, "Azariah, my brother, I have heard that she already has been married to seven husbands and

---

q 5.16 Gk *He*

r 5.17 Gk *he*

s 5.17 Other ancient authorities read *So he made preparations for the journey and*

t 5.21 Gk *He*

---

u 6.6 Q ms: S lacks *for the journey*

v 6.9 Gk *they*

w 6.11 Gk *he*

x 6.13 OL: S reads *Raguel*

that they died in the bridal chamber. On the night when they went in to her, they would die. And I have heard some say that a demon kills them.*y* 15 It does not harm her, but it kills anyone who desires to approach her. So now, since I am the only son my father has, I am afraid that I may die and bring my father's and mother's lives down to their graves, grieving for me—and they have no other son to bury them."

16 But Raphael*z* said to him, "Do you not remember your father's orders when he commanded you to take a wife from your father's house? Now listen to me, brother, and say no more about this demon. Take her. I know that this very night she will be given to you in marriage. 17 When you enter the bridal chamber, take some of the fish's liver and heart and put them on the embers of the incense. An odor will be given off; 18 the demon will smell it and flee and will never be seen near her any more. Now when you are about to go to bed with her, both of you must first stand up and pray, imploring the Lord of heaven that mercy and safety may be granted to you. Do not be afraid, for she has always been set apart for you. You will save her, and she will go with you. I know that you will have children by her, and they will be as brothers and sisters to you. Now say no more!" When Tobias heard the words of Raphael and learned that she was his sister, related through his father's lineage, he loved her very much, and his heart was drawn to her.

Arrival at Home of Raguel

7 Now when they*a* entered Ecbatana, Tobias*b* said to him, "Azariah, my brother, take me straight to our brother Raguel." So he took him to Raguel's house, where they found him sitting beside the courtyard door. They greeted him first, and he replied, "Many greetings, my brothers; welcome and good health!" Then he brought them into his house. 2 He said to his wife Edna, "How much this young man resembles my kinsman Tobit!" 3 Then Edna questioned them, saying, "Where are you from, my brothers?" They answered her, "We belong to the descendants of Naphtali who are exiles in Nineveh." 4 She said to them, "Do you know our kinsman Tobit?" And they replied, "Yes,

we know him." Then she asked them, "Is he in good health?" 5 They replied, "He is alive and in good health." And Tobias added, "He is my father!" 6 At that Raguel jumped up and kissed him and wept. 7 He also spoke to him as follows, "Blessings on you, my son, offspring of a good and noble father! O most miserable of calamities that such an upright and beneficent man has become blind!" He then embraced his kinsman Tobias and wept. 8 His wife Edna also wept for him, and their daughter Sarah likewise wept. 9 Then Raguel*c* slaughtered a ram from the flock and received them very warmly.

Marriage of Tobias and Sarah

When they had bathed and washed themselves and had reclined to dine, Tobias said to Raphael, "Azariah, my brother, ask Raguel to give me my sister Sarah." 10 But Raguel overheard it and said to the young man, "Eat and drink, and be merry tonight. For no one except you, brother, has the right to marry my daughter Sarah. Likewise I am not at liberty to give her to any other man than you because you are my nearest relative. But let me explain to you the true situation more fully, my son. 11 I have given her to seven men of our kinsmen, and all died on the night when they went in to her. But now, my son, eat and drink, and the Lord will act on behalf of you both." But Tobias said, "I will neither eat nor drink anything until you settle the things that pertain to me." So Raguel said, "I will do so. She is given to you in accordance with the decree in the book of Moses, and it has been decreed from heaven that she be given to you. Take your sister; from now on you are her brother, and she is your sister. She is given to you from today and forever. May the Lord of heaven, my son, guide and prosper you both this night and grant you mercy and peace." 12 Then Raguel summoned his daughter Sarah. When she came to him, he took her by the hand and gave her to Tobias,*d* saying, "Take her to be your wife in accordance with the law and decree written in the book of Moses. Take her and bring her safely to your father. And may the God of heaven let your journey go smoothly and in his peace." 13 Then he called her mother and told her to bring writing material, and he wrote out a copy of a marriage contract, to the effect that he gave her to him

---

y 6.14 Other ancient authorities lack *And I . . . kills them*
z 6.16 Gk *he*
a 7.1 Q ms OL: S *he*
b 7.1 Gk *he*

c 7.9 Gk *he*
d 7.12 Gk *him*

as wife according to the decree of the law of Moses.[e] [14]Then they began to eat and drink.

[15]Raguel called his wife Edna and said to her, "Sister, get the other room ready, and take her there." [16]So she went and made the bed in the room as he had told her and brought Sarah[f] there. She wept for her daughter.[g] Then, wiping away the tears, she said to her, "Take courage, my daughter; the Lord of heaven grant you joy in place of your sorrow. Take courage, my daughter." Then she went out.

Tobias Routs the Demon

8 When they had finished eating and drinking, they wanted to retire, so they took the young man and brought him into the bedroom. [2]Then Tobias remembered the words of Raphael, and he took the fish's liver and heart out of the bag where he had them and put them on the embers of the incense. [3]The odor of the fish so repelled the demon that he fled to the remotest parts[h] of Egypt. But Raphael followed him and at once bound him there hand and foot.

[4]When the parents[i] had gone out and shut the door of the room, Tobias got out of bed and said to Sarah,[j] "Sister, get up, and let us pray and implore our Lord that he grant us mercy and safety." [5]So she got up, and they began to pray and implore that they might be kept safe. Tobias[k] began by saying,

"Blessed are you, O God of our ancestors,
　and blessed is your name in all
　　generations forever.
Let the heavens and the whole creation
　bless you forever.
[6] You made Adam, and for him you made
　his wife Eve
　as a helper and support.
From the two of them the human race
　has sprung.
You said, 'It is not good that the man
　should be alone;
　let us make a helper for him like himself.'
[7] I now am taking this sister of mine,
　not for sexual gratification,
　but with sincerity.

Grant that she and I may find mercy
　and that we may grow old together."
[8]And they both together said, "Amen, Amen."
[9]Then they went to sleep for the night.

But Raguel arose and called his servants to him, and they went and dug a grave, [10]for he said, "It is possible that he will die, and we will become an object of ridicule and derision." [11]When they had finished digging the grave, Raguel went into his house and called his wife, [12]saying, "Send one of the female slaves and have her go in to see if he is alive. But if he is dead, let us bury him without anyone knowing it." [13]So they sent the female slave, lit a lamp, and opened the door; and she went in and found them lying in bed asleep together. [14]Then the female slave came out and informed them that he was alive and that nothing was wrong. [15]So they blessed the God of heaven, and Raguel[l] said,

"Blessed are you, O God, with every pure
　blessing;
　let all your chosen ones bless you.[m]
Let them bless you forever.
[16] Blessed are you because you have made me
　glad.
　It has not turned out as I expected,
　but you have dealt with us according to
　　your great mercy.
[17] Blessed are you because you had
　compassion
　on two only children.
Be merciful to them, O Master, and keep
　them safe;
　bring their lives to fulfillment
　in happiness and mercy."
[18]Then he ordered his servants to fill in the grave before daybreak.

Wedding Feast

[19]After this he asked his wife to bake many loaves of bread, and he went out to the herd and brought two steers and four rams and ordered them to be slaughtered. So they began to make preparations. [20]Then he called for Tobias and[n] said to him: "You shall not leave here for fourteen days but shall stay here eating and drinking with me, and you shall cheer up my daughter, who has been depressed. [21]Take at once half of what I own and return in safety to your father; the other half will be yours when my wife and

---

e 7.13 Other ancient authorities add *and put his seal
　to it*
f 7.16 Gk *her*
g 7.16 Gk *her*
h 8.3 Or *fled through the air to the parts*
i 8.4 Gk *they*
j 8.4 Gk *her*
k 8.5 Gk *He*

l 8.15 Gk *they*
m 8.15 Other ancient authorities lack this line
n 8.20 OL reads *swore on oath, saying*

I die. Take courage, my son. I am your father, and Edna is your mother, and we belong to you as well as to your sister now and forever. Take courage, my son."

The Money Recovered

9 Then Tobias called Raphael and said to him, 2"Azariah, my brother, take four servants and two camels with you and travel to Rages. Go to the home of Gabael, give him the bond, get the money, and then bring him with you to the wedding celebration. 4For you know that my father must be counting the days, and if I delay even one day I will upset him very much. 3You are witness to the oath Raguel has sworn, and I cannot violate his oath."*o* 5So Raphael with the four servants and two camels went to Rages in Media and stayed with Gabael. Raphael*p* gave him the bond and informed him that Tobit's son Tobias had married and was inviting him to the wedding celebration. So Gabael*q* got up and counted out to him the money bags, with their seals intact, and they put them together. 6In the morning they both got up early and went to the wedding celebration. When they came into Raguel's house, they found Tobias reclining at table. He sprang up and greeted Gabael,*r* who wept and blessed him with the words, "Good and noble son of a father good and noble, upright and generous! May the Lord grant the blessing of heaven to you and your wife and to your father and to the mother of your wife. Blessed be God, for I see in Tobias the very image of my cousin Tobit."

Anxiety of the Parents

10 Now day by day Tobit kept counting how many days Tobias*s* would need for going and for returning. And when the days had passed and his son did not appear, 2he said, "Is it possible that he has been detained? Or that Gabael has died, and there is no one to give him the money?" 3And he began to worry. 4His wife Anna said, "My son has perished and is no longer among the living." And she began to weep and mourn for her son, saying, 5"Woe to me, my child, the light of my eyes, that I let you make the journey." 6But Tobit kept saying to her, "Be quiet and stop worrying, my sister;

he is all right. Something must have happened to delay them. The man who went with him is trustworthy and is one of our own kin. Do not grieve for him, my sister; he will be here soon." 7She answered him, "Be quiet yourself! Stop trying to deceive me! My son has perished." She would rush out every day and watch the road her son had taken and would heed no one.*t* When the sun had set she would go in and mourn and weep all night long, getting no sleep.

Tobias and Sarah Start for Home

Now when the fourteen days of the wedding celebration had ended that Raguel had sworn to observe for his daughter, Tobias came to him and said, "Send me back, for I know that my father and mother do not believe that they will see me again. So I beg of you, father, to let me go so that I may return to my own father. I have already explained to you how I left him." 8But Raguel said to Tobias, "Stay, my son, stay with me; I will send messengers to your father Tobit, and they will inform him about you." 9But he said to him, "No! I beg you to send me back to my father." 10So Raguel stood and gave Tobias his wife Sarah, as well as half of all his property: male and female slaves, oxen and sheep, donkeys and camels, clothing, money, and household goods. 11Then he saw them safely off; he embraced Tobias*u* and said to him, "Farewell, my son; have a safe journey. The Lord of heaven prosper you and your wife Sarah, and may I see children of yours before I die." 12Then he said to his daughter Sarah, "My daughter, go to your father-in-law and your mother-in-law,*v* since from now on they are as much your parents as those who gave you birth. Go in peace, daughter, and may I hear a good report about you as long as I live." Then he bade them farewell and let them go. Then Edna said to Tobias, "My child and dear brother, the Lord of heaven bring you back safely, and may I live long enough to see children from you and of my daughter Sarah before I die. In the sight of the Lord I entrust my daughter to you; do nothing to make her unhappy all the days of your life. Go in peace, my son. From now on I am your mother, and Sarah is your sister. May we all prosper together

---

o **9.3** In other ancient authorities 9.3 precedes 9.4
p **9.5** Gk *He*
q **9.5** Gk *he*
r **9.6** Gk *him*
s **10.1** Gk *he*

---

t **10.7** Other ancient authorities read *would eat nothing*
u **10.11** Gk *him*
v **10.12** Other ancient authorities lack parts of *Then . . . mother-in-law*

all the days of our lives." Then she kissed them both and saw them safely off. ¹³Tobias parted from Raguel with happiness and joy, praising the Lord of heaven and earth, King over all, because he had made his journey a success, and he blessed Raguel and his wife Edna and said,ʷ "May it come to pass that I honorˣ them all the days of their lives."ʸ

Homeward Journey

11 When they came near to Kaserin, which is opposite Nineveh, Raphael said, ²"You are aware of how we left your father. ³Let us run ahead of your wife and prepare the house while they are still on the way." ⁴As they went on together, Raphaelᶻ said to him, "Have the gall ready in your hand." And the dogᵃ went along behind them.

⁵Meanwhile Anna sat looking intently down the road by which her son would come. ⁶When she caught sight of him coming, she said to his father, "Look, your son is coming, and the man who went with him!"

Tobit's Sight Restored

⁷Raphael said to Tobias before he had approached his father, "I know that his eyes will be opened. ⁸Smear the gall of the fish on his eyes; the medicine will make the white films shrink and peel off from his eyes, and your father will regain his sight and see the light."

⁹Then Anna ran up to her son and threw her arms around her son, saying, "Now that I have seen you, my son, I am ready to die." And she wept. ¹⁰Then Tobit got up and came stumbling out through the courtyard door. Tobias went up to him, ¹¹with the gall of the fish in his hand, and blew it into his eyes, then took hold of him, saying, "Take courage, father." With this he applied the medicine on his eyes, ¹²and it stung.ᵇ ¹³Next, with both his hands he peeled off the white films from the corners of his eyes. Then Tobitᶜ threw his arms around him, ¹⁴and he wept and said to him, "I see you, my son, the light of my eyes!" Then he said,

"Blessed be God.
May his great name be upon us,

and blessed be all the angelsᵈ
throughout all the ages.
¹⁵ Though he afflicted me,ᵉ
now I see my son Tobias!"

So Tobit went in rejoicing and praising God at the top of his voice. Tobias reported to his father that his journey had been successful, that he had brought the money, that he had married Raguel's daughter Sarah, and that she was, indeed, on her way there, very near to the gate of Nineveh.

¹⁶Then Tobit,ᶠ rejoicing and praising God, went out to meet his daughter-in-law at the gate of Nineveh. When the people of Nineveh saw him coming, walking along in full vigor and with no one leading him, they were amazed. ¹⁷Before them all, Tobit acknowledged that God had been merciful to him and had restored his sight. When Tobit met Sarah the wife of his son Tobias, he blessed her, saying, "Come in, my daughter, and be welcome. Blessed be your God who has brought you to us, my daughter. Blessed be your father and your mother, blessed be my son Tobias, and blessed be you, my daughter. Come in now to your home, and be welcome, with blessing and joy. Come in, my daughter." So on that day there was rejoicing among all the Jews who were in Nineveh. ¹⁸Ahikar and his nephew Nadab were also present to share Tobit's joy.ᵍ

Raphael's Wages

12 When the wedding celebration was ended, Tobit called his son Tobias and said to him, "My son, see to paying the wages of the man who went with you, and give him a bonus as well." ²He replied, "Father, how much shall I pay him? It would do me no harm to give him half of the possessions brought back with me. ³For he has led me back safely, cured my wife, brought the money back with me, and healed you. How much extra shall I give him as a bonus?" ⁴Tobit replied, "He deserves, my son, to receive half of all that he brought back." ⁵So Tobiasʰ called him and said, "Take for your wages half of all that you brought back, and farewell."

w 10.13 OL: S *And he said to him*
x 10.13 Cn: S *May it go well for you to honor*
y 10.13 OL: Meaning of Gk uncertain
z 11.4 Gk *he*
a 11.4 OL: S reads *And the Lord*
b 11.12 Cn: S *and he applied*
c 11.13 Gk *he*

d 11.14 Other ancient authorities lack *May his great . . . angels*
e 11.15 OL adds *he has had mercy upon me*
f 11.16 Gk *he*
g 11.18 Other ancient authorities add *With merriment they celebrated Tobias's wedding feast for seven days, and many gifts were given to him*
h 12.5 Gk *he*

Raphael's Exhortation

6 Then Raphael[i] called the two of them privately and said to them, "Bless God and acknowledge him in the presence of all the living for the good things he has done for you. Bless and sing praise to his name. With fitting honor declare to all people the deeds[j] of God. Do not be slow to acknowledge him. 7 It is good to conceal the secret of a king and to acknowledge and reveal the works of God with proper honor. Do good, and evil will not overtake you. 8 Prayer with fidelity is good, and almsgiving with righteousness is better than wealth with injustice. It is better to give alms than to lay up gold, 9 for almsgiving saves from death and purges away every sin. Those who give alms will enjoy a full life, 10 but those who commit sin and do wrong are their own enemies.

Raphael Discloses His Identity

11 "I will now declare the whole truth to you and will conceal nothing from you. Already I have declared it to you when I said, 'It is good to conceal the secret of a king but to reveal with due honor the works of God.' 12 So now when you and Sarah prayed, it was I who brought the record of your prayers before the glory of the Lord, and likewise whenever you would bury the dead. 13 And that time when you did not hesitate to get up and leave your dinner to go and lay out that corpse, 14 I was sent to you to test you. And at the same time God sent me to heal you and Sarah your daughter-in-law. 15 I am Raphael, one of the seven angels who stand ready and enter before the glory of the Lord."

16 The two of them were shaken and threw themselves face down, for they were afraid. 17 But he said to them, "Do not be afraid; peace be with you. Bless God forevermore. 18 As for me, when I was with you, I was not acting on my own will but by the will of God. Bless him each and every day; sing his praises. 19 When you were watching me, I was not really eating[k] anything, but what you saw was a vision. 20 So now bless the Lord on the earth[l] and acknowledge God. See, I am ascending to him who sent me. Write down all these things that have happened to you." And he ascended. 21 Then they stood up and could see him no more. 22 They kept blessing God and singing his praises, and they acknowledged God for these marvelous deeds of his, that an angel of God had appeared to them.

Tobit's Thanksgiving to God

13 Then Tobit[m] said:
"Blessed be God who lives forever,
  and blessed be his kingdom.
2 For he afflicts, and he shows mercy;
  he leads down to Hades in the lowest
    regions of the earth,
  and he brings up from the great abyss,
  and there is nothing that can escape his
    hand.
3 Acknowledge him before the nations,
    O children of Israel,
  for he has scattered you among them.
4 He has shown you his greatness even
    there.
Exalt him in the presence of every living
    being,
  because he is our[n] Lord, and he is our
    God;
  he is our Father, and he is God forever.
5 He will afflict[o] you for your iniquities,
  but he will again show mercy on all of
    you.
He will gather you from all the nations
  among whom you have been scattered.
6 If you turn to him with all your heart and
    with all your soul,
  to do what is true before him,
then he will turn to you
  and will no longer hide his face from you.
So now see what he has done for you;
  acknowledge him at the top of your voice.
Bless the Lord of righteousness,
  and exalt the King of the ages.[p]
In the land of my exile I acknowledge him
  and show his power and majesty to a
    nation of sinners:
'Turn back, you sinners, and do what is
    right before him;
  perhaps he may look with favor upon you
    and show you mercy.'
7 As for me, I exalt my God,
  and my soul rejoices in the King of
    heaven.

---

i 12.6 Gk *he*
j 12.6 Gk *words*; other ancient authorities read *words of the deeds*
k 12.19 Other ancient authorities add *and drinking*
l 12.20 Other ancient authorities read *get up from the ground*

m 13.1 Gk *he*
n 13.4 Q mss read *your*
o 13.5 Other ancient authorities read *He afflicted*
p 13.6 S lacks 13.6b–10a and is filled in from other ancient authorities

8 Let all people speak of his majesty
    and acknowledge him in Jerusalem.
9 O Jerusalem, the holy city,
    he afflicted*q* you for the deeds of your
      hands*r*
    but will again have mercy on the children
      of the righteous.
10 Acknowledge the Lord worthily,
    and bless the King of the ages,
    so that your tent*s* may be rebuilt for you*t*
      with joy.
    May he cheer all those within you who are
      captives
    and love all those within you who are
      distressed,
    to all generations forever.
11 A bright light will shine to all the remotest
      parts of the earth;
    many nations will come to you from far
      away,
    the inhabitants of the ends of the earth to
      your holy name,
    bearing gifts in their hands for the King
      of heaven.
    Generation after generation will give joyful
      praise in you;
    the name of the chosen city will endure
      forever.
12 Cursed are all who reject you
    and all who blaspheme you;
    cursed are all who hate you*u*
    and all who speak a harsh word against
      you;
    cursed are all who conquer you
    and pull down your walls,
    all who overthrow your towers
    and set your homes on fire.
    But blessed forever will be all who build
      you up.*v*
13 Rejoice,*w* then, and exult over the children
      of the righteous,
    for they will all be gathered together
    and will bless the Lord of the ages.
14 Happy will be those who love you,
    and happy are those who will rejoice in
      your peace.

Happy also all people who grieve with
      you
    because of your afflictions,
    for they will rejoice with you
    and witness all your joy forever.
15 My soul blesses*x* the Lord, the great King,
16   for Jerusalem will be rebuilt as his house
      for all ages.
    How happy I will be if a remnant of my
      descendants should survive
    to see your glory and acknowledge the
      King of heaven.
    The gates of Jerusalem will be built with
      sapphire and emerald
    and all your walls with precious
      stones.
    The towers of Jerusalem will be built with
      gold
    and their battlements with pure gold.
17 The streets of Jerusalem will be paved
    with ruby and with stones of Ophir.
18 The gates of Jerusalem will sing hymns of
      joy,
    and all her houses will cry,
    'Hallelujah!
    Blessed be the God of Israel!'—
    and the blessed will bless the holy name
      forever and ever."

Tobit's Final Counsel

14 So ended Tobit's words of praise.
2 He died in peace when he was one
hundred twelve years old and was buried with
great honor in Nineveh. He was fifty-eight*y*
years old when he lost his eyesight, and after
regaining it he lived in prosperity, giving alms.
He continued to bless God and to acknowledge
God's greatness.

3 When he was about to die, he called his
son Tobias and his seven children*z* and gave
this command: "My son, take your children
4 and escape off to Media, for I believe the word
of God that Nahum spoke about Nineveh, that
all these things will occur and will happen to
Assyria and Nineveh. Indeed, everything that
was spoken by the prophets of Israel whom
God sent will occur. None of all their words will
fail, but all will come true at their appointed
times. So it will be safer in Media than among
the Assyrians or in Babylon. For I know and

---

q 13.9 Other ancient authorities read *will afflict*
r 13.9 Other ancient authorities read *your children*
s 13.10 Or *tabernacle*
t 13.10 Q ms: Gk reads *in you*
u 13.12 Q ms: S lacks *reject . . . hate you*
v 13.12 OL: S *who fear you*
w 13.13 Q mss: S *Go*

---

x 13.15 OL reads *O my soul, bless*
y 14.2 Q mss OL: S *sixty-two*
z 14.3 OL: S lacks *and his seven children*

believe that whatever God has said will be fulfilled and will occur; not a single word of the prophecies will fail. All of our kindred, inhabitants of the land of Israel, will be counted and taken as captives from the good land, and the whole land of Israel will be desolate; even Samaria and Jerusalem will be desolate. And the temple of God in it will be burned to the ground and will be desolate for a while.*

5 "But God will again have mercy on them, and God will bring them back into the land of Israel, and they will rebuild the temple but not like the first one until the appointed time is completed. After this they all will return from their exile and will rebuild Jerusalem in splendor, and in it the temple of God will be rebuilt, just as the prophets of Israel have said concerning it. 6Then all the nations in the whole world will all be converted and will truly fear God. They will all abandon all their idols who deceitfully have led them into their error, 7and in righteousness they will praise the eternal God. All the Israelites who are saved in those days and are truly mindful of God will be gathered together; they will go to Jerusalem and live in safety forever in the land of Abraham, and it will be given over to them. Those who sincerely love God will rejoice, but those who commit sin and injustice will vanish from all the earth.

9 "So now, my children, I command you, serve God faithfully and do what is pleasing in his sight. Your children are also to be commanded to do what is right and to give alms and to be mindful of God and to bless his name at all times with sincerity and with all their strength. 8So now, my son, leave Nineveh; do not remain here.b 10On whatever day you bury your mother beside me, do not stay overnight within the confines of the city, for I see that there is much injustice within it and that much deceit is practiced within it, while the people are without shame. See, my son, what Nadab did to Ahikar, who had reared him. Was he not, while still alive, brought down into the earth? For God repaid him to his face for this shameful treatment. Ahikar came out into the light, but Nadab went into the eternal darkness because he tried to kill Ahikar. Because he gave alms, he escaped the fatal trap that Nadab had set for him, but Nadab fell into it himself and was destroyed. 11So now, my children, see what almsgiving accomplishes and what injustice does—it brings death! But now my breath fails me."

Death of Tobit and Anna

Then they laid him on his bed, and he died, and he received an honorable funeral. 12When Tobias's mother died, he buried her beside his father. Then he and his wifec returned to Media and settled in Ecbatana with Raguel his father-in-law. 13He looked after his parents-in-lawd with great respect in their old age and buried them in Ecbatana of Media. He inherited both the property of Raguel and that of his father Tobit. 14He died highly respected at the age of one hundred seventeen years. 15Before he died he saw and hearde of the destruction of Nineveh, and he saw its prisoners being led into Media, those whom King Cyaxaresf of Media had taken captive. Tobiasg blessed God for all he had done to the people of Nineveh and Assyria; before he died he rejoiced over Nineveh, and he blessed the Lord God forever and ever. Amen.

---

a 14.4 OL: Other ancient authorities read *of God will be in distress and will be burned for a while*

b 14.8 In other ancient authorities 14.8 precedes 14.9

c 14.12 Other ancient authorities add *and children*

d 14.13 Gk *them*

e 14.15 Other ancient authorities lack *saw and*

f 14.15 Cn: S *Ahikar*

g 14.15 Gk *He*

JUDITH

Arphaxad Fortifies Ecbatana

1 It was the twelfth year of the reign of Nebuchadnezzar, who ruled over the Assyrians in the great city of Nineveh. In those days Arphaxad ruled over the Medes in Ecbatana. ²He built walls around Ecbatana with hewn stones three cubits thick and six cubits long; he made the walls seventy cubits high and fifty cubits wide. ³At its gates he raised towers one hundred cubits high and sixty cubits wide at the foundations. ⁴He made its gates seventy cubits high and forty cubits wide to allow his armies to march out in force and his infantry to form their ranks. ⁵Then King Nebuchadnezzar made war against King Arphaxad in the great plain that is on the borders of Ragau. ⁶There rallied to him all the people of the hill country and all those who lived along the Euphrates, the Tigris, and the Hydaspes, and, on the plain, Arioch, king of the Elymeans. Thus many nations joined the forces of the Cheleoudites.ᵃ

Nebuchadnezzar Issues Ultimatum

⁷Then Nebuchadnezzar, king of the Assyrians, sent messengers to all who lived in Persia and to all who lived in the west, those who lived in Cilicia and Damascus, Lebanon and Antilebanon, and all who lived along the seacoast, ⁸and those among the nations of Carmel and Gilead, and Upper Galilee and the great plain of Esdraelon, ⁹and all who were in Samaria and its towns, and beyond the Jordan as far as Jerusalem and Bethany and Chelous and Kadesh and the river of Egypt, and Tahpanhes and Raamses and the whole land of Goshen, ¹⁰even beyond Tanis and Memphis, and all who lived in Egypt as far as the borders of Ethiopia. ¹¹But all who lived in the whole region showed contempt for the summons of Nebuchadnezzar, king of the Assyrians, and refused to join him in the war, for they were not afraid of him but regarded him as only one man.ᵇ So they sent back his messengers empty-handed and in disgrace.

¹²Then Nebuchadnezzar became very angry with this whole region and swore by his throne and kingdom that he would take revenge on the whole territory of Cilicia and Damascus and Syria, that he would kill with his sword also all the inhabitants of the land of Moab, and the people of Ammon, and all Judea, and every one in Egypt, as far as the coasts of the two seas.

Arphaxad Is Defeated

¹³In the seventeenth year he led his forces against King Arphaxad and defeated him in battle, overthrowing the whole army of Arphaxad and all his cavalry and all his chariots. ¹⁴Thus he took possession of his towns and came to Ecbatana, captured its towers, plundered its markets, and turned its glory into disgrace. ¹⁵He captured Arphaxad in the mountains of Ragau and struck him down with his spears, thus destroying him once and for all. ¹⁶Then he returned to Nineveh, he and all his combined forces, a vast body of troops, and there he and his forces rested and feasted for one hundred twenty days.

The Expedition against the West

2 In the eighteenth year, on the twenty-second day of the first month, there was talk in the palace of Nebuchadnezzar, king of the Assyrians, about carrying out his revenge on the whole region, just as he had said. ²He summoned all his attendants and all his nobles and set before them his secret plan and recounted fully, with his own lips, all the wickedness of the region.ᶜ ³They decided that all who had not obeyed his command should be destroyed.

⁴When he had completed his plan, Nebuchadnezzar, king of the Assyrians, called Holofernes, the chief general of his army, second

---

a 1.6 Syr: Gk *Chaldeans*

b 1.11 Or *a man*

c 2.2 Meaning of Gk uncertain

only to himself, and said to him, ⁵"Thus says the Great King, the lord of the whole earth: Leave my presence and take with you men confident in their strength, one hundred twenty thousand foot soldiers and twelve thousand cavalry. ⁶March out against all the land to the west, because they disobeyed my orders. ⁷Tell them to prepare earth and water, for I am coming against them in my anger and will cover the whole face of the earth with the feet of my troops, to whom I will hand them over to be plundered. ⁸Their wounded shall fill their ravines and gullies, and the swelling river shall be filled with their dead. ⁹I will lead them away captive to the ends of the whole earth. ¹⁰You shall go and seize all their territory for me in advance. They must yield themselves to you, and you shall hold them for me until the day of their punishment. ¹¹But to those who resist, show no mercy but hand them over to slaughter and plunder throughout your whole region. ¹²For as I live and by the power of my kingdom, what I have spoken I will accomplish by my own hand. ¹³And you—take care not to transgress any of your lord's commands, but carry them out exactly as I have ordered you; do it without delay."

Campaign of Holofernes

14 So Holofernes left the presence of his lord and summoned all the commanders, generals, and officers of the Assyrian army. ¹⁵He mustered the picked troops by divisions as his lord had ordered him to do, one hundred twenty thousand of them, together with twelve thousand archers on horseback, ¹⁶and he organized them as a great army is marshaled for a campaign. ¹⁷He took along a vast number of camels and donkeys and mules for transport and innumerable sheep and oxen and goats for food, ¹⁸also ample rations for everyone and a huge amount of gold and silver from the royal palace.

19 Then he set out with his whole army to go ahead of King Nebuchadnezzar and to cover the whole face of the earth to the west with their chariots and cavalry and picked foot soldiers. ²⁰Along with them went a mixed crowd like a swarm of locusts, like the dust*ᵈ* of the earth, a multitude that could not be counted.

21 They marched for three days from Nineveh to the plain of Bectileth and camped opposite Bectileth near the mountain that is to the north

of Upper Cilicia. ²²From there Holofernes*ᵉ* took his whole army, the infantry, cavalry, and chariots, and went up into the hill country. ²³He ravaged Put and Lud and plundered all the Rassisites and the Ishmaelites on the border of the desert, south of the country of the Chelleans. ²⁴Then he followed*ᶠ* the Euphrates and passed through Mesopotamia and destroyed all the fortified towns along the Wadi Abron, as far as the sea. ²⁵He also seized the territory of Cilicia and killed everyone who resisted him. Then he came to the southern borders of Japheth, facing Arabia. ²⁶He surrounded all the Midianites and burned their tents and plundered their sheepfolds. ²⁷Then he went down into the plain of Damascus during the wheat harvest and burned all their fields and destroyed their flocks and herds and sacked their towns and ravaged their lands and put all their young men to the sword.

28 So fear and dread of him fell upon all the people who lived along the seacoast, at Sidon and Tyre, and those who lived in Sur and Ocina and all who lived in Jamnia. Those who lived in Azotus and Ascalon feared him greatly.

Entreaties for Peace

3 They therefore sent messengers to him to sue for peace in these words: ²"We, the servants of Nebuchadnezzar, the Great King, lie prostrate before you. Do with us whatever you will. ³See, our buildings and all our land and all our wheat fields and our flocks and herds and all our encampments*ᵍ* lie before you; do with them as you please. ⁴Our towns and their inhabitants are also your slaves; come and deal with them as you see fit."

5 The men came to Holofernes and told him all this. ⁶Then he went down to the seacoast with his army and stationed garrisons in the fortified towns and took picked men from them as auxiliaries. ⁷These people and all in the countryside welcomed him with garlands and dances and tambourines. ⁸Yet he demolished all their shrines*ʰ* and cut down their sacred groves, for he had been commissioned to destroy all the gods of the land, so that all nations should worship Nebuchadnezzar alone and that all their dialects and tribes should call upon him as a god.

9 Then he came toward Esdraelon, near Dothan, facing the great ridge of Judea; ¹⁰he

---

d 2.20 Gk *sand*

e 2.22 Gk *he*

f 2.24 Or *crossed*

g 3.3 Gk *all the sheepfolds of our tents*

h 3.8 Syr: Gk *borders*

camped between Geba and Scythopolis and remained for a whole month in order to collect all
the supplies for his army.

Judea on the Alert

4 When the Israelites living in Judea heard of
everything that Holofernes, the general of
Nebuchadnezzar, the king of the Assyrians, had
done to the nations and how he had plundered
and destroyed all their temples, ²they were
therefore greatly terrified at his approach; they
were alarmed both for Jerusalem and for the
temple of the Lord their God. ³For they had only
recently returned from exile, and all the people
of Judea had just now gathered together, and the
sacred vessels and the altar and the temple had
been consecrated after their profanation. ⁴So
they sent word to every district of Samaria, and
to Kona, Beth-horon, Belmain, and Jericho, and
to Choba and Aesora, and the valley of Salem.
⁵They immediately seized all the high hilltops
and fortified the villages on them and stored up
food in preparation for war, since their fields
had recently been harvested.

6 The high priest Joakim, who was in Jerusalem at the time, wrote to the people of Bethulia
and Betomesthaim, which faces Esdraelon opposite the plain near Dothan, ⁷ordering them to
seize the mountain passes, since by them Judea
could be invaded, and it would be easy to stop
any who tried to enter, for the approach was narrow, wide enough for only two at a time to pass.

Prayer and Penance

8 So the Israelites did as they had been ordered by the high priest Joakim and the council
of the whole people of Israel, in session at Jerusalem. ⁹And every man of Israel cried out to
God with great fervor, and they humbled themselves with much fasting. ¹⁰They and their wives
and their children and their cattle and every
resident alien and hired laborer and purchased
slave—they all put sackcloth around their
waists. ¹¹And all the Israelite men, women, and
children living at Jerusalem prostrated themselves before the temple and put ashes on their
heads and spread out their sackcloth before the
Lord. ¹²They even draped the altar with sackcloth and cried out in unison, praying fervently
to the God of Israel not to allow their infants
to be carried off and their wives to be taken as
plunder, and the towns they had inherited to be
destroyed, and the sanctuary to be profaned and
desecrated to the malicious joy of the nations.

13 The Lord heard their prayers and had
regard for their distress, for the people fasted
many days throughout Judea and in Jerusalem
before the sanctuary of the Lord Almighty.
¹⁴The high priest Joakim and all the priests
who stood before the Lord and ministered to
the Lord, with sackcloth around their loins,
offered the daily burnt offerings, the votive
offerings, and freewill offerings of the people.
¹⁵With ashes on their turbans, they cried out to
the Lord with all their might to look with favor
on the whole house of Israel.

Council against the Israelites

5 It was reported to Holofernes, the general of
the Assyrian army, that the people of Israel
had prepared for war and had closed the mountain passes and fortified all the high hilltops and
set up barricades in the plains. ²In great anger
he called together all the princes of Moab and
the commanders of Ammon and all the governors of the coastland ³and said to them, "Tell
me, you Canaanites, what people is this that
lives in the hill country? What towns do they
inhabit? How large is their army, and in what
does their power and strength consist? Who
rules over them as king and leads their army?
⁴And why have they alone, of all who live in the
west, refused to come out and meet me?"

Achior's Report

5 Then Achior, the leader of all the Ammonites, said to him, "May my lord please listen to
a report from the mouth of your servant, and I
will tell you the truth about this people that lives
in the mountain district near you. No falsehood
shall come from your servant's mouth. ⁶These
people are descended from the Chaldeans. ⁷At
one time they lived in Mesopotamia because
they did not wish to follow the gods of their
ancestors who were in Chaldea. ⁸Since they
had abandoned the ways of their ancestors and
worshiped the God of heaven, the God they had
come to know, their ancestors[i] drove them out
from the presence of their gods. So they fled to
Mesopotamia and lived there for a long time.
⁹Then their God commanded them to leave the
place where they were living and go to the land
of Canaan. There they settled and grew very
prosperous in gold and silver and very much
livestock. ¹⁰When a famine spread over the
land of Canaan they went down to Egypt and

---

i 5.8 Gk *they*

lived there as long as they had food. There they became so great a multitude that their number could not be counted. ¹¹ So the king of Egypt became hostile to them; he exploited them and forced them to make bricks, reducing them to slaves. ¹² They cried out to their God, and he afflicted the whole land of Egypt with incurable plagues. So the Egyptians drove them out of their sight. ¹³ Then God dried up the Red Sea before them, ¹⁴ and he led them by the way of Sinai and Kadesh-barnea. They drove out all the people of the desert ¹⁵ and took up residence in the land of the Amorites and by their might destroyed all the inhabitants of Heshbon, and crossing over the Jordan they took possession of all the hill country. ¹⁶ They drove out before them the Canaanites, the Perizzites, the Jebusites, the Shechemites, and all the Gergesites and lived there a long time.

¹⁷ "As long as they did not sin against their God they prospered, for the God who hates iniquity is with them. ¹⁸ But when they departed from the way he had prescribed for them, they were utterly defeated in many battles and were led away captive to a foreign land. The temple of their God was razed to the ground, and their towns were occupied by their enemies. ¹⁹ But now they have returned to their God and have come back from the places where they were scattered and have occupied Jerusalem, where their sanctuary is, and have settled in the hill country, because it was uninhabited.

²⁰ "So now, my master and lord, if there is any oversight in this people and they sin against their God and we find out their offense, then we can go up and defeat them. ²¹ But if they are not a guilty nation, then let my lord pass them by, for their Lord and God will defend them, and we shall become the laughingstock of the whole world."

²² When Achior had finished saying these things, all the people standing around the tent began to complain; Holofernes's officers and all the inhabitants of the seacoast and Moab insisted that he should be cut to pieces. ²³ They said, "We are not afraid of the Israelites; they are a people with no strength or power for making war. ²⁴ Therefore let us go ahead, Lord Holofernes, and your vast army will swallow them up."

Achior Handed Over to the Israelites

6 When the disturbance made by the people outside the council had died down, Holofernes, the commander of the Assyrian army,

said to Achior[j] in the presence of all the foreign contingents:

² "Who are you, Achior and you mercenaries of Ephraim, to prophesy among us as you have done today and tell us not to make war against the people of Israel because their God will defend them? What god is there except Nebuchadnezzar? He will send his forces and destroy them from the face of the earth. Their God will not save them; ³ we the king's[k] servants will destroy them as one person. They cannot resist the might of our cavalry. ⁴ We will overwhelm them;[l] their mountains will be drunk with their blood, and their fields will be full of their dead. Not even their footprints will survive our attack; they will utterly perish. So says King Nebuchadnezzar, lord of the whole earth. For he has spoken; none of his words shall be in vain.

⁵ "As for you, Achior, you Ammonite mercenary, you have said these words in a moment of perversity; you shall not see my face again from this day until I take revenge on this people that came out of Egypt. ⁶ Then at my return the sword of my army and the spear[m] of my servants shall pierce your sides, and you shall fall among their wounded. ⁷ Now my slaves are going to take you back into the hill country and put you in one of the towns beside the passes. ⁸ You will not die until you perish along with them. ⁹ If you really hope in your heart that they will not be taken, then do not look downcast! I have spoken, and none of my words shall fail to come true."

¹⁰ Then Holofernes ordered his slaves who waited on him in his tent to seize Achior and take him away to Bethulia and hand him over to the Israelites. ¹¹ So the slaves took him and led him out of the camp into the plain, and from the plain they went up into the hill country and came to the springs below Bethulia. ¹² When the men of the town saw them,[n] they seized their weapons and ran out of the town to the top of the hill, and all the slingers kept them from coming up by throwing stones at them. ¹³ So having taken shelter below the hill, they bound Achior and left him lying at the foot of the hill and returned to their master.

---

j **6.1** Other ancient authorities add *and to all the Moabites*
k **6.3** Gk *his*
l **6.4** Other ancient authorities add *with it*
m **6.6** OL Syr: Gk *people*
n **6.12** Other ancient authorities add *on the top of the hill*

14 Then the Israelites came down from their town and found him; they untied him and brought him into Bethulia and placed him before the magistrates of their town, 15 who in those days were Uzziah son of Micah, of the tribe of Simeon, and Chabris son of Gothoniel, and Charmis son of Melchiel. 16 They called together all the elders of the town, and all their young men and women ran to the assembly. They set Achior in the midst of all their people, and Uzziah questioned him about what had happened. 17 He answered and told them what had taken place at the council of Holofernes, and all that he had said in the presence of the Assyrian leaders, and all that Holofernes had boasted he would do against the house of Israel. 18 Then the people fell down and worshiped God and cried out:

19 "O Lord God of heaven, see their arrogance, and have pity on our people in their humiliation, and look kindly today on the faces of those who are consecrated to you."

20 Then they reassured Achior and praised him highly. 21 Uzziah took him from the assembly to his own house and gave a banquet for the elders, and all that night they called on the God of Israel for help.

The Campaign against Bethulia

7 The next day Holofernes ordered his whole army and all the allies who had joined him to break camp and move against Bethulia and seize the passes up into the hill country and make war on the Israelites. 2 So all their warriors marched off that day; their fighting forces numbered one hundred seventy thousand infantry and twelve thousand cavalry, not counting the baggage and the foot soldiers handling it, a very great multitude. 3 They encamped in the valley near Bethulia, beside the spring, and they spread out in breadth over Dothan as far as Balbaim and in length from Bethulia to Cyamon, which faces Esdraelon.

4 When the Israelites saw their vast numbers, they were greatly terrified and said to one another, "They will now strip clean the whole land; neither the high mountains nor the valleys nor the hills will bear their weight." 5 Yet they all seized their weapons, and when they had kindled fires on their towers, they remained on guard all that night.

6 On the second day Holofernes led out all his cavalry in full view of the Israelites in Bethulia. 7 He reconnoitered the approaches to their town and visited the springs that supplied their water; he seized them and set guards of soldiers over them and then returned to his army.

8 Then all the chieftains of the Edomites and all the leaders of the Moabites and the commanders of the coastland came to him and said, 9 "Listen to what we have to say, my lord, and your army will suffer no losses. 10 This people, the Israelites, do not rely on their spears but on the height of the mountains where they live, for it is not easy to reach the tops of their mountains. 11 Therefore, my lord, do not fight against them in regular formation, and not a man of your army will fall. 12 Remain in your camp, and keep all the men in your forces with you; let your servants take possession of the spring of water that flows from the foot of the mountain, 13 for this is where all the people of Bethulia get their water. So thirst will destroy them, and they will surrender their town. Meanwhile, we and our people will go up to the tops of the nearby mountains and camp there to keep watch to see that no one gets out of the town. 14 They and their wives and children will waste away with famine, and before the sword reaches them they will be strewn about in the streets where they live. 15 Thus you will pay them back with evil because they rebelled and did not receive you peaceably."

16 These words pleased Holofernes and all his attendants, and he gave orders to do as they had said. 17 So the army of the Ammonites moved forward, together with five thousand Assyrians, and they encamped in the valley and seized the water supply and the springs of the Israelites. 18 And the Edomites and Ammonites went up and encamped in the hill country opposite Dothan, and they sent some of their men toward the south and the east, toward Egrebeh, which is near Chusi beside the Wadi Mochmur. The rest of the Assyrian army encamped in the plain and covered the whole face of the land. Their tents and supply trains spread out in great number, and they formed a vast multitude.

The Distress of the Israelites

19 The Israelites then cried out to the Lord their God, for their courage failed, because all their enemies had surrounded them, and there was no way of escape from them. 20 The whole Assyrian army, their infantry, chariots, and cavalry, surrounded them for thirty-four days, until all the water containers of every inhabitant of Bethulia were empty; 21 their cisterns were

going dry, and on no day did they have enough water to drink, for their drinking water was rationed. 22 Their children were listless, and the women and young men fainted from thirst and were collapsing in the streets of the town and in the gateways; they no longer had any strength.

23 Then all the people, the young men, the women, and the children, gathered around Uzziah and the rulers of the town and cried out with a loud voice and said before all the elders, 24 "Let God judge between you and us! You have done us a great injury in not making peace with the Assyrians. 25 For now we have no one to help us; God has sold us into their hands to be strewn before them in thirst and exhaustion. 26 Now summon them and surrender the whole town as plunder to the army of Holofernes and to all his forces. 27 For it would be better for us to be captured by them.*o* We shall indeed become slaves, but our lives will be spared, and we shall not witness our little ones dying before our eyes and our wives and children drawing their last breath. 28 We call to witness against you heaven and earth and our God, the Lord of our ancestors, who punishes us for our sins and the sins of our ancestors; do today the things that we have described!"

29 Then great and general lamentation arose throughout the assembly, and they cried out to the Lord God with a loud voice. 30 But Uzziah said to them, "Courage, my brothers and sisters! Let us hold out for five days more; by that time the Lord our God will turn his mercy to us again, for he will not forsake us utterly. 31 But if these days pass by and no help comes for us, I will do as you say."

32 Then he dismissed the people to their various posts, and they went up on the walls and towers of their town. The women and children he sent home. In the town they were in great misery.

The Character of Judith

8 Now in those days Judith heard about these things: she was the daughter of Merari son of Ox son of Joseph son of Oziel son of Elkiah son of Ananias son of Gideon son of Raphain son of Ahitub son of Elijah son of Hilkiah son of Eliab son of Nathanael son of Salamiel son of Sarasadai son of Israel. 2 Her husband Manasseh, who belonged to her tribe and family, had

died during the barley harvest. 3 For as he stood overseeing those who were binding sheaves in the field, he was overcome by the burning heat and took to his bed and died in his town Bethulia. So they buried him with his ancestors in the field between Dothan and Balamon. 4 Judith remained as a widow for three years and four months 5 at home, where she set up a tent for herself on the roof of her house. She put sackcloth around her waist and dressed in widow's clothing. 6 She fasted all the days of her widowhood except the day before the Sabbath and the Sabbath itself, the day before the new moon and the day of the new moon, and the festivals and days of rejoicing of the house of Israel. 7 She was beautiful in appearance and was very lovely to behold. Her husband Manasseh had left her gold and silver, male and female slaves, livestock, and fields, and she maintained this estate. 8 No one spoke ill of her, for she feared God with great devotion.

Judith and the Elders

9 When Judith heard the harsh words spoken by the people against the ruler because they were faint for lack of water, and when she heard all that Uzziah said to them and how he promised them under oath to surrender the town to the Assyrians after five days, 10 she sent her maid in charge of all she possessed to summon Uzziah and*p* Chabris and Charmis, the elders of her town. 11 They came to her, and she said to them,

"Listen to me, rulers of the people of Bethulia! What you have said to the people today is not right; you have even sworn and pronounced this oath between God and you, promising to surrender the town to our enemies unless the Lord turns and helps us within so many days. 12 Who are you to put God to the test today and to set yourselves up in the place of*q* God in human affairs? 13 You are putting the Lord Almighty to the test, but you will never learn anything! 14 You cannot plumb the depths of the human heart or understand the workings of the human mind; how do you expect to search out God, who made all these things, and find out his mind or comprehend his thought? No, my brothers, do not anger the Lord our God. 15 For if he does not choose to help us within these five days, he has power to protect us within

---

o 7.27 Other ancient authorities add *than to die of thirst*

p **8.10** Other ancient authorities lack *Uzziah and*

q **8.12** Or *above*

any time he pleases or even to destroy us in the presence of our enemies. ¹⁶Do not try to bind the purposes of the Lord our God, for God is not like a human being, to be threatened, or like a mere mortal, to be won over by pleading. ¹⁷Therefore, while we wait for his deliverance, let us call upon him to help us, and he will hear our voice, if it pleases him.

18 "For never in our generation nor in these present days has there been any tribe or family or people or town of ours that worships gods made with hands, as was done in days gone by. ¹⁹That was why our ancestors were handed over to the sword and to pillage, and so they suffered a great catastrophe before our enemies. ²⁰But we know no other god but him, and so we hope that he will not disdain us or any of our people. ²¹For if we are captured, all Judea will fall, and our sanctuary will be plundered, and he will make us pay for its desecration with our blood. ²²The slaughter of our kindred and the captivity of the land and the desolation of our inheritance—all this he will bring on our heads among the nations, wherever we serve as slaves, and we shall be an offense and a disgrace in the eyes of those who acquire us. ²³For our slavery will not bring us into favor, but the Lord our God will turn it to dishonor.

24 "Therefore, my brothers, let us set an example for our kindred, for their lives depend upon us, and the sanctuary—both the temple and the altar—rests upon us. ²⁵In spite of everything, let us give thanks to the Lord our God, who is putting us to the test as he did our ancestors. ²⁶Remember what he did with Abraham and how he tested Isaac and what happened to Jacob in Syrian Mesopotamia, while he was tending the sheep of Laban, his mother's brother. ²⁷For he has not tried us with fire, as he did them, to search their hearts, nor has he taken vengeance on us, but the Lord scourges those who are close to him in order to admonish them."

28 Then Uzziah said to her, "All that you have said was spoken out of a true heart, and there is no one who can deny your words. ²⁹Today is not the first time your wisdom has been shown, but from the beginning of your life all the people have recognized your understanding, for your heart's disposition is right. ³⁰But the people were so thirsty that they compelled us to do for them what we have promised and made us take an oath that we cannot break. ³¹Now since you are a God-fearing woman, pray for us, so that

the Lord may send us rain to fill our cisterns. Then we will no longer feel faint from thirst."

32 Then Judith said to them, "Listen to me. I am about to do something that will go down through all generations of our people. ³³Stand at the town gate tonight so that I may go out with my maid, and within the days after which you have promised to surrender the town to our enemies, the Lord will deliver Israel by my hand. ³⁴Only, do not try to find out what I am doing, for I will not tell you until I have finished what I am about to do."

35 Uzziah and the rulers said to her, "Go in peace, and may the Lord God go before you, to take vengeance on our enemies." ³⁶So they returned from the tent and went to their posts.

The Prayer of Judith

9 Then Judith prostrated herself, put ashes on her head, and uncovered the sackcloth she was wearing. At the very time when the evening incense was being offered in the house of God in Jerusalem, Judith cried out to the Lord with a loud voice and said,

2 "O Lord God of my ancestor Simeon, to whom you gave a sword to take revenge on those strangers who had torn off a virgin's clothing^r to defile her and exposed her thighs to put her to shame and profaned her womb to disgrace her, for you said, 'It shall not be done'— yet they did it, ³so you gave up their rulers to be killed, and their bed, which was ashamed of the deceit they had practiced, was stained with blood, and you struck down slaves along with princes and princes on their thrones. ⁴You gave up their wives for plunder and their daughters to captivity and all their spoils to be divided among your beloved children who burned with zeal for you and abhorred the pollution of their blood and called on you for help. O God, my God, hear me also, a widow.

5 "For you have done these things and those that went before and those that followed. You have designed the things that are now and those that are to come. What you had in mind has happened; ⁶the things you decided on presented themselves and said, 'Here we are!' For all your ways are prepared in advance, and your judgment is with foreknowledge.

7 "Here now are the Assyrians, a greatly increased force, priding themselves in their horses and riders, boasting in the strength of their foot

---

r 9.2 Cn: Gk *loosed her womb*

soldiers, and trusting in shield and spear, in bow and sling. They do not know that you are the Lord who crushes wars; the Lord is your name. ⁸Break their strength by your might, and bring down their power in your anger, for they intend to profane your sanctuary and to pollute the tabernacle where your glorious name resides and to break off the horns^s of your altar with the sword. ⁹Look at their pride, and send your wrath upon their heads. Give to me, a widow, the strong hand to do what I plan. ¹⁰By the deceit of my lips strike down the slave with the prince and the prince with his attendant; crush their arrogance by the hand of a woman.

¹¹"For your strength does not depend on numbers nor your might on the powerful. But you are the God of the lowly, helper of the oppressed, upholder of the weak, protector of the forsaken, savior of those without hope. ¹²Please, please, God of my father, God of the heritage of Israel, Lord of heaven and earth, Creator of the waters, King of all your creation, hear my prayer! ¹³Make my deceitful words bring wound and bruise on those who have planned cruel things against your covenant and against your sacred house and against Mount Zion and against the house your children possess. ¹⁴Let your whole nation and every tribe know and understand that you are God, the God of all power and might, and that there is no other who protects the people of Israel but you alone!"

Judith Prepares to Go to Holofernes

10 When Judith^t had stopped crying out to the God of Israel and had ended all these words, ²she rose from where she lay prostrate. She called her maid and went down into the house where she lived on Sabbaths and on her festal days. ³She removed the sackcloth she had been wearing, took off her widow's garments, bathed her body with water, and anointed herself with precious ointment. She combed her hair, put on a tiara, and dressed herself in the festive attire that she used to wear while her husband Manasseh was living. ⁴She put sandals on her feet and put on her anklets, bracelets, rings, earrings, and all her other jewelry. Thus she made herself very beautiful, to entice the eyes of all the men who might see her. ⁵She gave her maid a skin of wine and a flask of oil and filled a bag with roasted grain, dried fig cakes,

and fine bread;^{u} then she wrapped up all her dishes and gave them to her to carry.

⁶Then they went out to the town gate of Bethulia and found Uzziah standing there with the elders of the town, Chabris and Charmis. ⁷When they saw her transformed in appearance and dressed differently, they were very greatly astounded at her beauty and said to her, ⁸"May the God of our ancestors grant you favor and fulfill your plans, so that the people of Israel may glory and Jerusalem may be exalted." She bowed down to God.

⁹Then she said to them, "Order the gate of the town to be opened for me so that I may go out and accomplish the things you have just said to me." So they ordered the young men to open the gate for her, as she requested. ¹⁰When they had done this, Judith went out, accompanied by her maid. The men of the town watched her until she had gone down the mountain and passed through the valley, where they lost sight of her.

Judith Is Captured

¹¹As the women^v were going straight on through the valley, an Assyrian patrol met her ¹²and took her into custody. They asked her, "To what people do you belong, and where are you coming from, and where are you going?" She replied, "I am a daughter of the Hebrews, but I am fleeing from them, for they are about to be handed over to you to be devoured. ¹³I am on my way to see Holofernes the commander of your army, to give him a true report; I will show him a way by which he can go and capture all the hill country without losing one of his men, captured or slain."

¹⁴When the men heard her words and observed her face—she was in their eyes marvelously beautiful—they said to her, ¹⁵"You have saved your life by hurrying down to see our lord. Go at once to his tent; some of us will escort you and hand you over to him. ¹⁶When you stand before him, have no fear in your heart, but tell him what you have just said, and he will treat you well."

¹⁷They chose from their number a hundred men to accompany her and her maid, and they brought them to the tent of Holofernes. ¹⁸There was great excitement in the whole camp, for her arrival was reported from tent to tent. They came and gathered around her as she stood

---

s **9.8** Syr: Gk *horn*
t **10.1** Gk *she*

u **10.5** Other ancient authorities add *and cheese*
v **10.11** Gk *they*

outside the tent of Holofernes, waiting until they told him about her. ¹⁹They marveled at her beauty and admired the Israelites, judging them by her. They said to one another, "Who can despise these people, who have women like this among them? It is not wise to leave one of their men alive, for if we let them go they will be able to beguile the whole world!"

Judith Is Brought before Holofernes

20 Then the guards of Holofernes and all his attendants came out and led her into the tent. ²¹Holofernes was resting on his bed under a canopy that was woven with purple, gold, emeralds, and other precious stones. ²²When they told him of her, he came to the front of the tent, with silver lamps carried before him. ²³When Judith came into the presence of Holofernes^w and his attendants, they all marveled at the beauty of her face. She prostrated herself and did obeisance to him, but his slaves raised her up.

11 Then Holofernes said to her, "Take courage, woman, and do not be afraid in your heart, for I have never hurt anyone who chose to serve Nebuchadnezzar, king of all the earth. ²Even now, if your people who live in the hill country had not slighted me, I would never have lifted my spear against them. They have brought this on themselves. ³But now tell me why you have fled from them and have come over to us. In any event, you have come to safety. Take courage! You will live tonight and ever after. ⁴No one will hurt you. Rather, all will treat you well, as they do the servants of my lord King Nebuchadnezzar."

Judith Explains Her Presence

5 Judith answered him, "Accept the words of your slave, and let your servant speak in your presence. I will say nothing false to my lord this night. ⁶If you follow the words of your servant, God will accomplish something through you, and my lord will not fail to achieve his purposes. ⁷By the life of Nebuchadnezzar, king of the whole earth, and by the power of him who has sent you to direct every living being! Not only do humans serve him because of you, but also the animals of the field and the cattle and the birds of the air will live because of your power, under Nebuchadnezzar and all his house. ⁸For we have heard of your wisdom and skill, and

it is reported throughout the whole world that you alone are the best in the whole kingdom, the most informed and the most astounding in military strategy.

9 "Now as for Achior's speech in your council, we have heard his words, for the people of Bethulia spared him and he told them all he had said to you. ¹⁰Therefore, lord and master, do not disregard what he said, but keep it in your mind, for it is true. Indeed, our people cannot be punished nor can the sword prevail against them unless they sin against their God.

11 "But now, in order that my lord may not be defeated and his purpose frustrated, death will fall upon them, for a sin has overtaken them by which they are about to provoke their God to anger when they do what is wrong. ¹²Since their food supply is exhausted and their water has almost given out, they have planned to kill their livestock and have determined to use all that God by his laws has forbidden them to eat. ¹³They have decided to consume the first fruits of the grain and the tithes of the wine and oil, which they had consecrated and set aside for the priests who minister in the presence of our God in Jerusalem—things it is not lawful for any of the people even to touch with their hands. ¹⁴Since even the people in Jerusalem have been doing this, they have sent messengers there in order to bring back permission from the council of the elders. ¹⁵When the response reaches them and they act upon it, on that very day they will be handed over to you to be destroyed.

16 "So when I, your slave, learned all this, I fled from them. God has sent me to accomplish with you things that will astonish the whole world wherever people shall hear about them. ¹⁷Your servant is indeed God-fearing and serves the God of heaven night and day. So, my lord, I will remain with you, but every night your servant will go out into the valley and pray to God. He will tell me when they have committed their sins. ¹⁸Then I will come and tell you, so that you may go out with your whole army, and not one of them will be able to withstand you. ¹⁹Then I will lead you through Judea until you come to Jerusalem; there I will set your throne.^x You will drive them like sheep that have no shepherd, and no dog will so much as growl at you. For this was told me to give me foreknowledge; it was announced to me, and I was sent to tell you."

---

w **10.23** Gk *him*

x **11.19** Or *chariot*

20 Her words pleased Holofernes and all his attendants. They marveled at her wisdom and said, 21 "No other woman from one end of the earth to the other looks so beautiful or speaks so wisely!" 22 Then Holofernes said to her, "God has done well to send you ahead of the people, to strengthen our hands and bring destruction on those who have despised my lord. 23 You are not only beautiful in appearance but wise in speech. If you do as you have said, your God shall be my God, and you shall live in the palace of King Nebuchadnezzar and be renowned throughout the whole world."

Judith as a Guest of Holofernes

12 Then he commanded them to bring her in where his silver dinnerware was kept and ordered them to set a table for her with some of his own delicacies and with some of his own wine to drink. 2 But Judith said, "I cannot partake of them, or it will be an offense, but I will have enough with the things I brought with me." 3 Holofernes said to her, "If your supply runs out, where can we get you more of the same? For none of your people are here with us." 4 Judith replied, "As surely as you live, my lord, your servant will not use up the supplies I have with me before the Lord carries out by my hand what he has determined."

5 Then the attendants of Holofernes brought her into the tent, and she slept until midnight. Toward the morning watch she got up 6 and sent this message to Holofernes: "Let my lord now give orders to allow your servant to go out and pray." 7 So Holofernes commanded his guards not to hinder her. She remained in the camp three days. She went out each night to the valley of Bethulia and bathed at the spring in the camp.y 8 After bathing, she prayed the Lord God of Israel to direct her way for the triumph of hisz people. 9 Then she returned purified and stayed in the tent until she ate her food toward evening.

Judith Attends Holofernes's Banquet

10 On the fourth day Holofernes held a banquet for his slaves only and did not invite any of his officers. 11 He said to Bagoas, the eunuch who had charge of his personal affairs, "Go and persuade the Hebrew woman who is in your care to join us and to eat and drink with us. 12 For it would be a disgrace if we let such a

woman go without being intimate with her. If we do not seduce her, she will laugh at us."

13 So Bagoas left the presence of Holofernes and approached her and said, "Let this pretty servant not hesitate to come to my lord to be honored in his presence and to enjoy drinking wine with us and to become today like one of the Assyrian women who serve in the palace of Nebuchadnezzar." 14 Judith replied, "Who am I to refuse my lord? Whatever pleases him I will do at once, and it will be a joy to me until the day of my death." 15 So she proceeded to dress herself in all her woman's finery. Her maid went ahead and spread for her on the ground before Holofernes the lambskins she had received from Bagoas for her daily use in reclining.

16 Then Judith came in and lay down. Holofernes's heart was ravished with her and his passion was aroused, for he had been waiting for an opportunity to be with her from the day he first saw her. 17 So Holofernes said to her, "Have a drink and be merry with us!" 18 Judith said, "I will gladly drink, my lord, because today is the greatest day in my whole life." 19 Then she took what her maid had prepared and ate and drank before him. 20 Holofernes was greatly pleased with her and drank a great quantity of wine, much more than he had ever drunk in any one day since he was born.

Judith Beheads Holofernes

13 When evening came, his slaves quickly withdrew. Bagoas closed the tent from outside and shut out the attendants from his master's presence. They went to bed, for they all were weary because the banquet had lasted so long. 2 But Judith was left alone in the tent, with Holofernes stretched out on his bed, for he was dead drunk.

3 Now Judith had told her maid to stand outside the bedchamber and to wait for her to come out, as she did on the other days, for she said she would be going out for her prayers. She had said the same thing to Bagoas. 4 So everyone went out, and no one, either small or great, was left in the bedchamber. Then Judith, standing beside his bed, said in her heart, "O Lord God of all might, look in this hour on the work of my hands for the exaltation of Jerusalem. 5 Now indeed is the time to help your heritage and to carry out my design to destroy the enemies who have risen up against us."

6 She went up to the bedpost near Holofernes's head and took down his sword that hung there.

---

y 12.7 Other ancient authorities lack *in the camp*
z 12.8 Other ancient authorities read *her*

[7] She came close to his bed, took hold of the hair of his head, and said, "Give me strength today, O Lord God of Israel!" [8] Then she struck his neck twice with all her might and cut off his head. [9] Next she rolled his body off the bed and pulled down the canopy from the posts. Soon afterward she went out and gave Holofernes's head to her maid, [10] who placed it in her food bag.

Judith Returns to Bethulia

Then the two of them went out together, as they were accustomed to do for prayer. They passed through the camp, circled around the valley, went up the mountain to Bethulia, and came to its gates. [11] From a distance Judith called out to the sentries at the gates, "Open, open the gate! God, our God, is with us, still showing his power in Israel and his strength against our enemies, as he has done today!"

[12] When the people of her town heard her voice, they hurried down to the town gate and summoned the elders of the town. [13] They all ran together, both small and great, for it seemed unbelievable that she had returned. They opened the gate and welcomed them. Then they lit a fire to give light and gathered around them. [14] Then she said to them with a loud voice, "Praise God, O praise him! Praise God, who has not withdrawn his mercy from the house of Israel but has destroyed our enemies by my hand this very night!"

[15] Then she pulled the head out of the bag and showed it to them and said, "See here, the head of Holofernes, the commander of the Assyrian army, and here is the canopy beneath which he lay in his drunken stupor. The Lord has struck him down by the hand of a woman. [16] As the Lord lives, who has protected me in the way I went, I swear that it was my face that seduced him to his destruction and that he committed no sin with me, to defile and shame me."

[17] All the people were greatly astonished. They bowed down and worshiped God and said with one accord, "Blessed are you, our God, who have this day humiliated the enemies of your people."

[18] Then Uzziah said to her, "O daughter, you are blessed by the Most High God above all other women on earth, and blessed be the Lord God, who created the heavens and the earth, who has guided you to cut off the head of the leader of our enemies. [19] Your hope[a] will never

---

a 13.19 Other ancient authorities read *praise*

depart from the hearts of those who remember the power of God. [20] May God grant this to be a perpetual honor to you, and may he reward you with blessings because you risked your own life when our people was brought low, and you averted our ruin, walking in the straight path before our God." And all the people said, "Amen. Amen."

Judith's Counsel

14 Then Judith said to them, "Listen to me, my friends. Take this head and hang it upon the parapet of your wall. [2] As soon as day breaks and the sun rises on the earth, each of you take up your weapons, and let every able-bodied man go out of the town; set a captain over them, as if you were going down to the plain against the Assyrian outpost; only do not go down. [3] Then they will seize their arms and go into the camp and rouse the officers of the Assyrian army. They will rush into the tent of Holofernes and will not find him. Then panic will come over them, and they will flee before you. [4] Then you and all who live within the borders of Israel will pursue them and cut them down in their tracks. [5] But before you do all this, bring Achior the Ammonite to me so that he may see and recognize the man who despised the house of Israel and sent him to us as if to his death."

[6] So they summoned Achior from the house of Uzziah. When he came and saw the head of Holofernes in the hand of one of the men in the assembly of the people, he fell down on his face in a faint. [7] When they raised him up he threw himself at Judith's feet and did obeisance to her and said, "Blessed are you in every tent of Judah! In every nation those who hear your name will be alarmed. [8] Now tell me what you have done during these days."

So Judith told him in the presence of the people all that she had done from the day she left until the moment she began speaking to them. [9] When she had finished, the people raised a great shout and made a joyful noise in their town. [10] When Achior saw all that the God of Israel had done, he believed firmly in God. So he was circumcised and joined the house of Israel, remaining so to this day.

Holofernes's Death Is Discovered

[11] As soon as it was dawn, they hung the head of Holofernes on the wall. Then they all took their weapons and went out in companies to the mountain passes. [12] When the Assyrians

saw them, they sent word to their commanders, who then went to the generals and the captains and to all their other officers. ¹³They came to Holofernes's tent and said to the steward in charge of all his personal affairs, "Wake up our lord, for the slaves have been so bold as to come down against us to give battle, to their utter destruction."

¹⁴So Bagoas went in and knocked at the entry of the tent, for he supposed that he was sleeping with Judith. ¹⁵But when no one answered, he opened it and went into the bedchamber and found him dead, sprawled over the footstool, with his head missing. ¹⁶He cried out with a loud voice and wept and groaned and shouted and tore his clothes. ¹⁷Then he went to the tent where Judith had stayed, and when he did not find her, he rushed out to the people and shouted, ¹⁸"The slaves have foiled us! One Hebrew woman has brought disgrace on the house of King Nebuchadnezzar. Look, Holofernes is lying on the ground, and his head is missing!"

¹⁹When the leaders of the Assyrian army heard this, they tore their tunics and were greatly dismayed, and their loud cries and shouts rose up throughout the camp.

The Assyrians Flee in Panic

15 When the men in the tents heard it, they were amazed at what had happened. ²Overcome with fear and trembling, they did not wait for one another, but with one impulse all rushed out and fled by every path across the plain and through the hill country. ³Those who had camped in the hills around Bethulia also took to flight. Then the Israelites, everyone who was a soldier, rushed out upon them. ⁴Uzziah sent men to Betomasthaim*ᵇ* and Choba and Kola and to all the frontiers of Israel to tell what had taken place and to urge all to rush out upon the enemy to destroy them. ⁵When the Israelites heard it, with one accord they fell upon the enemy*ᶜ* and cut them down as far as Choba. Those in Jerusalem and all the hill country also came, for they were told what had happened in the camp of the enemy. The men in Gilead and in Galilee outflanked them with great slaughter, even beyond Damascus and its borders. ⁶The rest of the people of Bethulia fell upon the Assyrian camp and plundered it, acquiring great riches. ⁷And the Israelites, when they returned

from the slaughter, took possession of what remained. Even the villages and towns in the hill country and in the plain got a great amount of plunder, since there was a vast quantity of it.

The Israelites Celebrate Their Victory

⁸Then the high priest Joakim and the council of the Israelites who lived in Jerusalem came to witness the good things that the Lord had done for Israel and to see Judith and to wish her well. ⁹When they met her, they all blessed her with one accord and said to her, "You are the glory of Jerusalem, you are the great boast of Israel, you are the great pride of our people! ¹⁰You have done all this with your own hand; you have done great good to Israel, and God is well pleased with it. May the Almighty Lord bless you forever!" And all the people said, "Amen."

¹¹All the people plundered the camp for thirty days. They gave Judith the tent of Holofernes and all his silver dinnerware, his beds, his bowls, and all his furniture. She took them and loaded her mules and hitched up her carts and piled the things on them.

¹²All the women of Israel gathered to see her and blessed her, and some of them performed a dance in her honor. She took ivy-wreathed wands in her hands and distributed them to the women who were with her, ¹³and she and those who were with her crowned themselves with olive wreaths. She went before all the people in the dance, leading all the women, while all the men of Israel followed, bearing their arms and wearing garlands and singing hymns.

Judith Offers Her Hymn of Praise

¹⁴Judith began this thanksgiving before all Israel, and all the people loudly sang this song

16 of praise. ¹And Judith said,
"Begin a song to my God with
   tambourines;
  sing to my Lord with cymbals.
Raise to him a new psalm;*ᵈ*
  exalt him and call upon his name.
² For the Lord is a God who crushes wars;
  he sets up his camp among his people;
  he delivered me from the hands of my
    pursuers.
³ The Assyrian came down from the
   mountains of the north;
  he came with myriads of his warriors;

---

b 15.4 Other ancient authorities add *and Bebai*
c 15.5 Gk *them*

d 16.1 Other ancient authorities read *a psalm and praise*

their numbers blocked up the wadis,
   and their cavalry covered the hills.
4 He boasted that he would burn up my
    territory
   and kill my young men with the sword
   and dash my infants to the ground
   and seize my children as plunder
   and take my virgins as spoil.

5 "But the Lord Almighty has foiled them
   by the hand of a woman.*e*
6 For their mighty one did not fall by the
    hands of the young men,
   nor did the sons of the Titans strike him
    down,
   nor did tall giants set upon him,
  but Judith daughter of Merari
   with the beauty of her countenance undid
    him.

7 "For she put away her widow's clothing
   to exalt the oppressed in Israel.
  She anointed her face with perfume;
8   she fastened her hair with a tiara
   and put on a linen gown to beguile
    him.
9 Her sandal ravished his eyes,
   her beauty captivated his mind,
   and the sword severed his neck!
10 The Persians trembled at her boldness;
   the Medes were daunted at her daring.

11 "Then my oppressed people shouted;
   my weak people cried out,*f* and the
    enemy*g* trembled;
   they lifted up their voices, and the enemy*h*
    were turned back.
12 Sons of female slaves pierced them
    through
   and wounded them like the children of
    fugitives;
   they perished before the army of my
    Lord.

13 "I will sing to my God a new song:
  O Lord, you are great and glorious,
   wonderful in strength, invincible.
14 Let all your creatures serve you,
   for you spoke, and they were made.

You sent forth your spirit,*i* and it formed them;*j*
   there is none that can resist your voice.
15 For the mountains shall be shaken to their
    foundations with the waters;
   before your glance the rocks shall melt
    like wax.
  But to those who fear you
   you show mercy.
16 For every sacrifice as a fragrant offering is a
    small thing,
   and the fat of all whole burnt offerings to
    you is a very little thing,
  but whoever fears the Lord is great forever.

17 "Woe to the nations that rise up against my
    people!
  The Lord Almighty will take vengeance
   on them in the day of judgment;
  he will send fire and worms into their flesh;
   they shall weep in pain forever."

18 When they arrived at Jerusalem, they worshiped God. As soon as the people were purified, they offered their burnt offerings, their freewill offerings, and their gifts. 19 Judith also dedicated to God all the possessions of Holofernes that the people had given her, and the canopy that she had taken for herself from his bedchamber she gave as a votive offering. 20 For three months the people continued feasting in Jerusalem before the sanctuary, and Judith remained with them.

The Renown and Death of Judith

21 After this they all returned home to their own inheritances. Judith went to Bethulia and remained on her estate. For the rest of her life she was honored throughout the whole country. 22 Many desired to marry her, but she gave herself to no man all the days of her life after her husband Manasseh died and was gathered to his people. 23 She became more and more famous and grew old in her husband's house, reaching the age of one hundred five. She set her maid free. She died in Bethulia, and they buried her in the cave of her husband Manasseh, 24 and the house of Israel mourned her for seven days. Before she died she distributed her property to all those who were next of kin to her husband Manasseh and to her own nearest kindred. 25 No one ever again spread terror among the Israelites during the lifetime of Judith or for a long time after her death.

---

e 16.5 Other ancient authorities add *he has confounded them*
f 16.11 Other ancient authorities read *feared*
g 16.11 Gk *they*
h 16.11 Gk *they*

i 16.14 Or *breath*
j 16.14 Other ancient authorities read *they were created*

ESTHER (GREEK)

(The Greek Version Containing the Additional Chapters)

Note: The deuterocanonical portions of the book of Esther are several additional passages found in the Greek translation of the Hebrew book of Esther, a translation that differs also in other respects from the Hebrew text (the latter is translated in the NRSVue Old Testament). The disordered chapter numbers come from the displacement of the additions to the end of the canonical book of Esther by Jerome in his Latin translation and from the subsequent division of the Bible into chapters by Stephen Langton, who numbered the additions consecutively as though they formed a direct continuation of the Hebrew text. So that the additions may be read in their proper context, the whole of the Greek version is here translated, though certain familiar names are given according to their Hebrew rather than their Greek form, for example, Mordecai and Vashti instead of Mardocheus and Astin. The order followed is that of the Greek text, but the chapter and verse numbers conform to those of the King James, or Authorized, Version. The additions, conveniently indicated by the letters A–F, are located as follows: A before 1.1; B after 3.13; C and D after 4.17; E after 8.12; F after 10.3.

ADDITION A

Mordecai's Dream

11 2 *a*In the second year of the reign of Artaxerxes the Great, on the first day of Nisan, Mordecai son of Jair son of Shimei son of Kish, of the tribe of Benjamin, had a dream. 3 He was a Jew living in the city of Susa, a great man serving in the court of the king. 4 He was one of the captives whom King Nebuchadnezzar of Babylon had taken captive from Jerusalem with King Jeconiah of Judea. And this was his dream: 5 Noises*b* and confusion, thunder and earthquake, tumult on the earth! 6 Then two great dragons came forward, both ready to fight, and they roared terribly. 7 At their roaring every nation prepared for war, to fight against a nation of righteous people. 8 It was a day of darkness and gloom, of tribulation and distress, affliction and great tumult on the earth! 9 And the whole righteous nation was troubled; they feared the evils that threatened them*c* and were ready to perish. 10 Then they cried out to God, and at their outcry, as though from a tiny spring, there came a great river with abundant water; 11 light came, and the sun rose, and the lowly were exalted and devoured those held in honor.

12 Mordecai saw in this dream what God had determined to do, and after he awoke he had it on his mind, seeking all day to understand it in every detail.

A Plot against the King

12 Now Mordecai took his rest in the courtyard with Gabatha and Tharra, the two eunuchs of the king who kept watch in the courtyard. 2 He overheard their conversation and inquired into their purposes and learned that they were preparing to lay hands on King Artaxerxes, and he informed the king concerning them. 3 Then the king examined the two eunuchs, and after they had confessed it, they were led away. 4 The king wrote these things down as a commemoration, and Mordecai wrote an account of them. 5 And the king ordered Mordecai to serve in the court and rewarded him for these things. 6 But Haman son of Hammedatha, a Bougean, who was in great honor with the king, determined to injure Mordecai and his people because of the two eunuchs of the king.

END OF ADDITION A

---

a **11.2** 11.2–12.6 corresponds to A 1–17 in some translations.
b **11.5** Or *Voices*
c **11.9** Gk *their own evils*

Artaxerxes's Banquet

1 It was after this that the following things happened in the days of Artaxerxes, the same Artaxerxes who ruled over one hundred twenty-seven provinces from India to Ethiopia.*[d]* ²In those days, when King Artaxerxes was enthroned in the city of Susa, ³in the third year of his reign, he gave a banquet for his Friends and other persons of various nations, the Persians and Median nobles, and the governors of the satrapies. ⁴After this, when he had displayed to them the riches of his kingdom and the splendor of his bountiful celebration during the course of one hundred eighty days, ⁵at the end of the wedding feast the king gave a drinking party for the people of various nations who lived in the city. This was held for six days in the courtyard of the royal palace, ⁶which was adorned with curtains of fine linen and cotton, held by cords of linen and purple fabric attached to gold and silver blocks on pillars of marble and other stones. Gold and silver couches were placed on a mosaic floor of emerald, mother-of-pearl, and marble. There were coverings of gauze, embroidered in various colors, with roses scattered around them. ⁷The cups were of gold and silver, and a miniature cup was displayed, made of ruby, worth thirty thousand talents. There was abundant sweet wine, such as the king himself drank. ⁸This drinking party was not in accordance with established custom, but the king wished to have it so, and he commanded his stewards to comply with his pleasure and with that of the guests.

⁹Meanwhile, Queen Vashti gave a drinking party for the women in the palace where King Artaxerxes was.

Dismissal of Queen Vashti

¹⁰On the seventh day, when the king was in good humor, he told Haman, Bazan, Tharra, Boraze, Zatholtha, Abataza, and Tharaba, the seven eunuchs who served King Artaxerxes, ¹¹to escort the queen to him in order to proclaim her as queen and to place the diadem on her head and to have her display her beauty to all the governors and the people of various nations, for she was indeed a beautiful woman. ¹²But Queen Vashti refused to obey him and would not come with the eunuchs. This offended the king, and he became furious. ¹³He said to his Friends, "This is how Vashti has answered me.*[e]* Give,

therefore, your ruling and judgment on this matter." ¹⁴Arkesaeus, Sarsathaeus, and Malesear, the governors of the Persians and Medes who were closest to the king, who sat beside him in the chief seats, came to him ¹⁵and told him what, according to the law, was to be done to Queen Vashti for not obeying the order that the king had sent her by the eunuchs. ¹⁶Then Muchaeus said to the king and the governors, "Queen Vashti has wronged not only the king but also all the king's governors and officials" ¹⁷(for he had reported to them what the queen had said and how she had defied the king). "And just as she defied King Artaxerxes, ¹⁸so now the other noble wives of the Persian and Median governors, on hearing what she has said to the king, will likewise dare to dishonor their husbands. ¹⁹If, therefore, it pleases the king, let him issue a royal decree, inscribed in accordance with the laws of the Medes and Persians so that it may not be altered, that the queen may no longer come into his presence, and let the king give her royal rank to a woman better than she. ²⁰Let whatever law the king enacts be proclaimed in his kingdom, and thus all women will give honor to their husbands, rich and poor alike." ²¹This speech pleased the king and the governors, and the king did as Muchaeus had recommended. ²²The king sent the decree*[f]* into all his kingdom, to every province in its own language, so that men would be feared in their households.

Esther Becomes Queen

2 After these things, the king's anger abated, and he no longer remembered Vashti or remembered what he*[g]* had said and how he had condemned her. ²Then the king's servants said, "Let beautiful and virtuous young women be sought out for the king. ³The king shall appoint officers in all the provinces of his kingdom, and they shall select beautiful young virgins to be brought to the harem in the city of Susa. Let them be entrusted to the king's eunuch who is in charge of the women, and let ointments and whatever else they need be given them. ⁴And the woman who pleases the king shall be queen instead of Vashti." This pleased the king, and he did so.

⁵Now there was a Jew in the city of Susa whose name was Mordecai son of Jair son of

---

d   **1.1** Other ancient authorities lack *to Ethiopia*

e   **1.13** Gk *has said thus and so*

f   **1.22** Gk lacks *the decree*

g   **2.1** Or *she*

Shimei son of Kish, of the tribe of Benjamin; [6]he had been taken captive from Jerusalem among those whom King Nebuchadnezzar of Babylon had captured. [7]And he had a foster child, the daughter of his father's brother, Aminadab, and her name was Esther. When her parents died, he brought her up as a wife for himself. The young woman was beautiful in appearance. [8]So when the decree of the king was proclaimed and many young women were gathered in the city of Susa in custody of Gai, Esther also was brought to Gai, who had custody of the women. [9]The young woman pleased him and won his favor, and he quickly provided her with ointments and her portion of food,[h] as well as seven young women chosen from the palace; he treated her and her maids with special favor in the harem. [10]Now Esther had not disclosed her people or country, for Mordecai had commanded her not to make it known. [11]And every day Mordecai walked in the courtyard of the harem, to see what would happen to Esther.

[12]Now the period after which a young woman was to go to the king was twelve months. During this time the days of cosmetic treatment are completed: six months while they are anointing themselves with oil of myrrh and six months with spices and ointments for women. [13]Then she goes in to the king; she is handed to the person appointed and goes with him from the harem to the king's palace.[i] [14]In the evening she enters, and in the morning she departs to the second harem, where Gai the king's eunuch is in charge of the women, and she does not go in to the king again unless she is summoned by name.

[15]When the time was fulfilled for Esther daughter of Aminadab, the brother of Mordecai's father, to go in to the king, she neglected none of the things that the eunuch in charge of the women had commanded. For Esther found favor in the eyes of all who saw her. [16]So Esther went in to King Artaxerxes in the twelfth month, which is Adar, in the seventh year of his reign. [17]And the king loved Esther passionately, and she found favor beyond all the other virgins, and he put on her the queen's diadem. [18]Then the king gave a drinking party lasting seven days for all his Friends and the officers to celebrate his marriage to Esther, and he granted a remission of taxes to those who were under his rule.

The Plot Discovered

[19]Meanwhile Mordecai was serving in the court. [20]Esther had not disclosed her country, for thus Mordecai had instructed her to fear God and keep his laws, just as she had done when she was with him. So Esther did not change her way of life.

[21]Now two of the king's eunuchs, who were chief bodyguards, were upset because of Mordecai's advancement, and they plotted to kill King Artaxerxes. [22]The matter became known to Mordecai, and he warned Esther, who in turn revealed the plot to the king. [23]He investigated the two eunuchs and hanged them. Then the king ordered that a record commemorating Mordecai's goodwill be deposited in the royal archive.

Mordecai Refuses to Do Obeisance

3 After these events King Artaxerxes honored Haman son of Hammedatha, a Bougean, and exalted him, and would seat him first among all the king's[j] Friends. [2]So all who were at court used to do obeisance to Haman,[k] for so the king had commanded to be done. Mordecai, however, did not do obeisance. [3]Then the king's courtiers said to Mordecai, "Mordecai, why do you disobey the king's command?" [4]Day after day they spoke to him, but he would not listen to them. Then they informed Haman that Mordecai was resisting the king's command. Mordecai had told them that he was a Jew. [5]So when Haman learned that Mordecai was not doing obeisance to him, he became furiously angry [6]and resolved to destroy all the Jews under Artaxerxes's rule.

[7]In the twelfth year of the reign of Artaxerxes, Haman[l] came to a decision and cast lots, taking the days and the months one by one, to fix on one day to destroy the whole people of Mordecai. The lot fell on the fourteenth[m] day of the month of Adar.

Decree against the Jews

[8]Then Haman[n] said to King Artaxerxes, "There is a certain nation scattered among the other nations in all your kingdom; their laws are different from those of every other nation, and they do not keep the laws of the king. It is

---

h 2.9 Gk lacks *of food*
i 2.13 Meaning of Gk uncertain
j 3.1 Gk *all his*
k 3.2 Gk *him*
l 3.7 Gk *he*
m 3.7 Other ancient witnesses read *thirteenth*
n 3.8 Gk *he*

not expedient for the king to tolerate them. [9] If it pleases the king, let him decree that they are to be destroyed, and I will pay ten thousand talents of silver into the king's treasury." [10] So the king took off his signet ring and gave it to Haman to seal the decree[o] that was to be written against the Jews. [11] The king told Haman, "Keep the money, and do whatever you want with that nation."

[12] So on the thirteenth day of the first month the king's secretaries were summoned, and in accordance with Haman's instructions they wrote in the name of King Artaxerxes to the magistrates and the governors in every province from India to Ethiopia, one hundred twenty-seven provinces in all, and to the governors of the nations, each in his own language. [13] Instructions were sent by couriers throughout all the empire of Artaxerxes to destroy the Jewish people in a single day of the twelfth month, which is Adar, and to plunder their goods.

ADDITION B

The King's Letter

13 [p] This is a copy of the letter: "The Great King, Artaxerxes, writes the following to the governors of the hundred twenty-seven provinces from India to Ethiopia and to the officials under them:

[2] "Having become ruler of many nations and master of the whole world (not elated with presumption of authority but always acting reasonably and with kindness), I have determined to settle the lives of my subjects in lasting tranquility and, in order to make my kingdom peaceable and open to travel throughout all its extent, to restore the peace desired by all people.

[3] "When I asked my counselors how this might be accomplished, Haman—who excels among us in sound judgment and is distinguished for his unchanging goodwill and steadfast fidelity and has attained the second place of honor in the kingdom—[4] pointed out to us that among all the nations in the world there is scattered a certain hostile people who have laws contrary to those of every nation and continually disregard the ordinances of kings, so that the unifying of the kingdom that we honorably intend cannot be brought about. [5] We understand

that this people, and it alone, stands constantly in opposition to all humanity, perversely following a strange manner of life and laws, and is ill-disposed to our interests, doing all the harm they can so that our kingdom may not attain stability.

[6] "Therefore we have decreed that those indicated to you in the letters written by Haman, who is in charge of affairs and is our second father, shall all—wives and children included—be utterly destroyed by the swords of their enemies, without pity or restraint, on the fourteenth day of the twelfth month, Adar, of this present year, [7] so that those who have long been hostile and remain so may in a single day go down in violence to Hades and leave our interests secure and untroubled hereafter."

END OF ADDITION B

---

3 [14] Copies of the letter were posted in every province, and all the nations were ordered to be prepared for that day. [15] The matter was expedited also in Susa. And while the king and Haman caroused together, the city was thrown into confusion.

Mordecai Seeks Esther's Aid

4 When Mordecai learned of all that had been done, he tore his clothes, put on sackcloth, and sprinkled himself with ashes; then he rushed through the street of the city, shouting loudly: "An innocent nation is being destroyed!" [2] He got as far as the king's gate, and there he stopped, because no one was allowed to enter the courtyard clothed in sackcloth and ashes. [3] And in every province where the letter had been posted there was crying, lamentation, and great mourning among the Jews, and they put on sackcloth and ashes. [4] When the queen's[q] maids and eunuchs came and told her, she was deeply troubled by what she heard had happened and sent instructions to clothe Mordecai and to remove his sackcloth, but he would not consent. [5] Then Esther summoned Hachratheus, the eunuch who attended her, and dispatched him to get accurate information for her from Mordecai.[r]

[7] So Mordecai told him what had happened and about the promise that Haman had

---

o **3.10** Gk lacks *the decree*
p **13.1** 13.1–7 corresponds to B 1–7 in some translations.

q **4.4** Gk *When her*
r **4.5** Other ancient witnesses add [6] *So Hachratheus went out to Mordecai in the street of the city opposite the city gate.*

promised the king: ten thousand talents for the royal treasury to bring about the destruction of the Jews. ⁸He also gave him a copy of what had been posted in Susa for their destruction, to show to Esther, and he told him to charge her to go in to the king and plead for his favor in behalf of the people. "Remember," he said, "the days when you were an ordinary person, being brought up under my care, for Haman, who is second to the king, has spoken against us and demands our death. Call upon the Lord; then speak to the king in our behalf and save us from death."

9 Hachratheus went in and told her all these things. ¹⁰And Esther said to him, "Go to Mordecai and say: ¹¹All nations of the realm know that if any man or woman goes to the king inside the inner court without being called, there is no escape for that person. Only the one to whom the king stretches out the golden scepter is safe—and it is now thirty days since I myself was called to go to the king."

12 So Hachratheus delivered Esther's entire message to Mordecai, ¹³and then Mordecai said to Hachratheus, "Go and say to her: Esther, do not say to yourself that you alone among all the Jews in the realm will escape alive. ¹⁴For if you take no heed at such a time as this, help and protection will come to the Jews from another quarter, but you and your father's family will perish. And who knows whether it was not for such a time as this that you were made queen?" ¹⁵Then Esther gave the messenger this answer to take back to Mordecai: ¹⁶"Go and gather the Jews who are in Susa and fast on my behalf; for three days and nights do not eat or drink, and my maids and I will also go without food. After that I will go to the king, contrary to the law, even if I must die." ¹⁷So Mordecai went away and did what Esther had told him to do.

Addition C

Mordecai's Prayer

13 ⁸ˢThen Mordecai*ᵗ* prayed to the Lord, calling to remembrance all the works of the Lord.

9 He said, "O Lord, Lord, King of all powers, for the universe is in your power and there is

no one who can oppose you when it is your will to save Israel, ¹⁰for you have made heaven and earth and every wonderful thing under heaven. ¹¹You are Lord of all, and there is no one who can resist you, the Lord. ¹²You know all things; you know, O Lord, that it was not in insolence or pride or for any love of glory that I did this and refused to bow down to this proud Haman, ¹³for I would have been willing to kiss the soles of his feet to save Israel! ¹⁴But I did this so that I might not set human glory above the glory of God, and I will not bow down to anyone but you, who are my Lord, and I will not do these things in pride. ¹⁵And now, O Lord God and King, God of Abraham, spare your people, for the eyes of our foes are upon usᵘ to annihilate us, and they desire to destroy the inheritance that has been yours from the beginning. ¹⁶Do not neglect your portion, which you redeemed for yourself out of the land of Egypt. ¹⁷Hear my prayer and have mercy upon your inheritance; turn our mourning into feasting that we may live and sing praise to your name, O Lord; do not destroy the lipsᵛ of those who praise you."

18 And all Israel cried out with all their might, for their death was before their eyes.

Esther's Prayer

14 Then Queen Esther, seized with mortal anguish, fled to the Lord. ²She took off the garments of her honor and put on the garments of distress and mourning, and instead of costly perfumes she covered her head with ashes and dung, and she utterly humbled her body; every part that she loved to adorn she covered with her tangled hair. ³She prayed to the Lord God of Israel and said: "O my Lord, you alone are our king; help me, who am alone and have no helper but you, ⁴for my danger is in my hand. ⁵Ever since I was born I have heard in the tribe of my family that you, O Lord, took Israel out of all the nations and our ancestors from among all their forebears for an everlasting inheritance and that you did for them all that you said. ⁶And now we have sinned before you, and you have delivered us into the hands of our enemies ⁷because we glorified their gods. You are righteous, O Lord! ⁸And now they are not satisfied that we are in bitter slavery, but they have set their hands on the hands of their idols ⁹to abolish what your mouth has ordained

---

s **13.8** 13.8–15.16 corresponds to C 1–30 and D 1–16 in some translations.
t **13.8** Gk *he*

u **13.15** Gk *for they are eying us*
v **13.17** Gk *mouth*

and to destroy your inheritance, to stop the mouths of those who praise you and to quench your altar and the glory of your house, 10to open the mouths of the nations for the praise of vain idols and to magnify forever a mortal king.

11 "O Lord, do not surrender your scepter to what has no being, and do not let them laugh at our downfall, but turn their plan against them and make an example of him who began this against us. 12Remember, O Lord; make yourself known in this time of our affliction and give me courage, O King of the gods and Master of all dominion! 13Put eloquent speech in my mouth before the lion and turn his heart to hate the man who is fighting against us, so that there may be an end of him and those who agree with him. 14But save us by your hand and help me, who am alone and have no helper but you, O Lord. You have knowledge of all things, 15and you know that I hate the splendor of the lawless and abhor the bed of the uncircumcised and of any alien. 16You know my necessity, that I abhor the sign of my proud position that is upon my head on days when I appear in public. I abhor it like a menstrual cloth, and I do not wear it on the days when I am at rest. 17And your servant has not eaten at Haman's table, and I have not honored the king's feast or drunk the wine of libations. 18Your servant has had no joy since the day that I was brought here until now, except in you, O Lord God of Abraham. 19O God, whose might is over all, hear the voice of the despairing and save us from the hands of evildoers. And save me from my fear!"

END OF ADDITION C

ADDITION D

Esther Is Received by the King

15 On the third day, when she ended her prayer, she took off the garments in which she had worshiped and arrayed herself in the garments of her honor. 2Then, majestically adorned, after invoking the aid of the all-seeing God and Savior, she took two maids with her; 3on one she leaned gently for support, 4while the other followed, carrying her train. 5She was radiant with perfect beauty, and she looked happy, as if beloved, but her heart was frozen with fear. 6When she had gone through all the doors, she stood before the king. He was seated on his royal throne, clothed in the full array of his majesty, all covered with gold and precious stones. He was most terrifying.

7Lifting his face, ablaze with glory, he looked at her in fierce anger. The queen faltered, turned pale and faint, and collapsed on the head of the maid who went in front of her. 8Then God changed the spirit of the king to gentleness, and in alarm he sprang from his throne and took her in his arms until she came to herself. He comforted her with soothing words and said to her, 9"What is it, Esther? I am your kin.w Take courage. 10You shall not die, for our law applies only to our subjects.x Come near."

11Then he raised the golden scepter and touched her neck with it; 12he embraced her and said, "Speak to me." 13She said to him, "I saw you, my lord, like an angel of God, and my heart was shaken with fear at your glory. 14For you are wonderful, my lord, and your countenance is full of grace." 15And while she was speaking, she fainted and fell. 16Then the king was agitated, and all his attendants tried to comfort her.

END OF ADDITION D

5 3yThe king said to her, "What do you wish, Esther? What is your request? It shall be yours, even to half of my kingdom." 4And Esther said, "Today is a special day for me. If it pleases the king, let him and Haman come to the banquet that I shall prepare today." 5Then the king said, "Bring Haman quickly, so that we may do as Esther desires." So they both came to the banquet that Esther had spoken about. 6While they were drinking wine, the king said to Esther, "What is it, Queen Esther? It shall be granted you." 7She said, "My petition and request is: 8if I have found favor in the sight of the king, let the king and Haman come again tomorrow to the banquet that I shall prepare them, and tomorrow I will do the same."

Haman's Plot against Mordecai

9So Haman went out from the king joyful and glad of heart. But when he saw Mordecai the Jew in the courtyard, he was filled with anger. 10Nevertheless, he went home and summoned his friends and his wife Zosara. 11And he told

---

w 15.9 Gk brother
x 15.10 Meaning of Gk uncertain
y 5.3 In Greek, Addition D replaces 5.1–2 in Hebrew.

them about his riches and the honor that the king had bestowed on him and how he had advanced him to be the first in the kingdom. ¹²And Haman said, "The queen did not invite anyone to the banquet with the king except me, and I am invited again tomorrow. ¹³But these things give me no pleasure as long as I see Mordecai the Jew in the courtyard." ¹⁴His wife Zosara and his friends said to him, "Let a pole be cut, fifty cubits high, and in the morning tell the king and have Mordecai hung on it. Then, go with the king to the banquet and enjoy yourself." This advice pleased Haman, so the pole was prepared.

Mordecai's Reward from the King

6 That night the Lord took sleep from the king, so he told his teacher to bring the book of daily records and to read to him. ²He found the words written about Mordecai, how he had told the king about the two royal eunuchs who were on guard and sought to lay hands on Artaxerxes. ³The king said, "What honor or favor did we bestow on Mordecai?" The king's servants said, "You have not done anything for him." ⁴While the king was inquiring about the goodwill shown by Mordecai— Look! Haman was in the courtyard. The king asked, "Who is in the courtyard?" Now Haman had come to speak to the king about hanging Mordecai on the pole that he had prepared. ⁵The servants of the king said, "Look! Haman is standing in the courtyard." And the king said, "Summon him." ⁶Then the king said to Haman, "What shall I do for the person whom I wish to honor?" And Haman said to himself, "Whom would the king wish to honor more than me?" ⁷So he said to the king, "For a person whom the king wishes to honor, ⁸let the king's servants bring out the fine linen robe that the king wears and the horse on which the king rides, ⁹and let them be given to one of the king's honored Friends, and let him robe the person whom the king loves and mount him on the horse, and let him proclaim through the open square of the city, saying, 'Thus shall it be done to everyone whom the king honors.'" ¹⁰Then the king said to Haman, "You have spoken well! Do just as you have said for Mordecai the Jew who serves at court. And let not a word of what you have said be omitted." ¹¹So Haman got the robe and the horse; he put the robe on Mordecai, mounted him on the horse, and went through the open square of the city, proclaiming, "Thus shall it be done to everyone whom the king wishes to honor." ¹²Then Mordecai returned to the courtyard, but Haman returned home, mourning and

with his head covered. ¹³Haman told his wife Zosara and his friends what had befallen him. His friends and his wife said to him, "If Mordecai is of the Jewish people and you have begun to be humiliated before him, you will surely fall. You will not be able to defend yourself, because a living god is with him."

Haman at Esther's Banquet

¹⁴While they were still talking, the eunuchs arrived and hurriedly brought Haman to the **7** drinking party that Esther had prepared. ¹So the king and Haman went in to drink with the queen. ²And the second day, as they were drinking wine, the king said, "What is it, Queen Esther? What is your petition, and what is your request? It shall be granted to you, even to half of my kingdom." ³She answered and said, "If I have found favor with the king, let my life be granted me at my petition and my people at my request. ⁴For we have been sold, I and my people, to be destroyed, plundered, and made slaves—we and our children—male and female slaves. I took no heed, but now our adversary brings shame on^z the king's court." ⁵Then the king said, "Who is the person who would dare to do this thing?" ⁶Esther said, "Our enemy is this evil man Haman!" At this, Haman was terrified in the presence of the king and queen.

Punishment of Haman

⁷The king rose from the banquet and went into the garden, and Haman began to beg for his life from the queen, for he saw that he was in serious trouble. ⁸When the king returned from the garden, Haman had thrown himself on the couch, pleading with the queen. The king said, "Will you dare even assault my wife in my own house?" Haman, when he heard, turned away his face. ⁹Then Bugathan, one of the eunuchs, said to the king, "Look, Haman has even prepared a pole for Mordecai, who gave information of concern to the king; it is standing at Haman's house, a pole fifty cubits high." So the king said, "Let Haman be executed on that." ¹⁰So Haman was hung on the pole that had been prepared for Mordecai. With that the anger of the king abated.

Royal Favor Shown the Jews

8 On that very day King Artaxerxes granted to Esther all the property of the adversary Haman. Mordecai was summoned by the king,

---

z 7.4 Gk *is not worthy of*

for Esther had told the king*ᵃ* that he was related to her. ²The king took his ring, which he had taken back from Haman, and gave it to Mordecai, and Esther set Mordecai over everything that had been Haman's.

3 Then she spoke once again to the king, and, falling at his feet, she asked him to avert all the evil that Haman had planned against the Jews. ⁴The king extended his golden scepter to Esther, and she rose and stood before the king. ⁵Esther said, "If it pleases you, and if I have found favor, let an order be sent rescinding the letters that Haman wrote and sent to destroy the Jews in your kingdom. ⁶How can I look on the ruin of my people? How can I be safe if my ancestral nation*ᵇ* is destroyed?" ⁷The king said to Esther, "Now that I*ᶜ* have granted all of Haman's property to you and have hung him on a pole because he laid hands on the Jews, what else do you request? ⁸Write in my name what you think best and seal it with my ring, for whatever is written at the king's command and sealed with my ring cannot be contravened."

9 The secretaries were summoned on the twenty-third day of the first month, that is, Nisan, in the same year, and all that she commanded with respect to the Jews was given in writing to the administrators and governors of the satrapies from India to Ethiopia, one hundred twenty-seven satrapies, to each province in its own language. ¹⁰The edict was written*ᵈ* with the king's authority and sealed with his ring, and they sent out the letters by couriers. ¹¹He ordered the Jews*ᵉ* in every city to observe their laws, to defend themselves, and to act as they wished against their opponents and enemies ¹²on a single day, the thirteenth of the twelfth month, which is Adar, throughout all the kingdom of Artaxerxes.

ADDITION E

The Decree of Artaxerxes

16⟨*ᶠ*⟩ The following is a copy of this letter: "The Great King, Artaxerxes, to the governors of the provinces from India to Ethiopia, one hundred twenty-seven provinces, and to those who are loyal to our government, greetings.

2 "Many people, the more they are honored with the most generous kindness of their benefactors, the more proud do they become, ³and not only seek to injure our subjects, but in their inability to stand prosperity, they even undertake to scheme against their own benefactors. ⁴They not only take away thankfulness from others, but, carried away by the boasts of those who know nothing of goodness, they even assume that they will escape the evil-hating justice of God, who always sees everything. ⁵And often many of those who are set in places of authority have been made in part responsible for the shedding of innocent blood and have been involved in irremediable calamities, by the persuasion of friends who have been entrusted with the administration of public affairs, ⁶when these persons by the false trickery of their evil natures beguile the sincere goodwill of their sovereigns.

7 "What has been wickedly accomplished through the pestilent behavior of those who exercise authority unworthily can be seen not so much from the more ancient records that we hand on as from investigation of matters close at hand.*ᵍ* ⁸In the future we will take care to render our kingdom quiet and peaceable for all, ⁹by changing our methods and always judging what comes before our eyes with more equitable consideration. ¹⁰For Haman son of Hammedatha, a Macedonian (really an alien to the Persian blood and quite devoid of our kindliness), having become our guest, ¹¹enjoyed so fully the goodwill that we have for every nation that he was called our father and was continually bowed down to by all as the person second to the royal throne. ¹²But, unable to restrain his arrogance, he undertook to deprive us of our kingdom and our life*ʰ* ¹³and with intricate craft and deceit asked for the destruction of Mordecai, our savior and perpetual benefactor, and of Esther, the blameless partner of our kingdom, together with their whole nation. ¹⁴He thought that by these methods he would catch us undefended and would transfer the kingdom of the Persians to the Macedonians.

15 "But we find that the Jews, who were consigned to annihilation by this thrice-accursed man, are not evildoers but are governed by most righteous laws ¹⁶and are children of the living

---

a 8.1 Gk *him*
b 8.6 Gk *country*
c 8.7 Gk *If I*
d 8.10 Gk *It was written*
e 8.11 Gk *them*
f 16.1 16.1–24 corresponds to E 1–24 in some translations.

g 16.7 Gk *matters beside* (your) *feet*
h 16.12 Gk *our spirit*

God, most high, most mighty,[i] who has directed the kingdom both for us and for our ancestors in the most excellent order.

17 "You will therefore do well not to put in execution the letters sent by Haman son of Hammedatha, [18] since he, the one who did these things, has been executed at the gates of Susa with all his household—for God, who rules over all things, has speedily inflicted on him the punishment that he deserved.

19 "Therefore post a copy of this letter publicly in every place and permit the Jews to live according to their own customs. [20] And lend them support, so that on the thirteenth day of the twelfth month, Adar, on that very day, they may defend themselves against those who attack them at the time of affliction. [21] For God, who rules over all things, has made this day to be a joy for his chosen people instead of a day of destruction for them.

22 "Therefore you shall observe this with all good cheer as a notable day among your commemorative festivals, [23] so that both now and hereafter it may represent deliverance for us and for those loyal to the Persians but a reminder of destruction for those who plot against us.

24 "Every city and country, without exception, that does not act accordingly shall be destroyed in wrath with spear and fire. It shall be made not only impassable for humans but also most hateful to wild animals and birds for all time.

END OF ADDITION E

---

8 [13] "Let copies of the decree be posted conspicuously in all the kingdom, and let all the Jews be ready on that day to fight against their enemies."

14 So the messengers on horseback set out with all speed to perform what the king had commanded, and the decree was posted also in Susa. [15] Mordecai went out dressed in the royal robe and wearing a gold crown and a turban of purple linen. The people in Susa rejoiced on seeing him. [16] And the Jews had light and gladness [17] in every city and province wherever the decree was published; wherever the proclamation was made, the Jews had joy and gladness, a banquet and a holiday. And many of the nations were circumcised and became Jews out of fear of the Jews.

Victory of the Jews

9 Now on the thirteenth day of the twelfth month, which is Adar, the letter written by the king arrived. [2] On that same day the enemies of the Jews perished; no one resisted, because they feared them. [3] The governors of the satrapies, the princes, and the royal secretaries were paying honor to the Jews, because fear of Mordecai weighed upon them. [4] The king's decree required that Mordecai's name be held in honor throughout the kingdom.[j] [6] Now in the city of Susa the Jews killed five hundred men, [7] including Pharsannestain, Delphon, Phasga, [8] Pharadatha, Barea, Sarbacha, [9] Marmasima, Aruphaeus, Arsaeus, Zabutheus, [10] the ten sons of Haman son of Hammedatha, the Bougean, the enemy of the Jews—and they indulged themselves in plunder.

11 That same day, the number of those killed in Susa was reported to the king. [12] The king said to Esther, "In the city of Susa, the Jews have destroyed five hundred people. What do you suppose they have done in the surrounding countryside? Whatever more you ask will be done for you." [13] And Esther said to the king, "Let the Jews be allowed to do the same tomorrow. Also, hang up the bodies of Haman's ten sons." [14] So he permitted this to be done and handed over to the Jews of the city the bodies of Haman's sons to hang up. [15] The Jews who were in Susa gathered on the fourteenth and killed three hundred men but took no plunder.

16 Now the other Jews in the kingdom gathered to defend themselves and got relief from their enemies. They destroyed fifteen thousand of them on the thirteenth of Adar but did not engage in plunder. [17] On the fourteenth day of the same month they rested and kept it as a day of rest with joy and gladness. [18] The Jews who were in the city of Susa came together also on the fourteenth but did not rest. They celebrated the fifteenth with joy and gladness. [19] On this account, then, the Jews who are scattered around the countryside keep the fourteenth of Adar as a joyful holiday and send presents of food to one another, while those who live in the large cities keep the fifteenth day of Adar as their joyful holiday, also sending presents to one another.

---

i 16.16 Gk *greatest*

j 9.4 Meaning of Gk uncertain. Some ancient authorities add 9.5, *So the Jews struck down all their enemies with the sword, killing and destroying them, and they did as they pleased to those who hated them.*

The Festival of Purim

20 Mordecai recorded these things in a book and sent it to the Jews in the kingdom of Artaxerxes both near and far, 21 to institute these days as holidays and to keep the fourteenth and fifteenth days of Adar, 22 for on these days the Jews got relief from their enemies. The whole month (namely, Adar) in which their condition had been changed from sorrow into gladness and from a time of distress to a holiday was to be celebrated as a time for feasting*k* and gladness and for sending presents of food to their friends and to the poor.

23 So the Jews accepted what Mordecai had written to them: 24 how Haman son of Hammedatha, the Macedonian, fought against them, how he made a decree and cast lots*l* to destroy them, 25 and how he went in to the king, telling him to hang Mordecai, but the wicked plot he had devised against the Jews came back upon himself, and he and his sons were hanged. 26 Therefore these days were called "Purim," because of the lots (for in their language this is the word that means "lots"). And so, because of what was written in this letter and because of what they had experienced in this affair and what had befallen them, Mordecai established this festival,*m* 27 and the Jews took upon themselves, upon their descendants, and upon all who would join them to observe it without fail.*n* These days of Purim should be a memorial and kept from generation to generation, in every city, family, and country. 28 These days of Purim shall be observed for all time, and the commemoration of them shall never cease among their descendants.

29 Then Queen Esther daughter of Aminadab along with Mordecai the Jew wrote down what they had done and gave full authority to the letter about Purim.*o* 31 And Mordecai and Queen Esther established this decision on their own responsibility, pledging their own well-being to the plan.*p* 32 Esther established it by a decree forever, and it was written for a memorial.

10 The king levied a tax upon his kingdom both by land and sea. 2 And as for his power and bravery and the wealth and glory of his kingdom, they were recorded in the annals of the kings of the Persians and the Medes. 3 Mordecai succeeded King Artaxerxes and was great in the kingdom, as well as honored by the Jews. His way of life was such as to make him beloved to his whole nation.

ADDITION F

Mordecai's Dream Fulfilled

4 *q* And Mordecai said, "These things have come from God, 5 for I remember the dream that I had concerning these matters, and none of them has failed to be fulfilled. 6 There was the little spring that became a river, and there was light and sun and abundant water. The river is Esther, whom the king married and made queen. 7 The two dragons are Haman and myself. 8 The nations are those that gathered to destroy the name of the Jews. 9 And my nation, this is Israel, who cried out to God and was saved. The Lord has saved his people; the Lord has rescued us from all these evils; God has done great signs and wonders, wonders that have never happened among the nations. 10 For this purpose he made two lots, one for the people of God and one for all the nations, 11 and these two lots came to the hour and moment and to the day of judgment before God and among all the nations. 12 And God remembered his people and vindicated his inheritance. 13 So they will observe these days in the month of Adar, on the fourteenth and fifteenth*r* of that month, with an assembly and joy and gladness before God, from generation to generation forever among his people Israel."

Postscript

11 1 In the fourth year of the reign of Ptolemy and Cleopatra, Dositheus, who said that he was a priest and a Levite,*s* and his son Ptolemy brought to Egypt*t* the preceding letter about Purim, which they said was authentic and had been translated by Lysimachus son of Ptolemy, one of the residents of Jerusalem.

END OF ADDITION F

---

k **9.22** Gk *of weddings*
l **9.24** Gk *a lot*
m **9.26** Gk *he established* (it)
n **9.27** Meaning of Gk uncertain
o **9.29** 9.30 in Heb is lacking in Gk: *Letters were sent to all the Jews, to the one hundred twenty-seven provinces of the kingdom of Ahasuerus, in words of peace and truth.*
p **9.31** Meaning of Gk uncertain

q **10.4** 10.4–13 and 11.1 correspond to F 1–11 in some translations.
r **10.13** Other ancient authorities lack *and fifteenth*
s **11.1** Or *priest, and Levitas*
t **11.1** Cn: Gk *brought in*

THE WISDOM OF SOLOMON

Exhortation to Uprightness

1 Love righteousness, you rulers of the earth;
  think of the Lord in goodness
and seek him with sincerity of heart,
² because he is found by those who do not
      put him to the test
  and manifests himself to those who do not
      distrust him.
³ For perverse thoughts separate people from
      God,
  and when his power is tested, it exposes the
      foolish,
⁴ because wisdom will not enter a deceitful
      soul
  or dwell in a body enslaved to sin.
⁵ For a holy and disciplined spirit will flee
      from deceit
  and will leave foolish thoughts behind
  and will be ashamed at the approach of
      unrighteousness.

⁶ For wisdom is a kindly spirit,
  but it will not free blasphemers from the
      guilt of their words,
  because God is witness of their inmost
      feelings
  and a true observer of their hearts and a
      hearer of their tongues.
⁷ Because the spirit of the Lord has filled the
      world
  and that which holds all things together
      knows what is said,
⁸ therefore those who utter unrighteous
      things will not escape notice,
  and justice, when it punishes, will not pass
      them by.
⁹ For inquiry will be made into the counsels
      of the ungodly,
  and a report of their words will come to the
      Lord,
  to convict them of their lawless deeds,
¹⁰ because a jealous ear hears all things,
  and the sound of grumbling does not go
      unheard.

¹¹ Beware, then, of useless grumbling,
  and keep your tongue from slander,
  because no secret word is without result,[a]
  and a lying mouth destroys the soul.

¹² Do not court death by the error of your life
  or bring on destruction by the works of
      your hands,
¹³ because God did not make death,
  and he does not delight in the destruction
      of the living.
¹⁴ For he created all things so that they might
      exist;
  the generative forces[b] of the world are
      wholesome,
  and there is no destructive poison in them,
  and the dominion[c] of Hades is not on
      earth.
¹⁵ For righteousness is immortal.[d]

Life as the Ungodly See It

¹⁶ But the ungodly by their words and deeds
      summoned death;[e]
  considering him a friend, they pined away
  and made a covenant with him,
  because they are fit to belong to his
      company.
2 For they reasoned unsoundly, saying to
      themselves,
  "Short and sorrowful is our life,
  and there is no remedy when a life comes
      to its end,
  and no one has been known to return from
      Hades.
² For we were born by mere chance,
  and hereafter we shall be as though we had
      never been,
  for the breath in our nostrils is smoke,

---

a **1.11** Or *will go unpunished*
b **1.14** Or *the creatures*
c **1.14** Or *palace*
d **1.15** OL adds *but unrighteousness is the acquisition*
  of death
e **1.16** Gk *him*

and reason is a spark kindled by the
   beating of our hearts;
³ when it is extinguished, the body will turn
   to ashes,
   and the spirit will dissolve like empty air.
⁴ Our name will be forgotten in time,
   and no one will remember our works;
   our life will pass away like the traces of a
      cloud
   and be scattered like mist
   that is chased by the rays of the sun
   and overcome by its heat.
⁵ For our allotted time is the passing of a
      shadow,
   and there is no return from our death,
   because it is sealed up and no one turns
      back.

⁶ "Come, therefore, let us enjoy the good
      things that exist
   and make use of the creation to the full as
      in youth.
⁷ Let us take our fill of costly wine and
      perfumes,
   and let no flower of spring pass us by.
⁸ Let us crown ourselves with rosebuds
      before they wither.
⁹ Let no meadow be free from our revelry;
   everywhere let us leave signs of enjoyment,
   because this is our portion, and this our lot.
¹⁰ Let us oppress the righteous poor man;
   let us not spare the widow
   or regard the gray hairs of the aged.
¹¹ But let our might be our law of right,
   for what is weak proves itself to be useless.

¹² "Let us lie in wait for the righteous man,
   because he is inconvenient to us and
      opposes our actions;
   he reproaches us for sins against the law
   and accuses us of sins against our training.
¹³ He professes to have knowledge of God
   and calls himself a child of the Lord.
¹⁴ He became to us a reproof of our
      thoughts;
   the very sight of him is a burden to us,
¹⁵ because his manner of life is unlike that of
      others,
   and his ways are strange.
¹⁶ We are considered by him as something
      base,
   and he avoids our ways as unclean;
   he calls the last end of the righteous happy
   and boasts that God is his father.

¹⁷ Let us see if his words are true,
   and let us test what will happen at the end
      of his life,
¹⁸ for if the righteous man is God's child, he
      will help him
   and will deliver him from the hand of his
      adversaries.
¹⁹ Let us test him with insult and torture,
   so that we may find out how reasonable he is
   and make trial of his forbearance.
²⁰ Let us condemn him to a shameful death,
   for, according to what he says, he will be
      protected."

Error of the Wicked

²¹ Thus they reasoned, but they were led
      astray,
   for their wickedness blinded them,
²² and they did not know the secret purposes
      of God,
   nor hoped for the wages of holiness,
   nor discerned the prize for blameless souls,
²³ for God created us for incorruption
   and made us in the image of his own
      eternity,ᶠ
²⁴ but through an adversary'sᵍ envy death
      entered the world,
   and those who belong to his company
      experience it.

The Destiny of the Righteous

3 But the souls of the righteous are in the
      hand of God,
   and no torment will ever touch them.
² In the eyes of the foolish they seemed to
      have died,
   and their departure was thought to be a
      disaster
³ and their going from us to be their
      destruction,
   but they are at peace.
⁴ For though in the sight of others they were
      punished,
   their hope is full of immortality.
⁵ Having been disciplined a little, they will
      receive great good,
   because God tested them and found them
      worthy of himself;
⁶ like gold in the furnace he tried them,
   and like a sacrificial burnt offering he
      accepted them.

ƒ 2.23 Other ancient authorities read *nature*
g 2.24 Or *a devil's*

7 In the time of their visitation they will
   shine forth
   and will run like sparks through the
   stubble.
8 They will govern nations and rule over
   peoples,
   and the Lord will reign over them forever.
9 Those who trust in him will understand
   truth,
   and the faithful will abide with him in
   love,
   because grace and mercy are upon his holy
   ones,
   and he watches over his elect.[h]

The Destiny of the Ungodly

10 But the ungodly will be punished as their
   reasoning deserves,
   those who disregarded the righteous[i]
   and rebelled against the Lord,
11 for those who despise wisdom and
   instruction are miserable.
   Their hope is vain, their labors are
   unprofitable,
   and their works are useless.
12 Their wives are foolish and their children
   evil;
   their offspring are accursed.

On Childlessness

13 For blessed is the barren woman who is
   undefiled,
   who has not entered into a sinful union;
   she will have fruit when God examines
   souls.
14 Blessed also is the eunuch whose hands
   have done no lawless deed
   and who has not devised wicked things
   against the Lord,
   for special favor will be shown him for his
   faithfulness
   and a place of great delight in the temple of
   the Lord.
15 For the fruit of good labors is renowned,
   and the root of understanding does not
   fail.
16 But children of adulterers will not come to
   maturity,
   and the offspring of an unlawful union will
   perish.

17 Even if they live long they will be held of no
   account,
   and finally their old age will be without
   honor.
18 If they die young, they will have no hope
   and no consolation on the day of judgment.
19 For the end of an unrighteous generation is
   grievous.

4 Better than this is childlessness with
   virtue,
   for in the memory of virtue[j] is immortality,
   because it is known both by God and by
   mortals.
2 When it is present, people imitate[k] it,
   and they long for it when it has gone;
   throughout all time it marches, crowned in
   triumph,
   victor in the contest for prizes that are
   undefiled.
3 But the prolific brood of the ungodly will
   be of no use,
   and none of their illegitimate seedlings will
   strike a deep root
   or take a firm hold.
4 For even if they put forth boughs for a
   while,
   standing insecurely they will be shaken by
   the wind,
   and by the violence of the winds they will
   be uprooted.
5 The branches will be broken off before they
   come to maturity,
   and their fruit will be useless,
   not ripe enough to eat and good for nothing.
6 For children born of unlawful unions
   are witnesses of evil against their parents
   when God examines them.[l]
7 But the righteous, even if they die early, will
   be at rest.
8 For old age is not honored for length of
   time
   or measured by number of years,
9 but understanding is gray hair for anyone,
   and a blameless life is ripe old age.

10 There was one who pleased God and was
   loved by him
   and while living among sinners was
   taken up.

---

h 3.9 Text of this line uncertain; omitted by some
   ancient authorities
i 3.10 Or what is right

j 4.1 Gk it
k 4.2 Other ancient authorities read honor
l 4.6 Gk at their examination

11 He was caught up so that evil might not
   change his understanding
or guile deceive his soul.
12 For the fascination of wickedness obscures
   what is good,
and roving desire perverts the innocent
   mind.
13 Being perfected in a short time, he fulfilled
   long years,
14 for his soul was pleasing to the Lord;
therefore he hastened him from the midst
   of wickedness.
Yet the peoples saw and did not understand
   or take such a thing to heart,
15 that God's grace and mercy are with his
   elect
and that he watches over his holy ones.

The Triumph of the Righteous

16 The righteous who have died will condemn
   the ungodly who are living,
and youth that is quickly perfected^m will
   condemn the prolonged old age of the
   unrighteous.
17 For they will see the end of the wise
and will not understand what the Lord
   purposed for them
and for what he kept them safe.
18 The unrighteous^n will see and will have
   contempt for them,
but the Lord will laugh them to scorn.
19 After this they will become dishonored
   corpses
and an outrage among the dead forever,
because he will dash them speechless to the
   ground
and shake them from the foundations;
they will be left utterly dry and barren,
and they will suffer anguish,
and the memory of them will perish.

The Final Judgment

20 They will come with dread when their sins
   are reckoned up,
and their lawless deeds will convict them to
   their face.

5 Then the righteous will stand with great
   confidence
in the presence of those who have
   oppressed them
and those who make light of their labors.

2 When the unrighteous^o see them, they will
   be shaken with dreadful fear,
and they will be amazed at the unexpected
   salvation of the righteous.
3 They will speak to one another in
   repentance,
and in anguish of spirit they will groan,
4 "These are persons whom we once held in
   derision
and made a byword of reproach—fools that
   we were!
We thought that their lives were madness
and that their end was without honor.
5 Why have they been numbered among the
   children of God?
And why is their lot among the holy ones?
6 So it was we who strayed from the way of
   truth,
and the light of righteousness did not shine
   on us,
and the sun did not rise upon us.
7 We took our fill of the paths of lawlessness
   and destruction,
and we journeyed through trackless
   deserts,
but the way of the Lord we have not
   known.
8 What has our arrogance profited us?
And what good has our boasted wealth
   brought us?

9 "All those things have vanished like a
   shadow
and like a rumor that passes by;
10 like a ship that sails through the billowy
   water,
and when it has passed no trace can be
   found,
no track of its keel in the waves;
11 or as, when a bird flies through the air,
no evidence of its passage is found;
the light air, lashed by the beat of its
   pinions
and pierced by the force of its rushing
   flight,
is traversed by the movement of its wings,
and afterward no sign of its coming is
   found there;
12 or as, when an arrow is shot at a target,
the air, thus divided, comes together at
   once,
so that no one knows its pathway.

---

m **4.16** Or *ended*
n **4.18** Gk *They*

o **5.2** Gk *they*

13 So we also, as soon as we were born, ceased
   to be,
and we had no sign of virtue to show
but were consumed in our wickedness."
14 Because the hope of the ungodly is like
   thistledown*p* carried by the wind
and like a light frost*q* driven away by a storm;
it is dispersed like smoke before the wind,
and it passes like the remembrance of a
   guest who stays but a day.

The Reward of the Righteous

15 But the righteous live forever,
and their reward is with the Lord;
the Most High takes care of them.
16 Therefore they will receive a glorious crown
and a beautiful diadem from the hand of
   the Lord,
because with his right hand he will cover
   them,
and with his arm he will shield them.
17 The Lord*r* will take his zeal as his whole
   armor
and will arm all creation to repel*s* his
   enemies;
18 he will put on righteousness as a breastplate
and wear impartial justice as a helmet;
19 he will take holiness as an invincible shield
20 and sharpen stern wrath for a sword,
and the world will join him to fight against
   the senseless.
21 Shafts of lightning will fly with true aim
and will leap from the clouds to the target,
   as from a well-drawn bow,
22 and hailstones full of wrath will be hurled
   as from a catapult;
the water of the sea will rage against them,
and rivers will relentlessly overwhelm them;
23 a mighty wind will rise against them,
and like a tempest it will winnow them away.
Lawlessness will lay waste the whole earth,
and evildoing will overturn the thrones of
   rulers.

Kings Should Seek Wisdom

6 Listen therefore, O kings, and understand;
  learn, O judges of the ends of the earth.
2 Give ear, you who rule over multitudes
and boast of many nations.

---

p 5.14 Other ancient authorities read *dust*
q 5.14 Other ancient authorities read *spider's web*
r 5.17 Gk *He*
s 5.17 Or *punish*

3 For your dominion was given you from the
   Lord
and your sovereignty from the Most High;
he will search out your works and inquire
   into your plans.
4 Because as servants of his kingdom you did
   not rule rightly
or keep the law
or walk according to the purpose of God,
5 he will come upon you terribly and
   swiftly,
because severe judgment falls on those in
   high places.
6 For the lowliest may be pardoned in
   mercy,
but the mighty will be mightily tested.
7 For the Lord of all will not stand in awe of
   anyone
or show deference to greatness,
because he himself made both small and
   great,
and he takes thought for all alike.
8 But a strict inquiry is in store for the
   mighty.
9 To you then, O monarchs, my words are
   directed,
so that you may learn wisdom and not
   transgress.
10 For they will be made holy who observe
   holy things in holiness,
and those who have been taught them will
   find a defense.
11 Therefore set your desire on my words;
long for them, and you will be instructed.

Description of Wisdom

12 Wisdom is radiant and unfading,
and she is easily discerned by those who
   love her
and is found by those who seek her.
13 She hastens to make herself known to those
   who desire her.
14 One who rises early to seek her will have
   no difficulty,
for she will be found sitting at the gate.
15 To fix one's thought on her is perfect
   understanding,
and one who is vigilant on her account will
   soon be free from care,
16 because she goes about seeking those
   worthy of her,
and she graciously appears to them in their
   paths
and meets them in every thought.

17 The beginning of wisdom[t] is the most
    sincere desire for instruction,
18 and concern for instruction is love of her,
    and love of her is the keeping of her laws,
    and giving heed to her laws is assurance of
    immortality,
19 and immortality brings one near to God,
20 so the desire for wisdom leads to a
    kingdom.

21 Therefore if you delight in thrones and
    scepters, O monarchs over the
    peoples,
    honor wisdom, so that you may reign
    forever.
22 I will tell you what wisdom is and how she
    came to be,
    and I will hide no secrets from you,
    but I will trace her course from the
    beginning of creation
    and make knowledge of her clear,
    and I will not pass by the truth,
23 nor will I travel in the company of sickly
    envy,
    for envy[u] does not associate with wisdom.
24 The multitude of the wise is the salvation of
    the world,
    and a sensible king is the stability of any
    people.
25 Therefore be instructed by my words, and
    you will profit.

The King Is Like Other Mortals

7 I also am mortal like everyone else,
    a descendant of the first-formed child of
    earth,
    and in the womb of a mother I was molded
    into flesh,
2 within the period of ten months,
    compacted with blood,
    from the seed of a man and the pleasure of
    marriage.
3 And when I was born, I began to breathe
    the common air
    and fell upon the kindred earth;
    my first sound was a cry, as is true of all.
4 I was nursed with care in swaddling cloths.
5 For no king has had a different beginning
    of existence;
6 there is for all one entrance into life and
    one way out.

Respect for Wisdom

7 Therefore I prayed, and understanding was
    given me;
    I called on God, and the spirit of wisdom
    came to me.
8 I preferred her to scepters and thrones,
    and I accounted wealth as nothing in
    comparison with her.
9 Neither did I liken to her any priceless gem,
    because all gold is but a little sand in her
    sight,
    and silver will be accounted as clay before
    her.
10 I loved her more than health and beauty,
    and I chose to have her rather than light
    because her radiance never ceases.
11 All good things came to me along with her,
    and in her hands uncounted wealth.
12 I rejoiced in them all because wisdom leads
    them,
    but I did not know that she was their
    mother.
13 I learned without guile, and I impart
    without grudging;
    I do not hide her wealth,
14 for it is an unfailing treasure for mortals;
    those who get it obtain friendship with God,
    commended for the gifts that come from
    instruction.

Prayer for Wisdom

15 May God grant me to speak with judgment
    and to have thoughts worthy of what I have
    received,
    for he is the guide even of wisdom
    and the corrector of the wise.
16 For both we and our words are in his hand,
    as are all understanding and skill in crafts.
17 For it is he who gave me unerring
    knowledge of what exists,
    to know the structure of the world and the
    activity of the elements,
18 the beginning and end and middle of
    times,
    the alternations of the solstices and the
    changes of the seasons,
19 the cycles of the year and the constellations
    of the stars,
20 the natures of animals and the tempers of
    wild animals,
    the powers of spirits[v] and the thoughts of
    human beings,

---

t **6.17** Gk *Her beginning*
u **6.23** Gk *this*

v **7.20** Or *winds*

the varieties of plants and the virtues of
roots;

²¹ I learned both what is secret and what is
manifest,

²² for wisdom, the fashioner of all things,
taught me.

The Nature of Wisdom

There is in her a spirit that is intelligent,
holy,
unique, manifold, subtle,
agile, clear, unpolluted,
distinct, invulnerable, loving the good, keen,

²³ irresistible, beneficent, humane,
steadfast, sure, free from anxiety,
all-powerful, overseeing all,
and penetrating through all spirits
that are intelligent, pure, and altogether
subtle.

²⁴ For wisdom is more mobile than any
motion;
because of her pureness she pervades and
penetrates all things.

²⁵ For she is a breath of the power of God
and a pure emanation of the glory of the
Almighty;
therefore nothing defiled gains entrance
into her.

²⁶ For she is a reflection of eternal light,
a spotless mirror of the working of God,
and an image of his goodness.

²⁷ Although she is but one, she can do all
things,
and while remaining in herself, she renews
all things;
in every generation she passes into holy souls
and makes them friends of God and
prophets,

²⁸ for God loves nothing so much as the
person who lives with wisdom.

²⁹ She is more beautiful than the sun
and excels every constellation of the stars.
Compared with the light she is found to be
more radiant,

³⁰ for it is succeeded by the night,
but against wisdom evil does not prevail.

8 She reaches mightily from one end of the
earth to the other,
and she orders all things well.

Love for Wisdom

² I loved her and sought her from my youth;
I desired to take her for my bride
and became enamored of her beauty.

³ She glorifies her noble birth by living with
God,
and the Lord of all loves her.

⁴ For she is an initiate in the knowledge of
God
and an associate in his works.

⁵ If riches are a desirable possession in life,
what is richer than wisdom, the active
cause of all things?

⁶ And if understanding is effective,
who more than she is fashioner of what
exists?

⁷ And if anyone loves righteousness,
her labors are virtues,
for she teaches self-control and prudence,
justice and courage;
nothing in life is more profitable for
mortals than these.

⁸ And if anyone longs for wide experience,
she knows the things of old and infers the
things to come;
she understands turns of speech and the
solutions of riddles;
she has foreknowledge of signs and
wonders
and of the outcome of seasons and times.

Wisdom Indispensable to Rulers

⁹ Therefore I determined to take her to live
with me,
knowing that she would give me good
counsel
and encouragement in cares and grief.

¹⁰ Because of her I shall have glory among the
multitudes
and honor in the presence of the elders,
though I am young.

¹¹ I shall be found keen in judgment,
and in the sight of rulers I shall be admired.

¹² When I am silent they will wait for me,
and when I speak they will give heed;
if I speak at greater length,
they will put their hands on their mouths.

¹³ Because of her I shall have immortality
and leave an everlasting remembrance to
those who come after me.

¹⁴ I shall govern peoples,
and nations will be subject to me;

¹⁵ dread monarchs will be afraid of me when
they hear of me;
among the people I shall show myself
capable and courageous in war.

¹⁶ When I enter my house, I shall find rest
with her,

for companionship with her has no
   bitterness,
and life with her has no pain but gladness
   and joy.
17 When I considered these things inwardly
   and pondered in my heart
that in kinship with wisdom there is
   immortality,
18 and in friendship with her, pure delight,
and in the labors of her hands, unfailing
   wealth,
and in the experience of her company,
   understanding,
and renown in sharing her words,
I went about seeking how to get her for
   myself.
19 As a child I was naturally gifted,
and a good soul fell to my lot,
20 or rather, being good, I entered an
   undefiled body.
21 But I perceived that I would not possess
   wisdom unless God gave her to me—
and it was a mark of insight to know whose
   gift she was—
so I appealed to the Lord and implored him,
and with my whole heart I said,

Prayer for Wisdom

9 "O God of my ancestors and Lord of mercy,
   who have made all things by your word
2 and by your wisdom have formed
   humankind
to have dominion over the creatures you
   have made
3 and rule the world in holiness and
   righteousness
and pronounce judgment in uprightness
   of soul,
4 give me the wisdom that sits by your
   throne,
and do not reject me from among your
   children.
5 For I am your servant, the son of your
   female servant,
a man who is weak and short-lived,
with little understanding of judgment and
   laws,
6 for even one who is perfect among humans
will be regarded as nothing without the
   wisdom that comes from you.
7 You have chosen me to be king of your
   people
and to be judge over your sons and
   daughters.

8 You have given command to build a temple
   on your holy mountain
and an altar in the city of your habitation,
a copy of the holy tent that you prepared
   from the beginning.
9 With you is wisdom, she who knows your
   works
and was present when you made the world;
she understands what is pleasing in your
   sight
and what is right according to your
   commandments.
10 Send her forth from the holy heavens,
and from the throne of your glory send her,
that she may labor at my side
and that I may learn what is pleasing to
   you.
11 For she knows and understands all things,
and she will guide me wisely in my actions
and guard me with her glory.
12 Then my works will be acceptable,
and I shall judge your people justly
and shall be worthy of the throne^w of my
   father.
13 For who can learn the counsel of God?
Or who can discern what the Lord wills?
14 For the reasoning of mortals is worthless,
and our designs are likely to fail,
15 for a perishable body weighs down the
   soul,
and this earthy tent burdens the
   thoughtful^x mind.
16 We can hardly guess at what is on earth,
and what is at hand we find with labor,
but who has traced out what is in the
   heavens?
17 Who has learned your counsel
unless you have given wisdom
and sent your holy spirit from on high?
18 And thus the paths of those on earth were
   set right,
and people were taught what pleases you
and were saved by wisdom."

The Work of Wisdom

10 Wisdom^y protected the first-formed
   father of the world,
when he alone had been created;
she delivered him from his transgression
2 and gave him strength to rule all things.

---

w 9.12 Gk *thrones*
x 9.15 Or *anxious*
y 10.1 Gk *She*

³ But when an unrighteous man departed
     from her in his anger,
he perished because in rage he killed his
     brother.
⁴ When the earth was flooded because of
     him, wisdom again saved it,
steering the righteous man by a paltry piece
     of wood.

⁵ Wisdom*ᶻ* also, when the nations in wicked
     agreement had been put to confusion,
recognized the righteous man and
     preserved him blameless before God
and kept him strong in the face of his
     compassion for his child.

⁶ Wisdom*ᵃ* rescued a righteous man when
     the ungodly were perishing;
he escaped the fire that descended on the
     Five Cities.*ᵇ*
⁷ Evidence of their wickedness still remains:
a continually smoking wasteland,
plants bearing fruit that does not ripen,
and a pillar of salt standing as a monument
     to an unbelieving soul.
⁸ For because they passed wisdom by,
they not only were hindered from
     recognizing the good
but also left for humankind a reminder of
     their folly,
so that their failures could never go
     unnoticed.

⁹ Wisdom rescued from troubles those who
     served her.
¹⁰ When a righteous man fled from his
     brother's wrath,
she guided him on straight paths;
she showed him the kingdom of God
and gave him knowledge of holy things;
she prospered him in his labors
and increased the fruit of his toil.
¹¹ When his oppressors were covetous,
she stood by him and made him rich.
¹² She protected him from his enemies
and kept him safe from those who lay in
     wait for him;
in his arduous contest she declared him
     victorious,

so that he might learn that godliness is
     more powerful than anything else.
¹³ When a righteous man was sold, wisdom*ᶜ*
     did not desert him
but delivered him from sin.
¹⁴ She descended with him into the dungeon,
and when he was in prison she did not
     leave him,
until she brought him the scepter of a
     kingdom
and authority over his masters.
Those who accused him she showed to be
     false,
and she gave him everlasting honor.

Wisdom Led the Israelites out of Egypt

¹⁵ Holy people and blameless offspring
wisdom*ᵈ* delivered from a nation of
     oppressors.
¹⁶ She entered the soul of a servant of the Lord
and withstood dread kings with wonders
     and signs.
¹⁷ She gave to holy people the reward of their
     labors;
she guided them along a marvelous way
and became a shelter to them by day
and a starry flame through the night.
¹⁸ She brought them over the Red Sea
and led them through deep waters,
¹⁹ but she drowned their enemies
and cast them up from the depth of the sea.
²⁰ Therefore the righteous plundered the
     ungodly;
they sang hymns, O Lord, to your holy
     name
and praised with one accord your
     defending hand,
²¹ for wisdom opened the mouths of those
     who were mute
and made the tongues of infants speak
     clearly.

Wisdom Led the Israelites through the Desert

11 ¹ Wisdom*ᵉ* prospered their works by
     the hand of a holy prophet.
² They journeyed through an uninhabited
     wilderness
and pitched their tents in untrodden places.

---

z **10.5** Gk *She*
a **10.6** Gk *She*
b **10.6** Or *on Pentapolis*

c **10.13** Gk *she*
d **10.15** Gk *she*
e **11.1** Gk *She*

3 They withstood their enemies and fought
off their foes.
4 When they were thirsty, they called upon
you,
and water was given them out of flinty
rock
and from hard stone a remedy for their
thirst.
5 For through the very things by which their
enemies were punished,
they themselves received benefit in their
need.
6 Instead of the fountain of an ever-flowing
river,
stirred up and defiled with blood
7 in rebuke for the decree to kill the infants,
you gave them abundant water
unexpectedly,
8 showing by their thirst at that time
how you punished their enemies.
9 For when they were tried, though they
were being disciplined in mercy,
they learned how the ungodly were
tormented when judged in wrath.
10 For you tested them as a parent*f* does in
warning,
but you examined the ungodly*g* as a stern
king does in condemnation.
11 Whether absent or present, they were
equally distressed,
12 for a twofold grief possessed them
and a groaning at the memory of what had
occurred.
13 For when they heard that through their
own punishments
the righteous*h* had received benefit, they
perceived it was the Lord's doing.
14 For though they had mockingly rejected
him who long before had been cast
out and exposed,
at the end of the events they marveled at
him,
when they felt thirst in a different way from
the righteous.

Punishment of the Wicked
15 In return for their foolish and wicked
thoughts,
which led them astray to worship irrational
serpents and worthless animals,

you sent upon them a multitude of
irrational creatures to punish them,
16 so that they might learn that one is
punished by the very things by which
one sins.
17 For your all-powerful hand,
which created the world out of formless
matter,
did not lack the means to send upon
them a multitude of bears or bold
lions
18 or newly created unknown beasts full of
rage
or such as breathe out fiery breath
or belch forth a thick pall of smoke
or flash terrible sparks from their eyes;
19 not only could the harm they did destroy
people,*i*
but the mere sight of them could kill by
fright.
20 Even apart from these, people*j* could fall at
a single breath
when pursued by justice
and scattered by the breath of your power.
But you have arranged all things by
measure and number and weight.

God Is Powerful and Merciful
21 For it is always in your power to show great
strength,
and who can withstand the might of your
arm?
22 Because the whole world before you is like
a speck that tips the scales
and like a drop of morning dew that falls
on the ground.
23 But you are merciful to all, for you can do
all things,
and you overlook people's sins, so that they
may repent.
24 For you love all things that exist
and detest none of the things that you have
made,
for you would not have formed anything if
you had hated it.
25 How would anything have endured if you
had not willed it?
Or how would anything not called forth by
you have been preserved?
26 You spare all things, for they are yours,
O Lord, you who love the living.

---

f 11.10 Gk *a father*
g 11.10 Gk *those*
h 11.13 Gk *they*

---

i 11.19 Gk *them*
j 11.20 Gk *they*

12

For your immortal spirit is in all things.
²Therefore you correct little by little
    those who trespass,
and you remind and warn them of the
    things through which they sin,
so that they may be freed from wickedness
    and put their trust in you, O Lord.

The Sins of the Canaanites

³ Those who lived long ago in your holy land
⁴ you hated for their detestable practices,
    their works of sorcery and unholy rites,
⁵ their merciless slaughter[k] of children,
    and their sacrificial feasting on human
        flesh and blood.
These initiates from the midst of a bloody
    revelry,[l]
⁶ these parents who murder helpless lives,
    you willed to destroy by the hands of our
        ancestors,
⁷ so that the land most precious of all to you
    might receive a worthy colony of the
        children of God.
⁸ But even these you spared, since they were
    but mortals,
and sent wasps[m] as forerunners of your
    army
to destroy them little by little,
⁹ though you were not unable to give
    the ungodly into the hands of the
        righteous in battle
or to destroy them at one blow by dread
    wild animals or your stern word.
¹⁰ But judging them little by little you gave
    them an opportunity to repent,
though you were not unaware that their
    origin[n] was evil
and their wickedness inborn
and that their way of thinking would never
    change.
¹¹ For their offspring were accursed from the
    beginning,
and it was not through fear of anyone that
    you left them unpunished for their
    sins.

God Is Sovereign

¹² For who will say, "What have you done?"
    or will resist your judgment?

Who will accuse you for the destruction of
    nations that you made?
Or who will come before you to plead as an
    advocate for the unrighteous?
¹³ For neither is there any god besides you
    whose care is for all people,[o]
to whom you should prove that you have
    not judged unjustly,
¹⁴ nor can any king or monarch confront you
    about those whom you have punished.
¹⁵ You are righteous, and you rule all things
    righteously,
deeming it alien to your power
to condemn anyone who does not deserve
    to be punished.
¹⁶ For your strength is the source of
    righteousness,
and your sovereignty over all causes you to
    spare all.
¹⁷ For you show your strength when people
    doubt the completeness of your power,
and you rebuke any insolence among those
    who know it.[p]
¹⁸ Although you are sovereign in strength,
    you judge fairly,
and with great forbearance you govern us,
for you have power to act whenever you
    choose.

God's Lessons for Israel

¹⁹ Through such works you have taught your
    people
that the righteous must be kind,
and you have filled your children with
    good hope,
because you give repentance for sins.
²⁰ For if you punished with such great care
    and indulgence[q]
the enemies of your children and those
    deserving of death,
granting them time and opportunity to give
    up their wickedness,
²¹ with what strictness you have judged your
    children,[r]
to whose ancestors you gave oaths and
    covenants full of good promises!
²² So while chastening us you scourge our
    enemies ten thousand times more,

---

k 12.5 Gk *slaughterers*
l 12.5 Meaning of Gk uncertain
m 12.8 Or *hornets*
n 12.10 Or *nature*

o 12.13 Or *all things*
p 12.17 Meaning of Gk uncertain
q 12.20 Other ancient authorities lack *and indulgence*;
    others read *and entreaty*
r 12.21 Gk *sons*

so that when we judge we may meditate
    upon your goodness,
and when we are judged we may expect
    mercy.

The Punishment of the Egyptians

23 Therefore those who lived unrighteously, in
    a life of folly,
you tormented through their own
    abominations.
24 For they went far astray on the paths of
    error,
accepting as gods those animals that even
    their enemies[s] despised;
they were deceived like foolish infants.
25 Therefore, as though to children who
    cannot reason,
you sent your judgment to mock them.
26 But those who have not heeded the
    warning of mild rebukes
will experience the deserved judgment of
    God.
27 For when in their suffering they became
    incensed
at those creatures that they had thought to
    be gods, being punished by means of
    them,
they saw and recognized as the true God
    the one whom they had before refused
    to know.
Therefore the utmost condemnation came
    upon them.

The Foolishness of Nature Worship

13 For all people who were ignorant of
    God were foolish by nature,
and they were unable from the good things
    that are seen to know the one who
    exists,
nor did they recognize the artisan while
    paying heed to his works;
2 but they supposed that either fire or wind
    or swift air
or the circle of the stars or turbulent water
or the luminaries of heaven were the gods
    that rule the world.
3 If through delight in the beauty of these
    things people assumed them to be
    gods,
let them know how much better than these
    is their Lord,
for the author of beauty created them.

4 And if people[t] were amazed at their power
    and working,
let them perceive from them
how much more powerful is the one who
    formed them.
5 For from the greatness and beauty of
    created things
comes a corresponding perception of their
    Creator.
6 Yet these people are little to be blamed,
for perhaps they go astray
while seeking God and desiring to find
    him.
7 For while they live among his works, they
    keep searching
and trust in what they see because the
    things that are seen are beautiful.
8 Yet again, not even they are to be excused,
9 for if they had the power to know so much
    that they could investigate the world,
how did they not more quickly find the
    Lord of these things?

The Foolishness of Idolatry

10 But miserable, with their hopes set on dead
    things, are those
who give the name "gods" to the works of
    human hands,
gold and silver fashioned with skill
and likenesses of animals
or a useless stone, the work of an ancient
    hand.
11 A skilled woodcutter may saw down a tree
    easy to handle
and skillfully strip off all its bark
and then with pleasing workmanship
make a useful vessel that serves life's needs
12 and burn the cast-off pieces of his work
to prepare his food and eat his fill.
13 But a cast-off piece from among them,
    useful for nothing,
a stick crooked and full of knots,
he takes and carves with care in his leisure
and shapes it with skill gained in idleness;[u]
he forms it in the likeness of a human
    being
14 or makes it like some worthless animal,
giving it a coat of red paint and coloring its
    surface red
and covering every blemish in it with paint;

---

s 12.24 Gk *they*

t 13.4 Gk *they*
u 13.13 Other ancient authorities read *with intelligent
    skill*

15 then he makes a suitable niche for it
    and sets it in the wall and fastens it there
        with iron.
16 He takes thought for it so that it may not fall,
    because he knows that it cannot help itself,
    for it is only an image and has need of help.
17 When he prays about possessions and his
        marriage and children,
    he is not ashamed to address a lifeless thing.
    For health he appeals to a thing that is weak;
18 for life he prays to a thing that is dead;
    for aid he entreats a thing that is utterly
        inexperienced;
    for a prosperous journey, a thing that
        cannot take a step;
19 for money-making and work and success
        with his hands,
    he asks strength of a thing whose hands
        have no strength.

Folly of a Navigator Praying to an Idol

14 Again, one preparing to sail and about
        to voyage over raging waves
    calls upon a piece of wood more fragile
        than the ship that carries him.
2 For it was desire for gain that planned that
        vessel,
    and wisdom was the artisan who built it,
3 but it is your providence, O Father, that
        steers its course,
    because you have given it a path in the sea
    and a safe way through the waves,
4 showing that you can save from every
        danger,
    so that even a person who lacks skill may
        put to sea.
5 It is your will that works of your wisdom
        should not be without effect;
    therefore people trust their lives even to the
        smallest piece of wood,
    and passing through the billows on a raft
        they come safely to land.
6 For even in the beginning, when arrogant
        giants were perishing,
    the hope of the world took refuge on a raft
    and guided by your hand left to the world
        the seed of a new generation.
7 For blessed is the wood by which
        righteousness comes.

8 But the idol made with hands is accursed,
        and so is the one who made it—
    he for having made it, and the perishable
        thing because it was named a god.

9 For equally hateful to God are the ungodly
        and their ungodliness,
10 for what was done will be punished
        together with the one who did it.
11 Therefore there will be a visitation also
        upon the idols of the nations,
    because, though part of what God created,
        they became an abomination,
    stumbling blocks for human souls
    and a trap for the feet of the foolish.

The Origin and Evils of Idolatry

12 For the idea of making idols was the
        beginning of sexual immorality,
    and the invention of them was the
        corruption of life,
13 for they did not exist from the beginning,
    nor will they last forever.
14 For through human vanity they entered the
        world,
    and therefore their speedy end has been
        planned.

15 For a father, consumed with grief at an
        untimely bereavement,
    made an image of his child, who had been
        suddenly taken from him;
    he now honored as a god what was once a
        dead human being
    and handed on to his dependents secret
        rites and initiations.
16 Then the ungodly custom, grown strong
        with time, was kept as a law,
    and at the command of monarchs carved
        images were worshiped.
17 When people could not honor monarchs[v]
        in their presence, since they lived at a
        distance,
    they imagined their appearance far away
    and made a visible image of the king whom
        they honored,
    so that by their zeal they might flatter the
        absent one as though present.

18 Then the ambition of the artisan impelled
    even those who did not know the king[w] to
        intensify their worship.
19 For he, perhaps wishing to please his
        ruler,
    skillfully forced the likeness to take more
        beautiful form,

_____

v **14.17** Gk *them*
w **14.18** Gk lacks *the king*

²⁰ and the multitude, attracted by the charm
    of his work,
now regarded as an object of worship the
    one whom shortly before they had
    honored as a human.
²¹ And this became a hidden trap for
    humankind,
because people, in bondage to misfortune
    or to royal authority,
bestowed on objects of stone or wood the
    name that ought not to be shared.

²² Then it was not enough for them to err
    about the knowledge of God,
but though living in great strife due to
    ignorance,
they call such great evils peace.
²³ For whether they kill children in their
    initiations or celebrate secret
    mysteries
or hold frenzied revels with strange
    customs,
²⁴ they no longer keep either their lives or
    their marriages pure,
but they either treacherously kill one
    another or grieve one another by
    adultery,
²⁵ and all is a raging riot of blood and
    murder, theft and deceit, corruption,
    faithlessness, tumult, perjury,
²⁶ confusion over what is good, forgetfulness
    of favors,
defiling of souls, sexual perversion,
disorder in marriages, adultery, and
    debauchery.
²⁷ For the worship of idols not to be named
is the beginning and cause and end of every
    evil.
²⁸ For their worshipers^x either rave in
    exultation
or prophesy lies or live unrighteously or
    readily commit perjury,
²⁹ for because they trust in lifeless idols
they swear wicked oaths and expect to
    suffer no harm.
³⁰ But just penalties will overtake them on
    two counts:
because they thought wrongly about God
    in devoting themselves to idols
and because in deceit they swore
    unrighteously through contempt for
    holiness.

³¹ For it is not the power of the things by
    which people swear^y
but the just penalty for those who sin
that always pursues the transgression of the
    unrighteous.

Benefits of Worshiping the True God

15 But you, our God, are kind and true,
    patient, and ruling all things^z in mercy.
² For even if we sin we are yours, knowing
    your power;
but we will not sin because we know that
    you acknowledge us as yours.
³ For to know you is complete righteousness,
and to know your power is the root of
    immortality.
⁴ For neither has the evil intent of human art
    misled us,
nor the fruitless toil of painters,
a figure stained with varied colors,
⁵ whose appearance arouses yearning in
    fools,
so that they desire^a the lifeless form of a
    dead image.
⁶ Lovers of evil things and fit for such objects
    of hope^b
are those who either make or desire or
    worship them.

The Foolishness of Worshiping Clay Idols

⁷ A potter kneads the soft earth
and laboriously molds each vessel for our
    service,
fashioning out of the same clay
both the vessels that serve clean uses
and those for contrary uses, making all alike,
but which shall be the use of each of them
the worker in clay decides.
⁸ With misspent toil, these workers form a
    futile god from the same clay—
these mortals who were made of earth a
    short time before
and after a little while go to the earth from
    which all mortals are taken,
when the time comes to return the souls
    that were borrowed.
⁹ But the workers are not concerned that
    mortals are destined to die
or that their life is brief,

---

x 14.28 Gk *they*

y 14.31 Or *of the oaths people swear*
z 15.1 Or *ruling the universe*
a 15.5 Gk *and he desires*
b 15.6 Gk *such hopes*

but they compete with workers in gold and
silver
and imitate workers in copper,
and they count it a glorious thing to mold
counterfeit gods.

10 Their heart is ashes, their hope is cheaper
than dirt,
and their lives are of less worth than clay,

11 because they failed to know the one who
formed them
and inspired them with active souls
and breathed a living spirit into them.

12 But they considered our existence an idle
game
and life a festival held for profit,
for they say one must get money however
one can, even by base means.

13 For these persons, more than all others,
know that they sin
when they make from earthy matter fragile
vessels and carved images.

14 But most foolish and more miserable than
an infant
are all the enemies who oppressed your
people.

15 For they thought that all the idols of the
nations were gods,
though these have neither the use of their
eyes to see with,
nor nostrils with which to draw breath,
nor ears with which to hear,
nor fingers to feel with,
and their feet are of no use for walking.

16 For a human made them,
and one whose spirit is borrowed formed
them,
for none can form gods that are like
themselves.

17 People are mortal, and what they make
with lawless hands is dead,
for they are better than the objects they
worship,
since*c* they have life, but the idols*d* never
had.

Serpents in the Desert

18 Moreover, they worship even the most
hateful animals,
which are worse than all others when
judged by their lack of intelligence,

19 and even as animals they are not so
beautiful in appearance that one
would desire them,
but they have escaped both the praise of
God and his blessing.

16 Therefore those people*e* were
deservedly punished through such
creatures
and were tormented by a multitude of
animals.

2 Instead of this punishment you showed
kindness to your people,
and you prepared quails to eat,
a delicacy to satisfy the desire of appetite,

3 in order that those people, when they
desired food,
might lose the least remnant of appetite*f*
because of the odious creatures sent to
them,
while your people,*g* after suffering want a
short time,
might partake of delicacies.

4 For it was necessary that upon those
oppressors inescapable want should
come,
while to these others it was merely shown
how their enemies were being
tormented.

5 For when the terrible rage of wild animals
came upon your people*h*
and they were being destroyed by the bites
of writhing serpents,
your wrath did not continue to the end;

6 they were troubled for a little while as a
warning
and received a symbol of deliverance to
remind them of your law's command.

7 For the one who turned toward it was
saved not by the thing that was
beheld
but by you, the Savior of all.

8 And by this also you convinced our
enemies
that it is you who deliver from every evil.

9 For they were killed by the bites of locusts
and flies,
and no healing was found for them

---

c **15.17** Other ancient authorities read *of which*
d **15.17** Gk *but they*

e **16.1** Gk *they*
f **16.3** Gk *loathed the necessary appetite*
g **16.3** Gk *they*
h **16.5** Gk *them*

because they deserved to be punished by
such things.
10 But your children were not conquered even
by the fangs of venomous serpents,
for your mercy came to their help and
healed them.
11 To remind them of your oracles they were
bitten
and then were quickly delivered,
so that they would not fall into deep
forgetfulness
and become unresponsive^i to your kindness.
12 For neither herb nor poultice cured them,
but it was your word, O Lord, that heals all
people.
13 For you have power over life and death;
you lead mortals down to the gates of
Hades and back again.
14 A person in wickedness kills another
but cannot bring back the departed spirit
or set free the imprisoned soul.

Disastrous Storms Strike Egypt
15 To escape from your hand is impossible,
16 for the ungodly, refusing to know you,
were flogged by the strength of your arm,
pursued by unusual rains and hail and
relentless storms
and utterly consumed by fire.
17 For—most incredible of all—in water,
which quenches all things,
the fire had still greater effect,
for the universe defends the righteous.
18 At one time the flame was restrained,
so that it might not consume the creatures
sent against the ungodly,
but that seeing this they might know
that they were being pursued by the
judgment of God,
19 and at another time even in the midst of
water it burned more intensely than
fire,
to destroy the crops of the unrighteous
land.

The Israelites Receive Manna
20 Instead of these things you gave your
people food of angels,
and without their toil you supplied them
from heaven with bread ready to eat,
providing every pleasure and suited to
every taste.

21 For your sustenance manifested your
sweetness toward your children,
and the bread, ministering^j to the desire of
the one who took it,
was changed to suit everyone's liking.
22 Snow and ice withstood fire without
melting,
so that they might know that the crops of
their enemies
were being destroyed by the fire that blazed
in the hail
and flashed in the showers of rain;
23 whereas the fire,^{k} in order that the
righteous might be fed,
even forgot its native power.

24 For creation, serving you who made it,
exerts itself to punish the unrighteous
and in kindness relaxes on behalf of those
who trust in you.
25 Therefore at that time also, changed into all
forms,
it served your all-nourishing bounty,
according to the desire of those who had
need,^{l}
26 so that your children, whom you loved,
O Lord, might learn
that it is not the production of crops that
feeds humankind
but that your word sustains those who trust
in you.
27 For what was not destroyed by fire
was melted when simply warmed by a
fleeting ray of the sun,
28 to make it known that one must rise before
the sun to give you thanks
and must pray to you at the dawning of the
light,
29 for the hope of an ungrateful person will
melt like wintry frost
and flow away like wastewater.

Terror Strikes the Egyptians at Night
17 Great are your judgments and hard to
describe;
therefore uninstructed souls have gone
astray.
2 For when lawless people supposed that
they held the holy nation in their
power,

---
i 16.11 Meaning of Gk uncertain
j 16.21 Gk *and it, ministering*
k 16.23 Gk *this*
l 16.25 Or *who made supplication*

they themselves lay as captives of darkness
and prisoners of long night,
shut in under their roofs, exiles from
eternal providence.
3 For thinking that in their secret sins they
were unobserved
behind a dark curtain of forgetfulness,
they were scattered, terribly[m] alarmed
and appalled by specters.
4 For not even the inner chamber that held
them protected them from fear,
but terrifying sounds rang out around
them,
and dismal phantoms with gloomy faces
appeared.
5 And no power of fire was able to give light,
nor did the brilliant flames of the stars
avail to illumine that hateful night.
6 Nothing was shining through to them
except a dreadful, self-kindled fire,
and in terror they deemed the things that
they saw
to be worse than that unseen appearance.
7 The delusions of their magic art lay
humbled,
and their boasted wisdom was scornfully
rebuked.
8 For those who promised to drive off the
fears and disorders of a sick soul
were sick themselves with ridiculous fear.
9 For even if nothing disturbing frightened
them,
yet, scared by the passing of wild animals
and the hissing of snakes
10 they perished in trembling fear,
refusing to look even at the air, though it
nowhere could be avoided.
11 For wickedness is a cowardly thing,
condemned by its own testimony;[n]
distressed by conscience, it has always
exaggerated[o] the difficulties.
12 For fear is nothing but a giving up of the
helps that come from reason,
13 and hope, being weaker, prefers ignorance
of what causes the torment.
14 But throughout the night, which was really
powerless
and which came upon them from the
recesses of powerless Hades,

they all slept the same sleep
15 and now were driven by monstrous
specters
and now were paralyzed by their souls'
surrender,
for sudden and unexpected fear
overwhelmed them.
16 And whoever was there fell down
and thus was kept shut up in a prison not
made of iron;
17 for whether they were farmers or
shepherds
or workers who toiled in the wilderness,
they were seized and endured the
inescapable fate,
for with one chain of darkness they all were
bound.
18 Whether there came a whistling wind,
or a melodious sound of birds in
wide-spreading branches,
or the rhythm of violently rushing water,
19 or the harsh crash of rocks hurled down,
or the unseen running of leaping animals,
or the sound of the most savage roaring
beasts,
or an echo thrown back from a hollow of
the mountains,
it paralyzed them with terror.
20 For the whole world was illumined with
brilliant light
and went about its work unhindered,
21 while over those people alone heavy night
was spread,
an image of the darkness that was destined
to receive them,
but still heavier than darkness were they to
themselves.

Light Shines on the Israelites

18 But for your holy ones there was very
great light.
Their enemies[p] heard their voices but did
not see their forms
and counted them happy for not having
suffered
2 and were thankful that your holy ones,[q]
though previously wronged, were
doing them no injury,
and they begged their pardon for having
been at variance with them.[r]

---

m 17.3 Other ancient authorities read *unobserved,*
they were darkened behind a dark curtain of
forgetfulness, terribly
n 17.11 Meaning of Gk uncertain
o 17.11 Other ancient authorities read *anticipated*

---

p 18.1 Gk *They*
q 18.2 Meaning of Gk uncertain
r 18.2 Meaning of Gk uncertain

3 Therefore you provided a flaming pillar of
fire
as a guide for your people's[s] unknown
journey
and a harmless sun for their glorious
wandering.
4 For their enemies[t] deserved to be deprived
of light and imprisoned in darkness,
those who had kept your children
imprisoned,
through whom the imperishable light of
the law was to be given to the world.

The Death of the Egyptian Firstborn

5 When they had resolved to kill the infants
of your holy ones,
and one child had been abandoned and
rescued,
you in punishment took away a multitude
of their children,
and you destroyed them all together by a
mighty flood.
6 That night was made known beforehand to
our ancestors
so that they might rejoice in sure knowledge
of the oaths in which they trusted.
7 The deliverance of the righteous and the
destruction of their enemies
were expected by your people.
8 For by the same means by which you
punished our enemies
you called us to yourself and glorified us.
9 For in secret the holy children of good
people offered sacrifices
and with one accord agreed to the divine
law,
so that the holy ones would share alike the
same things,
both blessings and dangers,
and already they were singing the praises of
the ancestors.[u]
10 But the discordant cry of their enemies
echoed back,
and their piteous lament for their children
was spread abroad.
11 The slave was punished with the same
penalty as the master,
and the commoner suffered the same loss
as the king,

12 and they all together by the one form[v] of
death
had corpses too many to count.
For the living were not sufficient even to
bury them,
since in one instant their most valued
children had been destroyed.
13 For though they had disbelieved everything
because of their magic arts,
yet when their firstborn were destroyed
they acknowledged your people to be
God's child.
14 For while gentle silence enveloped all things
and night in its swift course was now
half-gone,
15 your all-powerful word leaped from
heaven, from the royal throne,
into the midst of the land that was doomed,
a stern warrior
16 carrying the sharp sword of your authentic
command,
and stood and filled all things with death
and touched heaven while standing on the
earth.
17 Then at once apparitions in dreadful
dreams greatly troubled them,
and unexpected fears assailed them,
18 and one here and another there, hurled
down half-dead,
made known why they were dying,
19 for the dreams that disturbed them
forewarned them of this,
so that they might not perish without
knowing why they suffered.

Threat of Annihilation in the Desert

20 The experience of death touched also the
righteous,
and a plague came upon the multitude in
the desert,
but the wrath did not long continue.
21 For a blameless man was quick to act as
their champion;
he brought forward the shield of his ministry,
prayer and propitiation by incense;
he withstood the anger and put an end to
the disaster,
showing that he was your servant.
22 He conquered the wrath[w] not by strength
of body,
not by force of arms,

---

s 18.3 Gk *their*
t 18.4 Gk *those persons*
u 18.9 Other ancient authorities read *dangers, the*
    ancestors already leading the songs of praise

v 18.12 Gk *name*
w 18.22 Cn: Gk *multitude*

but by his word he subdued the avenger,
  appealing to the oaths and covenants given
    to our ancestors.
23 For when the dead had already fallen on
    one another in heaps,
  he intervened and held back the assault
  and cut off its way to the living.
24 For on his long robe the whole world was
    depicted,
  and the glories of the ancestors were
    engraved on the four rows of stones,
  and your majesty was on the diadem upon
    his head.
25 To these the destroyer yielded, these he[x]
    feared,
  for merely to test the wrath was enough.

The Red Sea

19 But the ungodly were assailed to the
    end by pitiless anger,
  for God[y] knew in advance even their future
    actions:
2 how, though they themselves had
    permitted[z] your people to depart
  and hastily sent them out,
  they would change their minds and pursue
    them.
3 For while they were still engaged in
    mourning
  and were lamenting at the graves of their
    dead,
  they reached another foolish decision
  and pursued as fugitives those whom they
    had begged and compelled to leave.
4 For the fate they deserved drew them on to
    this end
  and made them forget what had happened,
  in order that they might fill up the
    punishment that their torments still
    lacked
5 and that your people might experience[a] an
    incredible journey,
  but they themselves might meet a strange
    death.

God Guides and Protects His People

6 For the whole creation in its nature was
    fashioned anew,
  complying with your commands,

so that your children might be kept
    unharmed.
7 The cloud was seen overshadowing the
    camp
  and dry land emerging where water had
    stood before,
  an unhindered way out of the Red Sea
  and a grassy plain out of the raging waves,
8 where those protected by your hand passed
    through as one nation,
  after gazing on marvelous wonders.
9 For they ranged like horses
  and leaped like lambs,
  praising you, O Lord, who delivered them.
10 For they still recalled the events of their
    sojourn,
  how instead of producing animals the earth
    brought forth gnats,
  and instead of fish the river spewed out vast
    numbers of frogs.
11 Afterward they saw also a new kind of bird,
  when desire led them to ask for luxurious
    food,
12 for, to give them relief, quails came up from
    the sea.

The Punishment of the Egyptians

13 The punishments did not come upon the
    sinners
  without prior signs in the violence of
    thunder,
  for they justly suffered because of their
    wicked acts,
  for they practiced a more bitter hatred of
    strangers.
14 Others had refused to receive strangers
    when they came to them,
  but these made slaves of guests who were
    their benefactors.
15 And not only so, but while punishment of
    some sort will come upon the former
  for having received strangers with hostility,
16 the latter, having first received them with
    festal celebrations,
  afterward afflicted with terrible sufferings
  those who had already shared the same
    rights.
17 They were stricken also with loss of
    sight—
  just as were those at the door of the
    righteous man—
  when, surrounded by yawning darkness,
  all of them tried to find the way through
    their own doors.

---

x 18.25 Other ancient authorities read *they*
y 19.1 Gk *he*
z 19.2 Other ancient authorities read *had changed their
    minds to permit*
a 19.5 Other ancient authorities read *accomplish*

A New Harmony in Nature

18 For the elements changed[b] places with one
        another,
    as on a harp the notes vary the nature of
        the rhythm,
    while each note remains the same.[c]
    This may be clearly inferred from the sight
        of what took place.
19 For land animals were transformed into
        water creatures,
    and creatures that swim moved over to the
        land.
20 Fire even in water retained its normal
        power,
    and water forgot its fire-quenching
        nature.
21 Flames, on the contrary, failed to
        consume
    the flesh of perishable creatures that walked
        among them,
    nor did they melt[d] the crystalline,
        quick-melting kind of heavenly food.

Conclusion

22 For in everything, O Lord, you have exalted
        and glorified your people,
    and you have not neglected to help them at
        all times and in all places.

---

b **19.18** Gk *changing*
c **19.18** Meaning of Gk uncertain
d **19.21** Cn: Gk *nor could be melted*

Ecclesiasticus, or the Wisdom of Jesus Son of
SIRACH

The Prologue

1 Many great teachings have been given to us through the Law and the Prophets 2 and the others*a* that followed them, 3 and for these we should praise Israel for instruction and wisdom. 4 Now those who read them must not only themselves understand them 5 but must also as lovers of learning be able through 6 both speaking and writing to help the outsiders. 7 So my grandfather Jesus, who had devoted himself especially 8 to the reading of the Law 9 and the Prophets 10 and the other books of our ancestors 11 and had acquired considerable proficiency in them, 12 was himself also led to write something pertaining to instruction and wisdom, 13 so that by becoming familiar also with his book*b* those who love learning 14 might make even greater progress in living according to the law.

15 You are invited, therefore, 17 to read it 16 with goodwill and attention 18 and to be indulgent 19 in cases where we may seem 20 to have rendered some phrases imperfectly, despite our diligent labor in translating. 21-22 For what was originally expressed in Hebrew does not have exactly the same effect when translated into another language. 23 Not only this book, 24 but even the Law itself, the Prophets,*c* 25 and the rest of the books 26 differ not a little when read in the original.

27 In the thirty-eighth year of the reign of Euergetes, 28 when I came to Egypt and stayed for some time, 29 I found a copy affording*d* no little instruction. 30 It seemed highly necessary that I should myself devote some diligence and labor to the translation of this book. 31-32 During that time I have applied my skill day and night 33 to complete and publish the book 34 for those living abroad who wish to gain learning and are 35 preparing 36 to live according to the law.

In Praise of Wisdom

1 All wisdom is from the Lord,
  and with him it remains forever.
2 The sand of the sea, the drops of rain,
  and the days of eternity—who can count
  them?
3 The height of heaven, the breadth of the
  earth,
  the abyss, and wisdom*e*—who can search
  them out?
4 Wisdom was created before all things
  and prudent understanding from
  eternity.*f*
6 The root of wisdom—to whom has it been
  revealed?
  Her subtleties—who knows them?*g*
8 There is but one who is wise, greatly to be
  feared,
  seated upon his throne: the Lord.
9 It is he who created her;
  he saw her and took her measure;
  he poured her out upon all his works,
10 upon all the living according to his gift;
  he lavished her upon those who love him.*h*

---

a P.2 Or *other books*
b P.13 Gk *with these things*
c P.24 Gk *prophecies*
d P.29 Other ancient authorities read *found opportunity for*

e 1.3 Other ancient authorities read *the depth of the abyss*
f 1.4 Other ancient authorities add as 1.5: *The source of wisdom is God's word in the highest heaven, and her ways are the eternal commandments.*
g 1.6 Other ancient authorities add as 1.7: *The knowledge of wisdom—to whom was it manifested? And her abundant experience—who has understood it?*
h 1.10 Other ancient authorities add *Love of the Lord is glorious wisdom; to those to whom he appears he apportions her, that they may see him.*

Fear of the Lord Is True Wisdom

11 The fear of the Lord is glory and exultation
    and gladness and a crown of rejoicing.
12 The fear of the Lord delights the heart
    and gives gladness and joy and long life.[i]
13 Those who fear the Lord will have a happy
    end;
        on the day of their death they will be
        blessed.

14 To fear the Lord is the beginning of
    wisdom;
        she is created with the faithful in the
        womb.
15 She made[j] among humans an eternal
    foundation,
        and among their descendants she will
        abide faithfully.
16 To fear the Lord is fullness of wisdom;
        she inebriates mortals with her fruits;
17 she fills their[k] whole house with desirable
    goods
        and their[l] storehouses with her produce.
18 The fear of the Lord is the crown of
    wisdom,
        making peace and perfect health to
        flourish.[m]
19 She rained down knowledge and
    discerning comprehension,
        and she heightened the glory of those
        who held her fast.
20 To fear the Lord is the root of wisdom,
    and her branches are long life.[n]

22 Unjust anger cannot be justified,
        for anger tips the scale to one's ruin.
23 Those who are patient stay calm until the
    right moment,
        and then cheerfulness comes back to
        them.
24 They hold back their words until the right
    moment,

and then the lips of many tell of their
    good sense.

25 In the treasuries of wisdom is insightful
    analogy,
        but godliness is an abomination to a
        sinner.
26 If you desire wisdom, keep the
    commandments,
        and the Lord will lavish her upon you.
27 For the fear of the Lord is wisdom and
    discipline;
        fidelity and humility are his delight.

28 Do not disobey the fear of the Lord;
        do not approach him with a divided
        mind.
29 Do not be a hypocrite before others,
        and keep watch over your lips.
30 Do not exalt yourself, or you may fall
        and bring dishonor upon yourself.
    The Lord will reveal your secrets
        and overthrow you before the whole
        congregation,
    because you did not come in the fear of the
        Lord,
        and your heart was full of deceit.

Duties toward God

2 My child, when you come to serve the
    Lord,
        prepare yourself for testing.[o]
2 Set your heart right and be steadfast,
        and do not be impetuous in time of
        calamity.
3 Cling to him and do not depart,
        so that your last days may be
        prosperous.
4 Accept whatever befalls you,
        and in times of humiliation be patient.
5 For gold is tested in the fire,
        and those found acceptable, in the
        furnace of humiliation.[p]
6 Trust in him, and he will help you;
        make your ways straight and hope in him.

7 You who fear the Lord, wait for his mercy;
        do not stray, or else you may fall.
8 You who fear the Lord, trust in him,
        and your reward will not be lost.

---

i 1.12 Other ancient authorities add *The fear of the
    Lord is a gift from the Lord; also for love he makes
    firm paths.*
j 1.15 Gk *made as a nest*
k 1.17 Other ancient authorities read *her*
l 1.17 Other ancient authorities read *her*
m 1.18 Other ancient authorities add *Both are gifts of
    God for peace; exultation opens out for those who
    love him. He saw her and took her measure.*
n 1.20 Other ancient authorities add as 1.21: *The fear
    of the Lord drives away sins, and where it abides, it
    will turn away all anger.*

---

o 2.1 Or *trials*
p 2.5 Other ancient authorities add *in sickness and
    poverty put your trust in him*

9 You who fear the Lord, hope for good
  things,
    for lasting joy and mercy.*q*
10 Consider the generations of old and see:
  Has anyone trusted in the Lord and been
    disappointed?
  Or has anyone persevered in the fear of the
    Lord*r* and been forsaken?
  Or has anyone called upon him and been
    neglected?
11 For the Lord is compassionate and
    merciful;
  he forgives sins and saves in time of
    distress.

12 Woe to timid hearts and to slack hands
  and to the sinner who walks a double
    path!
13 Woe to the fainthearted who have no trust!
  Therefore they will have no shelter.
14 Woe to you who have lost patience!
  What will you do when the Lord's
    reckoning comes?

15 Those who fear the Lord will not disobey
    his words,
  and those who love him will keep his
    ways.
16 Those who fear the Lord will seek his favor,
  and those who love him will be filled with
    his law.
17 Those who fear the Lord will prepare their
    hearts
  and will humble themselves before him.
18 Let us fall into the hands of the Lord
  but not into the hands of mortals,
  for equal to his majesty is his mercy.*s*

Duties toward Parents

3 Listen to me your father, O children;
    act accordingly, that you may be safe.
2 For the Lord honors a father above his
    children,
  and he confirms a mother's judgment
    over her sons.
3 Those who honor their father atone for
    sins,
4   and those who respect their mother are
    like those who lay up treasure.

5 Those who honor their father will have joy
    in their children,
  and when they pray they will be heard.
6 Those who respect their father will have
    long life,
  and those who honor*t* their mother obey
    the Lord;*u*
7   they will serve their parents as their
    masters.*v*
8 Honor your father by word and deed,
  that his blessing may come upon you.
9 For a father's blessing strengthens the
    houses of the children,
  but a mother's curse uproots their
    foundations.
10 Do not glorify yourself by your father's
    dishonor,
  for your father's dishonor is no glory to
    you.
11 The honor of one's father is one's own glory,
  and a mother dishonored is a disgrace to
    her children.

12 My child, help your father in his old age,
  and do not grieve him as long as he lives;
13 even if his mind fails, be patient with him;
  do not despise him because you have all
    your faculties.
14 For kindness to a father will not be
    forgotten
  and will be credited to you against your
    sins;
15 in the day of your distress it will be
    remembered in your favor;
  like frost in fair weather, your sins will
    melt away.
16 Whoever forsakes a father is like a
    blasphemer,
  and whoever angers a mother is cursed by
    the Lord.

Humility
17 My child, perform your tasks with
    humility;
  then you will be loved more than a giver
    of gifts.*w*
18 The greater you are, the more you must
    humble yourself;

---

q **2.9** Other ancient authorities add *for his reward is an*
  everlasting gift with joy
r **2.10** Gk *of him*
s **2.18** Syr adds *and equal to his name are his works*

t **3.6** Heb: Other ancient authorities read *comfort*
u **3.6** Heb: Gk *and those who obey the Lord honor their*
  mother
v **3.7** In other ancient authorities this line is preceded
  by *Those who fear the Lord honor their father,*
w **3.17** Heb Syr: Gk *more than an acceptable person*

so you will find favor in the sight of the
   Lord.*

20 For great is the might of the Lord,
   but by the humble he is glorified.

21 Neither seek what is too difficult for you
   nor investigate what is beyond your
     power.

22 Reflect upon what you have been
     commanded,
   for what is hidden is not your concern.

23 In matters greater than your own affairs, do
   not meddle,
   for things beyond human understanding
   have been shown you.

24 For their conceit has led many astray,
   and wrong opinion has impaired their
     judgment.

25 Without eyes there is no light;
   without knowledge there is no wisdom.*

26 A stubborn mind will fare badly at the end,
   and whoever loves danger will perish
     in it.

27 A stubborn mind will be burdened by
     troubles,
   and the sinner adds sin to sins.

28 When calamity befalls the proud, there is
   no healing,
   for an evil plant has taken root in him.

29 The mind of the intelligent appreciates
     proverbs,
   and an attentive ear is the desire of the
     wise.

Alms for the Poor

30 As water extinguishes a blazing fire,
   so almsgiving atones for sin.

31 Those who repay favors give thought to the
     future;
   when they fall they will find support.

Duties toward the Poor and the Oppressed

4 My child, do not cheat the poor of their
   living,
   and do not keep needy eyes waiting.

2 Do not grieve the hungry
   or anger one in need.

3 Do not add to the troubles of the angry
   or delay giving to the needy.

4 Do not reject a suppliant in distress
   or turn your face away from the poor.

5 Do not avert your eye from the needy,
   and give no one reason to curse you,

6 for if in bitterness of soul some should
   curse you,
   their Creator will hear their prayer.

7 Endear yourself to the congregation;
   bow your head low to the great.

8 Give a hearing to the poor,
   and return their greeting kindly.

9 Rescue the oppressed from the oppressor,
   and do not be hesitant in giving a verdict.

10 Be a father to orphans,
   and be like a husband to their mother;
   you will then be like a son of the Most High,
   and he will love you more than does your
     mother.

The Rewards of Wisdom

11 Wisdom teaches* her children
   and takes hold of those who seek her.

12 Whoever loves her loves life,
   and those who seek her from early
     morning will be filled with joy.

13 Whoever holds her fast inherits glory,
   and the Lord blesses the place she* enters.

14 Those who serve her minister to the Holy
     One;
   the Lord loves those who love her.

15 Whoever obeys her will judge the nations,
   and whoever listens to her will live securely.

16 If they remain faithful, they will inherit her;
   their descendants will also obtain her.

17 For at first she will walk with them in
     disguise;
   she will bring fear and dread upon them
   and will torment them by her discipline
   until she trusts them,*
   and she will test them with her ordinances.

18 Then she will come straight back to them
     again and gladden them
   and will reveal her secrets to them.

19 If they go astray, she will forsake them
   and hand them over to their ruin.

20 Watch for the opportune time, and beware
   of evil,
   and do not be ashamed to be yourself.

---

x 3.18 Other ancient authorities add as 3.19, *Many are
   lofty and renowned, but to the humble he reveals
   his secrets.*

y 3.25 Heb: Other ancient authorities lack 3.25

z 4.11 Heb Syr: Gk *exalts*

a 4.13 Or *he*

b 4.17 Or *until they remain faithful in their heart*

21 For there is a shame that leads to sin,
    and there is a shame that is glory and
      favor.
22 Do not show partiality to your own harm
    or deference to your downfall.
23 Do not refrain from speaking at the proper
    moment,*c*
    and do not hide your wisdom.*d*
24 For wisdom becomes known through
    speech
    and education through the words of the
      tongue.
25 Never speak against the truth,
    but be ashamed of your ignorance.
26 Do not be ashamed to confess your sins,
    and do not try to stop the current of a
      river.
27 Do not subject yourself to a fool
    or show partiality to a ruler.
28 Fight to the death for truth,
    and the Lord God will fight for you.

29 Do not be reckless in your speech
    or sluggish and remiss in your deeds.
30 Do not be like a lion in your home
    or suspicious of your slaves.
31 Do not let your hand be stretched out to
    receive
    and closed when it is time to give back.

Precepts for Everyday Living

5 Do not rely on your wealth
    or say, "I have enough."
2 Do not follow your inclination and
    strength
    in pursuing the desires of your heart.
3 Do not say, "Who can have power over
    me?"
    for the Lord will surely punish you.

4 Do not say, "I sinned, yet what has
    happened to me?"
    for the Lord is slow to anger.
5 Do not be so confident of forgiveness*e*
    that you add sin to sins.
6 Do not say, "His mercy is great;
    he will forgive*f* the multitude of my sins,"
    for both mercy and wrath are with him,
    and his anger will rest on sinners.

7 Do not delay to turn back to the Lord,
    and do not postpone it from day to day,
    for suddenly the wrath of the Lord will
      come forth,
    and at the time of punishment you will
      perish.
8 Do not rely on dishonest wealth,
    for it will not benefit you on the day of
      calamity.

9 Do not winnow in every wind
    or follow every path.*g*
10 Stand firm in what you know,
    and let your speech be consistent.
11 Be quick to hear,
    and utter a reply patiently.
12 If you understand, answer your neighbor,
    but if not, put your hand over your
      mouth.

13 Honor and dishonor come from speaking,
    and the tongue of mortals may be their
      downfall.
14 Do not be called double-tongued*h*
    and do not lay traps with your tongue,
    for shame comes to the thief
    and severe condemnation to the
      double-tongued.
15 In great and small matters cause no harm,*i*

6 ¹and do not become an enemy instead of
    a friend,
    for a bad name incurs shame and reproach;
    so it is with the double-tongued sinner.

2 Do not fall into the grip of passion,*j*
    or you may be torn apart as by a bull.*k*
3 Your leaves will be devoured and your fruit
    destroyed,
    and you will be left like a withered tree.
4 Strong passion*l* destroys those who have it
    and makes them the laughingstock of
      their enemies.

Friendship, False and True

5 Pleasant speech multiplies friends,
    and a gracious tongue multiplies
      courtesies.

---

c 4.23 Heb: Gk *at a time of salvation*
d 4.23 Other ancient authorities lack *and do not hide*
    your wisdom
e 5.5 Heb: Gk *atonement*
f 5.6 Heb: Gk *he* (or *it*) *will atone for*

g 5.9 Gk adds *so it is with the double-tongued sinner*
h 5.14 Heb: Gk *a slanderer*
i 5.15 Heb Syr: Gk *be ignorant*
j 6.2 Heb: Meaning of Gk uncertain
k 6.2 Meaning of Gk uncertain
l 6.4 Heb: Gk *An evil soul*

6 Let those who are at peace with you be
        many,
    but let your advisers be one in a
        thousand.
7 When you gain friends, gain them through
        testing,
    and do not trust them hastily.
8 For there are friends who are such when it
        suits them,
    but they will not stand by you in time of
        trouble.
9 And there are friends who turn to enmity
    and tell of the quarrel to your disgrace.
10 And there are friends who are companions
        at the table,
    but they will not stand by you in time of
        trouble.
11 When you are prosperous, they become
        your second self
    and boldly command your slaves,
12 but if you are brought low, they turn
        against you
    and hide themselves from you.
13 Keep away from your enemies,
    and be on guard with your friends.

14 Faithful friends are a sturdy shelter;
    whoever finds one has found a treasure.
15 Faithful friends are beyond price;
    no amount can balance their worth.
16 Faithful friends are life-saving medicine,
    and those who fear the Lord will find
        them.
17 Those who fear the Lord direct their
        friendship aright,
    for as they are, so are their neighbors also.

Blessings of Wisdom
18 My child, from your youth choose
        discipline,
    and when you have gray hair you will find
        wisdom.
19 Come to her like one who plows and sows,
    and wait for her good harvest.
    For when you cultivate her you will toil but
        little,
    and soon you will eat of her produce.
20 She seems very harsh to the undisciplined;
    fools will not remain with her.
21 She will be like a heavy stone to test them,
    and they will not delay in casting her
        aside.
22 For wisdom is like her name;
    she is not readily perceived by many.

23 Listen, my child, and accept my judgment;
    do not reject my counsel.
24 Put your feet into her fetters
    and your neck into her collar.
25 Bend your shoulder and carry her,
    and do not become angry with her bonds.
26 Come to her with all your soul,
    and keep her ways with all your might.
27 Search out and seek, and she will become
        known to you,
    and when you get hold of her, do not let
        her go.
28 For at last you will find her rest,
    and she will be changed into joy for you.
29 Then her fetters will become for you a
        strong defense,
    and her collar a glorious robe.
30 Her yoke*m* is a golden ornament
    and her bonds a purple cord.
31 You will wear her like a glorious robe
    and put her on like a splendid crown.*n*

32 If you are willing, my child, you can be
        disciplined,
    and if you apply yourself you will become
        clever.
33 If you love to listen you will accept
        discipline,
    and if you pay attention you will become
        wise.
34 Stand in the company of the elders.
    Who is wise? Attach yourself to such a
        one.
35 Be ready to listen to every godly discourse,
    and let no wise proverbs escape you.
36 If you see an intelligent person, rise early to
        visit him;
    let your foot wear out his doorstep.
37 Reflect on the statutes of the Lord,
    and meditate at all times on his
        commandments.
    It is he who will give insight to*o* your mind,
    and your desire for wisdom will be
        granted.

Miscellaneous Advice
7 Do no evil, and evil will never overtake
        you.
2 Stay away from wrong, and it will turn
        away from you.

---
m **6.30** Heb: Gk *Upon her*
n **6.31** Heb: Gk *crown of gladness*
o **6.37** Heb: Gk *will confirm*

3 Do^p not sow in the furrows of injustice,
    and you will not reap a sevenfold crop.

4 Do not seek from the Lord high office
    or the seat of honor from the king.
5 Do not assert your righteousness before the
        Lord
    or display your wisdom before the king.
6 Do not seek to become a judge,
    or you may be unable to root out injustice;
    perhaps you will fear the powerful
    and so mar your integrity.
7 Commit no offense against the public,
    and do not disgrace yourself among the
        people.

8 Do not commit a sin twice;
    even for one you will not go unpunished.
9 Do not say, "He will consider the great
        number of my gifts,
    and when I make an offering to the Most
        High God, he will accept it."
10 Do not grow weary when you pray;
    do not neglect to give alms.
11 Do not ridicule a person who is embittered
        in spirit,
    for there is one who humbles and exalts.
12 Do not devise^q a lie against your brother
    or do the same to a friend.
13 Refuse to utter any lie,
    for it is a habit that results in no good.
14 Do not babble in the company of the
        elders,
    and do not repeat yourself when you pray.

15 Do not hate hard labor
    or farm work, which was created by the
        Most High.
16 Do not enroll in the ranks of sinners;
    remember that retribution will not delay.
17 Humble yourself to the utmost,
    for the punishment of the ungodly is fire
    and worms.^r

Relations with Others
18 Do not exchange a friend for money
    or a real brother for the gold of Ophir.
19 Do not dismiss^s a wise and good wife,
    for her charm is worth more than gold.

20 Do not abuse slaves who work faithfully
    or hired laborers who give of themselves.
21 Let your soul love intelligent slaves;^t
    do not withhold from them their
        freedom.

22 Do you have cattle? Look after them;
    if they are profitable to you, keep them.
23 Do you have children? Discipline them,
    and make them obedient^u from their
        youth.
24 Do you have daughters? Be concerned for
        their chastity,^v
    and do not show yourself too indulgent
        with them.^w
25 Give a daughter in marriage, and you
        complete a great task,
    but give her to a sensible man.
26 Do you have a wife who pleases you?^x Do
        not divorce her,
    but do not trust yourself to one whom
        you detest.

27 With all your heart honor your father,
    and do not forget the birth pangs of your
        mother.
28 Remember that it was of your parents^y you
        were born;
    how will you repay what they have given
        to you?

29 With all your soul fear the Lord
    and revere his priests.
30 With all your might love your Maker,
    and do not neglect his ministers.
31 Fear the Lord and honor the priest,
    and give him his portion, as you have
        been commanded:
    the first fruits, the purification offering, the
        gift of the shoulders,
    the sacrifice of sanctification, and the first
        fruits of the holy things.

32 Stretch out your hand to the poor,
    so that your blessing may be complete.
33 Give graciously to all the living;
    do not withhold kindness even from the
        dead.

---

p 7.3 Gk *My child, do*
q 7.12 Heb: Gk *plow*
r 7.17 Heb *for the expectation of mortals is worms*
s 7.19 Heb: Gk *deprive yourself of*

t 7.21 Heb *Love a wise slave as yourself*
u 7.23 Gk *bend their necks*
v 7.24 Gk *body*
w 7.24 Gk *do not brighten your face toward them*
x 7.26 Heb Syr lack *who pleases you*
y 7.28 Gk *them*

34 Do not lag behind those who weep,
   but mourn with those who mourn.
35 Do not hesitate to visit the sick,
   because for such deeds you will be loved.
36 In all you do, remember the end of your
   life,
   and then you will never sin.

Prudence and Common Sense

8 Do not contend with the powerful,
   or you may fall into their hands.
2 Do not quarrel with the rich,
   in case their resources outweigh yours,
   for gold has ruined many
   and has perverted the minds of kings.
3 Do not argue with the loud of mouth,
   and do not heap wood on their fire.

4 Do not make fun of one who is
   uneducated,
   or your ancestors may be insulted.
5 Do not reproach one who is turning away
   from sin;
   remember that we all deserve
   punishment.
6 Do not disdain one who is old,
   for some of us are also growing old.
7 Do not rejoice over anyone's death;
   remember that we must all die.

8 Do not slight the discourse of the sages,
   but turn to their maxims,
   because from them you will learn discipline
   and how to serve the great.
9 Do not ignore the discourse of the aged,
   for they themselves learned from their
   parents;[z]
   from them you learn how to understand
   and to give an answer when the need
   arises.

10 Do not kindle the coals of sinners,
   or you may be burned[a] in their flaming
   fire.
11 Do not let the insolent bring you to your
   feet,
   or they may lie in ambush against your
   words.
12 Do not lend to one who is stronger than you,
   but if you do lend anything, count it as a
   loss.

13 Do not give surety beyond your means,
   but if you give surety be prepared to pay.

14 Do not go to law against a judge,
   for the decision will favor him because of
   his standing.
15 Do not travel on the road with the reckless,
   or your troubles may become burdensome,
   for they will act as they please,
   and through their folly you will perish
   with them.
16 Do not pick a fight with the quick-tempered,
   and do not journey with them through a
   deserted region,
   because bloodshed means nothing to them,
   and where no help is at hand they will
   strike you down.
17 Do not consult with fools,
   for they cannot keep a secret.
18 In the presence of strangers do nothing that
   is to be kept secret,
   for you do not know what they will
   divulge.[b]
19 Do not reveal your thoughts to anyone,
   or you may drive away your happiness.[c]

Advice concerning Women

9 Do not be jealous of the wife whom you
   embrace,
   or you will teach her an evil lesson to
   your own hurt.
2 Do not give yourself to a woman
   and let her trample down your strength.
3 Do not go near a loose woman,[d]
   or you may fall into her snares.
4 Do not dally with a female singer,
   or you may be caught in her activities.
5 Do not look intently at a virgin,
   or you may stumble and incur penalties
   for her.
6 Do not give yourself to prostitutes,
   or you may lose your inheritance.
7 Do not look around in the streets of a city
   or wander about in its deserted sections.
8 Turn away your eyes from a shapely woman,
   and do not gaze at beauty belonging to
   another;
   many have been seduced by a woman's
   beauty,
   and by it passion is kindled like a fire.

z **8.9** Or *ancestors*
a **8.10** Heb: Gk *do not get burned*

b **8.18** Or *it will bring forth*
c **8.19** Heb: Gk *and let him not return a favor to you*
d **9.3** Heb *strange woman*

⁹ Never dine*e* with another man's wife
    or revel with her at wine,
    or your heart may turn aside to her,
    and in blood*f* you may plunge into
        destruction.

Choice of Friends

¹⁰ Do not abandon old friends,
    for new ones cannot equal them.
    A new friend is like new wine;
    when it has aged, you will drink it with
        pleasure.

¹¹ Do not envy the notoriety of sinners,
    for you do not know what their end will
        be like.
¹² Do not delight in what pleases the
        ungodly;*g*
    remember that they will not be held
        guiltless until Hades.

¹³ Keep far from those who have power to
        kill,
    and you will not be haunted by the fear
        of death.
    But if you approach them, make no misstep,
    or they may rob you of your life.
    Know that you are stepping among snares
    and that you are walking on the city
        battlements.

¹⁴ As much as you can, aim to know your
        neighbors,
    and consult with the wise.
¹⁵ Let your conversation be with intelligent
        people,
    and let all your discussion be about the
        law of the Most High.
¹⁶ Let the righteous be your dinner
        companions,
    and let your boast be in the fear of the
        Lord.

Concerning Rulers

¹⁷ A work is praised for the skill of the artisan,
    so a people's leader is proved wise by his
        words.
¹⁸ The loud of mouth are feared in their city,
    and the one who is reckless in speech is
        hated.

10 ¹ A wise magistrate educates his people,
    and the rule of an intelligent person is
        well ordered.
² As the people's judge is, so are his
        officials;
    as the ruler of the city is, so are all its
        inhabitants.
³ An undisciplined king ruins his people,
    but a city becomes fit to live in through
        the understanding of its rulers.
⁴ The government of the earth is in the hand
        of the Lord,
    and over it he will raise up the right
        leader for the time.
⁵ Human success is in the hand of the Lord,
    and it is he who confers honor upon the
        lawgiver.*h*

The Sin of Pride

⁶ Do not get angry with your neighbor for
        every injury,
    and do not resort to acts of insolence.
⁷ Arrogance is hateful to the Lord and to
        mortals,
    and injustice is outrageous to both.
⁸ Sovereignty passes from nation to nation
    on account of injustice and insolence and
        wealth.*i*
⁹ How can dust and ashes be proud?
    Even in life the human body is infested
        with worms.*j*
¹⁰ A long illness mocks the physician;
    the king of today will die tomorrow.
¹¹ For when humans die
    they inherit maggots and vermin*k* and
        worms.
¹² The beginning of human pride is to forsake
        the Lord;
    the heart has withdrawn from its Maker.
¹³ For the beginning of pride is sin,
    and the one who clings to it pours out
        abominations.
    Therefore the Lord brought upon them
        unheard-of calamities
    and destroyed them completely.*l*
¹⁴ The Lord overthrew the thrones of rulers
    and enthroned the lowly in their place.

---

e 9.9 Heb: Gk *sit down*
f 9.9 Heb: Gk *by your spirit*
g 9.12 Gk: Heb *the success of the arrogant*

h 10.5 Heb: Gk *scribe*
i 10.8 Other ancient authorities add here or after 10.9a:
    Nothing is more wicked than one who loves money,
    for such a person puts his own soul up for sale.
j 10.9 Heb: Meaning of Gk uncertain
k 10.11 Gk: Heb *wild animals*
l 10.13 Gk: Heb *brings upon them . . . destroys them*

15 The Lord plucked up the roots of the
nations[m]
and planted the humble in their place.
16 The Lord laid waste the lands of the nations
and destroyed them to the foundations of
the earth.
17 He removed some of them and destroyed
them
and erased the memory of them from the
earth.
18 Pride was not created for human beings
or violent anger for those born of women.

Persons Deserving Honor

19 Whose offspring are worthy of honor?
Human offspring.
Whose offspring are worthy of honor?
Those who fear the Lord.
Whose offspring are unworthy of honor?
Human offspring.
Whose offspring are unworthy of honor?
Those who break the commandments.
20 Among family members their leader is
worthy of honor,
but those who fear the Lord are worthy of
honor in his eyes.[n]
22 The guest and the stranger[o] and the poor—
their boast is the fear of the Lord.
23 It is not right to despise one who is
intelligent but poor,
and it is not proper to honor one who is
sinful.
24 The prince and the judge and the ruler are
honored,
but none of them is greater than the one
who fears the Lord.
25 Free people will serve a wise slave,
and an intelligent person will not complain.

Concerning Humility

26 Do not make a display of your wisdom
when you do your work,
and do not extol yourself when you are in
difficulty.
27 Better those who work and have plenty
than those who boast and lack bread.

28 My child, honor yourself with humility,
and give yourself the esteem you deserve.

29 Who will acquit those who condemn[p]
themselves,
and who will honor those who dishonor
themselves?[q]
30 The poor are honored for their knowledge,
while the rich are honored for their
wealth.
31 One who is honored in poverty, how much
more in wealth!
And one dishonored in wealth, how
much more in poverty!

The Deceptiveness of Appearances

11 The wisdom of the humble lifts their
heads high
and seats them among the great.
2 Do not praise individuals for their good
looks
or loathe anyone because of appearance
alone.
3 The bee is small among flying creatures,
but what it produces is the origin of sweet
things.
4 Do not mock those wearing only a
loincloth
or make fun of those whose day is bitter,[r]
for the works of the Lord are wonderful
and his works are concealed from
humans.
5 Many oppressed have sat upon a throne,[s]
and one whom no one expected has worn
a crown.
6 Many rulers have been utterly disgraced,
and the honored have been handed over
to others.

Deliberation and Caution

7 Do not find fault before you investigate;
examine first and then criticize.
8 Do not answer before you listen,
and do not interrupt when another is
speaking.
9 Do not argue about a matter that does not
concern you,
and do not sit with sinners when they
judge a case.

10 My child, do not busy yourself with many
matters;

---

m 10.15 Other ancient authorities read *proud nations*
n 10.20 Other ancient authorities add as 10.21: *The
fear of the Lord is the beginning of acceptance;
obduracy and pride are the beginning of rejection.*
o 10.22 Heb: Gk *The rich and the eminent*

p 10.29 Heb: Gk *sin against*
q 10.29 Heb Lat: Gk *their own life*
r 11.4 Heb: Gk *Do not boast about wearing fine clothes,
and do not exalt yourself when you are honored*
s 11.5 Heb: Gk *Many sovereigns have sat on the ground*

if you multiply activities, you will not be
held blameless.
If you pursue, you will not overtake,
and by fleeing you will not escape.
11 There are those who work and struggle and
hurry
but are so much the more in want.
12 There are others who are slow and need
help,
who lack strength and abound in poverty,
but the eyes of the Lord look kindly upon
them;
he lifts them out of their lowly condition
13 and raises up their heads
to the amazement of the many.

14 Good things and bad, life and death,
poverty and wealth, come from the
Lord.*t*
17 The Lord's gift remains with the devout,
and his favor brings lasting success.
18 A person becomes rich through diligence
and self-denial,
and the reward allotted to him is this:
19 when he says, "I have found rest,
and now I shall feast on my goods!"
he does not realize how time passes by;
he will leave them to others and will die.

20 Stand by your agreement and attend to it,
and grow old in your work.
21 Do not wonder at the works of a sinner,
but trust in the Lord and keep at your job,
for it is easy in the sight of the Lord
to make the poor person suddenly rich,
in an instant.
22 The blessing of the Lord is*u* the reward of
the pious,
and quickly his blessing flourishes.
23 Do not say, "What do I need,
and what further benefit can be mine?"
24 Do not say, "I have enough,
and what harm can come to me now?"
25 In the day of prosperity, adversity is
forgotten,
and in the day of adversity, prosperity is
not remembered.

26 For it is easy for the Lord on the day of
death
to reward individuals according to their
conduct.
27 An hour's misery makes one forget
delights,
and at the close of one's life one's deeds
are revealed.
28 Call no one happy before his death;
by how he ends, a person becomes
known.*v*

Care in Choosing Friends
29 Do not invite everyone into your home,
for many are the tricks of the crafty.
30 Like a decoy partridge in a cage, so is the
mind of the proud,
and like spies they observe your
weakness,*w*
31 for they lie in wait, turning good into evil,
and to worthy actions they attach blame.
32 From a spark many coals are kindled,
and a sinner lies in wait to shed blood.
33 Beware of scoundrels, for they devise evil,
and they may ruin your reputation
forever.
34 Receive strangers into your home, and they
will stir up trouble for you
and will make you a stranger to your own
family.

12 If you do good, know to whom you
do it,
and you will be thanked for your good
deeds.
2 Do good to the devout, and you will be
repaid—
if not by them, certainly by the Most
High.
3 No good comes to one who persists in evil
or to one who does not give alms.
4 Give to the devout, but do not help the
sinner.
5 Do good to the humble, but do not give
to the ungodly;
hold back their bread, and do not give it to
them,
for by means of it they might subdue you;
then you will receive twice as much evil
for all the good you have done to them.

---

t 11.14 Other ancient authorities add as 11.15–16:
*15 Wisdom, understanding, and knowledge of the
law come from the Lord; affection and the ways of
good works come from him. 16 Error and darkness
were created with sinners; evil grows old with those
who take pride in malice.*
u 11.22 Heb: Gk *is in*

v 11.28 Heb: Gk *and through his children a person
becomes known*
w 11.30 Heb: Gk *downfall*

6 For the Most High also hates sinners
  and will inflict punishment on the
     ungodly.*

7 Give to the one who is good, but do not
   help the sinner.

8 A friend is not known* in prosperity,
   nor is an enemy hidden in adversity.

9 One's enemies are friendly* when one
   prospers,
   but in adversity even one's friend
     disappears.

10 Never trust your enemy,
   for like corrosion in copper, so is his
     wickedness.

11 Even if he humbles himself and walks
     bowed down,
   take care to be on your guard against him.
   Be to him like one who polishes a mirror,
   to be sure it does not become completely
     tarnished.

12 Do not put him next to you,
   or he may overthrow you and take your
     place.
   Do not let him sit at your right hand,
   or else he may try to take your own seat,
   and at last you will acknowledge my words
   and be stung by what I have said.

13 Who pities a snake charmer when he is
     bitten
   or all those who go near wild animals?

14 So no one pities people who associate with
     sinners
   and become involved in their sins.

15 They stand by you for a while,
   but if you falter, they will not be there.

16 Enemies speak sweetly with their lips,
   but in their hearts they plan to throw you
     into a pit;
   enemies may have tears in their eyes,
   but if they find an opportunity they will
     never have enough of your blood.

17 If evil comes upon you, you will find them
     there ahead of you;
   pretending to help, they will trip you up.

18 Then they will shake their heads and clap
     their hands
   and whisper much and show their true
     faces.

Caution Regarding Associates

13 Whoever touches pitch gets dirty,
   and whoever associates with the proud
     will become like them.

2 Do not lift a weight too heavy for you
   or associate with one mightier and richer
     than you.
   How can the clay pot associate with the
     iron kettle?
   The pot will strike against it and be
     smashed.

3 A rich person does wrong and even adds
     insults;
   a poor person suffers wrong and must
     add apologies.

4 Rich people* will exploit you* if you can be
     of use to them,
   but if you are in need they will abandon
     you.

5 If you own something, they will live with
     you;
   they will drain your resources without a
     qualm.

6 When they need you, they will deceive you
   and will smile at you and encourage you;
   they will speak to you kindly and say,
     "What do you need?"

7 They will embarrass you with their
     delicacies,
   until they have drained you two or three
     times,
   and finally they will laugh at you.
   Should they see you afterwards, they will
     pass you by
   and shake their heads at you.

8 Take care not to be led astray
   and humiliated when you are enjoying
     yourself.*

9 When the influential invite you, be
     reserved,
   and they will invite you more insistently.

10 Do not be forward, or you may be rebuffed;
   do not stand aloof, or you will be
     forgotten.

11 Do not try to treat them as equals
   or trust their lengthy conversations,
   for they will test you by prolonged talk,
   and while they smile they will be
     examining you.

---

x **12.6** Other ancient authorities add *and he is keeping*
   them for the day of their punishment
y **12.8** Other ancient authorities read *punished*
z **12.9** Heb: Gk *grieved*

---

a **13.4** Gk *He*
b **13.4** Heb: Gk *work with you*
c **13.8** Other ancient authorities read *in your folly*

12 Cruel are those who do not keep your
  secrets;
  they will not spare you harm or
  imprisonment.
13 Be on your guard and very careful,
  for you are walking about with your own
  downfall.*d*

15 Every creature loves its like
  and every person a neighbor.
16 All living beings associate with their own
  kind,
  and people stick close to those like
  themselves.
17 What does a wolf have in common with a
  lamb?
  No more has a sinner with the devout.
18 What peace is there between a hyena and a
  dog,
  and what peace between the rich and the
  poor?
19 Wild asses in the wilderness are the prey of
  lions;
  likewise the poor are feeding grounds for
  the rich.
20 Humility is an abomination to the proud;
  likewise the poor are an abomination to
  the rich.

21 When the rich person totters, he is
  supported by friends,
  but when the humble*e* falls, he is pushed
  away by friends.
22 If the rich person slips, many come to the
  rescue;
  he speaks unseemly words, but they
  justify him.
  If the humble person slips, they even
  criticize him;
  he talks sense but is not given a hearing.
23 The rich person speaks, and all are silent;
  they extol to the clouds what he says.
  The poor person speaks, and they say,
  "Who is this fellow?"
  And should he stumble, they push him
  down.
24 Riches are good if they are free from sin;
  poverty is evil only in the opinion of the
  ungodly.

25 The heart changes the countenance
  either for good or for evil.*f*
26 The sign of a happy heart is a cheerful face,
  but to devise proverbs requires strenuous
  thinking.

14 Happy are those who do not blunder
  with their lips
  and are not stricken with grief for sin.
2 Happy are those whose hearts do not
  condemn them
  and who have not given up their hope.

Responsible Use of Wealth
3 Riches are inappropriate for the
  small-minded,
  and of what use is wealth to misers?
4 What they deny themselves they collect for
  others,
  and others will live in luxury on their
  goods.
5 If they are mean to themselves, to whom
  will they be generous?
  They will not enjoy their own riches.
6 No one is worse than those who are
  grudging to themselves;
  this is the repayment for their meanness.
7 If ever they do good, it is by mistake,*g*
  and in the end they reveal their meanness.
8 Misers are evil people;
  they turn away and disregard people.
9 The eyes of the greedy are not satisfied with
  their share;
  greedy injustice withers the soul.
10 Misers begrudge bread,
  and it is lacking at their tables.

11 My child, treat yourself well, according to
  your means,
  and present worthy offerings to the Lord.
12 Remember that death does not tarry,
  and the decree*h* of Hades has not been
  shown to you.
13 Do good to friends before you die,
  and reach out and give to them as much
  as you can.
14 Do not deprive yourself of a day's
  enjoyment;
  do not let your share of desired good pass
  by you.

---

d 13.13 Other ancient authorities add as 13.14: *When
  you hear these things in your sleep, wake up!
  During all your life love the Lord, and call on him
  for your salvation.*
e 13.21 Other ancient authorities read *poor*

---

f 13.25 Other ancient authorities add *and a glad heart
  makes a cheerful countenance*
g 14.7 Syr: Gk *through forgetfulness*
h 14.12 Heb Syr: Gk *covenant*

15 Will you not leave the fruit of your labors
    to another,
  and what you acquired by toil to be
    divided by lot?
16 Give and take and indulge yourself,
  because in Hades one cannot look for
    luxury.
17 All living beings become old like a
    garment,
  for the decree*i* from of old is, "You must
    die!"
18 Like abundant leaves on a spreading tree
  that sheds some and puts forth others,
  so are the generations of flesh and blood:
  one dies, and another is born.
19 Every work decays and ceases to exist,
  and the one who made it will pass away
    with it.

The Happiness of Seeking Wisdom
20 Happy are those who meditate on*j* wisdom
  and who reason intelligently,
21 who reflect in their hearts on her ways
  and ponder her secrets,
22 pursuing her like a hunter
  and lying in wait on her paths;
23 who peer through her windows
  and listen at her doors;
24 who camp near her house
  and fasten their tent pegs to her walls;
25 who pitch their tents near her
  and so occupy an excellent lodging place;
26 who place their children under her shelter
  and lodge under her boughs;
27 who are sheltered by her from the heat
  and dwell in the midst of her glory.

15 Whoever fears the Lord will do this,
  and whoever holds to the law will
    obtain wisdom.*k*
2 She will come to meet him like a mother,
  and like a young bride she will welcome
    him.
3 She will feed him with the bread of
    understanding
  and give him the water of wisdom to
    drink.
4 He will lean on her and not fall,
  and he will rely on her and not be put to
    shame.

5 She will exalt him above his neighbors
  and will open his mouth in the midst of
    the assembly.
6 Gladness*l* and a crown of rejoicing
  and an everlasting name he will inherit.
7 The foolish will not obtain her,
  and sinners will not see her.
8 She is far from arrogance,
  and liars will never think of her.
9 Praise is unseemly on the lips of a sinner,
  for it has not been sent from the Lord.
10 For in wisdom must praise be uttered,
  and the Lord will make it prosper.

Freedom of Choice
11 Do not say, "It was the Lord's doing that I
    fell away,"
  for he does not do*m* what he hates.
12 Do not say, "It was he who led me astray,"
  for he has no need of the sinful.
13 The Lord hates all abominations;
  such things are not loved by those who
    fear him.
14 It was he who created humans in the
    beginning,
  and he left them in the power of their
    own inclinations.*n*
15 If you choose, you can keep the
    commandments,
  and to act faithfully is a matter of your
    choice.
16 He has placed before you fire and water;
  stretch out your hand for whichever you
    choose.
17 Before each person are life and death,
  and whichever one chooses will be given.
18 For great is the wisdom of the Lord;
  he is mighty in power and sees everything;
19 his eyes are on those who fear him,
  and he knows every human action.
20 He has not commanded anyone to be
    ungodly,
  and he has not given anyone permission
    to sin.

God's Punishment of Sinners
16 Do not desire a multitude of worthless*o*
    children,
  and do not rejoice in ungodly offspring.

---

i **14.17** Heb: Gk *covenant*
j **14.20** Other ancient authorities read *die in*
k **15.1** Gk *her*
l **15.6** Other ancient authorities read *He will find
    gladness*
m **15.11** Heb: Gk *you ought not to do*
n **15.14** Heb: Gk *deliberation*
o **16.1** Heb: Gk *unprofitable*

2 If they multiply, do not rejoice in them,
   unless the fear of the Lord is in them.
3 Do not trust in their survival
   or rely on their numbers,[p]
   for one can be better than a thousand,
   and to die childless is better than to have
   ungodly children.
4 For through one intelligent person a city
   can be filled with people,
   but through a clan of outlaws it becomes
   desolate.

5 Many such things my eye has seen,
   and my ear has heard things more
   striking than these.
6 In an assembly of sinners a fire is kindled,
   and in a disobedient nation wrath has
   blazed up.
7 He did not forgive the ancient giants[q]
   who revolted in their might.
8 He did not spare the neighbors of Lot,
   whom he loathed on account of their
   arrogance.
9 He showed no pity on the doomed nation,
   on those dispossessed because of their
   sins,[r]
10 or on the six hundred thousand foot
   soldiers
   who assembled in their stubbornness.[s]
11 Even if there were only one stiff-necked
   person,
   it would be a wonder if he remained
   unpunished.
   For mercy and wrath are with the Lord;[t]
   he acquits and forgives,[u] but he also pours
   out wrath.
12 Great as is his mercy, so also is his
   chastisement;
   he judges people according to their
   deeds.
13 The sinner will not escape with plunder,
   and the patience of the godly will not be
   frustrated.

14 He makes room for every act of
   almsgiving;
   everyone receives in accordance with his
   or her deeds.[v]

17 Do not say, "I am hidden from the Lord,
   and who from on high has me in mind?
   Among so many people I am unknown,
   for what am I in a boundless creation?
18 Look, heaven and the highest heaven,
   the abyss and the earth tremble at his
   visitation![w]
19 Together the mountains and the
   foundations of the earth
   shake and tremble when he looks upon
   them.
20 But no human mind can grasp this,
   and who can comprehend his ways?
21 Like a tempest that no one can see,
   so most of his works are concealed.[x]
22 Who is to announce his acts of justice?
   Or who can await them? For his decree[y]
   is far off."[z]
23 Such are the thoughts of one devoid of
   understanding;
   a senseless and misguided person thinks
   foolishly.

God's Wisdom Seen in Creation

24 Listen to me, my child, and acquire
   knowledge,
   and pay close attention to my words.
25 I will impart discipline precisely[a]
   and declare knowledge accurately.

26 When the Lord created[b] his works from the
   beginning
   and, in making them, determined their
   boundaries,

---

p 16.3 Other ancient authorities add *for you will groan
   in untimely mourning, and will know of their
   sudden end*
q 16.7 Gk: Heb *princes*
r 16.9 Other ancient authorities add *all these things
   he did to the hard-hearted nations, and by the
   multitude of his holy ones he was not appeased*
s 16.10 Other ancient authorities add *chastising,
   showing mercy, striking, healing, the Lord persisted
   in mercy and discipline*
t 16.11 Gk *him*
u 16.11 Heb: Gk *a master of propitiations*

v 16.14 Other ancient authorities add 16.15–16:
   *[15]The Lord hardened Pharaoh so that he did not
   recognize him, in order that his works might be
   known under heaven. [16]His mercy is manifest to the
   whole of creation, and he apportioned his light and
   darkness to Adam.*
w 16.18 Other ancient authorities add *The whole world
   past and present is in his will.*
x 16.21 Meaning of Gk uncertain: Heb Syr *If I sin, no
   eye can see me, and if I am disloyal all in secret,
   who is to know?*
y 16.22 Heb: Gk *the covenant*
z 16.22 Other ancient authorities add *and a scrutiny
   for all comes at the end*
a 16.25 Gk *by weight*
b 16.26 Heb: Gk *judged*

27 he arranged their works in an eternal order
and their dominion[c] for all generations.
They neither hunger nor grow weary,
and they do not abandon their tasks.
28 They do not crowd one another,
and they never disobey his word.
29 Then the Lord looked upon the earth
and filled it with his good things.
30 With all kinds of living beings he covered
its surface,
and into it they must return.

17

The Lord created humans out of earth
and makes them return to it again.
2 He gave them a fixed number of days
but granted them authority over
everything on the earth.[d]
3 He endowed them with strength like his
own[e]
and made them in his own image.
4 He put the fear of them[f] in all living beings
and gave them dominion over beasts and
birds.[g]
6 Discretion and tongue and eyes,
ears and a mind for thinking he gave
them.
7 He filled them with knowledge and
understanding
and showed them good and evil.
8 He put the fear of him into[h] their hearts
to show them the majesty of his works.[i]
10 And they will praise his holy name,
9 to proclaim the grandeur of his works.
11 He bestowed knowledge upon them
and allotted to them the law of life.[j]
12 He established with them an eternal
covenant
and revealed to them his decrees.
13 Their eyes saw his glorious majesty,
and their ears heard the glory of his
voice.

14 He said to them, "Beware of all iniquity."
And he gave commandment to each of
them concerning the neighbor.
15 Their ways are always before him;
they will not be hidden from his eyes.[k]
17 He appointed a ruler for every nation,
but Israel is the Lord's own portion.[l]
19 All their works are as the sun before him,
and his eyes are ever upon their ways.
20 Their iniquities are not hidden from him,
and all their sins are before the Lord.[m]
22 One's almsgiving is like a signet ring with
the Lord,[n]
and he will keep a person's kindness like
the apple of his eye.[o]
23 Afterward he will rise up and repay them,
and he will bring their recompense on
their heads.
24 Yet to those who repent he grants a return,
and he encourages those who are losing
hope.

A Call to Repentance

25 Turn back to the Lord and forsake your
sins;
pray in his presence and lessen your
offense.
26 Return to the Most High and turn away
from iniquity[p]
and hate intensely what is abhorrent.
27 Who will sing praises to the Most High in
Hades
in place of the living who give thanks?
28 From the dead, as from one who does not
exist, thanksgiving has ceased;
those who are alive and well sing the
Lord's praises.

---

c 16.27 Or *elements*
d 17.2 Lat: Gk *it*
e 17.3 Lat: Gk *proper to them*
f 17.4 Syr: Gk *him*
g 17.4 Other ancient authorities add as 17.5: *They
obtained the use of the five faculties of the Lord; as
sixth he distributed to them the gift of mind, and as
seventh, reason, the interpreter of one's faculties.*
h 17.8 Other ancient authorities read *He set his eye
upon*
i 17.8 Other ancient authorities add *and he gave them
to boast of his marvels forever*
j 17.11 Other ancient authorities add *so that they may
know that they who are alive now are mortal*

k 17.15 Other ancient authorities add [16]*Their ways
from youth tend toward evil, and they are unable
to make for themselves hearts of flesh in place
of their stony hearts.* [17]*For in the division of the
nations of the whole earth,*
l 17.17 Other ancient authorities add as 17.18: *whom,
being his firstborn, he brings up with discipline,
and allotting to him the light of his love, he does
not neglect him.*
m 17.20 Other ancient authorities add as 17.21: *But
the Lord, who is gracious and knows how they are
formed, has neither left them nor abandoned them
but has spared them.*
n 17.22 Gk *him*
o 17.22 Other ancient authorities add *apportioning
repentance to his sons and daughters*
p 17.26 Other ancient authorities add *for he will lead
you out of darkness to the light of health.*

²⁹ How great is the mercy of the Lord
 and his forgiveness for those who return
 to him!
³⁰ For not everything is within human
 capability,
 since human beings are not immortal.
³¹ What is brighter than the sun? Yet it can be
 eclipsed.
 So flesh and blood devise evil.
³² He marshals the host of the height of heaven,
 but all humans are dust and ashes.

The Majesty of God

18 He who lives forever created the whole
 universe;
² the Lord alone will be justified.*q*
⁴ To none has he given power to proclaim his
 works,
 and who can search out his mighty deeds?
⁵ Who can measure his majestic power,
 and who can fully recount his mercies?
⁶ It is not possible to diminish or increase
 them,
 nor is it possible to fathom the wonders
 of the Lord.
⁷ When humans have finished, they are just
 beginning,
 and when they stop, they are still
 perplexed.
⁸ What are humans, and of what use are they?
 What is good in them, and what is evil?
⁹ The number of days in their life is great if
 they reach one hundred years.*r*
¹⁰ Like a drop of water from the sea and a
 grain of sand,
 so are a few years among the days of
 eternity.
¹¹ That is why the Lord is patient with them
 and pours out his mercy upon them.
¹² He sees and recognizes that their end is
 miserable;
 therefore he grants his forgiveness all the
 more.
¹³ The compassion of humans is for their
 neighbors,
 but the compassion of the Lord is for
 every living thing.

He rebukes and trains and teaches them
 and turns them back, as a shepherd his
 flock.
¹⁴ He has compassion on those who accept
 his discipline
 and who are eager for his decrees.

The Right Spirit in Giving Alms

¹⁵ My child, do not mix reproach with your
 good deeds
 or harsh words with any gift.
¹⁶ Does not the dew give relief from the
 scorching heat?
 So a word is better than a gift.
¹⁷ Indeed, does not a word surpass a good
 gift?
 Both are to be found in a gracious
 person.
¹⁸ A fool will rebuke ungraciously,
 and the gift of a grudging giver makes the
 eyes weary.

The Need of Reflection and Self-control

¹⁹ Before you speak, learn,
 and before you fall ill, take care of
 yourself.
²⁰ Before judgment comes, examine yourself,
 and at the time of scrutiny you will find
 forgiveness.
²¹ Before falling ill, humble yourself,
 and when you have sinned, repent.
²² Let nothing hinder you from paying a vow
 promptly,
 and do not wait until death to be released
 from it.
²³ Before making a vow, prepare yourself;
 do not be like one who puts the Lord to
 the test.
²⁴ Think of his wrath on the day of death
 and of the moment of vengeance when he
 turns away his face.
²⁵ In the time of plenty think of the time of
 hunger;
 in days of wealth think of poverty and
 need.
²⁶ From morning to evening conditions
 change;
 all things move swiftly before the Lord.

²⁷ One who is wise is cautious in everything;
 when sin is all around, one guards against
 wrongdoing.
²⁸ Every intelligent person knows wisdom
 and praises the one who finds her.

---

q 18.2 Other ancient authorities add *and there is no
 other beside him; ³he steers the world with the span
 of his hand, and all things obey his will, for he is
 king of all things by his power, separating among
 them the holy things from the profane.*
r 18.9 Other ancient authorities add *but the death of
 each one is beyond the calculation of all*

²⁹ Those who are skilled in words become
    wise themselves
    and pour forth apt proverbs.ˢ

SELF-CONTROLᵗ
³⁰ Do not follow your base desires
    but restrain your appetites.
³¹ If you allow your soul to take pleasure in
    base desire,
    it will make you the laughingstock of
    your enemies.
³² Do not revel in great luxury,
    or you may become impoverished by
    contact with it.
³³ Do not become a beggar by feasting with
    borrowed money,
    when you have nothing in your purse.ᵘ

19 The one who does thisᵛ will not
    become rich;
    one who despises small things will fail
    little by little.
² Wine and women lead intelligent men
    astray,
    and the man who consorts with
    prostitutes is reckless.
³ Decay and worms will take possession of
    him,
    and the reckless person will be snatched
    away.

Against Loose Talk
⁴ One who trusts quickly has a shallow
    mind,
    and one who sins does wrong to himself.
⁵ One who rejoices in wickednessʷ will be
    condemned,ˣ
⁶ but one who hates discussion lacks
    understanding.
⁷ Never repeat a conversation,
    and you will lose nothing at all.
⁸ With friend or foe do not report it,
    and unless it would be a sin for you do
    not reveal it,

⁹ for someone may have heard you and
    watched you
    and in time will hate you.
¹⁰ Have you heard something? Let it die with
    you.
    Be brave; it will not make you burst!
¹¹ Having heard something, the fool suffers
    birth pangs
    like a woman in labor with a child.
¹² Like an arrow stuck in a person's thigh,
    so is gossip in the belly of a fool.
¹³ Question a friend; perhaps he did not do it;
    or if he did, so that he may not do it
    again.
¹⁴ Question a neighbor; perhaps he did not
    say it;
    or if he said it, so that he may not repeat
    it.
¹⁵ Question a friend, for often it is slander;
    so do not believe every word.
¹⁶ A person may make a slip without
    intending it.
    Who has not sinned with his tongue?
¹⁷ Question your neighbor before you
    threaten him,
    and make room for the law of the Most
    High.ʸ

True and False Wisdom
²⁰ The whole of wisdom is fear of the Lord,
    and in all wisdom there is the fulfillment
    of the law.ᶻ
²² The knowledge of wickedness is not
    wisdom,
    nor is there prudence in the counsel of
    sinners.
²³ There is a cleverness that is detestable,
    and there is a fool who merely lacks
    wisdom.
²⁴ Better are the God-fearing who lack
    understanding
    than the highly intelligent who transgress
    the law.

---

s **18.29** Other ancient authorities add *Better is
   confidence in a single master than clinging with a
   dead heart to a dead one.*
t **18.30** This heading is included in the Gk text.
u **18.33** Other ancient authorities add *for you will be
   plotting against your own life*
v **19.1** Heb: Gk *A worker who is a drunkard*
w **19.5** Other ancient authorities read *heart*
x **19.5** Other ancient authorities add *but one who
   withstands pleasures crowns his life.* ⁶*One who
   controls the tongue will live without strife,*

y **19.17** Other ancient authorities add *and do not be
   angry.* ¹⁸*The fear of the Lord is the beginning of
   acceptance, and wisdom obtains his love.* ¹⁹*The
   knowledge of the Lord's commandments is life-giving
   discipline, and those who do what is pleasing to him
   enjoy the fruit of the tree of immortality.*
z **19.20** Other ancient authorities add *and the
   knowledge of his omnipotence.* ²¹*When a slave says
   to his master, "I will not act as you wish," even if
   later he does it, he angers the one who supports him.*

25 There is a cleverness that is exact but unjust,
and there are people who abuse favors to
gain a verdict.*

26 There are villains bowed down in
mourning,
but inwardly they are full of deceit.

27 They hide their faces and pretend not to
hear,
but when no one notices, they will take
advantage of you.

28 Even if lack of strength keeps them from
sinning,
they will nevertheless do evil when they
find the opportunity.

29 People will be known by their appearances,
and sensible people will be known when
first met face to face.

30 People's attire and hearty laughter
and the way they walk proclaim things
about them.

Silence and Speech

20 There is a rebuke that is untimely,
and there is the person who is wise
enough to keep silent.

2 How much better it is to rebuke than to
fume!

3 And the one who admits his fault will be
kept from ridicule.

4 Like a eunuch lusting to violate a young
woman
is the person who makes decisions under
compulsion.

5 Some people keep silent and are found* to
be wise,
while others are detested for being
talkative.

6 Some people keep silent because they have
nothing to say,
while others keep silent because they
know when to speak.

7 The wise remain silent until the right
moment,
but the arrogant and the fool miss the
right moment.

8 Whoever talks too much is detested,
and whoever pretends to authority is
hated.*

Paradoxes

9 There may be good fortune for a person in
adversity,
and a windfall may result in a loss.

10 There is the gift that profits you nothing
and the gift to be paid back double.

11 There are losses for the sake of glory,
and there are some who have raised their
heads from humble circumstances.

12 Some buy much for little
but pay for it seven times over.

13 The wise make themselves beloved by only
few words,*
but the courtesies of fools are wasted.

14 A fool's gift will profit you nothing,*
for he looks for recompense sevenfold.*

15 He gives little and insults much;
he opens his mouth like a town crier.
Today he lends, and tomorrow he asks it
back;
such a one is hateful.*

16 The fool says, "I have no friends,
and I get no thanks for my good deeds."
Those who eat his bread are evil-tongued.

17 How many will ridicule him, and how
often!*

Inappropriate Speech

18 A slip on the pavement is better than a slip
of the tongue;
the downfall of the wicked will occur just
as speedily.

19 A coarse person is like an inappropriate
story,
continually on the lips of the ignorant.

20 A proverb from a fool's lips will be
rejected,
for he does not tell it at the proper time.

21 One may be prevented from sinning by
poverty,
so when he rests he feels no remorse.

22 One may lose his life through shame
or lose it because of a foolish person.*

---

a 19.25 Other ancient authorities add *and the one who
justifies is wise in judgment.*

b 20.5 Gk: Heb *thought*

c 20.8 Other ancient authorities add *How good it is to
show repentance when you are reproved, for so you
will escape deliberate sin!*

d 20.13 Heb: Gk *by words*

e 20.14 Other ancient authorities add *so it is with the
envious who give under compulsion*

f 20.14 Syr: Gk *he has many eyes instead of one*

g 20.15 Other ancient authorities add *to God and
humans*

h 20.17 Other ancient authorities add *for he has not
honestly received what he has, and what he does
not have is unimportant to him*

i 20.22 Other ancient authorities read *human respect*

23 One may make promises to a friend out of
     shame
   and so make an enemy for nothing.

Lying

24 A lie is an ugly blot on a person;
   it is continually on the lips of the
     ignorant.
25 A thief is preferable to a habitual liar,
   but both will inherit ruin.
26 The character of liars leads to disgrace,
   and their shame is ever with them.

PROVERBIAL SAYINGS*j*

27 Wise persons advance themselves by their
     words,
   and those who are sensible please the
     great.
28 Those who cultivate the soil heap up their
     harvest,
   and those who please the great atone for
     injustice.
29 Favors and gifts blind the eyes of the wise;
   like a muzzle on the mouth they stop
     reproofs.
30 Hidden wisdom and unseen treasure—
   of what value is either?
31 Better are those who hide their folly
   than those who hide their wisdom.*k*

Various Sins

21 Have you sinned, my child? Do so no
       more,
   but ask forgiveness for your past sins.
2 Flee from sin as from a snake,
   for if you approach sin it will bite you.
   Its teeth are lion's teeth
   and can destroy human lives.
3 All lawlessness is like a two-edged sword;
   there is no healing for the wound it
     inflicts.

4 Panic and insolence will waste away riches;
   thus the house of the proud will be
     uprooted.*l*
5 The prayer of the poor goes from their lips
   to the ears of God,*m*
   and his judgment comes speedily.

6 Those who hate reproof walk in the sinner's
     steps,
   but those who fear the Lord repent in
     their heart.
7 The mighty in speech are widely known;
   when they slip, the sensible person knows
     it.
8 Those who build their houses with other
     people's money
   are like those who gather stones for their
     own burial mounds.
9 An assembly of the lawless is like a bundle
     of tinder,
   and their end is a blazing fire.
10 The way of sinners is paved with smooth
     stones,
   but at its end is the pit of Hades.

Wisdom and Foolishness

11 Those who keep the law control their
     thoughts,
   and the fulfillment of the fear of the Lord
     is wisdom.
12 Those who are not clever cannot be taught,
   but there is a cleverness that increases
     bitterness.
13 The knowledge of the wise will increase like
     a flood
   and their counsel like a life-giving spring.
14 The mind*n* of a fool is like a broken jar;
   it can hold no knowledge.

15 When intelligent people hear a wise saying,
   they praise it and add to it;
   when fools*o* hear it, they laugh at*p* it
   and throw it behind their backs.
16 The chatter*q* of fools is like a burden on a
     journey,
   but delight is found in the speech of the
     intelligent.
17 The utterance of sensible people is sought
     in the assembly,
   and they ponder their words in their
     minds.
18 Like a house in ruins is wisdom to a fool,
   and the knowledge of the ignorant is
     meaningless talk.

---

j **20.27** This heading is included in the Gk text.
k **20.31** Other ancient authorities add 20.32:
       Unwearied endurance in seeking the Lord is better
       than a masterless charioteer of one's own life.
l **21.4** Other ancient authorities read *laid waste*
m **21.5** Gk *his ears*

---

n **21.14** Syr Lat: Gk *entrails*
o **21.15** Syr: Gk *revelers*
p **21.15** Syr: Gk *dislike*
q **21.16** Syr: Gk *explanation*

¹⁹ To the senseless, education is fetters on
      their feet
    and like manacles on their right hands.
²⁰ Fools raise their voices when they laugh,
    but the wise^r smile quietly.
²¹ To the sensible, education is like a golden
      ornament
    and like a bracelet on the right arm.

²² The foot of a fool rushes into a house,
    but an experienced person waits
      respectfully outside.
²³ A boor peers into the house from the door,
    but a cultivated person remains outside.
²⁴ It is ill-mannered for a person to listen at a
      door;
    the discreet would be grieved by the
      disgrace.

²⁵ The lips of babblers speak of what is not
      their concern,^s
    but the words of the prudent are weighed
      in the balance.
²⁶ The mind of fools is in their mouth,
    but the mouth of the wise is in^t their
      mind.
²⁷ When ungodly people curse an adversary,
    they curse themselves.
²⁸ Whisperers degrade themselves
    and are hated in their neighborhoods.

The Idler

22 ¹ The idler is like a filthy stone,
    and every one hisses at his disgrace.
² The idler is like a lump of dung;
    anyone who picks it up will shake it off
      his hand.

Degenerate Children
³ It is a disgrace to be the father of an
      undisciplined son,
    and the birth of a daughter is a loss.
⁴ A sensible daughter obtains a husband of
      her own,
    but one who acts shamefully is a grief to
      her father.
⁵ An impudent daughter disgraces father and
      husband
    and is despised by both.

⁶ Like music in time of mourning is ill-timed
      conversation,
    but a thrashing and discipline are at all
      times wisdom.^u

Wisdom and Folly
⁹ Whoever teaches a fool is like one who
      glues potsherds together
    or who rouses a sleeper from deep
      slumber.
¹⁰ Whoever tells a story to a fool tells it to a
      drowsy man,
    and at the end he will say, "What is it?"
¹¹ Weep for the dead, for they have left the
      light behind,
    and weep for the fool, for they have left
      intelligence behind.
    Weep less bitterly for the dead, for they are
      at rest,
    but the life of the fool is worse than
      death.
¹² Mourning for the dead lasts seven days,
    but for the foolish or the ungodly it lasts
      all the days of their lives.

¹³ Do not talk much with senseless people
    or visit unintelligent people.^v
    Stay clear of them, or you may have trouble
    and be spattered when they shake
      themselves off.
    Avoid them and you will find rest,
    and you will never be wearied by their
      lack of sense.
¹⁴ What is heavier than lead?
    And what is its name except "Fool"?
¹⁵ Sand, salt, and a piece of iron
    are easier to bear than a stupid person.

¹⁶ A wooden beam firmly bonded into a
      building
    is not loosened by an earthquake;
    so the mind firmly resolved after due
      reflection
    will not be afraid in a crisis.
¹⁷ A mind settled on an intelligent thought
    is like plaster decoration that makes a
      wall smooth.

---

r 21.20 Syr Lat: Gk *clever*
s 21.25 Other ancient authorities read *The lips of
      strangers speak of these things*
t 21.26 Other ancient authorities omit *in*

u 22.6 Other ancient authorities add 22.7–8: ⁷*Children
      who are brought up in a good life conceal the
      lowly birth of their parents.* ⁸*Children who glory in
      contempt and ignorance stain the nobility of their
      kindred.*
v 22.13 Other ancient authorities add *For being
      without sense he will despise everything about you*

¹⁸ Fences[w] set on a high place
     will not stand firm against the wind;
   so a timid mind with a fool's resolve
     will not stand firm against any fear.

The Preservation of Friendship

¹⁹ One who pricks the eye brings tears,
     and one who pricks the heart makes clear
       its feelings.
²⁰ One who throws a stone at birds scares
       them away,
     and one who reviles a friend destroys a
       friendship.
²¹ Even if you draw your sword against a
       friend,
     do not despair, for there is a way back.
²² If you open your mouth against your
       friend,
     do not worry, for reconciliation is
       possible.
   But as for reviling, arrogance, disclosure of
       secrets, or a treacherous blow—
     in these cases any friend will take to flight.

²³ Gain the trust of your neighbor in his
       poverty,
     so that you may rejoice[x] with him in his
       prosperity.
   Stand by him in time of distress,
     so that you may share with him in his
       inheritance.[y]
²⁴ The vapor and smoke of the furnace
       precede the fire;
     so insults precede bloodshed.
²⁵ I am not ashamed to shelter a friend,
     and I will not hide from him,
²⁶ but if harm should come to me because of
       him,
     whoever hears of it will beware of him.

A Prayer for Help against Sinning

²⁷ Who will set a guard over my mouth
     and an effective seal upon my lips,
   so that I may not fall because of them
     and my tongue may not destroy me?

23 O Lord, Father and Master of my life,
     do not abandon me to their designs,
     and do not let me fall among them!

² Who will set whips over my thoughts
     and the discipline of wisdom over my
       mind,
   so as not to spare me in my errors
     and not overlook my[z] sins?
³ Otherwise my mistakes may be multiplied,
     and my sins may abound,
   and I may fall before my adversaries,
     and my enemy may rejoice over me.[a]
⁴ O Lord, Father and God of my life,
     do not give me haughty eyes,
⁵   and remove desire from me.
⁶ Let neither gluttony nor lust overcome me,
     and do not give me over to shameless
       passion.

DISCIPLINE OF THE TONGUE[b]
⁷ Listen, my children, to instruction
       concerning the mouth;
     the one who observes it will never be
       caught.
⁸ Sinners are overtaken through their lips;
     by them the reviler and the arrogant are
       tripped up.
⁹ Do not accustom your mouth to oaths
     nor habitually utter the name of the Holy
       One,
¹⁰ for as a slave who is constantly under
       scrutiny
     will not lack bruises,
   so also the person who always swears and
       utters the Name
     will never be cleansed[c] from sin.
¹¹ The one who swears many oaths is full of
       iniquity,
     and the scourge will not leave his house.
   If he swears in error, his sin remains on him,
     and if he disregards it, he sins doubly;
   if he swears a false oath, he will not be
       justified,
     for his house will be filled with calamities.

Foul Language

¹² There is a manner of speaking comparable
       to death;[d]
     may it never be found in the inheritance
       of Jacob!

---

w 22.18 Other ancient authorities read *Pebbles*
x 22.23 Other ancient authorities read *you also may
     be filled*
y 22.23 Other ancient authorities add *For one should
     not always despise restricted circumstances or
     admire a rich person who has no resolve.*

z 23.2 Gk *their*
a 23.3 Other ancient authorities add *From them the
     hope of your mercy is remote*
b 23.7 This heading is included in the Gk text.
c 23.10 Syr *be free*
d 23.12 Other ancient authorities read *clothed about
     with death*

Such conduct will be far from the godly,
and they will not wallow in sins.

13 Do not accustom your mouth to lewd
ignorance,
for it involves sinful speech.

14 Remember your father and mother
when you sit among the great,
or you may forget yourself in their
presence,
and behave like a fool through habit;
then you will wish that you had never been
born,
and you will curse the day of your birth.

15 Those who are accustomed to using abusive
language
will never become disciplined as long as
they live.

Concerning Sexual Sins

16 Two kinds of individuals multiply sins,
and a third incurs wrath.
Hot passion that blazes like a fire
will not be quenched until it burns itself
out;
those who commit incest with their near
of kin
will never cease until the fire burns
them up.

17 To the sexually immoral all bread is sweet;
he will never weary until he dies.

18 The one who sins against his marriage bed
says to himself, "Who can see me?
Darkness surrounds me, the walls hide me,
and no one sees me. Why should I worry?
The Most High will not remember my
sins."

19 His fear is confined to human eyes,
and he does not realize that the eyes of
the Lord
are ten thousand times brighter than the
sun;
they look upon every aspect of human
behavior
and see into hidden corners.

20 Before the universe was created, it was
known to him,
and so it is since its completion.

21 This man will be punished in the streets of
the city,
and where he least suspects it he will be
seized.

22 So it is with a woman who leaves her
husband

and presents him with an heir by another
man.

23 For, first of all, she has disobeyed the law of
the Most High;
second, she has committed an offense
against her husband;
and third, through sexual immorality she
has committed adultery
and brought forth children by another
man.

24 She herself will be brought before the
assembly,
and her punishment will extend to her
children.

25 Her children will not take root,
and her branches will not bear fruit.

26 She will leave behind an accursed memory,
and her disgrace will never be blotted out.

27 Those who survive her will recognize
that nothing is better than the fear of the
Lord
and nothing sweeter than to heed the
commandments of the Lord.*e* ·

THE PRAISE OF WISDOM*f*

24 Wisdom praises herself
and tells of her glory in the midst of
her people.

2 In the assembly of the Most High she opens
her mouth,
and in the presence of his hosts she tells
of her glory:

3 "I came forth from the mouth of the Most
High
and covered the earth like a mist.

4 I encamped in the heights,
and my throne was in a pillar of cloud.

5 Alone I compassed the vault of heaven
and traversed the depths of the abyss.

6 Over waves of the sea, over all the earth,
and over every people and nation I have
held sway.*g*

7 Among all these I sought a resting place;
in whose inheritance should I abide?

8 "Then the Creator of all things gave me a
command,
and my Creator pitched my tent.

---

e 23.27 Other ancient authorities add as 23.28: *It is a
great honor to follow God, and to be received by
him is long life.*

f 24.1 This heading is included in the Gk text.

g 24.6 Other ancient authorities read *I have acquired
a possession*

He said, 'Encamp in Jacob,
and in Israel receive your inheritance.'
⁹ Before the ages, in the beginning, he
created me,
and for all the ages I shall not cease to be.
¹⁰ In the holy tent I ministered before him,
and so I was established in Zion.
¹¹ Thus in the beloved city he gave me a
resting place,
and in Jerusalem was my domain.
¹² I took root in an honored people;
in the portion of the Lord is my
inheritance.

¹³ "I grew tall like a cedar in Lebanon
and like a cypress on the heights of
Hermon.
¹⁴ I grew tall like a palm tree in En-gedi^h
and like rosebushes in Jericho;
like a fair olive tree in the field
and like a plane tree beside water^i I grew
tall.
¹⁵ Like cassia and camel's thorn I gave forth
perfume,
and like choice myrrh I spread my
fragrance,
like galbanum, onycha, and stacte,
and like the odor of incense in the tent.
¹⁶ Like a terebinth I spread out my
branches,
and my branches are glorious and
graceful.
¹⁷ Like the vine I bud forth delights,
and my blossoms become glorious and
abundant fruit.^j

¹⁹ "Come to me, you who desire me,
and eat your fill of my fruits.
²⁰ For the memory of me is sweeter than
honey
and the possession of me sweeter than the
honeycomb.
²¹ Those who eat of me will hunger for more,
and those who drink of me will thirst for
more.
²² Whoever obeys me will not be put to
shame,
and those who work with me will not sin."

Wisdom and the Law

²³ All this is the book of the covenant of the
Most High God,
the law that Moses commanded us
as an inheritance for the congregations of
Jacob.^k
²⁵ It becomes full, like the Pishon, with
wisdom
and like the Tigris at the time of the
spring harvest.
²⁶ It fills up, like the Euphrates, with
understanding,
and like the Jordan at harvest time.
²⁷ It pours forth instruction like the Nile,^l
like the Gihon at the time of vintage.
²⁸ The first man did not know wisdom^m fully,
nor will the last one fathom her.
²⁹ For her thoughts are more abundant than
the sea
and her counsel deeper than the great
abyss.

³⁰ I came forth like a canal from a river,
like a water channel into a garden.
³¹ I said, "I will water my garden
and drench my flower beds."
And look, my canal became a river
and my river a sea.
³² I will again make instruction shine forth
like the dawn,
and I will make it clear from far away.
³³ I will again pour out teaching like prophecy
and leave it to all future generations.
³⁴ Observe that I have not labored for myself
alone
but for all who seek wisdom.^n

Those Who Are Worthy of Praise

25 I take pleasure in three things,
and they are beautiful in the sight of
God and of mortals:^o
agreement among brothers and sisters,
friendship among neighbors,
and a wife and a husband who live in
harmony.

---

h 24.14 Other ancient authorities read *on the beaches*
i 24.14 Other ancient authorities omit *beside water*
j 24.17 Other ancient authorities add as 24.18: *I am the
mother of beautiful love, of fear, of knowledge, and
of holy hope; I give to all my children; these things
are eternal for those who are named by him.*

k 24.23 Other ancient authorities add as 24.24: *Do not
cease to be strong in the Lord, cling to him so that
he may strengthen you; the Lord Almighty alone is
God, and besides him there is no savior.*
l 24.27 Syr: Gk *It makes instruction shine forth like light*
m 24.28 Gk *her*
n 24.34 Gk *her*
o 25.1 Syr Lat: Gk *In three things I was beautiful, and I
stood in beauty before the Lord and mortals*

2 I hate three kinds of people,
  and I loathe their manner of life:
a pauper who boasts, a rich person who
    lies,
  and an old adulterer who lacks sense.

3 If you gathered nothing in your youth,
  how can you find anything in your old
    age?
4 How attractive is sound judgment in
    gray-haired women
  and for aged men to possess good
    counsel!
5 How attractive is wisdom in the aged
  and understanding and counsel in the
    venerable!
6 Rich experience is the crown of the aged,
  and their boast is the fear of the Lord.

7 I can think of nine whom I would call
    happy,
  and a tenth my tongue proclaims:
a man who can rejoice in his children,
  who lives to see the downfall of his foes.
8 Happy the man who lives with a sensible
    wife
  and who does not plow with ox and ass
    together,ᵖ
who does not slip with the tongue
  and who has not become enslaved to an
    inferior.
9 Happy is the one who finds good sense
  and the one who speaks to attentive
    listeners.
10 How great is the one who finds wisdom!
  But none is superior to the one who fears
    the Lord.
11 Fear of the Lord surpasses everything;
  to whom can we compare the one who
    has it?�q

Some Extreme Forms of Evil

13 Any wound, but not a wound of the heart!
  Any wickedness, but not the wickedness
    of a woman!
14 Any suffering, but not suffering from those
    who hate!
  And any vengeance, but not the
    vengeance of enemies!

15 There is no venomʳ worse than a snake's
    venomˢ
  and no anger worse than a woman'sᵗ
    wrath.

The Evil of a Wicked Woman

16 I would rather live with a lion and a dragon
  than live with an evil woman.
17 A woman's wickedness changes her
    appearance
  and darkens her face like that of a bear.
18 Her husband sitsᵘ among the neighbors,
  and he cannot help sighingᵛ bitterly.
19 Any iniquity is small compared to a
    woman's iniquity;
  may a sinner's lot befall her!
20 A sandy ascent for the feet of the aged—
  such is a garrulous wife to a quiet
    husband.
21 Do not be ensnared by a woman's beauty,
  and do not desire a woman for her
    possessions.ʷ
22 There is wrath and impudence and great
    disgrace
  when a wife supports her husband.
23 Dejected mind, gloomy face,
  and wounded heart come from an evil
    wife.
Drooping hands and weak knees
  come from the wife who does not make
    her husband happy.
24 From a woman sin had its beginning,
  and because of her we all die.
25 Allow no outlet to water
  and no boldness of speech to an evil wife.
26 If she does not go as you direct,
  separate her from yourself.

The Joy of a Good Wife

26 Happy is the husband of a good wife;
  the number of his days will be doubled.
2 A courageous wife brings joy to her
    husband,
  and he will complete his years in peace.
3 A good wife is a good portion;
  she will be granted as a portion to the
    man who fears the Lord.

---

p **25.8** Heb Syr: Gk lacks *and the one who does not plow
  with ox and ass together*
q **25.11** Other ancient authorities add as 25.12: *The fear
  of the Lord is the beginning of love for him, and
  faith is the beginning of clinging to him.*

---

r **25.15** Syr: Gk *head*
s **25.15** Syr: Gk *head*
t **25.15** Other ancient authorities read *an enemy's*
u **25.18** Heb Syr: Gk *loses heart*
v **25.18** Other ancient authorities read *and listening
  he sighs*
w **25.21** Heb Syr: Gk lacks *for her possessions*

4 Whether rich or poor, his heart is content,
  and at all times his face is cheerful.

The Worst of Evils: A Wicked Wife

5 Of three things my heart is frightened,
    and of a fourth I am in great fear:ˣ
  slander in the city, the gathering of a mob,
    and false accusation—all these are worse
      than death.
6 But it is heartache and sorrow when a wife
    has a rival,
  and a tongue-lashing makes it known to
    all.
7 A bad wife is a chafing yoke;
    taking hold of her is like grasping a
      scorpion.
8 A drunken wife arouses great anger;
    she cannot hide her shame.
9 The haughty stare betrays a sexually
    immoral wife;
  her eyelids give her away.

10 Keep strict watch over a headstrong
    daughter,
   or else, when she finds liberty, she will
     make use of it.
11 Be on guard against her impudent eye,
   and do not be surprised if she sins against
     you.
12 As a thirsty traveler opens his mouth
   and drinks from any water near him,
   so she will sit in front of every tent peg
   and open her quiver to the arrow.

The Blessing of a Good Wife

13 A wife's charm delights her husband,
   and her skill puts flesh on his bones.
14 A silent wife is a gift from the Lord,
   and nothing is so precious as her
     self-discipline.
15 A modest wife adds charm to charm,
   and no scales can weigh the value of her
     self-control.
16 Like the sun rising in the heights of the
     Lord,
   so is the beauty of a good wife in her
     well-ordered home.
17 Like the shining lamp on the holy
     lampstand,
   so is a beautiful face on a stately figure.
18 Like golden pillars on silver bases,
   so are shapely legs upon steadfast feet.

Other ancient authorities add verses 19–27:

19 *My child, keep sound the bloom of your
     youth,
   and do not give your strength to
     strangers.*
20 *Seek a fertile field within the whole plain,
   and sow it with your own seed, trusting in
     your fine stock.*
21 *So your offspring will prosper,
   and, having confidence in their good
     descent, will grow great.*
22 *A prostitute is regarded as spittle
   and a married woman as a tower of death
     to her lovers.*
23 *A godless wife is given as a portion to a
     lawless man,
   but a pious wife is given to the man who
     fears the Lord.*
24 *A shameless woman constantly acts
     disgracefully,
   but a modest daughter will even be
     embarrassed before her husband.*
25 *A headstrong wife is regarded as a dog,
   but one who has a sense of shame will fear
     the Lord.*
26 *A wife honoring her husband will seem wise
     to all,
   but if she dishonors him in her pride she
     will be known to all as ungodly.
   Happy is the husband of a good wife,
   for the number of his years will be doubled.*
27 *A loud-voiced and garrulous wife is like a
     trumpet sounding the charge,
   and every person like this lives in the
     anarchy of war.*

Three Depressing Things

28 At two things my heart is grieved,
   and because of a third anger comes over
     me:
   a warrior in want through poverty,
   intelligent men who are treated
     contemptuously,
   and a man who turns back from
     righteousness to sin—
   the Lord will prepare him for the sword!

The Temptations of Commerce

29 A merchant can hardly keep from
     wrongdoing,
   nor is a tradesman innocent of sin.

---

x 26.5 Syr: Meaning of Gk uncertain

27

Many have committed sin for gain,[y]
and those who seek to get rich will
avert their eyes.

2 As a stake is driven firmly into a fissure
between stones,
so sin is wedged in between selling and
buying.

3 If a person is not steadfast in the fear of the
Lord,
his house will be quickly overthrown.

Tests in Life

4 When a sieve is shaken, the refuse appears;
so does a person's waste when he speaks.

5 The kiln tests the potter's vessels,
and the test of a person is in his
conversation.

6 Its fruit discloses the cultivation of a tree;
so does speech[z] the thoughts of the
human mind.

7 Do not praise anyone before he speaks,
for this is the way people are tested.

Reward and Retribution

8 If you pursue justice, you will attain it
and wear it like a glorious robe.

9 Birds roost with their own kind,
so honesty comes home to those who
practice it.

10 A lion lies in wait for prey;
so does sin for evildoers.

Varieties of Speech

11 The conversation of the godly is always
wise,
but the fool changes like the moon.

12 Among stupid people limit your time,
but among thoughtful people linger on.

13 The talk of fools is offensive,
and their laughter is wantonly sinful.

14 Their cursing and swearing make one's hair
stand on end,
and their quarrels make others stop their
ears.

15 The strife of the proud leads to bloodshed,
and their abuse is grievous to hear.

Betraying Secrets

16 Whoever betrays secrets destroys
confidence
and will never find a congenial friend.

17 Love your friends and keep faith with them,
but if you betray their secrets, do not
follow after them.

18 For as a person destroys an enemy,[a]
so you have destroyed the friendship of
your neighbor.

19 And as you allow a bird to escape from
your hand,
so you have let your neighbor go and will
not catch him again.

20 Do not go after him, for he is too far off
and has escaped like a gazelle from a
snare.

21 For a wound may be bandaged,
and there is reconciliation after abuse,
but whoever has betrayed secrets is
without hope.

Hypocrisy and Retribution

22 Whoever winks the eye plots harm,
and those who know such a one will keep
their distance.

23 In your presence their mouths are all
sweetness,
and they admire your words,
but later they will twist their speech
and with your own words they will cause
a scandal.

24 I have hated many things but them above
all;
even the Lord hates them.

25 Those who throw a stone straight up throw
it on their own heads,
and a treacherous blow opens up many
wounds.

26 Whoever digs a pit will fall into it,
and whoever sets a snare will be caught
in it.

27 If people do evil, it will roll back upon them,
and they will not know where it came from.

28 Mockery and abuse issue from the proud,
but vengeance lies in wait for them like
a lion.

29 Those who rejoice in the fall of the godly
will be caught in a snare,
and pain will consume them before their
death.

Anger and Vengeance

30 Anger and wrath, these also are
abominations,
yet a sinner holds on to them.

---

y 27.1 Other ancient authorities read *a trifle*

z 27.6 Other ancient authorities read *reasoning*

a 27.18 Other ancient authorities read *corpse*

28

The vengeful will face the Lord's
vengeance,
for he keeps a strict account of[b] their sins.
2 Forgive your neighbor the wrong he has
done,
and then your sins will be pardoned when
you pray.
3 Does anyone harbor anger against
another
and expect healing from the Lord?
4 If people have no mercy toward those like
themselves,
can they then seek pardon for their own
sins?
5 If mere mortals harbor wrath,
who will make an atoning sacrifice for
their sins?
6 Remember the end of your life and set
enmity aside;
remember corruption and death and be
true to the commandments.
7 Remember the commandments and do not
be angry with your neighbor;
remember the covenant of the Most High
and overlook faults.

8 Refrain from strife, and your sins will be
fewer,
for the hot-tempered kindle strife
9 and the sinner disrupts friendships
and sows discord among those who are
at peace.
10 In proportion to the fuel, so will the fire
burn,
and in proportion to the obstinacy, so will
strife increase;[c]
in proportion to people's strength will be
their anger,
and in proportion to their wealth they
will increase their wrath.
11 A hasty quarrel kindles a fire,
and a hasty dispute sheds blood.

The Evil Tongue
12 If you blow on a spark, it will glow;
if you spit on it, it will be put out,
yet both come out of your mouth.

13 Curse the gossips and the double-tongued,
for they destroy the peace of many.

14 Slander[d] has shaken many
and scattered them from nation to nation;
it has destroyed strong cities
and overturned the houses of the great.
15 Slander[e] has driven courageous women
from their homes
and deprived them of the fruit of their
toil.
16 Those who pay heed to slander[f] will not
find rest,
nor will they settle down in peace.
17 The blow of a whip raises a welt,
but a blow of the tongue crushes the
bones.
18 Many have fallen by the edge of the sword,
but not as many as have fallen because of
the tongue.
19 Happy is the one who is protected from it,
who has not been exposed to its anger,
who has not borne its yoke,
and who has not been bound with its
fetters.
20 For its yoke is a yoke of iron,
and its fetters are fetters of bronze;
21 its death is an evil death,
and Hades is preferable to it.
22 It has no power over the godly;
they will not be burned in its flame.
23 Those who forsake the Lord will fall into its
power;
it will burn among them and will not be
put out.
It will be sent out against them like a lion;
like a leopard it will mangle them.
24a Look! Fence in your property with thorns,
25b and make a door and a bolt for your
mouth.
24b Lock up your silver and gold,
25a and make balances and scales for your
words.
26 Take care not to err with your tongue[g]
and fall victim to one lying in wait.

On Lending and Borrowing

29

The merciful lend to their neighbors;
by holding out a helping hand they
keep the commandments.
2 Lend to your neighbor in his time of need;
repay your neighbor when a loan falls due.

---

b 28.1 Other ancient authorities read *for he firmly
establishes*
c 28.10 Other ancient authorities read *burn*

d 28.14 Gk *A third tongue*
e 28.15 Gk *A third tongue*
f 28.16 Gk *it*
g 28.26 Gk *with it*

³ Keep your word and be honest with him,
    and on every occasion you will find what
    you need.
⁴ Many regard a loan as a windfall
    and cause trouble to those who help
    them.
⁵ One kisses another's hands until he gets a
    loan
    and is deferential in speaking of his
    neighbor's money,
    but at the time for repayment he delays
    and pays back with empty promises
    and finds fault with the time.
⁶ If he can pay, his creditor*ʰ* will hardly get
    back half
    and will regard that as a windfall.
    If he cannot pay, the borrower*ⁱ* has robbed
    the other of his money,
    and he has needlessly made him an
    enemy;
    he will repay him with curses and
    reproaches
    and instead of glory will repay him with
    dishonor.
⁷ Many refuse to lend, not because of
    meanness,
    but from fear*ʲ* of being defrauded
    needlessly.

⁸ Nevertheless, be patient with someone in
    humble circumstances,
    and do not keep him waiting for your
    alms.
⁹ Help the poor for the commandment's
    sake,
    and in their need do not send them away
    empty-handed.
¹⁰ Lose your silver for the sake of a brother or
    a friend,
    and do not let it rust under a stone and
    be lost.
¹¹ Lay up your treasure according to the
    commandments of the Most High,
    and it will profit you more than gold.
¹² Store up almsgiving in your treasury,
    and it will rescue you from every disaster;
¹³ better than a stout shield and a sturdy
    spear,
    it will fight for you against the enemy.

On Guaranteeing Debts

¹⁴ A good person will be surety for his
    neighbor,
    but the one who has lost all sense of
    shame will fail him.
¹⁵ Do not forget the kindness of your
    guarantor,
    for he has given his life for you.
¹⁶ A sinner wastes the property of his
    guarantor,
¹⁷ and the ungrateful person abandons his
    rescuer.
¹⁸ Being surety has ruined many who were
    prosperous
    and has tossed them about like waves of
    the sea;
    it has driven the influential into exile,
    and they have wandered among foreign
    nations.
¹⁹ The sinner comes to grief through surety;
    his pursuit of gain involves him in
    lawsuits.
²⁰ Assist your neighbor to the best of your
    ability,
    but be careful not to fall yourself.

Home and Hospitality

²¹ The necessities of life are water, bread, and
    clothing,
    and also a house to assure privacy.
²² Better is the life of the poor under their
    own crude roof
    than sumptuous food in the house of
    strangers.
²³ Be content with little or much,
    and you will hear no reproach for being
    a guest.*ᵏ*
²⁴ It is a miserable life to go from house to
    house;
    as a guest you should not open your
    mouth;
²⁵ you will play the host and provide drink
    without being thanked,
    and besides this you will hear rude words
    like these:
²⁶ "Come here, stranger, prepare the table;
    let me eat what you have there."
²⁷ "Be off, stranger, for an honored guest is
    here;
    my brother has come for a visit, and I
    need the house."

---

h **29.6** Gk *he*
i **29.6** Gk *he*
j **29.7** Other ancient authorities read *many refuse to
    lend, therefore, because of such meanness; they are
    afraid*

---

k **29.23** Lat: Gk *reproach from your family*; other
    ancient authorities lack this line

28 It is hard for a sensible person to bear
      scolding about lodging[l] and the insults of
      the moneylender.

CONCERNING CHILDREN[m]

30 He who loves his son will whip him
      often,
    so that he may rejoice at the way he turns
      out.
2 He who disciplines his son will profit by
      him
    and will boast of him among
      acquaintances.
3 He who teaches his son will make his
      enemies envious
    and will glory in him among his friends.
4 When the father dies, he will not seem to
      be dead,
    for he has left behind him one like
      himself,
5 whom in his life he looked upon with joy
    and at death, without grief.
6 He has left behind him an avenger against
      his enemies
    and one to repay the kindness of his
      friends.

7 Whoever cherishes his son will bind up his
      wounds,
    and at every cry his heart will be troubled.
8 An unbroken horse turns out stubborn,
    and an unchecked son turns out
      headstrong.
9 Pamper a child, and he will terrorize you;
    play with him, and he will grieve you.
10 Do not laugh with him, or you will have
      sorrow with him,
    and in the end you will gnash your teeth.
11 Give him no freedom in his youth;[n]
12 beat his sides while he is young,
    or else he will become stubborn and
      disobey you.[o]
13 Discipline your son and make his yoke
      heavy,[p]
    so that you may not be offended by his
      shamelessness.

14 Better off poor, healthy, and fit
    than rich and afflicted in body.
15 Health and fitness are better than any gold
    and a robust body[q] than countless riches.
16 There is no wealth better than health of body
    and no gladness above joy of heart.
17 Death is better than a life of misery
    and eternal sleep[r] than chronic sickness.

CONCERNING FOODS[s]
18 Good things poured out upon a mouth that
      is closed
    are like offerings of food placed upon a
      grave.
19 Of what use to an idol is a sacrifice?
    For it can neither eat nor smell.
    So is the one punished by the Lord;
20 he sees with his eyes and groans
    as a eunuch groans when embracing a
      young woman.[t]

21 Do not give yourself over to sorrow,
    and do not distress yourself deliberately.
22 A joyful heart is life itself,
    and rejoicing lengthens one's life span.
23 Indulge yourself[u] and take comfort,
    and remove sorrow far from you,
    for sorrow has destroyed many,
    and no advantage ever comes from it.
24 Jealousy and anger shorten life,
    and anxiety brings on premature old age.
25 Those who are cheerful and merry at table
    will benefit from their food.

Right Attitude toward Riches

31 Wakefulness over wealth wastes away
      one's flesh,
    and anxiety about it drives away sleep.
2 Wakeful anxiety prevents slumber,
    and a severe illness carries off sleep.[v]
3 Rich people toil to amass possessions,
    and when they rest, they fill themselves
      with their delicacies.
4 Poor people toil to make a meager living,
    and if ever they rest, they become needy.

---

l **29.28** Or *scolding from the household*
m **30.1** This heading is included in the Gk text.
n **30.11** Other ancient authorities add *and do not
    ignore his errors. Bow down his neck in his youth,*
o **30.12** Other ancient authorities add *and you will
    have sorrow of soul from him*
p **30.13** Heb: Gk *take pains with him*

q **30.15** Gk: Syr Heb read *spirit*
r **30.17** Other ancient authorities lack *eternal sleep*
s **30.18** This heading is included in the Gk text; other
    ancient authorities place the heading before 30.16
t **30.20** Other ancient authorities add *So is the person
    who does right under compulsion*
u **30.23** Other ancient authorities read *Beguile yourself*
v **31.2** Other ancient authorities read *sleep carries off a
    severe illness*

5 Those who love gold will not be justified;
  those who pursue money will be led
    astray[w] by it.
6 Many have come to ruin because of gold,
  and their destruction has met them face
    to face.
7 It is a stumbling block to those who are
    avid for it,
  and every fool will be taken captive by it.
8 Blessed are the rich who are found
    blameless
  and who do not go after gold.
9 Who are they, that we may call them happy?
  For they have done wonders among their
    people.
10 Who has been tested by it and been found
    perfect?
  Let it be for them a ground for boasting.
  Who has had the power to transgress and
    did not transgress
  and to do evil and did not do it?
11 Their prosperity will be established,[x]
  and the assembly will proclaim their acts
    of charity.

Table Etiquette

12[y] Are you seated at the table of the great?[z]
  Do not be greedy at it,
  and do not say, "How much food there is
    here!"
13 Remember that a greedy eye is a bad thing.
  What has been created more greedy than
    the eye?
  Therefore it covers the face with tears.
14 Do not reach out your hand for everything
    you see,
  and do not crowd your neighbor[a] at the
    dish.
15 Judge your neighbor's feelings by your own,
  and in every matter be thoughtful.
16 Eat what is set before you like a well
    brought-up person,[b]
  and do not chew greedily, or you will be
    despised.
17 Be the first to stop, as befits good manners,
  and do not be insatiable, or you will give
    offense.

18 If you are seated among many persons,
  do not help yourself[c] before they do.
19 How ample a little is for the well-disciplined!
  They do not breathe heavily when in bed.
20 Healthy sleep depends on moderate eating;
  they rise early and feel fit.
  The distress of sleeplessness and of nausea
  and colic are with the glutton.
21 If you are overstuffed with food,
  get up to vomit, and you will have relief.
22 Listen to me, my child, and do not
    disregard me,
  and in the end you will appreciate my
    words.
  In everything you do be moderate,[d]
  and no sickness will overtake you.
23 People bless those who are liberal with food,
  and the testimony to their generosity is
    trustworthy.
24 The city complains of those who are stingy
    with food,
  and the testimony to their stinginess is
    accurate.

Temperance in Drinking Wine

25 Do not try to prove your strength by
    wine-drinking,
  for wine has destroyed many.
26 As the furnace tests the work of the smith,[e]
  so wine tests hearts when the insolent
    quarrel.
27 Wine is very life to humans
  if taken in moderation.
  What is life to one who is without wine?
  It has been created to make people happy.
28 Wine drunk at the proper time and in
    moderation
  is rejoicing of heart and gladness of soul.
29 Wine drunk to excess leads to bitterness of
    spirit,
  to quarrels and stumbling.
30 Drunkenness increases the anger of fools to
    their own hurt,
  reducing their strength and adding
    wounds.
31 Do not reprove your neighbors at a
    banquet of wine,
  and do not despise them in their
    merrymaking;

---

w 31.5 Heb Syr: Gk *pursues destruction will be filled*
x 31.11 Other ancient authorities add *because of this*
y 31.12 Some ancient authorities add the title
    Concerning Food
z 31.12 Heb Syr: Gk *at a great table*
a 31.14 Gk *him*
b 31.16 Heb: Gk *like a human being*

c 31.18 Gk *reach out your hand*
d 31.22 Heb Syr: Gk *industrious*
e 31.26 Heb: Gk *tests the hardening of steel by dipping*

speak no word of reproach to them,
and do not distress them by making
demands of them.

Etiquette at a Banquet

32 If they make you master of the feast,
do not exalt yourself;
be among them as one of their number.
Take care of them first and then sit down;
2   when you have fulfilled all your duties,
take your place,
so that you may be merry along with them
and receive a wreath for your excellent
leadership.

3 Speak, you who are older, for it is your right,
but with accurate knowledge, and do not
interrupt the music.
4 Where there is entertainment, do not pour
out talk;
do not display your cleverness at the
wrong time.
5 A ruby seal in a setting of gold
is a concert of music at a banquet of wine.
6 A seal of emerald in a rich setting of gold
is the melody of music with good wine.

7 Speak, you who are young, if you are
obliged to,
but no more than twice and only if asked.
8 Be brief; say much in few words;
be as one who knows and can still hold
his tongue.
9 Among the great do not act as their equal;
and when another is speaking, do not
babble.

10 Lightning travels ahead of the thunder,
and approval goes before one who is
modest.
11 Leave in good time and do not be the last;
go home quickly and do not linger.
12 Amuse yourself there to your heart's
content,
but do not sin through proud speech.
13 But above all bless your Maker,
who intoxicates you with his good gifts.

The Providence of God

14 The one who seeks God^f will accept his
discipline,

and those who rise early to seek him^g will
find favor.
15 The one who seeks the law will be filled
with it,
but the hypocrite will stumble at it.
16 Those who fear the Lord will form true
judgments,
and they will kindle righteous deeds like
a light.
17 Sinners will shun reproof
and will find a decision according to their
liking.

18 A sensible person will not overlook a
thoughtful suggestion;
an insolent^h and proud person will not be
deterred by fear.^{i}
19 Do nothing without deliberation,
but when you have acted do not
regret it.
20 Do not go on a path full of hazards,
and do not stumble at an obstacle twice.^{j}
21 Do not be overconfident on a smooth^k
road,
22   and give good heed to your paths.^{l}
23 Guard^m yourself in every act,
for this is the keeping of the
commandments.

24 The one who keeps the law preserves
himself,^{n}
and the one who trusts the Lord will not
suffer loss.

33 No evil will befall the one who fears
the Lord,
but in trials such a one will be rescued
again and again.
2 The wise will not hate the law,
but the one who is hypocritical about it is
like a boat in a storm.
3 The sensible person will trust in the law,^{o}
for such a one the law is as dependable as
a divine oracle.

---

g **32.14** Other ancient authorities lack *to seek him*
h **32.18** Heb: Gk *alien*
i **32.18** Or *cower in fear*; other ancient authorities add
and after acting, with him, without deliberation
j **32.20** Heb: Gk *stumble on stony ground*
k **32.21** Or *an unexplored*
l **32.22** Heb Syr: Gk *and beware of your children*
m **32.23** Heb Syr: Gk *Trust*
n **32.24** Heb: Gk *who believes the law heeds the*
commandments
o **33.3** Heb *a word*

---

f **32.14** Heb: Gk *who fears the Lord*

4 Prepare what to say, and then you will be
   listened to;
   draw upon your training and give your
   answer.
5 The heart of a fool is like a cart wheel
   and his thoughts like a turning axle.
6 A mocking friend is like a stallion
   that neighs no matter who the rider is.

Differences in Nature and in Humankind

7 Why is one day more important than
   another,
   when all the daylight in the year is from
   the sun?
8 By the Lord's wisdom they were
   distinguished,
   and he appointed the different seasons
   and festivals.
9 Some days he exalted and hallowed,
   and some he made ordinary days.
10 All humans come from the ground,
   and humankind^p was created out of the
   dust.
11 In the fullness of his knowledge the Lord
   distinguished them
   and appointed their different ways.
12 Some he blessed and exalted,
   and some he made holy and brought near
   to himself,
   but some he cursed and brought low
   and turned them out of their place.
13 Like clay in the hand of the potter,
   to be molded as he pleases,
   so are humans in the hand of their Maker,
   to be given whatever he decides.

14 Good is the opposite of evil
   and life the opposite of death;
   so the sinner is the opposite of the godly.
15 Look at all the works of the Most High;
   they come in pairs, one the opposite of
   the other.

16 Now I was the last to keep vigil;
   I was like a gleaner following the
   grape-pickers;
17 by the blessing of the Lord I arrived first,
   and like a grape-picker I filled my
   winepress.
18 Consider that I have not labored for myself
   alone
   but for all who seek instruction.

19 Hear me, you who are great among the
   people,
   and you leaders of the congregation, pay
   heed!

The Advantage of Independence

20 To son or wife, to brother or friend,
   do not give power over yourself, as long
   as you live,
   and do not give your property to another,
   in case you change your mind and must
   ask for it.
21 While you are still alive and have breath in
   you,
   do not let anyone take your place.
22 For it is better that your children should
   ask from you
   than that you should look to the hand of
   your children.
23 Excel in all that you do;
   bring no stain upon your honor.
24 At the time when you end the days of your
   life,
   in the hour of death, distribute your
   inheritance.

The Treatment of Slaves

25 ^q Fodder and a stick and burdens for a
   donkey;
   bread and discipline and work for a
   slave.
26 Set your slaves to work,^r and you will find
   rest;
   leave their hands idle, and they will seek
   liberty.
27 Yoke and strap will bow the neck,
   and for wicked slaves there are racks and
   tortures.
28 Put them to work in order that they may
   not be idle,
29 for idleness teaches much evil.
30 Set them to work as is fitting for them,
   and if they do not obey make their fetters
   heavy.
   Do not be overbearing toward anyone,
   and do nothing without deliberation.

31 If you have but one slave, treat him like
   yourself,
   because you have bought him with blood.

---

p 33.10 Heb: Gk *Adam*

q 33.25 Some ancient authorities add the title
   Concerning Slaves

r 33.26 Heb: Gk *Work with instruction*

If you have but one slave, treat him like a
    brother,
  for you will need him as you need your
    life.

32 If you ill-treat him and he leaves you and
    runs away,

33 which way will you go to seek him?

Dreams Mean Nothing

34 The senseless have vain and false hopes,
    and dreams give wings to fools.

2 As one who catches at a shadow and
    pursues the wind,
  so is anyone who pays attention to
    dreams.

3 What is seen in dreams is but a reflection,
  the likeness of a face looking at itself.

4 From an unclean thing, what can be clean?
  And from something false, what can be
    true?

5 Divinations and omens and dreams are
    unreal,
  and like a woman in labor the mind has
    fantasies.

6 Unless they are sent by intervention from
    the Most High,
  pay no attention to them.

7 For dreams have deceived many,
  and those who put their hope in them
    have perished.

8 Without such deceptions the law will be
    fulfilled,
  and wisdom is complete in a trustworthy
    mouth.

Experience as a Teacher

9 People who have traveled[s] know many
    things,
  and those with much experience know
    what they are talking about.

10 The inexperienced know few things,

11 but those who have traveled acquire
    much cleverness.

12 I have seen many things in my travels,
  and I understand more than I can express.

13 I have often been in danger of death
  but have escaped because of these
    experiences.

Fear the Lord

14 The spirit of those who fear the Lord will
    live,

15 for their hope is in him who saves them.

16 Those who fear the Lord will not be timid
  or play the coward, for he is their hope.

17 Happy are souls that fear the Lord!

18 To whom do they look? And who is their
    support?

19 The eyes of the Lord are on those who love
    him,
  a mighty shield and strong support,
  a shelter from scorching heat and a shade
    from noonday sun,
  a guard against stumbling and a help
    against falling.

20 He lifts up the soul and makes the eyes
    sparkle;
  he gives health and life and blessing.

Offering Sacrifices

21 If one sacrifices ill-gotten goods, the
    offering is blemished;[t]

22 the gifts[u] of the lawless are not acceptable.

23 The Most High is not pleased with the
    offerings of the ungodly,
  nor for a multitude of sacrifices does he
    forgive sins.

24 Like one who kills a son before his father's
    eyes
  is the person who offers a sacrifice from
    the property of the poor.

25 The bread of the needy is the life of the
    poor;
  whoever deprives them of it is a
    murderer.

26 To take away a neighbor's living is to
    commit murder;

27 to deprive an employee of wages is to
    shed blood.

28 When one builds and another tears down,
  what do they gain but hard work?

29 When one prays and another curses,
  to whose voice will the Lord listen?

30 If one washes after touching a corpse and
    touches it again,
  what has been gained by washing?

31 So if one fasts for his sins
  and goes again and does the same things,
  who will listen to his prayer?
  And what has he gained by humbling
    himself?

---

s 34.9 Other ancient authorities read *are educated*

t 34.21 Other ancient authorities read *is made in
   mockery*

u 34.22 Other ancient authorities read *mockeries*

The Law and Sacrifices

35 The one who keeps the law makes many offerings;

2 one who heeds the commandments
makes an offering of well-being.

3 The one who returns a kindness offers
choice flour,

4 and one who gives alms sacrifices a thank
offering.

5 To keep from wickedness is pleasing to the
Lord,
and to forsake unrighteousness is an
atonement.

6 Do not appear before the Lord
empty-handed,

7 for all that you offer is in fulfillment of the
commandment.

8 The offering of the righteous enriches the
altar,
and its pleasing odor rises before the
Most High.

9 The sacrifice of the righteous is acceptable,
and it will never be forgotten.

10 Be generous when you worship the Lord,
and do not skimp the first fruits of your
hands.

11 With every gift show a cheerful face
and dedicate your tithe with gladness.

12 Give to the Most High as he has given to
you
and as generously as you can afford.

13 For the Lord is the one who repays,
and he will repay you sevenfold.

Divine Justice

14 Do not offer him a bribe, for he will not
accept it,

15 and do not rely on a dishonest sacrifice,
for the Lord is the judge,
and with him there is no partiality.

16 He will not show partiality to the poor,
but he will listen to the prayer of one who
is wronged.

17 He will not ignore the supplication of the
orphan
or the widow when she pours out her
complaint.

18 Do not the tears of the widow run down
her cheek

19 as she cries out against the one who
causes them to fall?

20 Those whose service is pleasing to the Lord
will be accepted,
and their prayers will reach to the clouds.

21 The prayer of the humble pierces the
clouds,
and it will not rest until it reaches its goal;
it will not desist until the Most High
responds

22 and does justice for the righteous and
executes judgment.
Indeed, the Lord will not delay,
and like a warrior[v] he will not be patient
until he crushes the loins of the unmerciful

23 and repays vengeance on the nations,
until he destroys the multitude of the
insolent
and breaks the scepters of the
unrighteous,

24 until he repays mortals according to their
deeds
and the works of all according to their
thoughts,

25 until he judges the case of his people
and makes them rejoice in his mercy.

26 His mercy is as welcome in time of distress
as clouds of rain in time of drought.

A Prayer for God's People

36 Have mercy upon us, O God[w] of all,
2and put all the nations in fear of you.

3 Lift up your hand against foreign nations
and let them see your might.

4 As you have used us to show your holiness
to them,
so use them to show your glory to us.

5 Then they will know,[x] as we have known,
that there is no God but you, O Lord.

6 Give new signs and work other wonders;

7 make your hand and right arm glorious.

8 Rouse your anger and pour out your wrath;

9 destroy the adversary and wipe out the
enemy.

10 Hasten the day, and remember the
appointed time,[y]
and let people recount your mighty
deeds.

11 Let survivors be consumed in the fiery
wrath,
and may those who harm your people
meet destruction.

12 Crush the heads of hostile rulers
who say, "There is no one but ourselves."

---

v 35.22 Heb: Gk *and with them*

w 36.1 Heb: Gk *O Master, the God*

x 36.5 Heb: Gk *And let them know you*

y 36.10 Other ancient authorities read *remember your oath*

13 Gather all the tribes of Jacob,*z*

16 and give them their inheritance, as at the
beginning.

17 Have mercy, O Lord, on the people called
by your name,
on Israel, whom you have named*a* your
firstborn.

18 Have pity on the city of your sanctuary,*b*
Jerusalem, the place of your dwelling.*c*

19 Fill Zion with your majesty*d*
and your temple*e* with your glory.

20 Bear witness to those whom you created in
the beginning,
and fulfill the prophecies spoken in your
name.

21 Reward those who wait for you,
and let your prophets be found
trustworthy.

22 Hear, O Lord, the prayer of your servants,
according to your goodwill toward*f*
your people,
and all who are on the earth will know
that you are the Lord, the God of the ages.

Concerning Discrimination

23 The stomach will take any food,
yet one food is better than another.

24 As the palate tastes the kinds of game,
so an intelligent mind detects false words.

25 A perverse mind will cause grief,
but a person with experience will pay him
back.

26 A woman will accept any man as a husband,
but one daughter is preferable to another.

27 A woman's beauty lights up a man's face,
and there is nothing he desires more.

28 If kindness and humility mark her speech,
her husband is more fortunate than other
men.

29 He who acquires a wife gets his best
possession,*g*
a helper fit for him and a pillar of support.*h*

30 Where there is no fence, the property will
be plundered,
and where there is no wife, a man will
become a fugitive and a wanderer.*i*

31 For who will trust a nimble robber
who skips from city to city?
So who will trust a man who has no nest
but lodges wherever nighttime finds him?

False Friends

37 Every friend says, "I, too, am a friend,"
but some friends are friends only in
name.

2 Does not sorrow draw near to death
when a companion and friend*j* turns into
an enemy?

3 O inclination to evil, why were you formed
to cover the land with deceit?

4 Some companions rejoice in the happiness
of friends,
but in time of trouble they are against them.

5 Some companions help a friend for their
stomachs' sake,
yet in battle they will carry his shield.

6 Do not forget friends during the battle,*k*
and do not be unmindful of them when
you distribute your spoils.*l*

Caution in Taking Advice

7 All counselors praise the counsel they give,
but some give counsel in their own interest.

8 Be wary of counselors
and learn first what is their interest,
for they will take thought for themselves.
They may cast the lot against you

9 and tell you, "Your way is good,"
and then stand aside to see what happens
to you.

10 Do not consult the one who regards you
with suspicion;
hide your intentions from those who are
jealous of you.

11 Do not consult with a woman about her
rival
or with a coward about war,
with a merchant about business
or with a buyer about selling,
with a miser about generosity*m*
or with the merciless about kindness,

---

z **36.13** Verse numbers 14 and 15 are not used in
chapter 36
a **36.17** Other ancient authorities read *you have likened
to*
b **36.18** Or *on your holy city*
c **36.18** Heb: Gk *your rest*
d **36.19** Heb Syr: Gk *the celebration of your wondrous
deeds*
e **36.19** Heb Syr: Gk Lat *people*
f **36.22** Heb and two Gk mss: Lat and most Gk mss
read *according to the blessing of Aaron for*
g **36.29** Heb: Gk *enters upon a possession*
h **36.29** Heb: Gk *rest*

i **36.30** Heb: Gk *wander about and sigh*
j **37.2** Heb reads *a friend like yourself*
k **37.6** Heb: Gk *in your heart*
l **37.6** Heb: Gk *him in your wealth*
m **37.11** Gk: Heb *with an evil person about generosity*

with an idler about any work
  or with a seasonal laborer about finishing
    the job,
with a lazy slave about a big task—
  pay no attention to any advice they give.
12 But associate with a godly person
  whom you know to be a keeper of the
    commandments,
who is like-minded with yourself,
  and who will grieve with you if you fail.
13 And heed[n] the counsel of your own heart,
  for no one is more faithful to you than
    it is.
14 For our own mind sometimes keeps us
    better informed
  than seven sentinels sitting high on a
    watchtower.
15 But above all pray to the Most High
  that he may direct your way in truth.

True and False Wisdom

16 Discussion is the beginning of every work,
  and counsel precedes every
    undertaking.
17 The mind is the root of all counsel;[o]
18   it sprouts four branches,[p]
good and evil, life and death,
  and it is the tongue that continually rules
    them.
19 Some people may be clever enough to
    teach many
  and yet be useless to themselves.
20 Skillful speakers may be hated;
  they will be destitute of all food,
21 for the Lord has withheld the gift of
    charm,
  since they are lacking in all wisdom.
22 If people are wise to their own advantage,
  the fruits of their good sense will be
    praiseworthy.[q]
23 The wise instruct their own people,
  and the fruits of their good sense are
    trustworthy.
24 The wise will have praise heaped upon
    them,
  and all who see them will call them
    happy.
25 The days of a person's life are numbered,
  but the days of Israel are without number.

26 Those who are wise among their people
  will inherit honor,[r]
and their names will live forever.

Concerning Moderation

27 My child, test yourself while you live;
  see what is bad for you, and do not give
    in to it.
28 For not everything is good for everyone,
  and no one enjoys everything.
29 Do not be greedy for every delicacy,
  and do not eat without restraint,
30 for overeating brings sickness,
  and gluttony leads to nausea.
31 Many have died of gluttony,
  but those who guard against it prolong
    their lives.

Concerning Physicians and Health

38 Honor physicians for their services,
  for the Lord created them,
2 for their gift of healing comes from the
    Most High,
  and they are rewarded by the king.
3 The skill of physicians makes them
    distinguished,
  and in the presence of the great they are
    admired.
4 The Lord created medicines out of the
    earth,
  and the sensible will not despise them.
5 Was not water made sweet with a tree
  in order that its[s] power might be known?
6 And he gave skill to human beings
  that he[t] might be glorified in his
    marvelous works.
7 By them the physician[u] heals and takes
    away pain;
8   the pharmacist makes a mixture from
      them.
God's[v] works will never be finished,
  and from him health spreads over all the
    earth.

9 My child, when you are ill, do not delay,
  but pray to the Lord, and he will heal you.
10 Give up your faults and direct your hands
    rightly,
  and cleanse your heart from all sin.

---

n 37.13 Heb: Gk *establish*
o 37.17 Heb: Gk *change*
p 37.18 Heb: Gk *four kinds of destiny appear*
q 37.22 Other ancient authorities read *trustworthy*

r 37.26 Other ancient authorities read *confidence*
s 38.5 Or *his*
t 38.6 Or *they*
u 38.7 Heb: Gk *he*
v 38.8 Gk *His*

11 Offer a sweet-smelling sacrifice and a
        memorial portion of choice flour,
     and pour oil on your offering, as much as
        you can afford.ʷ
12 Then give physicians their place, for the
        Lord created them;
     do not let them leave you, for you need
        them.
13 There may come a time when recovery lies
        in the hands of physicians,ˣ
14 for they, too, pray to the Lord
     that he grant them success in diagnosisʸ
     and in healing, for the sake of preserving
        life.
15 Those who sin against their Maker
     will be defiant toward the physician.ᶻ

On Mourning for the Dead

16 My child, let your tears fall for the dead,
     and as one in great pain begin the lament.
     Lay out the body according to custom,
     and do not neglect the burial.
17 Let your weeping be bitter and your wailing
        fervent;
     make your mourning worthy of the
        departed,
     for one day or two, to avoid criticism;
     then be comforted for your grief.
18 For grief may result in death,
     and a sorrowful heart saps one's strength.
19 In calamity, grief continues,
     but the life of the poor is a curse to the
        heart.
20 Do not give your heart to grief;
     drive it away and remember your own
        end.
21 Do not forget, there is no coming back;
     you do the deadᵃ no good, and you injure
        yourself.
22 Remember hisᵇ fate, for yours is like it;
     yesterday it was his,ᶜ and today it is yours.
23 When the dead are at rest, let their
        remembrance rest, too,
     and be comforted for them when their
        spirits have departed.

Trades and Crafts

24 The wisdom of the scribe depends on the
        opportunity of leisure;
     only the one who has little business can
        become wise.
25 How can one become wise who handles the
        plow
     and who glories in the shaft of a goad,
     who drives oxen and is occupied with their
        work,
     and whose talk is about the offspring of
        bulls?
26 He sets his heart on plowing furrows,
     and he loses sleep over fodder for the
        heifers.
27 So it is with every artisan and master
        artisan
     who labors by night as well as by day;
     those who carve the signets of seals—
     each is diligent in making a great
        variety;
     they set their heart on painting a lifelike
        image,
     and they lose sleep in order to finish their
        work.
28 So it is with the smith sitting by the anvil,
     intent on his ironwork;
     the breath of the fire melts his flesh,
     and he struggles with the heat of the
        furnace;
     the sound of the hammer deafens his
        ears,ᵈ
     and his eyes are on the pattern of the
        object.
     He sets his heart on finishing his
        handiwork,
     and he loses sleep to complete its
        decoration.
29 So it is with the potter sitting at his work
     and turning the wheel with his feet;
     he always lies down anxious about his
        work,
     and his every work is taken into
        account.
30 He molds the clay with his arm
     and makes it pliable with his feet;
     he sets his heart to finish the glazing,
     and he takes care in firingᵉ the kiln.

31 All these rely on their hands,
     and all are skillful in their own work.

---

w **38.11** Heb: Lat lacks *as much as you can afford*;
       meaning of Gk uncertain
x **38.13** Gk *in their hands*
y **38.14** Heb: Gk *rest*
z **38.15** Heb: Gk *may they fall into the hands of the
       physician*
a **38.21** Gk *him*
b **38.22** Heb: Gk *my*
c **38.22** Heb: Gk *mine*

d **38.28** Cn: Gk *renews his ear*
e **38.30** Cn: Gk *cleaning*

32 Without them no city can be inhabited,
  and wherever they live they will not go
    hungry.[f]
  Yet they are not sought out for the council
    of the people,[g]
33 nor do they attain eminence in the public
    assembly.
  They do not sit in the judge's seat,
    nor do they understand the decisions of
      the courts;
  they cannot expound discipline or
    judgment,
  and they are not found among the rulers.[h]
34 But they maintain the fabric of the world,
  and their concern is for[i] the exercise of
    their trade.

The Activity of the Scribe

  How different the one who devotes himself
    to the study of the law of the Most High!

39 They seek out the wisdom of all the
      ancients
  and are concerned with prophecies;
2 they preserve the sayings of the famous
  and penetrate the subtleties of parables;
3 they seek out the hidden meanings of
    proverbs
  and are at home with the obscurities of
    parables.
4 They serve among the great
  and appear before rulers;
  they travel in foreign nations
  and learn what is good and evil in the
    human lot.
5 They set their hearts to rise early
  to seek the Lord who made them
  and to petition the Most High;
  they open their mouths in prayer
  and ask pardon for their sins.

6 If the great Lord is willing,
  they will be filled with the spirit of
    understanding;
  they will pour forth words of wisdom of
    their own
  and give thanks to the Lord in prayer.
7 The Lord[j] will direct their counsel and
    knowledge

as they meditate on his mysteries.
8 They will show the discipline of their
    training
  and will glory in the law of the Lord's
    covenant.
9 Many will praise their understanding;
  it will never be blotted out.
  Their memory will not disappear,
  and their names will live through all
    generations.
10 Nations will speak of their wisdom,
  and the congregation will proclaim their
    praise.
11 If they live long, they will leave a name
  greater than a thousand,
  and if they go to rest, it is enough for them.

A Hymn of Praise to God

12 I have more on my mind to express;
  I am full like the full moon.
13 Listen to me, my faithful children, and
    blossom
  like a rose growing by a stream of water.
14 Send out fragrance like incense
  and put forth blossoms like a lily.
  Raise your voice[k] and sing a hymn of praise;
  bless the Lord for all his works.
15 Ascribe majesty to his name
  and give thanks to him with praise,
  with songs on your lips and with harps;
  this is what you shall say in thanksgiving:

16 "All the works of the Lord are very good,
  and whatever he commands will be done
    at the appointed time.
17 No one can say, 'What is this?' or 'Why is
    that?'—
  for at the appointed time everything will
    be made known.
  At his word the waters stood in a heap
  and the reservoirs of water at the word of
    his mouth.
18 At his command, his purpose is fulfilled,
  and none can limit his saving power.
19 The works of all are before him,
  and nothing can be hidden from his eyes.
20 From age to age he observes all,
  and nothing is too marvelous for him.
21 No one can say, 'What is this?' or 'Why is
    that?'—
  for everything has been created for its
    own purpose.

---

f **38.32** Syr: Gk *and people can neither live nor walk there*
g **38.32** Most ancient authorities lack this line
h **38.33** Cn: Gk *among parables*
i **38.34** Syr: Gk *prayer is in*
j **39.7** Gk *He himself*

---

k **39.14** Syr: Gk *fragrance*

22 "His blessing covers the dry land like a river
    and drenches it like a flood.
23 The nations will inherit his wrath,
    as when he turned a watered land into
        salt.
24 To the faithful his ways are straight
    but full of pitfalls for the lawless.
25 From the beginning good things were
        created for the good
    but for sinners good things and bad.[l]
26 The basic necessities of human life
    are water and fire and iron and salt
    and wheat flour and milk and honey,
    the blood of the grape and oil and clothing.
27 All these are good for the godly,
    but for sinners they turn into evils.

28 "There are winds created for vengeance,
    and in their anger they can dislodge
        mountains;[m]
    on the day of reckoning they will pour out
        their strength
    and calm the anger of their Maker.
29 Fire and hail and famine and pestilence—
    all these have been created for vengeance;
30 the fangs of wild animals and scorpions
        and vipers
    and the sword that punishes the ungodly
        with destruction.
31 They take delight in doing his bidding,
    always ready for his service on earth,
    and when their time comes they never
        disobey his command."

32 So from the beginning I have been steadfast
    and have thought it out and left it in
        writing:
33 All the works of the Lord are good,
    and he will supply every need in its time.
34 No one can say, "This is not as good as
        that,"
    for everything proves good in its
        appointed time.
35 So now sing praise with all your heart and
        voice,
    and bless the name of the Lord.

Human Wretchedness

40 Hard work was created for everyone,
    and a heavy yoke is laid on the
        children of Adam,

from the day they come forth from their
        mother's womb
    until the day they return to[n] the mother
        of all the living.[o]
2 Perplexities and fear of heart are theirs
    and anxious thought of the day of their
        death.
3 From the one who sits on a splendid throne
    to the one who grovels in dust and ashes,
4 from the one who wears purple and a
        crown
    to the one who is clothed in burlap,
5 there is anger and envy and trouble and
        unrest
    and fear of death and fury and strife.
    And when one rests upon his bed,
    his sleep at night confuses his mind.
6 He gets little or no rest;
    he struggles in his sleep as he did by day.[p]
    He is troubled by the visions of his mind
    like one who has escaped from the
        battlefield.
7 At the moment he reaches safety[q] he wakes
        up,
    astonished that his fears were groundless.
8 To all creatures, human and animal,
    but to sinners seven times more,
9 come death and bloodshed and strife and
        sword,
    calamities and famine and ruin and
        plague.
10 All these were created for the lawless,
    and on their account the flood came.
11 All that is of earth returns to earth,
    and what is from above returns above.[r]

Injustice Will Not Prosper

12 All bribery and injustice will be blotted out,
    but good faith will last forever.
13 The wealth of the unjust will dry up like a
        river
    and crash like a loud clap of thunder in a
        storm.
14 As a generous person has cause to rejoice,
    so lawbreakers will utterly fail.
15 The children of the ungodly put out few
        branches;
    they are unhealthy roots on sheer rock.

---

l 39.25 Heb Lat: Gk *sinners bad things*
m 39.28 Heb Syr: Gk *can scourge mightily*

n 40.1 Other Gk and Lat authorities read *are buried in*
o 40.1 Heb: Gk *of all*
p 40.6 Arm: Meaning of Gk uncertain
q 40.7 Other ancient authorities read *need*
r 40.11 Heb Syr: Gk Lat *from the waters returns to
    the sea*

16 The reeds by any water or river bank
    are plucked up before any grass,
17 but kindness is like a garden of blessings,
    and almsgiving endures forever.

The Joys of Life

18 A life of abundance and wages make life
    sweet,[s]
    but better than either is finding a treasure.
19 Children and the building of a city establish
    one's name,
    but better than either is the one who finds
    wisdom.
    Cattle and orchards make one prosperous,[t]
    but a blameless wife is accounted better
    than either.
20 Wine and music gladden the heart,
    but the love of friends[u] is better than
    either.
21 The flute and the harp make sweet melody,
    but a pleasant voice is better than either.
22 The eye desires grace and beauty,
    but the green shoots of grain more than
    either.
23 A friend or companion is always welcome,
    but a sensible wife[v] is better than either.
24 Kindred and helpers are for a time of
    trouble,
    but almsgiving rescues better than
    either.
25 Gold and silver make one stand firm,
    but good counsel is esteemed more than
    either.
26 Riches and strength build up confidence,
    but the fear of the Lord is better than
    either.
    There is no want in the fear of the Lord,
    and with it there is no need to seek for
    help.
27 The fear of the Lord is like a garden of
    blessing
    and covers a person better than any glory.

The Disgrace of Begging

28 My child, do not lead the life of a beggar;
    it is better to die than to beg.
29 When one looks to the table of another,
    one's way of life cannot be considered a
    life.

One loses self-respect with another person's
    food,
    but one who is intelligent and well
    instructed guards against that.
30 In the mouth of the shameless begging is
    sweet,
    but it kindles a fire inside them.

Concerning Death

41 O death, how bitter is the thought of
    you
    to the one at peace among possessions,
    who has nothing to worry about and is
    prosperous in everything
    and still is vigorous enough to enjoy
    pleasure![w]
2 O death, how welcome is your sentence
    to one who is needy and failing in
    strength,
    worn down by age and anxious about
    everything,
    to one who is contrary and has lost all
    patience!
3 Do not fear death's decree for you;
    remember those who went before you
    and those who will come after.
4 This is the Lord's decree for all flesh;
    why, then, should you reject the will of
    the Most High?
    Whether life lasts for ten years or a
    hundred or a thousand,
    there are no questions asked in Hades.

The Fate of the Wicked

5 The children of sinners are abominable
    children,
    and they frequent the haunts of the ungodly.
6 The inheritance of the children of sinners
    will perish,
    and on their offspring will be a perpetual
    disgrace.
7 Children will blame an ungodly father,
    for they suffer disgrace because of him.
8 Woe to you, the ungodly,
    who have forsaken the law of the Most
    High![x]
9 You[y] will beget them only for groaning.
    When you stumble, there is lasting joy,[z]
    and when you die, a curse is your lot.

---

s **40.18** Heb: Gk *Life is sweet for the self-reliant and
    hard-working*
t **40.19** Heb Syr: Gk lacks *but better . . . prosperous*
u **40.20** Heb: Gk *wisdom*
v **40.23** Heb Compare Syr: Gk *wife with her husband*

w **41.1** Heb: Gk *food*
x **41.8** Heb: Gk adds *God*
y **41.9** Other ancient authorities read *If you have
    children, calamity will be theirs; you*
z **41.9** Heb: Meaning of Gk uncertain

10 Whatever comes from earth returns to
        earth,
    so the ungodly go from curse to
        destruction.

11 The breath[a] of humans is in their bodies,
    but a virtuous name will never be blotted
        out.[b]
12 Have regard for your name, since it will
        outlive you
    longer than a thousand hoards of gold.
13 The days of a good life are numbered,
    but a good name lasts forever.

14 My children, be true to your training and
        be at peace;
    hidden wisdom and unseen treasure—
    of what value is either?

A Series of Contrasts

15 Better are those who hide their folly
    than those who hide their wisdom.
16 Therefore show respect for my words,
    for it is not good to feel shame in every
        circumstance,
    nor is every kind of shaming to be
        approved.[c]

17 Be ashamed of sexual immorality before
        your father or mother
    and of a lie before a prince or a ruler,
18 of a crime before a judge or magistrate
    and of a breach of the law before the
        congregation and the people,
    of unjust dealing before your partner or
        your friend
19 and of theft in the place where you live.
    Be ashamed of breaking an oath or
        agreement[d]
    and of leaning on your elbow at meals,
    of surliness in receiving or giving
20 and of silence before those who greet you,
    of looking at a prostitute
21 and of rejecting the appeal of a relative,
    of taking away someone's portion or gift
    and of gazing at another man's wife,
22 of meddling with his female servant—
    and do not approach her bed;

---

a 41.11 Heb: Gk *misery*
b 41.11 Heb: Gk *but the bad name of sinners will be
      blotted out*
c 41.16 Heb: Gk *and not everything is confidently
      esteemed by everyone*
d 41.19 Heb: Gk *before the truth of God and the covenant*

---

    of abusive words, before friends—
    and do not be insulting after making a
        gift.

42 Be ashamed of repeating what you
        hear
    and of betraying secrets.
    Then you will show proper shame
    and will find favor with everyone.

Of the following things do not be ashamed,
    and do not sin by showing partiality:
2 Do not be ashamed of the law of the Most
        High and his covenant
    and of rendering judgment to acquit the
        ungodly;
3 of keeping accounts with a partner or with
        traveling companions
    and of dividing the inheritance of friends;
4 of accuracy with scales and weights
    and of acquiring much or little;
5 of profit from dealing with merchants
    and of frequent disciplining of children
    and of drawing blood from the back of a
        wicked slave.
6 Where there is an untrustworthy wife, a
        seal is a good thing,
    and where there are many hands, lock
        things up.
7 When you make a deposit, be sure it is
        counted and weighed,
    and when you give or receive, put it all in
        writing.
8 Do not be ashamed to correct the stupid or
        foolish
    or the aged who are guilty of sexual
        immorality.
    Then you will show your sound training
    and will be approved by all.

Daughters and Fathers

9 A daughter is a secret anxiety to her father,
    and worry over her robs him of sleep;
    when she is young, for fear she may not
        marry,
    or if married, for fear she may be disliked;
10 while a virgin, for fear she may be seduced
    and become pregnant in her father's
        house;
    or having a husband, for fear she may go
        astray,
    or, though married, for fear she may be
        barren.
11 Keep strict watch over a headstrong
        daughter,

or she may make you a laughingstock to
  your enemies,
a byword in the city and the assembly of[e]
  the people,
and put you to shame in public
  gatherings.[f]
See that there is no lattice in her room,
  no spot that overlooks the approaches to
  the house.[g]
12 Do not let her parade her beauty before any
  man
  or spend her time among married
  women,[h]
13 for from garments comes the moth
  and from a woman comes woman's
  wickedness.
14 Better is the wickedness of a man than a
  woman who does good;
  it is a woman who brings shame and
  disgrace.

The Works of God in Nature

15 I will now call to mind the works of the
  Lord
  and will declare what I have seen.
  By the word of the Lord his works are
  made,
  and all his creatures do his will.[i]
16 The sun looks down on everything with its
  light,
  and the work of the Lord is full of his
  glory.
17 The Lord has not empowered even his holy
  ones
  to recount all his marvelous works,
  which the Lord the Almighty has
  established
  so that the universe may stand firm in his
  glory.
18 He searches out the abyss and the human
  heart;
  he understands their subtleties.[j]
  For the Most High knows all that may be
  known;
  he sees from of old the things that are to
  come.[k]

19 He discloses what has been and what is to be,
  and he reveals the traces of hidden things.
20 No thought escapes him,
  and not a single word is hidden from him.
21 He has set in order the splendors of his
  wisdom;
  he is from all eternity one and the same.
  Nothing can be added or taken away,
  and he needs no one to be his counselor.
22 How desirable are all his works,
  and how sparkling they are to see![l]
23 All these things live and remain forever;
  each creature is preserved to meet a
  particular need.[m]
24 All things come in pairs, one opposite the
  other,
  and he has made nothing incomplete.
25 Each supplements the virtues of the other.
  Who could ever tire of seeing his glory?

The Splendor of the Sun

43 The pride of the higher realms is the
  clear vault of the sky,
  as glorious to behold as the sight of the
  heavens.
2 The sun, when it appears, proclaims as it
  rises
  what a marvelous instrument it is, the
  work of the Most High.
3 At noon it parches the land,
  and who can withstand its burning heat?
4 A man tending[n] a furnace works in
  burning heat,
  but three times as hot is the sun scorching
  the mountains;
  when it breathes out fiery vapors
  and when it shines forth its rays, it blinds
  the eyes.
5 Great is the Lord who made it;
  at his orders it hurries on its course.

The Splendor of the Moon

6 It is the moon that marks the changing
  seasons,[o]
  governing the times, an everlasting sign.
7 From the moon comes the sign for festal
  days,
  a light that wanes when it completes its
  course.

---

e **42.11** Heb: Meaning of Gk uncertain
f **42.11** Heb: Gk *to shame before the great multitude*
g **42.11** Heb: Gk lacks *See . . . house*
h **42.12** Heb: Meaning of Gk uncertain
i **42.15** Syr Compare Heb: most Gk mss lack *and all . . .
  will*
j **42.18** Heb: Gk *wondrous feats*
k **42.18** Heb: Gk *he sees the sign(s) of the age*

l **42.22** Meaning of Gk uncertain
m **42.23** Heb: Gk *forever for every need, and all are
  obedient*
n **43.4** Other ancient authorities read *blowing upon*
o **43.6** Heb: Meaning of Gk uncertain

8 The new moon, as its name suggests,
      renews itself;[p]
   how marvelous it is in this change,
   a beacon to the hosts on high
   shining in the vault of the heavens!

The Glory of the Stars and the Rainbow

9 The glory of the stars is the beauty of
      heaven,
      a glittering array in the heights of the
      Lord.
10 On the orders of the Holy One they stand
      in their appointed places;
   they never relax in their watches.
11 Look at the rainbow and praise him who
      made it;
   it is exceedingly beautiful in its
      brightness.
12 It encircles the sky with its glorious arc;
   the hands of the Most High have
      stretched it out.

The Marvels of Nature

13 By his command he sends the driving
      snow
   and speeds the lightnings of his
      judgment.
14 Therefore the storehouses are opened,
   and the clouds fly out like birds.
15 In his majesty he gives the clouds their
      strength,
   and the hailstones are broken in pieces.
17a The voice of his thunder causes the earth to
      tremble;
16   when he appears, the mountains shake.
   At his will the south wind blows,
17b so do the storm from the north and the
      whirlwind.
   He scatters the snow like birds flying down,
   and its descent is like locusts alighting.
18 The eye is dazzled by the beauty of its
      whiteness,
   and the mind is amazed as it falls.
19 He pours frost over the earth like salt,
   and icicles form like pointed thorns.
20 The cold north wind blows,
   and ice freezes on the water;
   it settles on every pool of water,
   and the water puts it on like a breastplate.
21 He consumes the mountains and burns up
      the wilderness
   and withers the tender grass like fire.

22 A mist quickly heals all things;
   the falling dew gives refreshment from
      the heat.
23 By his plan he stilled the deep
   and planted islands in it.
24 Those who sail the sea tell of its dangers,
   and we marvel at what we hear.
25 In it are strange and marvelous creatures,
   all kinds of living things, and mighty[q] sea
      monsters.
26 Because of him each of his messengers
      succeeds,
   and by his word all things hold together.

27 We could say more but could never say
      enough;
   let the final word be: "He is the all."
28 Where can we find the strength to praise
      him?
   For he is greater than all his works.
29 Awesome is the Lord and very great,
   and marvelous is his power.
30 Glorify the Lord and exalt him as much as
      you can,
   for he surpasses even that.
   When you exalt him, summon all your
      strength,
   and do not grow weary, for you cannot
      praise him enough.
31 Who has seen him and can describe him?
   Or who can extol him as he is?
32 Many things greater than these lie hidden,
   for I[r] have seen but few of his works.
33 For the Lord has made all things,
   and to the godly he has given wisdom.

Hymn in Honor of Our Ancestors[s]

44
Let us now sing the praises of famous
      men,
      our ancestors in their generations.
2 The Lord apportioned to them[t] great glory,
   his majesty from the beginning.
3 There were those who ruled in their kingdoms
   and made a name for themselves by their
      strength;
   those who gave counsel because they were
      intelligent;
   those who spoke in prophetic oracles;

---

p **43.8** Heb: Gk *The month accords with its name*
q **43.25** Heb: Gk *a creation of*
r **43.32** Heb: Gk *we*
s **44.1** This title is included in the Gk text.
t **44.2** Heb: Gk *created*

4 those who led the people by their counsels
  and by their knowledge of the people's
    lore;
  they were wise in their words of
    instruction;
5 those who composed musical tunes
  or put verses in writing;
6 rich men endowed with resources,
  living peacefully in their homes—
7 all these were honored in their generations
  and were the pride of their times.
8 Some of them have left behind a name,
  so that others declare their praise.
9 But of others there is no memory;
  they have perished as though they had
    never existed;
  they have become as though they had
    never been born,
  they and their children after them.
10 But these also were men of compassion
  whose righteous deeds have not been
    forgotten;
11 their wealth will remain with their
    descendants
  and their inheritance with their children's
    children.*u*
12 Their descendants stand by the covenants;
  their children also, for their sake.
13 Their offspring will continue forever,
  and their glory will never be blotted out.
14 Their bodies are buried in peace,
  but their name lives on generation after
    generation.
15 The assembly declares*v* their wisdom,
  and the congregation proclaims their
    praise.

Enoch
16 Enoch pleased the Lord and was taken up,
  an example of repentance to all
    generations.

Noah
17 Noah was found perfect and righteous;
  in the time of wrath he kept humanity
    alive;*w*
  because of him*x* a remnant was left on the
    earth
  when the flood came.

18 Everlasting covenants were made with him
  that all flesh should never again be
    blotted out by a flood.

Abraham
19 Abraham was the great father of a
    multitude of nations,
  and no one has been found like him in
    glory.
20 He kept the law of the Most High
  and entered into a covenant with him;
  he certified the covenant in his flesh,
  and when he was tested he proved
    faithful.
21 Therefore the Lord*y* assured him with an
    oath
  that the nations would be blessed through
    his offspring,
  that he would make him as numerous as
    the dust of the earth
  and exalt his offspring like the stars
  and give them an inheritance from sea to
    sea
  and from the Euphrates*z* to the ends of
    the earth.

Isaac and Jacob
22 To Isaac also he gave the same assurance
  for the sake of his father Abraham.
  The blessing of all people and a covenant
23   he made to rest on the head of Jacob;
  he acknowledged him with his blessings
    and gave him his inheritance;
  he divided his portions
    and distributed them among twelve tribes.

Moses
From his descendants the Lord*a* brought
    forth a man of compassion
  who found favor in the sight of all

45 1 and was beloved by God and people,
         Moses, whose memory is blessed.
2 He made him equal in glory to the holy
    ones
  and made him great, to the terror of his
    enemies.
3 By his words he performed swift miracles;*b*
  the Lord*c* glorified him in the presence of
    kings.

---

u 44.11 Heb Compare Lat Syr: Meaning of Gk
  uncertain
v 44.15 Heb: Gk *Peoples declare*
w 44.17 Heb: Gk *was taken in exchange*
x 44.17 Cn: Gk *this*

y 44.21 Gk *he*
z 44.21 Syr: Heb Gk *River*
a 44.23 Gk *he*
b 45.3 Heb: Gk *caused signs to cease*
c 45.3 Gk *he*

He gave him commandments for his
    people
  and revealed to him his glory.
4 For his faithfulness and meekness he
    consecrated him,
  choosing him out of all humankind.
5 He allowed him to hear his voice
  and led him into the dark cloud
  and gave him the commandments face to
    face,
  the law of life and knowledge,
  so that he might teach Jacob the covenant
  and Israel his decrees.

Aaron

6 He exalted Aaron, a holy man like Moses,*d*
  who was his brother, of the tribe of Levi.
7 He made an everlasting covenant with him
  and gave him the priesthood of the
    people.
  He blessed him with stateliness
  and put a glorious robe on him.
8 He clothed him in perfect splendor*e*
  and strengthened him with the apparel of
    authority,
  the linen undergarments, the long robe,
    and the ephod.
9 And he encircled him with pomegranates,
  with many golden bells all around,
  to send forth a sound as he walked,
  to make their ringing heard in the temple
  as a reminder to his people;
10 with the sacred vestment, of gold and violet
  and purple, the work of an embroiderer;
  with the oracle of judgment, the
    manifestations of truth;
11 with twisted crimson, the work of an
    artisan;
  with precious stones engraved like seals,
  in a setting of gold, the work of a jeweler,
  to commemorate in engraved letters
  each of the tribes of Israel;
12 with a gold crown upon his turban,
  inscribed like a holy seal,
  majestic and glorious, a work of power,
  a delight to the eyes, richly adorned.
13 Before him such beautiful things did not
    exist.
  No outsider ever put them on,
  but only his sons
  and his descendants in perpetuity.

14 His sacrifices shall be wholly burned
  twice every day continually.
15 Moses ordained him
  and anointed him with holy oil;
  it was an everlasting covenant for him
  and for his descendants as long as the
    heavens endure,
  to minister to the Lord*f* and serve as priest
  and bless his people in his name.
16 He chose him out of all the living
  to offer sacrifice to the Lord,
  incense and a pleasing odor as a memorial,
  to make atonement for the*g* people.
17 In his commandments he gave him
    authority, by means of a decree, and*h*
      judgments,
  to teach Jacob the testimonies
  and to enlighten Israel with his law.
18 Outsiders conspired against him
  and envied him in the wilderness,
  Dathan and Abiram and their followers
  and the company of Korah, in wrath and
    anger.
19 The Lord saw it and was not pleased,
  and in the heat of his anger they were
    destroyed;
  he performed wonders against them
  to consume them in flaming fire.
20 He added glory to Aaron
  and gave him a heritage;
  he allotted to him the best of the first fruits
  and prepared bread of first fruits in
    abundance,
21 for they eat the sacrifices of the Lord,
  which he gave to him and his descendants.
22 But in the land of the people he has no
    inheritance,
  and he has no portion among the people,
  for the Lord*i* himself is his*j* portion and
    inheritance.

Phinehas

23 Phinehas son of Eleazar ranks third in
    glory
  for being zealous in the fear of the Lord
  and standing firm, when the people turned
    away,
  in the noble courage of his soul,
  and he made atonement for Israel.

---

d **45.6** Gk *him*
e **45.8** Heb: Gk *boasting*

f **45.15** Gk *him*
g **45.16** Other ancient authorities read *his* or *your*
h **45.17** Heb: Gk *authority in covenants of*
i **45.22** Gk *he*
j **45.22** Other ancient authorities read *your*

²⁴ Therefore a covenant of peace was
established with him,
that he should be leader of the sanctuary
and of his people,
that he and his descendants should have
the dignity of the priesthood forever.
²⁵ Just as a covenant was established with
David
son of Jesse of the tribe of Judah,
that the king's heritage passes only from
son to son,
so the heritage of Aaron is for his
descendants alone.

²⁶ And now bless the Lord
who has crowned you with glory.ᵏ
May the Lordˡ grant you wisdom of mind
to judge his people with justice,
so that their prosperity may not vanish
and that their glory may endure through
all their generations.

Joshua and Caleb

46 Joshua son of Nun was mighty in war
and was the successor of Moses in the
prophetic office.
He became, as his name implies,
a great savior of God'sᵐ elect,
to take vengeance on the enemies who rose
against them,
so that he might give Israel its
inheritance.
² How glorious he was when he lifted his
hands
and brandished his sword against the
cities!
³ Who before him ever stood so firm?
For he waged the wars of the Lord.
⁴ Was it not through him that the sun stood
still
and one day became as long as two?
⁵ He called upon the Most High, the Mighty
One,
when enemies pressed him on every
side,
and the great Lord answered him
with hailstones of mighty power.
⁶ He overwhelmed that nation in battle,
and on the slope he destroyed his
opponents,

so that the nations might know his
armament,
because their battle was againstⁿ the
Lord,
for he was a devoted follower of the
Mighty One.
⁷ And in the days of Moses he showed
compassion,
he and Caleb son of Jephunneh:
they opposed the congregation,ᵒ
restrained the people from sin,
and stilled their wicked grumbling.
⁸ And these two alone were spared
out of six hundred thousand infantry,
to lead the peopleᵖ into their inheritance,
the land flowing with milk and honey.
⁹ The Lord gave Caleb strength,
which remained with him in his old
age,
so that he went up to the hill country,
and his children obtained it for an
inheritance,
¹⁰ so that all the Israelites might see
how good it is to follow the Lord.

The Judges

¹¹ The judges also, with their respective
names,
whose hearts did not fall into idolatry
and who did not turn away from the
Lord—
may their memory be blessed!
¹² May their bones send forth new life from
where they lie,
and may the names of those who have
been honored
live again in their children!�q

¹³ Samuel was beloved by his Lord;
a prophet of the Lord, he established the
kingdom
and anointed rulers over his people.
¹⁴ By the law of the Lord he judged the
congregation,
and the Lord watched over Jacob.
¹⁵ By his faithfulness he was proved to be a
prophet,
and by his words he became known as a
trustworthy seer.

---

k 45.26 Heb: Gk lacks *And . . . glory*
l 45.26 Gk *he*
m 46.1 Gk *his*

n 46.6 Other ancient authorities read *for his battle was
before*
o 46.7 Other ancient authorities read *the enemy*
p 46.8 Gk *them*
q 46.12 Meaning of Gk uncertain

16 He called upon the Lord, the Mighty One,
    when his enemies pressed him on every
      side,
    and he offered in sacrifice a suckling
      lamb.
17 Then the Lord thundered from heaven
    and made his voice heard with a mighty
      sound;
18 he subdued the leaders of the enemy[r]
    and all the rulers of the Philistines.
19 Before the time of his eternal sleep,
    Samuel[s] bore witness before the Lord and
      his anointed:
  "No property, not so much as a pair of
      shoes,
    have I taken from anyone!"
    And no one accused him.
20 Even after he had fallen asleep, he
      prophesied
    and made known to the king his death
    and lifted up his voice from the ground
    in prophecy, to blot out the lawlessness of
      the people.

Nathan

47 After him Nathan rose up
    to prophesy in the days of David.

David

2 As the fat is set apart from the offering of
      well-being,
    so David was set apart from the Israelites.
3 He played with lions as though they were
      young goats
    and with bears as though they were lambs
      of the flock.
4 In his youth did he not kill a giant
    and take away the people's disgrace,
    when he whirled the stone in the sling
    and struck down the boasting Goliath?
5 For he called on the Lord, the Most High,
    and he gave strength to his right arm
    to strike down a mighty warrior
    and to exalt the power[t] of his people.
6 So they glorified him for the tens of
      thousands
    and praised him for the blessings
      bestowed by the Lord,
    when the glorious diadem was given to
      him.

7 For he wiped out his enemies on every side
    and scorned his adversaries the
      Philistines;
    he crushed their power[u] to our own day.
8 In all that he did he gave thanks
    to the Holy One, the Most High,
      proclaiming his glory;
    he sang praise with all his heart,
    and he loved his Maker.
9 He placed singers before the altar,
    to make sweet melody with their voices.[v]
10 He gave beauty to the festivals
    and arranged their times throughout the
      year,[w]
    while they praised God's[x] holy name
    and the sanctuary resounded from early
      morning.
11 The Lord took away his sins
    and exalted his power[y] forever;
    he gave him a covenant of kingship
    and a glorious throne in Israel.

Solomon

12 After him a wise son rose up
    who because of him lived in security:[z]
13 Solomon reigned in an age of peace,
    because God gave him rest all around,
    so that he might build a house in his name
    and provide a sanctuary to stand forever.
14 How wise you were when you were young!
    You overflowed like the Nile[a] with
      understanding.
15 Your influence spread throughout the
      earth,
    and you filled it with proverbs having
      deep meaning.
16 Your fame reached to far-off islands,
    and you were loved for your peaceful
      reign.
17 For your songs, proverbs, parables,
    and understanding the nations marveled
      at you.
18 In the name of the Lord God,
    who is called the God of Israel,
    you gathered gold like tin
    and amassed silver like lead.

---

r **46.18** Heb: Gk *leaders of the people of Tyre*
s **46.19** Gk *he*
t **47.5** Gk *horn*
u **47.7** Gk *horn*
v **47.9** Other ancient authorities add *and daily they sing
    their praises*
w **47.10** Gk *to completion*
x **47.10** Gk *his*
y **47.11** Gk *horn*
z **47.12** Heb: Gk *in a broad place*
a **47.14** Heb: Gk *a river*

19 But you brought in women to lie at your
        side,
     and through your body you were brought
        into subjection.
20 You stained your honor
     and defiled your family line,
  so that you brought wrath upon your
        children,
     and they were grieved[b] at your folly,
21 because the sovereignty was divided
     and a rebel kingdom arose out of
        Ephraim.
22 But the Lord will never give up his mercy
     or cause any of his words[c] to perish;
  he will never blot out the descendants of
        his chosen one
     or destroy the family line of him who
        loved him.
  So he gave a remnant to Jacob
     and to David a root from his own
        family.

Rehoboam and Jeroboam
23 Solomon rested with his ancestors
     and left behind him one of his sons
  broad in[d] folly and lacking in sense,
     Rehoboam, whose policy drove the
        people to revolt.
  Then Jeroboam son of Nebat led Israel into
        sin
     and started Ephraim on its sinful ways.
24 Their sins increased more and more
     until they were exiled from their land.
25 For they sought out every kind of
        wickedness
     until vengeance came upon them.

Elijah
48 Then Elijah arose, a prophet like fire,
        and his word burned like a torch.
2 He brought a famine upon them,
     and by his zeal he made them few in
        number.
3 By the word of the Lord he shut up the
        heavens
     and also three times brought down fire.
4 How glorious you were, Elijah, in your
        wondrous deeds!
  Who can boast[e] as you can?

5 You who raised a corpse from death
     and from Hades, by the word of the Most
        High,
6 who sent kings down to destruction
     and famous men from their sickbeds,
7 who heard rebuke at Sinai
     and judgments of vengeance at Horeb,
8 who anointed kings to inflict retribution
     and prophets to succeed you,[f]
9 who were taken up by a whirlwind of fire
     in a chariot with horses of fire,
10 who were prepared at the appointed time[g]
     to calm wrath before it breaks out in fury,
  to turn the hearts of parents to their
        children
     and to restore the tribes of Jacob.
11 Happy are those who saw you
     and were adorned[h] in love!
  For we also shall surely live.[i]

Elisha
12 When Elijah was enveloped in the whirlwind,
     Elisha was filled with his spirit.
  He performed twice as many signs
     and marvels with every utterance of his
        mouth.[j]
  Never in his lifetime did he tremble before
        any ruler,
     nor could anyone intimidate him at all.
13 Nothing was too hard for him,[k]
     and when he was dead his body
        prophesied.
14 In his life he did wonders,
     and in death his deeds were marvelous.

15 Despite all this the people did not repent,
     nor did they forsake their sins,
  until they were carried off as plunder from
        their land
     and were scattered over all the earth.
  The people were left very few in number
     but with a ruler from the house of David.
16 Some of them did what was right,
     but others sinned more and more.

Hezekiah
17 Hezekiah fortified his city
     and brought water into its midst;

---

b 47.20 Other ancient authorities read *I was grieved*
c 47.22 Heb Syr: Gk *works*
d 47.23 Heb Syr: Gk *the people's*
e 48.4 Or *be glorified*

f 48.8 Heb: Gk *him*
g 48.10 Heb: Gk *are for reproofs*
h 48.11 Other ancient authorities read *and have died*
i 48.11 Meaning of Gk uncertain
j 48.12 Heb: Gk lacks *He performed . . . mouth*
k 48.13 Heb: Gk *no word surpassed him*

he tunneled the rock with iron tools
  and built cisterns for the water.
18 In his days Sennacherib invaded the
      country;
  he sent his commander[l] and departed;
  he shook his fist against Zion
  and made great boasts in his arrogance.
19 Then their hearts and hands were shaken,
  and they were in anguish, like women in
      labor.
20 But they called upon the Lord who is
      merciful,
  spreading out their hands toward him.
  The Holy One quickly heard them from
      heaven
  and delivered them through Isaiah.
21 The Lord[m] struck down the camp of the
      Assyrians,
  and his angel wiped them out.
22 For Hezekiah did what was pleasing to the
      Lord,
  and he kept firmly to the ways of his
      ancestor David,
  as he was commanded by the prophet
      Isaiah,
  who was great and trustworthy in his
      visions.

Isaiah
23 In Isaiah's[n] days the sun went backward,
  and he prolonged the life of the king.
24 By his dauntless spirit he saw the future
  and comforted the mourners in Zion.
25 He revealed what was to occur to the end
      of time
  and the hidden things before they
      happened.

Josiah and Other Worthies

49
The name[o] of Josiah is like blended
      incense
  prepared by the skill of the perfumer;
  his memory[p] is as sweet as honey to every
      mouth
  and like music at a banquet of wine.
2 He did what was right by reforming the
      people
  and removing the lawless
      abominations.

3 He kept his heart fixed on the Lord;
  in lawless times he made godliness
      prevail.

4 Except for David and Hezekiah and
      Josiah,
  all of them were great sinners,
  for they abandoned the law of the Most
      High;
  the kings of Judah came to an end.
5 They[q] gave their power to others
  and their glory to a foreign nation,
6 who set fire to the chosen city of the
      sanctuary
  and made its streets desolate,
  as Jeremiah had foretold.[r]
7 For they had mistreated him,
  who even in the womb had been
      consecrated a prophet,
  to pluck up and ruin and destroy
  and likewise to build and to plant.

8 It was Ezekiel who saw the vision of glory,
  which God[s] showed him above the
      chariot of the cherubim.
9 For he also mentioned Job,
  who held fast to all the ways of justice.[t]
10 May the bones of the Twelve Prophets
  send forth new life from where they lie,
  for they comforted the people of Jacob
  and delivered them with confident hope.

11 How shall we magnify Zerubbabel?
  He was like a signet ring on the right
      hand,
12   and so was Jeshua son of Jozadak;
  in their days they built the house
  and raised a temple[u] holy to the Lord,
  prepared for everlasting glory.
13 The memory of Nehemiah also is lasting;
  he raised our fallen walls
  and set up gates and bars
  and rebuilt our ruined houses.

Retrospect
14 Few have[v] ever been created on earth like
      Enoch,
  for he was taken up from the earth.

---

l **48.18** Other ancient authorities add *from Lachish*
m **48.21** Gk *He*
n **48.23** Gk *his*
o **49.1** Heb: Gk *memory*
p **49.1** Heb: Gk *it*

q **49.5** Heb *He*
r **49.6** Gk *by the hand of Jeremiah*
s **49.8** Gk *He*
t **49.9** Heb Compare Syr: Meaning of Gk uncertain
u **49.12** Other ancient authorities read *people*
v **49.14** Heb Syr: Gk *No one has*

15 Nor was anyone ever born like Joseph;[w]
    even his bones were cared for.
16 Shem and Seth and Enosh were honored,[x]
    but above every other created living being
        was Adam.

Simon Son of Onias

50 The leader of his brothers and the
    pride of his people[y]
    was the high priest, Simon son of Onias,
    who in his life repaired the house
    and in his time fortified the temple.
2 He laid the foundations for the high double
        walls,
    the high retaining walls for the temple
        enclosure.
3 In his days a water cistern was dug,[z]
    a reservoir like the sea in circumference.
4 He considered how to save his people from
        ruin
    and fortified the city against siege.
5 How glorious he was as he gazed from the
        tent,[a]
    as he came out of the house of the curtain,
6 like the morning star among the clouds,
    like the full moon at the festal season,[b]
7 like the sun shining on the temple of the
        Most High,
    like the rainbow gleaming in splendid
        clouds,
8 like roses in the days of the spring harvest,
    like lilies by springs of water,
    like a green shoot on Lebanon on a
        summer day,
9 like fire and incense in the censer,
    like a vessel of hammered gold
        studded with all kinds of precious stones,
10 like an olive tree laden with fruit,
    and like a cypress towering in the clouds.
11 When he put on his glorious robe
    and clothed himself in perfect splendor,
    when he went up to the holy altar,
    he made the court of the sanctuary glorious.

12 When he received the portions from the
        hands of the priests,
    as he stood by the hearth of the altar

with a garland of brothers around him,
    he was like a young cedar on Lebanon
    surrounded by the trunks of palm trees.
13 All the sons of Aaron in their splendor
    held the Lord's offering in their hands
    before the whole congregation of Israel.
14 Finishing the service at the altars[c]
    and arranging the offering to the Most
        High, the Almighty,
15 he held out his hand for the cup
    and poured a drink offering of the blood
        of the grape;
    he poured it out at the foot of the altar,
    a pleasing odor to the Most High, the
        king of all.
16 Then the sons of Aaron shouted;
    they blew their trumpets of hammered
        metal;
    they sounded a mighty fanfare
    as a reminder before the Most High.
17 Then all the people together quickly
    fell to the ground on their faces
    to worship their Lord,
    the Almighty, God Most High.

18 Then the singers praised him with their
        voices
    in sweet and full-toned melody.[d]
19 And the people of the Lord Most High
        offered
    their prayer before the Merciful One,
    until the order of worship of the Lord was
        ended
    and they completed his ritual.
20 Then Simon[e] came down and raised his
        hands
    over the whole congregation of Israelites,
    to pronounce the blessing of the Lord with
        his lips
    and to glory in his name,
21 and they bowed down in worship a second
        time
    to receive the blessing from the Most High.

A Benediction
22 And now bless the God of all,
    who everywhere works great wonders,
    who exalts our days from birth[f]
    and deals with us according to his mercy.

---

w **49.15** Heb Syr: Gk adds *the leader of his brothers, the
    support of the people*
x **49.16** Heb: Gk *Shem and Seth were honored by people*
y **50.1** Heb Syr: Gk lacks this line.
z **50.3** Heb: Meaning of Gk uncertain
a **50.5** Heb: Gk *in his courses in the temple*
b **50.6** Heb: Meaning of Gk uncertain

c **50.14** Other ancient authorities read *altar*
d **50.18** Other ancient authorities read *in sweet melody
    throughout the house*
e **50.20** Gk *he*
f **50.22** Heb *who nurtures humankind from the womb*

23 May he give us[g] gladness of heart,
  and may there be peace in our[h] days
  in Israel, as in the days of old.
24 May he entrust to us his mercy,
  and may he deliver us in our[i] days!

Epilogue

25 Two nations my soul detests,
  and the third is not even a nation:
26 those who live in Seir[j] and the Philistines
  and the foolish people who live in
    Shechem.

27 Instruction in understanding and knowledge
  I have written in this book,
  Jesus son of Eleazar son of Sirach[k] of
    Jerusalem,
  whose mind poured forth wisdom.
28 Happy are those who concern themselves
    with these things,
  and those who lay them to heart will
    become wise.
29 For if they put them into practice, they will
    be equal to anything,
  for the fear[l] of the Lord is their path.[m]

PRAYER OF JESUS SON OF SIRACH[n]

51 I give you thanks, O Lord and King,
  and praise you, O God my Savior.
  I give thanks to your name,
2   for you have been my protector and
      helper
  and have delivered my body from destruction
    and from the trap laid by a slanderous
      tongue,
  from lips that fabricate lies.
  In the face of my adversaries,
    you have been my helper ³and delivered
      me,
  in the greatness of your mercy and of
    your name,
  from grinding teeth about to devour me,
  from the hand of those seeking my life,

from the many troubles I endured,
4 from choking fire on every side,
  and from the midst of fire that I had not
    kindled,
5 from the deep belly of Hades,
  from an unclean tongue and lying words,
6   the slander of an unrighteous tongue to
    the king.
  My soul drew near to death,
    and my life was on the brink of Hades
    below.
7 They surrounded me on every side,
  and there was no one to help me.
  I looked for human assistance,
    and there was none.
8 Then I remembered your mercy, O Lord,
  and your kindness[o] from of old,
  for you rescue those who wait for you
  and save them from the hand of their
    enemies.
9 And I sent up my prayer from the earth
  and begged for rescue from death.
10 I cried out, "Lord, you are my Father;[p]
  do not forsake me in the days of trouble,
  when there is no help against the proud.
11 I will praise your name continually
  and will sing hymns of thanksgiving."
  My prayer was heard,
12   for you saved me from destruction
  and rescued me in time of trouble.
  For this reason I thank you and praise you,
  and I bless the name of the Lord.

Heb adds:

*Give thanks to the LORD, for he is good,
  for his steadfast love endures forever.*

*Give thanks to the God of praises,
  for his steadfast love endures forever.*

*Give thanks to the guardian of Israel,
  for his steadfast love endures forever.*

*Give thanks to him who formed all things,
  for his steadfast love endures forever.*

*Give thanks to the redeemer of Israel,
  for his steadfast love endures forever.*

---

g **50.23** Other ancient authorities read *you*
h **50.23** Other ancient authorities read *your*
i **50.24** Other ancient authorities read *his*
j **50.26** Heb Compare Lat: Gk *on the mountain of
    Samaria*
k **50.27** Heb: Meaning of Gk uncertain
l **50.29** Heb: Other ancient authorities read *light*
m **50.29** Other ancient authorities add *And to the pious
    he gave wisdom. Blessed be the Lord forever. May
    it be; may it be.*
n **51.1** This title is included in the Gk text.

o **51.8** Other ancient authorities read *work*
p **51.10** Heb: Gk *the Father of my lord*

Give thanks to him who gathers the
  dispersed of Israel,
  for his steadfast love endures forever.

Give thanks to him who rebuilt his city and
  his sanctuary,
  for his steadfast love endures forever.

Give thanks to him who makes a horn to
  sprout for the house of David,
  for his steadfast love endures forever.

Give thanks to him who has chosen the sons
  of Zadok to be priests,
  for his steadfast love endures forever.

Give thanks to the shield of Abraham,
  for his steadfast love endures forever.

Give thanks to the rock of Isaac,
  for his steadfast love endures forever.

Give thanks to the mighty one of Jacob,
  for his steadfast love endures forever.

Give thanks to him who has chosen Zion,
  for his steadfast love endures forever.

Give thanks to the King of the kings of kings,
  for his steadfast love endures forever.

He has raised up a horn for his people,
  praise for all his loyal ones.

For the children of Israel, the people close to him.
  Praise the LORD!

Autobiographical Poem on Wisdom

13 While I was still young, before I went on
  my travels,
  I sought wisdom openly in my prayer.
14 Before the temple I asked for her,
  and I will search for her until the end.

15 From the first blossom to the ripening grape,
  my heart delighted in her;
  my foot walked on the straight path;
  from my youth I followed her steps.

16 I inclined my ear a little and received her,
  and I found for myself much instruction.
17 I made progress in her;
  to him who gives wisdom I will give glory.

18 For I resolved to practice wisdom,^{q}
  and I was zealous for the good,
  and I shall never be disappointed.
19 My soul grappled with wisdom,^{r}
  and in my conduct I was strict.^{s}

  I spread out my hands to the heavens
  and lamented my ignorance of her.
20 I directed my soul to her,
  and in purity I found her.

  With her I gained understanding from the
  first;
  therefore I will never be forsaken.
21 My heart was stirred to seek her;
  therefore I have gained a prize possession.
22 The Lord gave me my tongue as a reward,
  and I will praise him with it.

23 Draw near to me, you who are uneducated,
  and lodge in the house of instruction.
24 Why do you say you are lacking in these
  things,^{t}
  and why do you endure such great thirst?
25 I opened my mouth and said,
  "Acquire wisdom^u for yourselves without
  money.

26 "Put your neck under her^v yoke,
  and let your souls receive instruction;
  it is to be found close by."

27 See with your own eyes that I have labored
  but little
  and found for myself much serenity.
28 Hear but a little of my instruction,
  and through me you will acquire silver
  and gold.^{w}

29 May your soul rejoice in God's^x mercy,
  and may you never be ashamed to praise
  him.
30 Do your work in good time,
  and in his own time God^y will give you
  your reward.

---

q **51.18** Gk *her*
r **51.19** Gk *her*
s **51.19** Meaning of Gk uncertain
t **51.24** Cn Compare Heb Syr: Meaning of Gk uncertain
u **51.25** Heb: Gk lacks *wisdom*
v **51.26** Heb: other ancient authorities read *the*
w **51.28** Syr Compare Heb: Gk *Get instruction with a
  large sum of silver, and you will gain by it much gold.*
x **51.29** Gk *his*
y **51.30** Gk *he*

BARUCH

Baruch and the Jews in Babylon

1 These are the words of the book that Baruch son of Neriah son of Mahseiah son of Zedekiah son of Hasadiah son of Hilkiah wrote in Babylon, ²in the fifth year, on the seventh day of the month, at the time when the Chaldeans took Jerusalem and burned it with fire.

3 Baruch read the words of this book to Jeconiah son of Jehoiakim, king of Judah, and to all the people who came to hear the book ⁴and to the nobles and the princes and to the elders and to all the people, small and great, all who lived in Babylon by the River Sud.

5 Then they wept and fasted and prayed before the Lord; ⁶they collected as much silver as each could give ⁷and sent it to Jerusalem to the priest Jehoiakim son of Hilkiah son of Shallum the priest and to the priests and to all the people who were present with him in Jerusalem. ⁸At the same time, on the tenth day of Sivan, Baruch*ᵃ* took the vessels of the house of the Lord that had been carried away from the temple, to return them to the land of Judah—the silver vessels that Zedekiah son of Josiah, king of Judah, had made ⁹after King Nebuchadnezzar of Babylon had carried away from Jerusalem Jeconiah and the princes and the prisoners and the nobles and the people of the land and brought them to Babylon.

A Letter to Jerusalem

10 They said, "Here we send you silver, so buy with the silver burnt offerings and for sin and incense, and prepare a grain offering, and offer them on the altar of the Lord our God, ¹¹and pray for the life of King Nebuchadnezzar of Babylon and for the life of his son Belshazzar, so that their days on earth may be like the days of heaven. ¹²The Lord will give us strength and light to our eyes; we shall live under the protection*ᵇ* of King Nebuchadnezzar of Babylon and

under the protection of his son Belshazzar, and we shall serve them many days and find favor in their sight. ¹³Pray also for us to the Lord our God, for we have sinned against the Lord our God, and to this day the anger of the Lord and his wrath have not turned away from us. ¹⁴And you shall read aloud this scroll that we are sending you, to make your confession in the house of the Lord on the days of the festivals and at appointed seasons.

Confession of Sins

15 "And you shall say: To the Lord our God belongs righteousness, but to us, this day, public shame, on the people of Judah, on the inhabitants of Jerusalem, ¹⁶and on our kings, our rulers, our priests, our prophets, and our ancestors, ¹⁷because we have sinned before the Lord. ¹⁸We have disobeyed him and have not heeded the voice of the Lord our God, to walk in the statutes of the Lord that he set before us. ¹⁹From the time when the Lord brought our ancestors out of the land of Egypt until today, we have been disobedient to the Lord our God, and we have been negligent in not listening to his voice. ²⁰So to this day there have clung to us the calamities and the curse that the Lord declared through his servant Moses at the time when he brought our ancestors out of the land of Egypt to give to us a land flowing with milk and honey. ²¹We did not listen to the voice of the Lord our God in all the words of the prophets whom he sent to us, ²²but all of us followed the intent of our own wicked hearts by serving other gods and doing what is evil in the sight of the Lord our God.

2 "So the Lord carried out the threat*ᶜ* he spoke against us: against our judges who ruled Israel and against our kings and our rulers and the people of Israel and Judah. ²Under the whole heaven there has not been done the like of what he has done in Jerusalem, in accordance with what is written in the law of Moses, ³that

---

a 1.8 Gk *he*
b 1.12 Gk *in the shadow*

c 2.1 Gk *word*

we would each eat the flesh of our sons and the flesh of our daughters. ⁴ He made them subject to all the kingdoms around us, to be an object of scorn and a desolation among all the surrounding peoples, where the Lord has scattered them. ⁵ They were brought down and not raised up, because we sinned against the Lord our God and did not listen to his voice.

6 "To the Lord our God belongs righteousness, but to us, this day, open shame. ⁷ All those calamities with which the Lord threatened us have come upon us. ⁸ Yet we have not entreated the favor of the Lord by turning away, each of us, from the thoughts of our wicked hearts. ⁹ And the Lord has kept the calamities ready, and the Lord has brought them upon us, for the Lord is just in all the works that he has commanded us to do. ¹⁰ Yet we have not obeyed his voice, to walk in the statutes of the Lord that he set before us.

Prayer for Deliverance

11 "And now, O Lord God of Israel, who brought your people out of the land of Egypt with a mighty hand and with signs and wonders and with great power and outstretched arm and made yourself a name that continues to this day, ¹² we have sinned, we have been ungodly, we have done wrong, O Lord our God, against all your ordinances. ¹³ Let your anger turn away from us, for we are left few in number among the nations where you have scattered us. ¹⁴ Hear, O Lord, our prayer and our entreaty, and for your own sake deliver us and grant us favor in the sight of those who have carried us into exile, ¹⁵ so that all the earth may know that you are the Lord our God, for Israel and his descendants are called by your name.

16 "O Lord, look down from your holy dwelling and consider us. Incline your ear, O Lord, and hear; ¹⁷ open your eyes, O Lord, and see, for the dead who are in Hades, whose spirit has been taken from their bodies, will not ascribe glory or justice to the Lord, ¹⁸ but the person who is deeply grieved, who walks bowed and feeble, with failing eyes and famished soul, will declare your glory and righteousness, O Lord.

19 "For it is not because of any righteous deeds of our ancestors or our kings that we bring before you our prayer for mercy, O Lord our God. ²⁰ For you have sent your anger and your wrath upon us, as you declared by your servants the prophets, saying: ²¹ 'Thus says the Lord: Bend your shoulders and serve the king of Babylon, and you will remain in the land that I gave to your ancestors. ²² But if you will not obey the voice of the Lord and will not serve the king of Babylon, ²³ I will silence from the towns of Judah and from the region around Jerusalem the voice of joy and the voice of gladness, the voice of the bridegroom and the voice of the bride, and the whole land will be a desolation without inhabitants.'

24 "But we did not obey your voice to serve the king of Babylon, and you have carried out your threats^d that you spoke by your servants the prophets, that the bones of our kings and the bones of our ancestors would be brought out of their resting place, ²⁵ and indeed they have been thrown out to the heat of day and the frost of night. They perished in great misery, by famine and sword and pestilence. ²⁶ And the house that is called by your name you have made as it is today because of the wickedness of the house of Israel and the house of Judah.

God's Promise Recalled

27 "Yet you have dealt with us, O Lord our God, in all your kindness and in all your great compassion, ²⁸ as you spoke by your servant Moses on the day when you commanded him to write your law in the presence of the people of Israel, saying, ²⁹ 'If you will not obey my voice, this very great multitude will surely turn into a small number among the nations, where I will scatter them. ³⁰ For I know that they will not obey me, for they are a stiff-necked people. But in the land of their exile they will have a change of heart ³¹ and know that I am the Lord their God. I will give them a heart that obeys and ears that hear; ³² they will praise me in the land of their exile and will remember my name ³³ and turn from their stubbornness and their wicked deeds, for they will remember the ways of their ancestors, who sinned before the Lord. ³⁴ I will bring them again into the land that I swore to give to their ancestors, to Abraham, Isaac, and Jacob, and they will rule over it, and I will increase them, and they will not be diminished. ³⁵ I will make an everlasting covenant with them to be their God, and they shall be my people, and I will never again remove my people Israel from the land that I have given them.'

3 "O Lord Almighty, God of Israel, the soul in anguish and the wearied spirit cry out to you. ² Hear, O Lord, and have mercy, for we have sinned before you. ³ For you are enthroned

---

d 2.24 Gk *words*

forever, and we are perishing forever. ⁴O Lord Almighty, God of Israel, hear now the prayer of those of Israel who have died and of the children of those who sinned before you, who did not heed the voice of the Lord their God, so that calamities have clung to us. ⁵Do not remember the iniquities of our ancestors, but in this crisis remember your power and your name. ⁶For you are the Lord our God, and it is you, O Lord, whom we will praise. ⁷For you have put the fear of you in our hearts so that we would call upon your name, and we will praise you in our exile, for we have put away from our hearts all the iniquity of our ancestors who sinned against you. ⁸See, we are today in our exile where you have scattered us, to be reproached and cursed and punished for all the iniquities of our ancestors, who forsook the Lord our God."

In Praise of Wisdom

9 Hear, O Israel, the commandments of life;
  give ear and learn wisdom!
10 Why is it, O Israel, why is it that you are in
    the land of your enemies,
  that you are growing old in a foreign land,
11 that you are defiled with the dead,
    that you are counted among those in
    Hades?
12 You have forsaken the fountain of wisdom.
13 If you had walked in the way of God,
  you would be living in peace forever.
14 Learn where there is wisdom,
  where there is strength,
  where there is understanding,
  so that you may at the same time discern
  where there is length of days and life,
  where there is light for the eyes and
    peace.

15 Who has found her place,
  and who has entered her storehouses?
16 Where are the rulers of the nations
    and those who lorded it over the animals
    on earth;
17 those who made sport of the birds of the air
    and who hoarded up silver and gold
  in which people trust,
    and there is no end to their getting;
18 those who schemed to get silver and were
    anxious,
  but there is no trace of their works?
19 They have vanished and gone down to
    Hades,
  and others have arisen in their place.

20 Younger people have seen the light of day
    and have lived upon the earth,
  but they have not learned the way to
    knowledge,
  nor understood her paths,
  nor laid hold of her.
21 Their descendants have strayed far from
    theirᵉ way.
22 She has not been heard of in Canaan
  or seen in Teman;
23 the descendants of Hagar, who seek for
    understanding on the earth,
    the merchants of Merran and Teman,
    the storytellers and the seekers for
    understanding,
  have not learned the way to wisdom
  or given thought to her paths.

24 O Israel, how great is the house of God,
  how vast the territory that he possesses!
25 It is great and has no bounds;
  it is high and immeasurable.
26 The giants were born there, who were
    famous of old,
  great in stature, expert in war.
27 God did not choose them
  or give them the way to knowledge,
28 so they perished because they had no
    wisdom;
  they perished through their folly.

29 Who has gone up into heaven and taken
    her
  and brought her down from the clouds?
30 Who has gone over the sea and found her
  and will buy her for pure gold?
31 No one knows the way to her
  or is concerned about the path to her.
32 But the one who knows all things knows
    her;
  he found her by his understanding.
  The one who prepared the earth for all time
  filled it with four-footed creatures;
33 the one who sends forth the light and it
    goes,
  he called it, and it obeyed him, trembling;
34 the stars shone in their watches and were
    glad;
35 he called them, and they said, "Here we
    are!"
  They shone with gladness for him who
    made them.

---

e 3.21 Gk: Syr her

³⁶ This is our God;
  no other can be compared to him.
³⁷ He found the whole way to knowledge
  and gave her to his servant Jacob
  and to Israel, whom he loved.
³⁸ Afterward she appeared on earth
  and lived with humankind.

4 She is the book of the commandments of
    God,
  the law that endures forever.
  All who hold her fast will live,
  and those who forsake her will die.
² Turn, O Jacob, and take her;
  walk toward the shining of her light.
³ Do not give your glory to another
  or your advantages to a foreign nation.
⁴ Happy are we, O Israel,
  for we know what is pleasing to God.

Encouragement for Israel

⁵ Take courage, my people,
  who perpetuate Israel's name!
⁶ It was not for destruction
  that you were sold to the nations,
  but you were handed over to your enemies
  because you angered God.
⁷ For you provoked the one who made you
  by sacrificing to demons and not to God.
⁸ You forgot the everlasting God, who
    brought you up,
  and you grieved Jerusalem, who reared
    you.
⁹ For she saw the wrath that came upon you
    from God,
  and she said:
  "Listen, you neighbors of Zion;
  God has brought great sorrow upon me,
¹⁰ for I have seen the exile of my sons and
    daughters,
  which the Everlasting brought upon
    them.
¹¹ With joy I nurtured them,
  but I sent them away with weeping and
    sorrow.
¹² Let no one rejoice over me, a widow
  and bereaved of many;
  I was left desolate because of the sins of my
    children,
  because they turned away from the law
    of God.
¹³ They had no regard for his statutes;
  they did not walk in the ways of God's
    commandments

or tread the paths his righteousness
  showed them.
¹⁴ Let the neighbors of Zion come;
  remember the capture of my sons and
    daughters,
  which the Everlasting brought upon
    them.
¹⁵ For he brought a distant nation against
    them,
  a nation ruthless and of a strange
    language,
  which had no respect for the aged
  and no pity for a child.
¹⁶ They led away the widow's beloved sons
  and bereaved the lonely woman of her
    daughters.

¹⁷ "But I, how can I help you?
¹⁸ For he who brought these calamities
  will deliver you from the hand of your
    enemies.
¹⁹ Go, my children, go,
  for I have been left desolate.
²⁰ I have taken off the robe of peace
  and put on sackcloth for my supplication;
  I will cry to the Everlasting all my days.

²¹ "Take courage, my children, cry to God,
  and he will deliver you from the power
  and hand of the enemy.
²² For I have put my hope in the Everlasting
    to save you,
  and joy has come to me from the Holy
    One,
  because of the mercy that will soon come
    to you
  from your everlasting savior.ᶠ
²³ For I sent you out with sorrow and
    weeping,
  but God will give you back to me with joy
  and gladness forever.
²⁴ For as the neighbors of Zion have now seen
    your capture,
  so they soon will see your salvation by
    God,
  which will come to you with great glory
  and with the splendor of the Everlasting.
²⁵ My children, endure with patience the wrath
    that has come upon you from God.
  Your enemy has overtaken you,
  but you will soon see their destruction
  and will tread upon their necks.

_____
ᶠ 4.22 Or *from the Everlasting, your savior*

26 My pampered children have traveled rough
      roads;
   they were taken away like a flock carried
      off by the enemy.

27 "Take courage, my children, and cry to
      God,
   for you will be remembered by the one
      who brought this upon you.
28 For just as you were disposed to go astray
      from God,
   return with tenfold zeal to seek him.
29 For the one who brought these calamities
      upon you
   will bring you everlasting joy with your
      salvation."

Jerusalem Is Assured of Help
30 Take courage, O Jerusalem,
   for the one who named you will comfort
      you.
31 Wretched will be those who mistreated
      you
   and who rejoiced at your fall.
32 Wretched will be the cities that your
      children served as slaves;
   wretched will be the city that received
      your offspring.
33 For just as she rejoiced at your fall
   and was glad for your ruin,
   so she will be grieved at her own
      desolation.
34 I will take away her pride in her great
      population,
   and her insolence will be turned to grief.
35 For fire will come upon her from the
      Everlasting for many days,
   and for a long time she will be inhabited
      by demons.

36 Look toward the east, O Jerusalem,
   and see the joy that is coming to you from
      God.

37 Look, your children are coming, whom you
      sent away;
   they are coming, gathered from east and
      west,
   at the word of the Holy One,
   rejoicing in the glory of God.

5 Take off the garment of your sorrow and
      affliction, O Jerusalem,
   and put on forever the beauty of the glory
      from God.
2 Put on the robe of the righteousness that
      comes from God;
   put on your head the diadem of the glory
      of the Everlasting,
3 for God will show your splendor
      everywhere under heaven,
4 for God will give you evermore the name,
   "Righteous Peace, Godly Glory."

5 Arise, O Jerusalem, stand upon the height;
   look toward the east,
   and see your children gathered from west
      and east
   at the word of the Holy One,
   rejoicing that God has remembered them.
6 For they went out from you on foot,
   led away by their enemies,
   but God will bring them back to you,
   carried in glory, as on a royal throne.
7 For God has ordered that every high
      mountain and the everlasting hills be
      made low
   and the valleys filled up, to make level
      ground,
   so that Israel may walk safely in the glory
      of God.
8 The woods and every fragrant tree
   have shaded Israel at God's command.
9 For God will lead Israel with joy,
   in the light of his glory,
   with the mercy and righteousness that
      come from him.

THE LETTER OF JEREMIAH

A copy of a letter that Jeremiah sent to those who were to be taken to Babylon as exiles by the king of the Babylonians, to give them the message that God had commanded him.

The People Face a Long Captivity

1 Because of the sins that you have committed before God, you will be taken to Babylon as exiles by Nebuchadnezzar, king of the Babylonians. ²Therefore when you have come to Babylon you will remain there for many years, for a long time, up to seven generations; after that I will bring you away from there in peace. ³Now in Babylon you will see gods made of silver and gold and wood that people carry on their shoulders and that cause the nations to fear. ⁴So beware of becoming at all like the foreigners or of letting fear of these gods*a* possess you ⁵when you see the multitude before and behind them worshiping them. But say in your heart, "It is you, O Lord, whom we must worship." ⁶For my angel is with you, and he is watching over your lives.

The Helplessness of Idols

7 Their tongues are smoothed by the carpenter, and they themselves are overlaid with gold and silver, but they are false and cannot speak. ⁸People*b* take gold and make crowns for the heads of their gods, as they might for a young woman who loves ornaments. ⁹Sometimes the priests secretly take gold and silver from their gods and spend it on themselves ¹⁰or even give some of it to the prostitutes on the terrace. They deck their gods*c* out with garments like humans—these gods of silver and gold and wood ¹¹that cannot save themselves from rust and decay.*d* When they have been dressed in purple robes, ¹²their faces are wiped because of the dust from the temple, which is thick upon them. ¹³One of them holds a scepter like a district judge but is unable to destroy anyone who offends it. ¹⁴Another has a dagger in its right hand and an ax but cannot defend itself from war and robbers. ¹⁵From this it is evident that they are not gods, so do not fear them.

16 For just as someone's dish is useless when it is broken, ¹⁷so are their gods when they have been set up in the temples. Their eyes are full of the dust raised by the feet of those who enter. And just as the gates are shut on every side against anyone who has offended a king, as though under sentence of death, so the priests make their temples secure with doors and locks and bars in order that they may not be plundered by robbers. ¹⁸They light more lamps for them than they light for themselves, though their gods*e* can see none of them. ¹⁹They are*f* just like a beam of the temple, but their hearts, it is said, are eaten away when crawling creatures from the earth devour them and their robes. They do not notice ²⁰when their faces have been blackened by the smoke of the temple. ²¹Bats, swallows, and birds alight on their bodies and heads, and so do cats. ²²From this you will know that they are not gods, so do not fear them.

23 As for the gold that they wear for beauty, it*g* will not shine unless someone wipes off the tarnish, for even when they were being cast, they did not feel it. ²⁴They are bought without regard to cost, but there is no breath in them. ²⁵Having no feet, they are carried on the shoulders of others, revealing to humans their worthlessness. And those who serve them are put to shame ²⁶because, if any of these gods falls*h* to the ground, they themselves must pick it up. If anyone sets it upright, it cannot move itself, and if it is tipped over, it cannot straighten itself. Gifts are placed before them just as before

---

a **4** Gk *for them*
b **8** Gk *They*
c **10** Gk *them*
d **11** Gk *food*

e **18** Gk *they*
f **19** Gk *It is*
g **23** Lat Syr: Gk *they*
h **26** Gk *if they fall*

the dead. 27The priests sell the sacrifices that are offered to these gods[i] and use the money themselves. Likewise their wives preserve some of the meat[j] with salt but give none to the poor or helpless. 28Sacrifices to them may even be touched by women during their periods or after giving birth. Since you know by these things that they are not gods, do not fear them.

29For how can they be called gods? Women serve meals for gods of silver and gold and wood, 30and in their temples the priests sit with their clothes torn, their heads and beards shaved, and their heads uncovered. 31They howl and shout before their gods as some do at a funeral banquet. 32The priests take some of the clothing of their gods[k] to clothe their wives and children. 33Whether one does evil to them or good, they will not be able to repay it. They cannot set up a king or depose one. 34Likewise, they are not able to give either wealth or money; if one makes a vow to them and does not keep it, they will not require it. 35They cannot save anyone from death or rescue the weak from the strong. 36They cannot restore sight to the blind; they cannot rescue one who is in distress. 37They cannot take pity on a widow or do good to an orphan. 38These things that are made of wood and overlaid with gold and silver are like stones from the mountain, and those who serve them will be put to shame. 39Why then must anyone think that they are gods or call them gods?

The Foolishness of Worshiping Idols

Besides, even the Chaldeans themselves dishonor them, for when they see someone who cannot speak, they bring Bel and pray that the mute may speak, as though Bel[l] were able to understand! 40Yet they themselves cannot perceive this and abandon them, for they have no sense. 41And the women, with cords around them, sit along the passageways, burning bran for incense. 42When one of them is led off by one of the passers-by and is taken to bed by him, she derides the woman next to her because she was not as attractive as herself and her cord was not broken. 43Whatever is done for these idols[m] is false. Why then must anyone think that they are gods or call them gods?

44They are made by carpenters and goldsmiths; they can be nothing but what the artisans wish them to be. 45Those who make them will certainly not live very long themselves; 46how then can the things that are made by them be gods? They have left only lies and reproach for those who come after. 47For when war or calamity comes upon them, the priests consult together as to where they can hide themselves and their gods.[n] 48How then can one fail to see that these are not gods, for they cannot save themselves from war or calamity? 49Since they are made of wood and overlaid with gold and silver, it will afterward be known that they are false. 50It will be manifest to all the nations and kings that they are not gods but the work of human hands and that there is no work of God in them. 51Who, then, does not know that they are not gods?

52For they cannot set up a king over a country or give rain to people. 53They cannot judge their own cause or deliver one who is wronged, for they have no power; 54they are like crows between heaven and earth. When fire breaks out in a temple of wooden gods overlaid with gold or silver, their priests will flee and escape, but the gods[o] will be burned up like timbers. 55Besides, they can offer no resistance to king or enemy. Why then must anyone admit or think that they are gods?

56Gods made of wood and overlaid with silver and gold are unable to save themselves from thieves or robbers. 57Anyone who can will strip them of their gold and silver and of the robes they wear and go off with this plunder, and they will not be able to help themselves. 58So it is better to be a king who shows his courage or a household utensil that serves its owner's need than to be these false gods, better even the door of a house that protects its contents than these false gods, better also a wooden pillar in a palace than these false gods.

59For sun and moon and stars are bright and, when sent to do a service, they are obedient. 60So also the lightning when it flashes is widely seen, and the wind likewise blows in every land. 61When God commands the clouds to go over the whole world, they carry out his command. 62And the fire sent from above to consume mountains and woods does what it is ordered. But these idols[p] are not to be compared

---

i 27 Gk *to them*
j 27 Gk *of them*
k 32 Gk *some of their clothing*
l 39 Gk *he*
m 43 Gk *them*

---

n 47 Gk *them*
o 54 Gk *they*
p 62 Gk *these things*

with them in appearance or power. 63 Therefore one must not think that they are gods nor call them gods, for they are unable either to decide a case or to do good to anyone. 64 Since you know, then, that they are not gods, do not fear them.

65 They can neither curse nor bless kings; 66 they cannot show signs in the heavens for the nations or shine like the sun or give light like the moon. 67 The wild animals are better than they are, for they can flee to shelter and help themselves. 68 So we have no evidence whatever that they are gods; therefore do not fear them.

69 Like a scarecrow in a cucumber bed that guards nothing, so are their gods of wood, overlaid with gold and silver. 70 In the same way, their gods of wood, overlaid with gold and silver, are like a thornbush in a garden on which every bird perches or like a corpse thrown out in the darkness. 71 From the purple and linen*q* that rot upon them you will know that they are not gods, and they will finally be consumed themselves and be a reproach in the land. 72 Better, therefore, is someone upright who has no idols; such a person will be far above reproach.

---

q 71 Cn: Gk *marble*, Syr *silk*

The Prayer of

AZARIAH

and the Song of the Three Jews

(Additions to Daniel, inserted
between 3.23 and 3.24)

The Prayer of Azariah in the Furnace

1 They walked around in the midst of the
flames, singing hymns to God and blessing the
Lord. 2 Then Azariah stood still in the fire and
prayed aloud:

3 "Blessed are you, O Lord, God of our
    ancestors, and worthy of praise,
  and glorious is your name forever!
4 For you are just in all you have done;
  all your works are true and your ways
    right,
  and all your judgments are true.
5 You have executed true judgments in all
    you have brought upon us
  and upon Jerusalem, the holy city of our
    ancestors;
  by a true judgment you have brought all
    this upon us because of our sins.
6 For we have sinned and broken your law in
    turning away from you;
  in all matters we have sinned grievously.
7 We have not obeyed your commandments;
  we have not kept them or done what
    you have commanded us for our own
    good.
8 So all that you have brought upon us
  and all that you have done to us,
  you have done by a true judgment.
9 You have handed us over to our enemies,
  lawless and hateful rebels,
  and to an unjust king, the most wicked in
    all the world.
10 And now we cannot open our mouths;
  we, your servants who worship you, bear
    shame and reproach.

11 For your name's sake do not give us up
    forever,
  and do not annul your covenant.
12 Do not withdraw your mercy from us,
for the sake of Abraham your beloved
  and for the sake of Isaac your servant
  and Israel your holy one,
13 to whom you promised
  to multiply their descendants like the
    stars of heaven
  and like the sand on the shore of the sea.
14 For we, O Lord, have become fewer than
    any other nation
  and are brought low this day in all the
    world because of our sins.
15 In our day we have no ruler, or prophet, or
    leader,
  no burnt offering, or sacrifice, or oblation,
    or incense,
  no place to make an offering before you
    and to find mercy.
16 Yet with a contrite heart and a humble
    spirit may we be accepted,
17 as though it were with burnt offerings of
    rams and bulls
  or with tens of thousands of fat lambs;
  such may our sacrifice be in your sight
    today,
  and may we unreservedly follow you,*a*
  for no shame will come to those who
    trust in you.
18 And now with all our heart we follow you;
  we fear you and seek your presence.
19 Do not put us to shame,
  but deal with us in your patience
  and in your abundant mercy.

---

a 17 Meaning of Gk uncertain

20 Deliver us in accordance with your
    marvelous works,
    and bring glory to your name, O Lord.
21 Let all who do harm to your servants be
    put to shame;
    let them be disgraced and deprived of all
    power,
    and let their strength be broken.
22 Let them know that you alone are the Lord
    God,
    glorious over the whole world."

The Song of the Three Jews

23 Now the king's servants who threw them in kept stoking the furnace with naphtha, pitch, tinder, and brushwood. 24 And the flames poured out above the furnace forty-nine cubits 25 and spread out and burned those Chaldeans who were caught near the furnace. 26 But the angel of the Lord came down into the furnace to be with Azariah and his companions and drove the fiery flame out of the furnace 27 and made the inside of the furnace as though a moist wind were whistling through it. The fire did not touch them at all and caused them no pain or distress.

28 Then the three with one voice praised and glorified and blessed God in the furnace:
29 "Blessed are you, O Lord, God of our
    ancestors,
    and to be praised and highly exalted
    forever;
    And blessed is your glorious, holy name,
    and to be highly praised and highly
    exalted forever.
30 Blessed are you in the temple of your holy
    glory,
    and to be extolled and highly glorified
    forever.
31 Blessed are you who look into the depths
    from your throne on the cherubim,
    and to be praised and highly exalted
    forever.
32 Blessed are you on the throne of your
    kingdom,
    and to be extolled and highly exalted
    forever.
33 Blessed are you in the firmament of heaven,
    and to be sung and glorified forever.

34 "Bless the Lord, all you works of the Lord;
    sing praise to him and highly exalt him
    forever.
35 Bless the Lord, you heavens;

    sing praise to him and highly exalt him
    forever.
36 Bless the Lord, you angels of the Lord;
    sing praise to him and highly exalt him
    forever.
37 Bless the Lord, all you waters above the
    heavens;
    sing praise to him and highly exalt him
    forever.
38 Bless the Lord, all you powers of the Lord;
    sing praise to him and highly exalt him
    forever.
39 Bless the Lord, sun and moon;
    sing praise to him and highly exalt him
    forever.
40 Bless the Lord, stars of heaven;
    sing praise to him and highly exalt him
    forever.

41 "Bless the Lord, all rain and dew;
    sing praise to him and highly exalt him
    forever.
42 Bless the Lord, all you winds;
    sing praise to him and highly exalt him
    forever.
43 Bless the Lord, fire and heat;
    sing praise to him and highly exalt him
    forever.
44 Bless the Lord, winter cold and summer
    heat;
    sing praise to him and highly exalt him
    forever.
45 Bless the Lord, dews and falling snow;
    sing praise to him and highly exalt him
    forever.
46 Bless the Lord, nights and days;
    sing praise to him and highly exalt him
    forever.
47 Bless the Lord, light and darkness;
    sing praise to him and highly exalt him
    forever.
48 Bless the Lord, ice and cold;
    sing praise to him and highly exalt him
    forever.
49 Bless the Lord, frosts and snows;
    sing praise to him and highly exalt him
    forever.
50 Bless the Lord, lightnings and clouds;
    sing praise to him and highly exalt him
    forever.

51 "Let the earth bless the Lord;
    let it sing praise to him and highly exalt
    him forever.

52 Bless the Lord, mountains and hills;
　　sing praise to him and highly exalt him
　　　forever.
53 Bless the Lord, all that grows in the ground;
　　sing praise to him and highly exalt him
　　　forever.
54 Bless the Lord, seas and rivers;
　　sing praise to him and highly exalt him
　　　forever.
55 Bless the Lord, you springs;
　　sing praise to him and highly exalt him
　　　forever.
56 Bless the Lord, you sea monsters and all
　　　that swim in the waters;
　　sing praise to him and highly exalt him
　　　forever.
57 Bless the Lord, all birds of the air;
　　sing praise to him and highly exalt him
　　　forever.
58 Bless the Lord, all wild animals and cattle;
　　sing praise to him and highly exalt him
　　　forever.

59 "Bless the Lord, all people on earth;
　　sing praise to him and highly exalt him
　　　forever.
60 Bless the Lord, O Israel;
　　sing praise to him and highly exalt him
　　　forever.
61 Bless the Lord, you priests of the Lord;

　　sing praise to him and highly exalt him
　　　forever.
62 Bless the Lord, you servants of the Lord;
　　sing praise to him and highly exalt him
　　　forever.
63 Bless the Lord, spirits and souls of the
　　　righteous;
　　sing praise to him and highly exalt him
　　　forever.
64 Bless the Lord, you who are holy and
　　　humble in heart;
　　sing praise to him and highly exalt him
　　　forever.

65 "Bless the Lord, Hananiah, Azariah, and
　　　Mishael;
　　sing praise to him and highly exalt him
　　　forever.
For he has rescued us from Hades and
　　　saved us from the power[b] of death
and delivered us from the midst of the
　　　burning fiery furnace;
from the midst of the fire he has delivered
　　　us.
66 Give thanks to the Lord, for he is good,
　　for his mercy endures forever.
67 All who worship the Lord, bless the God of
　　　gods,
　　sing praise to him and give thanks to him,
　　for his mercy endures forever."

---

b 65 Gk *hand*

SUSANNA

(Chapter 13 of the Greek Version of Daniel)

Susanna's Beauty Attracts Two Elders

1 There was a man living in Babylon whose name was Joakim. 2 He married the daughter of Hilkiah, named Susanna, a very beautiful woman and one who feared the Lord. 3 Her parents were righteous and had trained their daughter according to the law of Moses. 4 Joakim was very rich and had a fine garden adjoining his house; the Jews used to come to him because he was the most honored of them all.

5 That year two elders from the people were appointed as judges. Concerning them the Lord had said: "Wickedness came forth from Babylon, from elders who were judges, who were supposed to govern the people." 6 These men were frequently at Joakim's house, and all who had a case to be tried came to them there.

7 When the people left at noon, Susanna would go into her husband's garden to walk. 8 Every day the two elders used to see her, going in and walking about, and they began to lust for her. 9 They suppressed their consciences and turned away their eyes from looking to heaven or remembering their duty to administer justice. 10 Both were overwhelmed with passion for her, but they did not tell each other of their distress, 11 for they were ashamed to disclose their lustful desire to have intercourse with her. 12 Day after day they watched eagerly to see her.

13 One day they said to each other, "Let us go home, for it is time for lunch." So they both left and parted from each other. 14 But turning back, they met again, and when each pressed the other for the reason, they confessed their lust. Then together they arranged for a time when they could find her alone.

The Elders Threaten Susanna

15 Once, while they were watching for an opportune day, she went in as before with only two maids and wished to bathe in the garden, for it was a hot day. 16 No one was there except the two elders, who had hidden themselves and were watching her. 17 She said to her maids, "Bring me olive oil and ointments, and shut the garden doors so that I can bathe." 18 They did as she told them: they shut the doors of the garden and went out by the side doors to bring what they had been commanded; they did not see the elders because they were hiding.

19 When the maids had gone out, the two elders got up and ran to her. 20 They said, "Look, the garden doors are shut, and no one can see us. We are burning with desire for you, so give your consent, and lie with us. 21 If you refuse, we will testify against you that a young man was with you, and this was why you sent your maids away."

22 Susanna groaned and said, "I am completely trapped. For if I do this, it will mean death for me; if I do not, I cannot escape your hands. 23 I choose not to do it; I will fall into your hands rather than sin in the sight of the Lord."

24 Then Susanna cried out with a loud voice, and the two elders shouted against her. 25 And one of them ran and opened the garden doors. 26 When the people in the house heard the shouting in the garden, they rushed in at the side door to see what had happened to her. 27 And when the elders told their story, the servants felt very much ashamed, for nothing like this had ever been said about Susanna.

The Elders Testify against Susanna

28 The next day, when the people gathered at the house of her husband Joakim, the two elders came, full of their wicked plot to have Susanna put to death. In the presence of the people they said, 29 "Send for Susanna daughter of Hilkiah, the wife of Joakim." 30 So they sent for her. And she came with her parents, her children, and all her relatives.

31 Now Susanna was a woman of great refinement and beautiful in appearance. 32 As she was veiled, the scoundrels ordered her to be unveiled, so that they might feast their eyes on her beauty. 33 Those who were with her and all who saw her were weeping.

34 Then the two elders stood up before the people and laid their hands on her head. 35 Through her tears she looked up toward heaven, for her heart trusted in the Lord. 36 The elders said, "While we were walking in the garden alone, this woman came in with two maids, shut the garden doors, and dismissed the maids. 37 Then a young man who was hiding there came to her and was intimate with her. 38 We were in a corner of the garden, and when we saw this wickedness we ran to them. 39 Although we saw him have intercourse with her, we could not hold the man because he was stronger than we, and he opened the doors and got away. 40 We did, however, seize this woman and asked who the young man was, 41 but she would not tell us. These things we testify."

Because they were elders of the people and judges, the assembly believed them and condemned her to death.

42 Then Susanna cried out with a loud voice and said, "O eternal God, you know what is secret and are aware of all things before they come to be; 43 you know that these men have given false evidence against me. And now I am to die, though I have done none of the wicked things that they have charged against me!"

44 The Lord heard her cry. 45 Just as she was being led off to execution, God stirred up the holy spirit of a young man named Daniel, 46 and he shouted with a loud voice, "I want no part in shedding this woman's blood!"

Daniel Rescues Susanna

47 All the people turned to him and asked, "What is this you are saying?" 48 Taking his stand among them he said, "Are you such fools, O Israelites, as to condemn a daughter of Israel without examination and without learning the facts? 49 Return to court, for these men have given false evidence against her."

50 So all the people hurried back. And the rest of the[a] elders said to him, "Come, sit among us and inform us, for God has given you the standing of an elder." 51 Daniel said to them,

"Separate them far from each other, and I will examine them."

52 When they were separated from each other, he summoned one of them and said to him, "You old relic of wicked days, your sins have now come home, which you have committed in the past, 53 pronouncing unjust judgments, condemning the innocent and acquitting the guilty, though the Lord said, 'You shall not put an innocent and righteous person to death.' 54 Now then, if you really saw this woman, tell me this: Under what tree did you see them being intimate with each other?" He answered, "Under a mastic tree."[b] 55 And Daniel said, "Very well! This lie has cost you your head, for the angel of God has received the sentence from God and will immediately cut[c] you in two."

56 Then, putting him to one side, he ordered them to bring the other. And he said to him, "You offspring of Canaan and not of Judah, beauty has beguiled you and lust has perverted your heart. 57 This is how you have been treating the daughters of Israel, and they were intimate with you through fear, but a daughter of Judah would not tolerate your wickedness. 58 Now then, tell me: Under what tree did you catch them being intimate with each other?" He answered, "Under an evergreen oak."[d] 59 Daniel said to him, "Very well! This lie has cost you also your head, for the angel of God is waiting with his sword to split[e] you in two, so as to destroy you both."

60 Then the whole assembly raised a great shout and blessed God, who saves those who hope in him. 61 And they took action against the two elders because out of their own mouths Daniel had convicted them of bearing false witness; they did to them as they had wickedly planned to do to their neighbor. 62 Acting in accordance with the law of Moses, they put them to death. Thus innocent blood was spared that day.

63 Hilkiah and his wife praised God for their daughter Susanna, and so did her husband Joakim and all her relatives, because she was found innocent of a shameful deed. 64 And from that day onward Daniel had a great reputation among the people.

---

b 54 The Greek words for *mastic tree* and *cut* are
    similar
c 55 The Greek words for *mastic tree* and *cut* are similar
d 58 The Greek words for *evergreen oak* and *split* are
    similar
e 59 The Greek words for *evergreen oak* and *split* are
    similar

---

a 50 Gk lacks *rest of the*

BEL AND THE DRAGON

(Chapter 14 of the Greek Version of Daniel)

Daniel and the Priests of Bel

1 When King Astyages was laid to rest with his ancestors, Cyrus the Persian succeeded to his kingdom. 2 Daniel was a companion of the king and was the most honored of all his Friends.

3 Now the Babylonians had an idol called Bel, and every day they provided for it twelve bushels of choice flour and forty sheep and six measures of wine. 4 The king revered it and went every day to worship it. But Daniel worshiped his own God.

So the king said to him, "Why do you not worship Bel?" 5 He answered, "Because I do not revere idols made with hands but the living God, who created heaven and earth and has dominion over all living creatures."

6 The king said to him, "Do you not think that Bel is a living god? Do you not see how much he eats and drinks every day?" 7 And Daniel laughed and said, "Do not be deceived, O king, for this thing is only clay inside and bronze outside, and it has never eaten or drunk anything."

8 Then the king was angry and called the priests of Bel*a* and said to them, "If you do not tell me who is eating these provisions, you shall die. 9 But if you prove that Bel is eating them, Daniel shall die because he has spoken blasphemy against Bel." Daniel said to the king, "Let it be done as you have said."

10 Now there were seventy priests of Bel, besides their wives and children. So the king went with Daniel into the temple of Bel. 11 The priests of Bel said, "See, we are now going outside; you yourself, O king, set out the food and prepare the wine and shut the door and seal it with your signet. 12 When you return in the morning, if you do not find that Bel has eaten

it all, we will die; otherwise Daniel will, who is telling lies about us." 13 They were unconcerned, for beneath the table they had made a hidden entrance through which they used to go in regularly and consume the provisions. 14 After they had gone out, the king set out the food for Bel. Then Daniel ordered his servants to bring ashes, and they scattered them throughout the whole temple in the presence of the king alone. Then they went out, shut the door and sealed it with the king's signet, and departed. 15 During the night the priests came as usual, with their wives and children, and they ate and drank everything.

16 Early in the morning the king rose and came, and Daniel with him. 17 The king said, "Are the seals unbroken, Daniel?" He answered, "They are unbroken, O king." 18 As soon as the doors were opened, the king looked at the table and shouted in a loud voice, "You are great, O Bel, and in you there is no deceit at all!"

19 But Daniel laughed and restrained the king from going in. "Look at the floor," he said, "and notice whose footprints these are." 20 The king said, "I see the footprints of men and women and children." 21 Then the king was enraged, and he arrested the priests and their wives and children. They showed him the secret doors through which they used to enter to consume what was on the table. 22 Therefore the king put them to death and gave Bel over to Daniel, who destroyed it and its temple.

Daniel Kills the Dragon

23 Now in that place*b* there was a great dragon*c* that the Babylonians revered. 24 The king said to Daniel, "You cannot deny that this

---

a **8** Gk *his priests*

b **23** Other ancient authorities lack *in that place*
c **23** Or *serpent*

is a living god, so worship him." 25 Daniel said, "I worship the Lord my God, for he is a living God. 26 But give me permission, O king, and I will kill the dragon*d* without sword or club." The king said, "I give you permission."

27 Then Daniel took pitch, fat, and hair and boiled them together and made cakes, which he fed to the dragon.*e* The dragon*f* ate them and burst open. Then Daniel said, "See what you have been worshiping!"

28 When the Babylonians heard about it, they were very indignant and conspired against the king, saying, "The king has become a Jew; he has destroyed Bel and killed the dragon*g* and slaughtered the priests." 29 Going to the king, they said, "Hand Daniel over to us, or else we will kill you and your household." 30 The king saw that they were pressing him hard, and under compulsion he handed Daniel over to them.

Daniel in the Lions' Den

31 They threw Daniel into the lions' den, and he was there for six days. 32 There were seven lions in the den, and every day they had been given two human bodies and two sheep, but now they were given nothing, so that they would devour Daniel.

33 Now the prophet Habakkuk was in Judea; he had made a stew and had broken bread into a bowl and was going into the field to take it to the reapers. 34 But the angel of the Lord said to Habakkuk, "Take the food that you have to Babylon, to Daniel, in the lions' den." 35 Habakkuk said, "Sir, I have never seen Babylon, and I know nothing about the den." 36 Then the angel of the Lord took him by the crown of his head and carried him by his hair; with a gust of wind*h* he set him down in Babylon, right over the den.

37 Then Habakkuk shouted, "Daniel, Daniel! Take the food that God has sent you." 38 Daniel said, "You have remembered me, O God, and have not abandoned those who love you." 39 So Daniel got up and ate. And the angel of God immediately returned Habakkuk to his own place.

40 On the seventh day the king came to mourn for Daniel. When he came to the den he looked in, and there sat Daniel! 41 The king shouted with a loud voice, "You are great, O Lord, the God of Daniel, and there is no other besides you!" 42 Then he pulled Daniel*i* out and threw into the den those who had attempted his destruction, and they were instantly eaten before his eyes.

---

d 26 Or *serpent*
e 27 Or *serpent*
f 27 Or *serpent*
g 28 Or *serpent*

h 36 Or *by the power of his spirit*
i 42 Gk *him*

1 MACCABEES

Alexander the Great

1 After Alexander son of Philip, the Macedonian, who came from the land of Kittim, had defeated*a* King Darius of the Persians and the Medes, he succeeded him as king. (He had previously become king of Greece.) ²He fought many battles, conquered strongholds, and slaughtered the kings of the earth. ³He advanced to the ends of the earth and plundered many nations. When the earth became quiet before him, he was exalted, and his heart was lifted up. ⁴He gathered a very strong army and ruled over countries, nations, and princes, and they paid him tribute.

5 After this he fell sick and perceived that he was dying. ⁶So he summoned his most honored officers, who had been brought up with him from youth, and divided his kingdom among them while he was still alive. ⁷And after Alexander had reigned twelve years, he died.

8 Then his officers began to rule, each in his own place. ⁹They all put on crowns after his death, and so did their descendants after them for many years, and they caused many evils on the earth.

Antiochus Epiphanes and Renegade Jews

10 From them came forth a sinful root, Antiochus Epiphanes, son of King Antiochus; he had been a hostage in Rome. He began to reign in the one hundred thirty-seventh year of the kingdom of the Greeks.

11 In those days certain renegades came out from Israel and misled many, saying, "Let us go and make a covenant with the nations around us, for since we separated from them many disasters have come upon us." ¹²This proposal pleased them, ¹³and some of the people eagerly went to the king, who authorized them to observe the ordinances of the nations. ¹⁴So they built a gymnasium in Jerusalem according to the customs of the nations, ¹⁵and made foreskins for themselves, and abandoned the holy covenant. They joined with the nations and sold themselves to do evil.

Antiochus in Egypt

16 When Antiochus saw that his kingdom was established, he determined to become king of the land of Egypt, in order that he might reign over both kingdoms. ¹⁷So he invaded Egypt with a strong force, with chariots and elephants and cavalry and with a large fleet. ¹⁸He engaged King Ptolemy of Egypt in battle, and Ptolemy turned and fled before him, and many were wounded and fell. ¹⁹They captured the fortified cities in the land of Egypt, and he plundered the land of Egypt.

Persecution of the Jews

20 After subduing Egypt, Antiochus turned back in the one hundred forty-third year and went up against Israel and came to Jerusalem with a strong force. ²¹He arrogantly entered the sanctuary and took the golden altar, the lampstand for the light, and all its utensils. ²²He took also the table for the bread of the Presence, the cups for drink offerings, the bowls, the golden censers, the curtain, the crowns, and the gold decoration on the front of the temple; he stripped it all off. ²³He took the silver and the gold and the costly vessels; he took also the hidden treasures that he found. ²⁴Taking them all, he went into his own land.

He shed much blood
  and spoke with great arrogance.

25 Israel mourned deeply in every community;
26   rulers and elders groaned;
  young women and young men became
    faint;
  the beauty of the women faded.
27 Every bridegroom took up the lament;
  she who sat in the bridal chamber was
    mourning.
28 Even the land trembled for its inhabitants,
  and all the house of Jacob was clothed
    with shame.

---

a 1.1 Gk adds *and he defeated*

The Occupation of Jerusalem

29 Two years later the king sent to the cities of Judah a chief collector of tribute, and he came to Jerusalem with a large force. 30 Deceitfully he spoke peaceable words to them, and they believed him, but he suddenly fell upon the city, dealt it a severe blow, and destroyed many people of Israel. 31 He plundered the city, burned it with fire, and tore down its houses and its surrounding walls. 32 They took captive the women and children and seized the livestock. 33 Then they fortified the city of David with a large strong wall and strong towers, and it became their citadel. 34 They stationed there a sinful nation, men who were renegades. These strengthened their position; 35 they stored up arms and food, and, collecting the spoils of Jerusalem, they stored them there and became a great menace,

36 for the citadel*b* became an ambush against
     the sanctuary,
   an evil adversary of Israel at all times.
37 On every side of the sanctuary they shed
     innocent blood;
   they even defiled the sanctuary.
38 Because of them the residents of Jerusalem
     fled;
   she became a dwelling of strangers;
   she became strange to her offspring,
   and her children forsook her.
39 Her sanctuary became desolate like a
     desert;
   her feasts were turned into mourning,
   her Sabbaths into a reproach,
   her honor into contempt.
40 Her dishonor now grew as great as her
     glory;
   her exaltation was turned into mourning.

Installation of Gentile Cults

41 Then the king wrote to his whole kingdom that all should be one people 42 and that all should give up their particular customs. All the nations accepted the command of the king. 43 Many even from Israel gladly adopted his religion; they sacrificed to idols and profaned the Sabbath. 44 And the king sent letters by messengers to Jerusalem and the towns of Judah; he directed them to follow customs strange to the land, 45 to forbid burnt offerings and sacrifices and drink offerings in the sanctuary, to profane Sabbaths and festivals, 46 to defile the sanctuary and the holy ones, 47 to build altars and sacred precincts and shrines for idols, to sacrifice pigs and other unclean animals, 48 and to leave their sons uncircumcised. They were to make themselves abominable by everything unclean and profane 49 so that they would forget the law and change all the ordinances. 50 He added,*c* "And whoever does not obey the command of the king shall die."

51 In such words he wrote to his whole kingdom. He appointed inspectors over all the people and commanded the towns of Judah to offer sacrifice, town by town. 52 Many of the people, everyone who forsook the law, joined them, and they did evil in the land; 53 they drove Israel into hiding in every place of refuge they had.

54 Now on the fifteenth day of Chislev, in the one hundred forty-fifth year, they erected a desolating sacrilege on the altar of burnt offering. They also built altars in the surrounding towns of Judah 55 and offered incense at the doors of the houses and in the streets. 56 The books of the law that they found they tore to pieces and burned with fire. 57 Anyone found possessing the book of the covenant or anyone who adhered to the law was condemned to death by decree of the king. 58 They kept using violence against Israel, against those who were found month after month in the towns. 59 On the twenty-fifth day of the month they offered sacrifice on the altar that was on top of the altar of burnt offering. 60 According to the decree, they put to death the women who had their children circumcised 61 and their families and those who circumcised them, and they hung the infants from their mothers' necks.

62 But many in Israel stood firm and were resolved in their hearts not to eat unclean food. 63 They chose to die rather than to be defiled by food or to profane the holy covenant, and they did die. 64 Very great wrath came upon Israel.

Mattathias and His Sons

2 In those days Mattathias son of John son of Simeon, a priest of the clan of Joarib, moved from Jerusalem and settled in Modein. 2 He had five sons: John surnamed Gaddi, 3 Simon called Thassi, 4 Judas called Maccabeus, 5 Eleazar called Avaran, and Jonathan called Apphus. 6 He saw the blasphemies being committed in Judah and Jerusalem 7 and said,

---

b 1.36 Gk *it*   *c* 1.50 Gk lacks *He added*

"Alas! Why was I born to see this,
  the ruin of my people, the ruin of the holy
    city?
The people sat idle there when it was given
    over to the enemy,
  the sanctuary given over to strangers.
8 Her temple has become like a person
    without honor;*d*
9 her glorious vessels have been carried
    into exile.
  Her infants have been killed in her streets,
    her youths by the sword of the foe.
10 What nation has not inherited her palaces*e*
    and has not seized her spoils?
11 All her adornment has been taken away;
    no longer free, she has become a slave.
12 And see, our holy place, our beauty,
    and our glory have been laid waste;
  the nations have profaned them.
13   Why should we live any longer?"

14 Then Mattathias and his sons tore their clothes, put on sackcloth, and mourned greatly.

Pagan Worship Refused

15 The king's officers who were enforcing the apostasy came to the town of Modein to make them offer sacrifice. 16 Many from Israel came to them, and Mattathias and his sons were assembled. 17 Then the king's officers spoke to Mattathias as follows: "You are a leader, honored and great in this town, and supported by sons and brothers. 18 Now be the first to come and do what the king commands, as all the nations and the people of Judah and those who are left in Jerusalem have done. Then you and your sons will be numbered among the Friends of the king, and you and your sons will be honored with silver and gold and many gifts."

19 But Mattathias answered and said in a loud voice: "Even if all the nations that live under the rule of the king obey him and have chosen to obey his commandments, every one of them abandoning the religion of their ancestors, 20 I and my sons and my brothers will continue to live by the covenant of our ancestors. 21 Far be it from us to desert the law and the ordinances. 22 We will not obey the king's words by turning aside from our religion to the right hand or to the left."

23 When he had finished speaking these words, a Jew came forward in the sight of all to offer sacrifice on the altar in Modein, according to the king's command. 24 When Mattathias saw it, he burned with zeal, and his heart was stirred. He gave vent to righteous anger; he ran and slaughtered him on the altar. 25 At the same time he killed the king's officer who was forcing them to sacrifice, and he tore down the altar. 26 Thus he burned with zeal for the law, just as Phinehas did against Zimri son of Salu.

27 Then Mattathias cried out in the town with a loud voice, saying: "Let every one who is zealous for the law and supports the covenant come out with me!" 28 Then he and his sons fled to the hills and left all that they had in the town.

29 At that time many who were seeking righteousness and justice went down to the wilderness to live there, 30 they, their sons, their wives, and their livestock, because troubles pressed heavily upon them. 31 And it was reported to the king's officers and to the troops in Jerusalem the city of David that those who had rejected the king's command had gone down to the hiding places in the wilderness. 32 Many pursued them and overtook them; they encamped opposite them and prepared for battle against them on the Sabbath day. 33 They said to them, "Enough of this! Come out and do what the king commands, and you will live." 34 But they said, "We will not come out, nor will we do what the king commands and so profane the Sabbath day." 35 Then the enemy*f* quickly attacked them. 36 But they did not answer them or hurl a stone at them or block up their hiding places, 37 for they said, "Let us all die in our innocence; heaven and earth testify for us that you are killing us unjustly." 38 So they attacked them on the Sabbath, and they died, with their wives and children and livestock, to the number of a thousand persons.

39 When Mattathias and his friends learned of it, they mourned for them deeply. 40 And all said to their neighbors: "If we all do as our kindred have done and refuse to fight with the nations for our lives and for our ordinances, they will quickly destroy us from the earth." 41 So they made this decision that day: "Let us fight against anyone who comes to attack us on the Sabbath day; let us not all die as our kindred died in their hiding places."

---

d 2.8 Meaning of Gk uncertain
e 2.10 Other ancient authorities read *has not had a
    part in her kingdom*

---

f 2.35 Gk *they*

Counter-Attack

42 Then there united with them a company of Hasideans, mighty warriors of Israel, all who offered themselves willingly for the law. 43 And all who became fugitives to escape their troubles joined them and reinforced them. 44 They organized an army and struck down sinners in their anger and renegades in their wrath; the survivors fled to the nations for safety. 45 And Mattathias and his friends went around and tore down the altars; 46 they forcibly circumcised all the uncircumcised boys whom they found within the borders of Israel. 47 They hunted down the arrogant, and the work prospered in their hands. 48 They rescued the law out of the hands of the nations and kings, and they never let the sinner gain the upper hand.

The Last Words of Mattathias

49 Now the days drew near for Mattathias to die, and he said to his sons: "Arrogance and scorn have now become strong; it is a time of ruin and furious anger. 50 Now, my children, show zeal for the law and give your lives for the covenant of our ancestors.

51 "Remember the deeds of the ancestors, which they did in their generations, and you will receive great honor and an everlasting name. 52 Was not Abraham found faithful when tested, and it was reckoned to him as righteousness? 53 Joseph in the time of his distress kept the commandment and became lord of Egypt. 54 Phinehas our ancestor, because he was deeply zealous, received the covenant of everlasting priesthood. 55 Joshua, because he fulfilled the command, became a judge in Israel. 56 Caleb, because he testified in the assembly, received an inheritance in the land. 57 David, because he was merciful, inherited the throne of the kingdom forever. 58 Elijah, because of great zeal for the law, was taken up into heaven. 59 Hananiah, Azariah, and Mishael believed and were saved from the flame. 60 Daniel, because of his innocence, was delivered from the mouth of the lions.

61 "And so observe, from generation to generation, that none of those who put their trust in him will lack strength. 62 Do not fear the words of sinners, for their splendor will turn into dung and worms. 63 Today they will be exalted, but tomorrow they will not be found, for they will have returned to the dust, and their plans will have perished. 64 My children, be courageous and grow strong in the law, for by it you will gain honor.

65 "Here is your brother Simeon, who I know is wise in counsel; always listen to him; he shall be your father. 66 Judas Maccabeus has been a mighty warrior from his youth; he shall command the army for you and fight the battle against the peoples.^{g} 67 You shall rally around you all who observe the law and avenge the wrong done to your people. 68 Pay back the nations in full, and obey the commands of the law."

69 Then he blessed them and was gathered to his ancestors. 70 He died in the one hundred forty-sixth year and was buried in the tomb of his ancestors at Modein. And all Israel mourned for him with great lamentation.

The Early Victories of Judas

3 Then his son Judas, who was called Maccabeus, took command in his place. 2 All his brothers and all who had joined his father helped him; they gladly fought for Israel.

3 He extended the glory of his people.
  Like a giant he put on his breastplate;
  he bound on his armor of war and waged battles,
    protecting the camp by his sword.
4 He was like a lion in his deeds,
  like a lion's cub roaring for prey.
5 He searched out and pursued those who broke the law;
  he burned those who troubled his people.
6 Lawbreakers shrank back for fear of him;
  all the evildoers were confounded;
  and deliverance prospered by his hand.
7 He embittered many kings,
  but he made Jacob glad by his deeds,
  and his memory is blessed forever.
8 He went through the cities of Judah;
  he destroyed the ungodly out of the land;^{h}
  thus he turned away wrath from Israel.
9 He was renowned to the ends of the earth;
  he gathered in those who were perishing.

10 Then Apollonius gathered together nations and a large force from Samaria to fight against Israel. 11 When Judas learned of it, he went out to meet him, and he defeated and killed him. Many were wounded and fell, and the rest fled. 12 Then they seized their spoils, and Judas took the sword of Apollonius and used it in battle the rest of his life.

13 When Seron, the commander of the Syrian army, heard that Judas had gathered a large

g 2.66 Or *of the people*
h 3.8 Gk *it*

company, including a body of faithful soldiers who stayed with him and went out to battle, [14]he said, "I will make a name for myself and win honor in the kingdom. I will make war on Judas and his companions, who scorn the king's command." [15]Once again a strong army of godless men joined him and went up with him to help him, to take vengeance on the Israelites.

[16]When he approached the ascent of Bethhoron, Judas went out to meet him with a small company. [17]But when they saw the army coming to meet them, they said to Judas, "How can we, few as we are, fight against so great and so strong a multitude? And we are faint, for we have eaten nothing today." [18]Judas replied, "It is easy for many to be hemmed in by few, for in the sight of heaven there is no difference between saving by many or by few. [19]It is not on the size of the army that victory in battle depends, but strength comes from heaven. [20]They come against us in great insolence and lawlessness to destroy us and our wives and our children and to despoil us, [21]but we fight for our lives and our laws. [22]He himself will crush them before us; as for you, do not be afraid of them."

[23]When he finished speaking, he rushed suddenly against Seron and his army, and they were crushed before him. [24]They pursued them[i] down the descent of Beth-horon to the plain; eight hundred of them fell, and the rest fled into the land of the Philistines. [25]Then Judas and his brothers began to be feared, and terror fell on the nations all around them. [26]His fame reached the king, and the nations talked of the battles of Judas.

The Policy of Antiochus

[27]When King Antiochus heard these reports, he was greatly angered, and he sent and gathered all the forces of his kingdom, a very strong army. [28]He opened his coffers and gave a year's pay to his forces and ordered them to be ready for any need. [29]Then he saw that the money in the treasury was exhausted and that the tribute payments from the country were small because of the dissension and disaster that he had caused in the land by abolishing the laws that had existed from the earliest days. [30]He feared that he might not have such funds as he had before for his expenses and for the gifts that he used to give more lavishly than preceding kings. [31]He was greatly perplexed in

mind; then he determined to go to Persia and collect the tribute payments from those regions and raise a large fund.

[32]He left Lysias, a distinguished man of royal lineage, in charge of the king's affairs from the River Euphrates to the borders of Egypt. [33]Lysias was also to take care of his son Antiochus until he returned. [34]And he turned over to Lysias[j] half of his forces and the elephants and gave him orders about all that he wanted done. As for the residents of Judea and Jerusalem, [35]Lysias was to send a force against them to wipe out and destroy the strength of Israel and the remnant of Jerusalem; he was to banish the memory of them from the place, [36]settle strangers in all their territory, and distribute their land by lot. [37]Then the king took the remaining half of his forces and left Antioch his capital in the one hundred and forty-seventh year. He crossed the Euphrates River and went through the upper provinces.

Preparations for Battle

[38]Lysias chose Ptolemy son of Dorymenes and Nicanor and Gorgias, able men among the Friends of the king, [39]and sent with them forty thousand infantry and seven thousand cavalry to go into the land of Judah and destroy it, as the king had commanded. [40]So they set out with their entire force, and when they arrived they encamped near Emmaus in the plain. [41]When the traders of the region heard what was said to them, they took silver and gold in immense amounts and fetters[k] and went to the camp to get the Israelites for slaves. And forces from Syria and the land of the Philistines[l] joined with them.

[42]Now Judas and his brothers saw that misfortunes had increased and that the forces were encamped in their territory. They also learned what the king had commanded to do to the people to cause their final destruction. [43]But they said to one another, "Let us restore the ruins of our people and fight for our people and the sanctuary." [44]So the congregation assembled to be ready for battle and to pray and ask for mercy and compassion.

[45] Jerusalem was uninhabited like a
   wilderness;
      not one of her children went in or out.

---

i 3.24 Other ancient authorities read *him*

j 3.34 Gk *him*
k 3.41 Syr: Gk Vg *slaves*
l 3.41 Gk *foreigners*

The sanctuary was trampled down,
  and strangers held the citadel;
  it was a lodging place for the nations.
Joy was taken from Jacob;
  the flute and the harp ceased to play.

46 Then they gathered together and went to Mizpah, opposite Jerusalem, because Israel formerly had a place of prayer in Mizpah. 47 They fasted that day, put on sackcloth, and sprinkled ashes on their heads, and tore their clothes. 48 And they opened the book of the law to inquire into those matters about which the nations consulted the likenesses of their gods. 49 They also brought the vestments of the priesthood and the first fruits and the tithes, and they stirred up the nazirites who had completed their days, 50 and they cried aloud to heaven, saying,

"What shall we do with these?
  Where shall we take them?
51 Your sanctuary is trampled down and
    profaned,
  and your priests mourn in humiliation.
52 Here the nations are assembled against us
    to destroy us;
  you know what they plot against us.
53 How will we be able to withstand them,
    if you do not help us?"

54 Then they sounded the trumpets and gave a loud shout. 55 After this Judas appointed leaders of the people in charge of thousands and hundreds and fifties and tens. 56 Those who were building houses or were about to be married or were planting a vineyard or were fainthearted, he told to go home, according to the law. 57 Then the army marched out and encamped to the south of Emmaus.

58 And Judas said, "Arm yourselves and be courageous. Be ready early in the morning to fight with these nations who have assembled against us to destroy us and our sanctuary. 59 It is better for us to die in battle than to see the misfortunes of our nation and of the sanctuary. 60 But as his will in heaven may be, so shall he do."

The Battle at Emmaus

4 Now Gorgias took five thousand infantry and one thousand picked cavalry, and this division moved out by night 2 to fall upon the camp of the Jews and attack them suddenly. Men from the citadel were his guides. 3 But Judas heard of it, and he and his warriors moved out to attack the king's force in Emmaus 4 while the division was still absent from the camp.

5 When Gorgias entered the camp of Judas by night, he found no one there, so he looked for them in the hills, because he said, "These men are running away from us."

6 At daybreak Judas appeared in the plain with three thousand men, but they did not have armor and swords such as they desired. 7 And they saw the camp of the nations, strong and fortified, with cavalry all around it, and these men were trained in war. 8 But Judas said to those who were with him, "Do not fear their numbers or be afraid when they charge. 9 Remember how our ancestors were saved at the Red Sea, when Pharaoh with his forces pursued them. 10 And now, let us cry to heaven to see whether he will favor us and remember his covenant with our ancestors and crush this army before us today. 11 Then all the nations will know that there is one who redeems and saves Israel."

12 When the foreigners looked up and saw them coming against them, 13 they went out from their camp to battle. Then the men with Judas blew their trumpets 14 and engaged in battle. The nations were crushed and fled into the plain, 15 and all those in the rear fell by the sword. They pursued them to Gazara and to the plains of Idumea and to Azotus and Jamnia, and three thousand of them fell. 16 Then Judas and his force turned back from pursuing them, 17 and he said to the people, "Do not be greedy for plunder, for there is a battle before us; 18 Gorgias and his force are near us in the hills. But stand now against our enemies and fight them and afterward seize the plunder boldly."

19 Just as Judas was finishing this speech, a detachment appeared coming out of the hills. 20 They saw that their army[m] had been put to flight and that the Jews[n] were burning the camp, for the smoke that was seen showed what had happened. 21 When they perceived this, they were greatly frightened, and when they also saw the army of Judas drawn up in the plain for battle, 22 they all fled into the land of the Philistines.[o] 23 Then Judas returned to plunder the camp, and they seized a great amount of gold and silver, and cloth dyed blue and sea purple, and great riches. 24 On their return they sang hymns and praises to heaven: "For he is good, for his mercy endures forever." 25 Thus Israel had a great deliverance that day.

---

m 4.20 Gk they
n 4.20 Gk they
o 4.22 Gk foreigners

First Campaign of Lysias

26 Those of the foreigners who escaped went and reported to Lysias all that had happened. 27 When he heard it, he was perplexed and discouraged, for things had not happened to Israel as he had intended, nor had they turned out as the king had ordered. 28 But the next year he mustered sixty thousand picked infantry and five thousand cavalry to subdue them. 29 They came into Idumea and encamped at Beth-zur, and Judas met them with ten thousand men.

30 When he saw that their army was strong, he prayed, saying, "Blessed are you, O Savior of Israel, who crushed the attack of the mighty warrior by the hand of your servant David and gave the camp of the Philistines into the hands of Jonathan son of Saul and of the man who carried his armor. 31 Hem in this army by the hand of your people Israel, and let them be ashamed of their troops and their cavalry. 32 Fill them with cowardice; melt the boldness of their strength; let them tremble in their destruction. 33 Strike them down with the sword of those who love you, and let all who know your name praise you with hymns."

34 Then both sides attacked, and there fell of the army of Lysias five thousand men; they fell before them.*p* 35 When Lysias saw the rout of his troops and observed the boldness that inspired those of Judas and how ready they were either to live or to die nobly, he withdrew to Antioch and enlisted mercenaries in order to invade Judea again with an even larger army.

Cleansing and Dedication of the Temple

36 Then Judas and his brothers said, "See, our enemies are crushed; let us go up to cleanse the sanctuary and dedicate it." 37 So all the army assembled and went up to Mount Zion. 38 There they saw the sanctuary desolate, the altar profaned, and the gates burned. In the courts they saw bushes sprung up as in a thicket or as on one of the mountains. They saw also the chambers of the priests in ruins. 39 Then they tore their clothes and mourned with great lamentation; they sprinkled themselves with ashes 40 and fell face down on the ground. And they blew the signal trumpets, and they cried out to heaven. 41 Then Judas detailed men to fight against those in the citadel until he had cleansed the sanctuary. 42 He chose blameless priests devoted to the law, 43 and they cleansed the sanctuary and

removed the defiled stones to an unclean place. 44 They deliberated what to do about the altar of burnt offering, which had been profaned. 45 And they thought it best to tear it down, so that it would not be a lasting shame to them that the nations had defiled it. So they tore down the altar 46 and stored the stones in a convenient place on the temple hill until a prophet should come to tell what to do with them. 47 Then they took unhewn*q* stones, as the law directs, and built a new altar like the former one. 48 They also rebuilt the sanctuary and the interior of the temple and consecrated the courts. 49 They made new holy vessels and brought the lampstand, the altar of incense, and the table into the temple. 50 Then they offered incense on the altar and lit the lamps on the lampstand, and these gave light in the temple. 51 They placed the bread on the table and hung up the curtains. Thus they finished all the work they had undertaken.

52 Early in the morning on the twenty-fifth day of the ninth month, which is the month of Chislev, in the one hundred forty-eighth year, 53 they rose and offered sacrifice, as the law directs, on the new altar of burnt offering that they had built. 54 At the very season and on the very day that the nations had profaned it, it was dedicated with songs and harps and lutes and cymbals. 55 All the people fell on their faces and worshiped and blessed heaven, who had prospered them. 56 So they celebrated the dedication of the altar for eight days and joyfully offered burnt offerings; they offered a sacrifice of well-being and a thanksgiving offering. 57 They decorated the front of the temple with golden crowns and small shields; they restored the gates and the chambers for the priests and fitted them with doors. 58 There was very great joy among the people, and the disgrace brought by the nations was removed.

59 Then Judas and his brothers and all the assembly of Israel determined that every year at that season the days of dedication of the altar should be observed with joy and gladness for eight days, beginning with the twenty-fifth day of the month of Chislev.

60 At that time they fortified Mount Zion with high walls and strong towers all around, to keep the nations from coming and trampling them down as they had done before. 61 Judas*r* stationed a garrison there to guard it; he also

---

p **4.34** Or *and some fell on the opposite side*

q **4.47** Gk *whole*
r **4.61** Gk *He*

fortified Beth-zur to guard it, so that the people might have a stronghold that faced Idumea.

Wars with Neighboring Peoples

5 When the nations all around heard that the altar had been rebuilt and the sanctuary dedicated as it was before, they became very angry, ²and they determined to destroy the descendants of Jacob who lived among them. So they began to kill and destroy among the people. ³But Judas made war on the descendants of Esau in Idumea, at Akrabattene, because they kept lying in wait for Israel. He dealt them a heavy blow and humbled them and despoiled them. ⁴He also remembered the wickedness of the sons of Baean, who were a trap and a snare to the people and ambushed them on the highways. ⁵They were shut up by him in towers, and he encamped against them, vowed their complete destruction, and burned with fire their towers and all who were in them. ⁶Then he crossed over to attack the Ammonites, where he found a strong band and many people, with Timothy as their leader. ⁷He engaged in many battles with them, and they were crushed before him; he struck them down. ⁸He also took Jazer and its villages; then he returned to Judea.

Liberation of Galilean Jews

9 Now the nations in Gilead gathered together against the Israelites who lived in their territory and planned to destroy them. But they fled to the stronghold of Dathema ¹⁰and sent to Judas and his brothers letters that said, "The nations around us have gathered together to destroy us. ¹¹They are preparing to come and capture the stronghold to which we have fled, and Timothy is leading their forces. ¹²Now then, come and rescue us from their hands, for many of us have fallen, ¹³and all our kindred who were in the land of Tobias have been killed; the enemy*s* have captured their wives and children and goods and have destroyed about a thousand persons there."

14 While the letters were still being read, other messengers, with their garments torn, came from Galilee and made a similar report; ¹⁵they said that the people of Ptolemais and Tyre and Sidon and all Galilee of the gentiles*t* had gathered together against them "to annihilate us." ¹⁶When Judas and the people heard these

messages, a great assembly was called to determine what they should do for their kindred who were in distress and were being attacked by enemies."*u* ¹⁷Then Judas said to his brother Simon, "Choose your men and go and rescue your kindred in Galilee; Jonathan my brother and I will go to Gilead." ¹⁸But he left Joseph, son of Zechariah, and Azariah, a leader of the people, with the rest of the forces in Judea to guard it, ¹⁹and he gave them this command, "Take charge of this people, but do not engage in battle with the nations until we return." ²⁰Then three thousand men were assigned to Simon to go to Galilee and eight thousand to Judas for Gilead.

21 So Simon went to Galilee and fought many battles against the nations, and the nations were crushed before him. ²²He pursued them to the gate of Ptolemais; as many as three thousand of the nations fell, and he despoiled them. ²³Then he took the Jews*v* of Galilee and Arbatta, with their wives and children, and all they possessed and led them to Judea with great rejoicing.

Judas and Jonathan in Gilead

24 Judas Maccabeus and his brother Jonathan crossed the Jordan and made three days' journey into the wilderness. ²⁵They encountered the Nabateans, who met them peaceably and told them all that had happened to their kindred in Gilead: ²⁶"Many of them have been shut up in Bozrah and Bosor, in Alema and Chaspho, Maked and Carnaim"—all these towns were strong and large—²⁷"and some have been shut up in the other towns of Gilead; the enemy*w* are getting ready to attack the strongholds tomorrow and capture and destroy all these people in a single day."

28 Then Judas and his army quickly turned back by the wilderness road to Bozrah, and he took the town and killed every male by the edge of the sword; then he seized all its spoils and burned it with fire. ²⁹He left the place at night, and they went all the way to the stronghold of Dathema.*x* ³⁰At dawn they looked out and saw a large company, which could not be counted, carrying ladders and engines of war to capture the stronghold and attacking the Jews within.*y* ³¹So Judas saw that the battle had begun and that the cry of the town went up to heaven,

---

s 5.13 Gk *they*
t 5.15 Gk *foreigners*

u 5.16 Gk *them*
v 5.23 Gk *those*
w 5.27 Gk *they*
x 5.29 Gk lacks *of Dathema*
y 5.30 Gk *and they were attacking them*

with trumpets and loud shouts, [32] and he said to the men of his forces, "Fight today for your kindred!" [33] Then he came up behind them in three companies, who sounded their trumpets and cried aloud in prayer. [34] And when the army of Timothy realized that it was Maccabeus, they fled before him, and he dealt them a heavy blow. As many as eight thousand of them fell that day.

[35] Next he turned aside to Maapha[z] and fought against it and took it, and he killed every male in it, plundered it, and burned it with fire. [36] From there he marched on and took Chaspho, Maked, and Bosor and the other towns of Gilead.

[37] After these things Timothy gathered another army and encamped opposite Raphon, on the other side of the stream. [38] Judas sent men to spy out the camp, and they reported to him, "All the nations around us have gathered to him; it is a very large force. [39] They also have hired Arabs to help them, and they are encamped across the stream ready to come and fight against you." And Judas went to meet them.

[40] Now as Judas and his army drew near to the stream of water, Timothy said to the officers of his forces, "If he crosses over to us first, we will not be able to resist him, for he will surely defeat us. [41] But if he shows fear and camps on the other side of the river, we will cross over to him and defeat him." [42] When Judas approached the stream of water, he stationed the officers[a] of the army at the stream and gave them this command, "Permit no one to encamp, but make them all enter the battle." [43] Then he crossed over against them first, and the whole army followed him. All the nations were defeated before him, and they threw away their arms and fled into the sacred precincts at Carnaim. [44] But he took the town and burned the sacred precincts with fire, together with all who were in them. Thus Carnaim was conquered; they could stand before Judas no longer.

The Return to Jerusalem

[45] Then Judas gathered together all the Israelites in Gilead, the small and the great, with their wives and children and goods, a very large company, to go to the land of Judah. [46] So they came to Ephron. This was a large and very strong town on the road, and they could not go around it to the right or to the left; they had to

go through it. [47] But the people of the town shut them out and blocked up the gates with stones.

[48] Judas sent them this friendly message, "Let us pass through your land to get to our land. No one will do you harm; we will simply pass by on foot." But they refused to open to him. [49] Then Judas ordered proclamation to be made to the army that all should encamp where they were. [50] So the men of the forces encamped, and he fought against the town all that day and all the night, and the town was delivered into his hands. [51] He destroyed every male by the edge of the sword and razed and plundered the town. Then he passed through the town over the bodies of the dead.

[52] Then they crossed the Jordan into the large plain before Beth-shan. [53] Judas kept rallying the laggards and encouraging the people all the way until he came to the land of Judah. [54] So they went up to Mount Zion with joy and gladness and offered burnt offerings because they had returned in safety; not one of them had fallen.

Joseph and Azariah Defeated

[55] Now while Judas and Jonathan were in Gilead and their[b] brother Simon was in Galilee before Ptolemais, [56] Joseph son of Zechariah and Azariah, the commanders of the forces, heard of their brave deeds and of the heroic war they had fought. [57] So they said, "Let us also make a name for ourselves; let us go and make war on the nations around us." [58] So they issued orders to the men of the forces that were with them and marched against Jamnia. [59] Gorgias and his men came out of the town to meet them in battle. [60] Then Joseph and Azariah were routed and were pursued to the borders of Judea; as many as two thousand of the people of Israel fell that day. [61] Thus the people suffered a great rout because, thinking to do a brave deed, they did not listen to Judas and his brothers. [62] But they did not belong to the family of those men through whom deliverance was given to Israel.

[63] The man Judas and his brothers were greatly honored in all Israel and among all the nations, wherever their name was heard. [64] People gathered to them and praised them.

Success at Hebron and Philistia

[65] Then Judas and his brothers went out and fought the descendants of Esau in the land to the south. He struck Hebron and its villages and

---

z 5.35 Other ancient authorities read *Alema*
a 5.42 Or *scribes*

b 5.55 Gk *his*

tore down its strongholds and burned its towers on all sides. ⁶⁶Then he marched off to go into the land of the Philistines*c* and passed through Marisa.*d* ⁶⁷On that day some priests who wished to do a brave deed fell in battle, for they went out to battle unwisely. ⁶⁸But Judas turned aside to Azotus in the land of the Philistines; he tore down their altars, and the carved images of their gods he burned with fire; he plundered the towns and returned to the land of Judah.

The Last Days of Antiochus Epiphanes

6 King Antiochus was going through the upper provinces when he heard that Elymais in Persia was a city famed for its wealth in silver and gold. ²Its temple was very rich, containing golden shields, breastplates, and weapons left there by Alexander son of Philip, the Macedonian king who first reigned over the Greeks. ³So he came and tried to take the city and plunder it, but he could not because his plan had become known to the citizens, ⁴and they withstood him in battle. So he fled and in great disappointment left there to return to Babylon.

⁵Then someone came to him in Persia and reported that the armies that had gone into the land of Judah had been routed; ⁶that Lysias had gone first with a strong force but had turned and fled before the Jews;*e* that the Jews*f* had grown strong from the arms, supplies, and abundant spoils that they had taken from the armies they had cut down; ⁷that they had torn down the abomination that he had erected on the altar in Jerusalem; and that they had surrounded the sanctuary with high walls as before, and also Beth-zur, his town.

⁸When the king heard this news, he was astounded and badly shaken. He took to his bed and became sick from disappointment because things had not turned out for him as he had planned. ⁹He lay there for many days because deep disappointment continually gripped him, and he realized that he was dying. ¹⁰So he called all his Friends and said to them, "Sleep has departed from my eyes, and I am downhearted with worry. ¹¹I said to myself, 'To what distress I have come! And into what a great flood I now am plunged! For I was kind and beloved in my power.' ¹²But now I remember the wrong I did

in Jerusalem. I seized all its vessels of silver and gold, and I sent to destroy the inhabitants of Judah without good reason. ¹³I know that it is because of this that these misfortunes have come upon me; here I am, perishing of bitter disappointment in a strange land."

¹⁴Then he called for Philip, one of his Friends, and made him ruler over all his kingdom. ¹⁵He gave him the crown and his robe and the signet so that he might guide his son Antiochus and bring him up to be king. ¹⁶Thus King Antiochus died there in the one hundred forty-ninth year. ¹⁷When Lysias learned that the king was dead, he set up Antiochus the king's*g* son to reign. Lysias*h* had brought him up from boyhood; he named him Eupator.

Renewed Attacks from Syria

¹⁸Meanwhile the garrison in the citadel kept hemming Israel in around the sanctuary. They were trying in every way to harm them and strengthen the nations. ¹⁹Judas therefore resolved to destroy them and assembled all the people to besiege them. ²⁰They gathered together and besieged the citadel*i* in the one hundred fiftieth year, and he built siege towers and engines of war. ²¹But some of the garrison escaped from the siege, and some of the ungodly Israelites joined them. ²²They went to the king and said, "How long will you fail to do justice and to avenge our kindred? ²³We were happy to serve your father, to live by what he said, and to follow his commands. ²⁴For this reason the sons of our people besieged the citadel*j* and became hostile to us; moreover, they have put to death as many of us as they have caught, and they have seized our inheritances. ²⁵It is not against us alone that they have stretched out their hands; they have also attacked all the lands on their borders. ²⁶And see, today they have encamped against the citadel in Jerusalem to take it; they have fortified both the sanctuary and Beth-zur; ²⁷unless you quickly prevent them, they will do still greater things, and you will not be able to stop them."

²⁸The king was enraged when he heard this. He assembled all his Friends, the commanders of his forces and those in authority.*k* ²⁹Mercenary forces also came to him from other

---

c 5.66 Gk *foreigners*

d 5.66 Other ancient authorities read *Samaria*

e 6.6 Gk *them*

f 6.6 Gk *they*

g 6.17 Gk *his*

h 6.17 Gk *He*

i 6.20 Gk *it*

j 6.24 Meaning of Gk uncertain

k 6.28 Gk *those over the reins*

kingdoms and from islands of the seas. [30] The number of his forces was one hundred thousand foot soldiers, twenty thousand horsemen, and thirty-two elephants accustomed to war. [31] They came through Idumea and encamped against Beth-zur, and for many days they fought and built engines of war, but the Jews[l] sallied out and burned these with fire and fought courageously.

The Battle at Beth-zechariah

[32] Then Judas marched away from the citadel and encamped at Beth-zechariah, opposite the camp of the king. [33] Early in the morning the king set out and took his army by a forced march along the road to Beth-zechariah, and his troops made ready for battle and sounded their trumpets. [34] They offered the elephants the juice of grapes and mulberries, to arouse them for battle. [35] They distributed the animals among the phalanxes; with each elephant they stationed a thousand men armed with coats of mail and with brass helmets on their heads, and five hundred picked horsemen were assigned to each beast. [36] These took their position beforehand wherever the animal was; wherever it went, they went with it, and they never left it. [37] On the elephants[m] were wooden towers, strong and covered; they were fastened on each animal by special harness, and on each were four[n] armed men who fought from there and also its Indian driver. [38] The rest of the cavalry were stationed on either side, on the two flanks of the army, to harass the enemy while being themselves protected by the phalanxes. [39] When the sun shone on the shields of gold and brass, the hills were ablaze with them and gleamed like flaming torches.

[40] Now a part of the king's army was spread out on the high hills, and some troops were on the plain, and they advanced steadily and in good order. [41] All who heard the noise made by their multitude, by the marching of the multitude and the clanking of their arms, trembled, for the army was very large and strong. [42] But Judas and his army advanced to the battle, and six hundred of the king's army fell. [43] Now Eleazar, called Avaran, saw that one of the animals was equipped with royal armor. It was taller than all the others, and he supposed that the king was on it. [44] So he gave his life to save his people and to win for himself an everlasting name. [45] He courageously ran into the midst of the phalanx to reach it; he killed men right and left, and they parted before him on both sides. [46] He got under the elephant, stabbed it from beneath, and killed it, but it fell to the ground upon him and he died. [47] When the Jews[o] saw the royal might and the fierce attack of the forces, they turned away in flight.

The Siege of the Temple

[48] The soldiers of the king's army went up to Jerusalem against them, and the king encamped in Judea and at Mount Zion. [49] He made peace with the people of Beth-zur, and they evacuated the town because they had no provisions there to withstand a siege, since it was a sabbatical year for the land. [50] So the king took Beth-zur and stationed a guard there to hold it. [51] Then he encamped before the sanctuary for many days. He set up siege towers, engines of war, devices to throw fire and stones, machines to shoot arrows, and catapults. [52] The Jews[p] also made engines of war to match theirs and fought for many days. [53] But they had no food in storage,[q] because it was the seventh year; those who had found safety in Judea from the nations had consumed the last of the stores. [54] Only a few men were left in the sanctuary; the rest scattered to their own homes, for the famine proved too much for them.

Syria Offers Terms

[55] Then Lysias heard that Philip, whom King Antiochus while still living had appointed to bring up his son Antiochus to be king, [56] had returned from Persia and Media with the forces that had gone with the king and that he was trying to seize control of the government. [57] So he quickly gave orders to withdraw and said to the king, to the commanders of the forces, and to the troops, "Daily we grow weaker, our food supply is scant, the place against which we are fighting is strong, and the affairs of the kingdom press urgently on us. [58] Now, then, let us come to terms with these people and make peace with them and with all their nation. [59] Let us agree to let them live by their laws as they did before, for it was on account of their laws that we abolished that they became angry and did all these things."

---

l **6.31** Gk *they*
m **6.37** Gk *them*
n **6.37** Cn: Ancient authorities read *thirty* or *thirty-two*

o **6.47** Gk *they*
p **6.52** Gk *They*
q **6.53** Other ancient authorities read *in the sanctuary*

60 The speech pleased the king and the commanders, and he sent to the Jews[r] an offer of peace, and they accepted it. 61 So the king and the commanders gave them their oath. On these conditions the Jews[s] evacuated the stronghold. 62 But when the king entered Mount Zion and saw what a strong fortress the place was, he broke the oath he had sworn and gave orders to tear down the wall all around. 63 Then he set off in haste and returned to Antioch. He found Philip in control of the city, but he fought against him and took the city by force.

Expedition of Bacchides and Alcimus

7 In the one hundred fifty-first year Demetrius son of Seleucus set out from Rome, sailed with a few men to a town by the sea, and there began to reign. 2 As he was entering the royal palace of his ancestors, the army seized Antiochus and Lysias to bring them to him. 3 But when this act became known to him, he said, "Do not let me see their faces!" 4 So the army killed them, and Demetrius took his seat on the throne of his kingdom.

5 Then there came to him all the renegade and godless men of Israel; they were led by Alcimus, who wanted to be high priest. 6 They brought to the king this accusation against the people: "Judas and his brothers have destroyed all your Friends and have driven us out of our land. 7 Now, then, send a man whom you trust; let him go and see all the ruin that Judas[t] has brought on us and on the land of the king, and let him punish them and all who help them."

8 So the king chose Bacchides, one of the king's Friends, governor of the province Beyond the River; he was a great man in the kingdom and was faithful to the king. 9 He sent him, and with him he sent the ungodly Alcimus, whom he made high priest, and he commanded him to take vengeance on the Israelites. 10 So they marched away and came with a large force into the land of Judah, and he sent messengers to Judas and his brothers with peaceable but treacherous words. 11 But they paid no attention to their words, for they saw that they had come with a large force.

12 Then a group of scribes appeared in a body before Alcimus and Bacchides to ask for just terms. 13 The Hasideans were first among the Israelites to seek peace from them, 14 for they said, "A priest of the line of Aaron has come with the army, and he will not harm us." 15 Alcimus[u] spoke peaceable words to them and swore this oath to them, "We will not seek to injure you or your friends." 16 So they trusted him, but he seized sixty of them and killed them in one day, in accordance with the word that was written, 17 "The flesh of your faithful ones and their blood

they poured out all around Jerusalem,
and there was no one to bury them."

18 Then the fear and dread of them fell on all the people, for they said, "There is no truth or justice in them, for they have violated the agreement and the oath that they swore."

19 Then Bacchides withdrew from Jerusalem and encamped in Beth-zaith. And he sent and seized many of the men who had deserted to him,[v] and some of the people, and killed them and threw them into a great pit. 20 He placed Alcimus in charge of the country and left with him a force to help him; then Bacchides went back to the king.

21 Alcimus struggled to maintain his high priesthood, 22 and all who were troubling their people joined him. They gained control of the land of Judah and did great damage in Israel. 23 And Judas saw all the wrongs that Alcimus and those with him had done among the Israelites; it was more than the nations had done. 24 So Judas[w] went out into all the surrounding parts of Judea, taking vengeance on those who had deserted and preventing those in the city[x] from going out into the country. 25 When Alcimus saw that Judas and those with him had grown strong and realized that he could not withstand them, he returned to the king and brought malicious charges against them.

Nicanor in Judea

26 Then the king sent Nicanor, one of his honored princes, who hated and detested Israel, and he commanded him to destroy the people. 27 So Nicanor came to Jerusalem with a large force and treacherously sent to Judas and his brothers this peaceable message, 28 "Let there be no fighting between you and me; I shall come with a few men to see you face to face in peace."

---

r 6.60 Gk them
s 6.61 Gk they
t 7.7 Gk he

u 7.15 Gk He
v 7.19 Or many of his men who had deserted
w 7.24 Gk he
x 7.24 Gk and they were prevented

29 So he came to Judas, and they greeted one another peaceably, but the enemy were preparing to kidnap Judas. 30 It became known to Judas that Nicanor*y* had come to him with treacherous intent, and he was afraid of him and would not meet him again. 31 When Nicanor learned that his plan had been disclosed, he went out to meet Judas in battle near Caphar-salama. 32 About five hundred of the army of Nicanor fell, and the rest*z* fled into the city of David.

Nicanor Threatens the Temple

33 After these events Nicanor went up to Mount Zion. Some of the priests from the sanctuary and some of the elders of the people came out to greet him peaceably and to show him the burnt offering that was being offered for the king. 34 But he mocked them and derided them and defiled them and spoke arrogantly, 35 and in anger he swore this oath, "Unless Judas and his army are delivered into my hands this time, then if I return safely I will burn up this house." And he went out in great anger. 36 At this the priests went in and stood before the altar and the temple; they wept and said,

37 "You chose this house to be called by your
    name
    and to be for your people a house of
      prayer and supplication.
38 Take vengeance on this man and on his
    army,
    and let them fall by the sword;
    remember their blasphemies,
    and let them live no longer."

The Death of Nicanor

39 Now Nicanor went out from Jerusalem and encamped in Beth-horon, and the Syrian army joined him. 40 Judas encamped in Adasa with three thousand men. Then Judas prayed and said, 41 "When the messengers from the king spoke blasphemy, your angel went out and struck down one hundred eighty-five thousand of the Assyrians.*a* 42 So also crush this army before us today; let the rest learn that Nicanor*b* has spoken wickedly against the sanctuary, and judge him according to this wickedness." 43 So the armies met in battle on the thirteenth day of the month of Adar. The army of Nicanor was crushed, and he himself was the first to fall in the battle. 44 When his army saw that Nicanor had fallen, they threw down their arms and fled. 45 The Jews*c* pursued them a day's journey, from Adasa as far as Gazara, and as they followed they kept sounding the battle call on the trumpets. 46 People came out of all the surrounding villages of Judea, and they outflanked the enemy*d* and drove them back to their pursuers,*e* so that they all fell by the sword; not even one of them was left. 47 Then the Jews*f* seized the spoils and the plunder; they cut off Nicanor's head and the right hand that he had so arrogantly stretched out and brought them and displayed them just outside Jerusalem. 48 The people rejoiced greatly and celebrated that day as a day of great gladness. 49 They decreed that this day should be celebrated each year on the thirteenth day of Adar. 50 So the land of Judah had rest for a few days.

A Eulogy of the Romans

8 Now Judas heard of the fame of the Romans, that they were very strong and were well-disposed toward all who made an alliance with them, that they pledged friendship to those who came to them, 2 and that they were very strong. He had been told of their wars and of the brave deeds that they were doing among the Gauls, how they had defeated them and forced them to pay tribute, 3 and what they had done in the land of Spain to get control of the silver and gold mines there, 4 and how they had gained control of the whole region by their planning and patience, even though the place was far distant from them. They also subdued the kings who came against them from the ends of the earth, until they crushed them and inflicted great disaster on them; the survivors paid them tribute every year. 5 They had crushed in battle and conquered Philip, and King Perseus of the Macedonians,*g* and the others who rose up against them. 6 They also had defeated Antiochus the Great, king of Asia, who went to fight against them with one hundred twenty elephants and with cavalry and chariots and a very large army. He was crushed by them; 7 they took him alive and decreed that he and those who would reign after him should pay a

---

y 7.30 Gk *he*
z 7.32 Gk *they*
a 7.41 Gk *of them*
b 7.42 Gk *he*
c 7.45 Gk *They*
d 7.46 Gk *them*
e 7.46 Gk *these*
f 7.47 Gk *they*
g 8.5 Or *Kittim*

heavy tribute and give hostages and surrender some of their best provinces: ⁸ the countries of India, Media, and Lydia. These they took from him and gave to King Eumenes. ⁹ The Greeks planned to come and destroy them, ¹⁰ but this became known to them, and they sent a general against the Greeks^h and attacked them. Many of them were wounded and fell, and the Romans^i took captive their wives and children; they plundered them, conquered the land, tore down their strongholds, and enslaved them to this day. ¹¹ The remaining kingdoms and islands, as many as ever opposed them, they destroyed and enslaved, ¹² but with their friends and those who rely on them they have kept friendship. They have subdued kings far and near, and as many as have heard of their fame have feared them. ¹³ Those whom they wish to help and to make kings, they make kings, and those whom they wish they depose, and they have been greatly exalted. ¹⁴ Yet for all this not one of them has put on a crown or worn purple as a mark of pride, ¹⁵ but they have built for themselves a senate chamber, and every day three hundred twenty senators constantly deliberate concerning the people, to govern them well. ¹⁶ They trust one man each year to rule over them and to control all their land; they all heed the one man, and there is no envy or jealousy among them.

An Alliance with Rome

17 So Judas chose Eupolemus son of John son of Accos, and Jason son of Eleazar, and sent them to Rome to establish friendship and alliance ¹⁸ and to free themselves from the yoke, for they saw that the kingdom of the Greeks was enslaving Israel completely. ¹⁹ They went to Rome, a very long journey, and they entered the senate chamber and spoke as follows: ²⁰ "Judas, who is also called Maccabeus, and his brothers and the people of the Jews have sent us to you to establish alliance and peace with you, so that we may be enrolled as your allies and friends." ²¹ The proposal pleased them, ²² and this is a copy of the letter that they wrote in reply, on bronze tablets, and sent to Jerusalem to remain with them there as a memorial of peace and alliance:

23 "May all go well with the Romans and with the nation of the Jews at sea and on land forever, and may sword and enemy be far from them. ²⁴ If war comes first to Rome or to any of their allies in all their dominion, ²⁵ the nation of the Jews shall act as their allies wholeheartedly, as the occasion may indicate to them. ²⁶ To the enemy that makes war they shall not give or supply grain, arms, money, or ships, just as Rome has decided, and they shall keep their obligations without receiving any return. ²⁷ In the same way, if war comes first to the nation of the Jews, the Romans shall willingly act as their allies, as the occasion may indicate to them. ²⁸ And to their enemies there shall not be given grain, arms, money, or ships, just as Rome has decided, and they shall keep these obligations and do so without deceit. ²⁹ Thus on these terms the Romans make a treaty with the Jewish people. ³⁰ If after these terms are in effect both parties shall determine to add or delete anything, they shall do so at their discretion, and any addition or deletion that they may make shall be valid.

31 "Concerning the wrongs that King Demetrius is doing to them, we have written to him as follows, 'Why have you made your yoke heavy on our friends and allies the Jews? ³² If now they appeal again for help against you, we will defend their rights and fight you on sea and on land.' "

Bacchides Returns to Judea

9 When Demetrius heard that Nicanor and his army had fallen in battle, he sent Bacchides and Alcimus into the land of Judah a second time, and with them the right wing of the army. ² They went by the road that leads to Gilgal and encamped against Mesaloth in Arbela, and they took it and killed many people. ³ In the first month of the one hundred fifty-second year they encamped against Jerusalem; ⁴ then they marched off and went to Berea with twenty thousand foot soldiers and two thousand cavalry.

5 Now Judas was encamped in Elasa, and with him were three thousand picked men. ⁶ When they saw the huge number of the enemy forces, they were greatly frightened, and many slipped away from the camp, until no more than eight hundred of them were left.

7 When Judas saw that his army had slipped away and the battle was imminent, he was crushed in spirit, for he had no time to assemble them. ⁸ He became faint, but he said to those who were left, "Let us get up and go against our enemies. We may have the strength to fight them." ⁹ But they tried to dissuade him, saying, "We do not have the strength. Let us rather save our own lives now, and let us come back with our kindred and fight them, for we are too few."

---

h **8.10** Gk *them*
i **8.10** Gk *they*

10 But Judas said, "Far be it from me to do such a thing as to flee from them. If our time has come, let us die bravely for our kindred and leave no cause to question our honor."

The Last Battle of Judas

11 Then the army of Bacchides*j* marched out from the camp and took its stand for the encounter. The cavalry was divided into two companies, and the slingers and the archers went ahead of the army, as did all the chief warriors. 12 Bacchides was on the right wing. Flanked by the two companies, the phalanx advanced to the sound of the trumpets, and the men with Judas also blew their trumpets. 13 The earth was shaken by the noise of the armies, and the battle raged from morning until evening.

14 Judas saw that Bacchides and the strength of his army were on the right; then all the courageous men went with him, 15 and they crushed the right wing, and he pursued them as far as Mount Azotus. 16 When those on the left wing saw that the right wing was crushed, they turned and followed close behind Judas and his men. 17 The battle became desperate, and many on both sides were wounded and fell. 18 Judas also fell, and the rest fled.

19 Then Jonathan and Simon took their brother Judas and buried him in the tomb of their ancestors at Modein 20 and wept for him. All Israel made great lamentation for him; they mourned many days and said,
21 "How is the mighty fallen,
  the savior of Israel!"
22 Now the rest of the acts of Judas, and his wars and the brave deeds that he did, and his greatness have not been recorded because they were very many.

Jonathan Succeeds Judas

23 After the death of Judas, the renegades emerged in all parts of Israel; all the wrongdoers reappeared. 24 In those days a very great famine occurred, and the country went over to their side. 25 Bacchides chose the godless and put them in charge of the country. 26 They made inquiry and searched for the friends of Judas and brought them to Bacchides, who took vengeance on them and made sport of them. 27 So there was great distress in Israel such as had not been since the time a prophet had last appeared among them.

28 Then all the friends of Judas assembled and said to Jonathan, 29 "Since the death of your brother Judas there has been no one like him to go against our enemies and Bacchides and to deal with those of our nation who hate us. 30 Now, therefore, we have chosen you today to take his place as our ruler and leader, to fight our battle." 31 So Jonathan accepted the leadership at that time in place of his brother Judas.

The Campaigns of Jonathan

32 When Bacchides learned of this, he tried to kill him. 33 But Jonathan and his brother Simon and all who were with him heard of it, and they fled into the wilderness of Tekoa and camped by the water of the pool of Asphar. 34 Bacchides found this out on the Sabbath day, and he with all his army crossed the Jordan.

35 So Jonathan*k* sent his brother as leader of the multitude and begged the Nabateans, who were his friends, for permission to store with them the great amount of baggage that they had. 36 But the family of Jambri from Medeba came out and seized John and all that he had and left with it.

37 After these things it was reported to Jonathan and his brother Simon, "The family of Jambri are celebrating a great wedding and are conducting the bride, a daughter of one of the great nobles of Canaan, from Nadabath with a large escort." 38 Remembering how their brother John had been killed, they went up and hid under cover of the mountain. 39 They looked out and saw a tumultuous procession with a great amount of baggage, and the bridegroom came out with his friends and his brothers to meet them with tambourines and musicians and many weapons. 40 Then they rushed on them from the ambush and began killing them. Many were wounded and fell, and the rest fled to the mountain, and the troops*l* took all their goods. 41 So the wedding was turned into mourning and the voice of their musicians into a funeral dirge. 42 After they had fully avenged the blood of their brother, they returned to the marshes of the Jordan.

43 When Bacchides heard of this, he came with a large force on the Sabbath day to the banks of the Jordan. 44 And Jonathan said to those with him, "Let us get up now and fight for our lives, for today things are not as they were

---

j **9.11** Gk lacks *of Bacchides*

k **9.35** Gk *he*
l **9.40** Gk *they*

before. ⁴⁵For look! The battle is in front of us and behind us; the water of the Jordan is on this side and on that, with marsh and thicket; there is no place to turn. ⁴⁶Cry out now to heaven that you may be delivered from the hands of our enemies." ⁴⁷So the battle began, and Jonathan stretched out his hand to strike Bacchides, but he eluded him and went to the rear. ⁴⁸Then Jonathan and the men with him leaped into the Jordan and swam across to the other side, and Bacchides's troops^m did not cross the Jordan to attack them. ⁴⁹And about one thousand of Bacchides's men fell that day.

Bacchides Builds Fortifications

50 Then Bacchides^n returned to Jerusalem and built strong cities in Judea: the fortress in Jericho, and Emmaus, and Beth-horon, and Bethel, and Timnath, and^o Pharathon, and Tephon, with high walls and gates and bars. ⁵¹And he placed garrisons in them to harass Israel. ⁵²He also fortified the town of Beth-zur, and Gazara, and the citadel, and in them he put troops and stores of food. ⁵³And he took the sons of the leading men of the land as hostages and put them under guard in the citadel at Jerusalem.

54 In the one hundred and fifty-third year, in the second month, Alcimus gave orders to tear down the wall of the inner court of the sanctuary. He tore down the work of the prophets! ⁵⁵But he only began to tear it down, for at that time Alcimus was stricken, and his work was hindered; his mouth was stopped, and he was paralyzed, so that he could no longer say a word or give commands concerning his house. ⁵⁶And Alcimus died at that time in great agony. ⁵⁷When Bacchides saw that Alcimus was dead, he returned to the king, and the land of Judah had rest for two years.

The End of the War

58 Then all the lawless plotted and said, "See! Jonathan and his men are living in quiet and confidence. So now let us bring Bacchides back, and he will capture them all in one night." ⁵⁹And they went and consulted with him. ⁶⁰He started to come with a large force and secretly sent letters to all his allies in Judea telling them to seize Jonathan and his men, but they were unable to do it, because their plan became known. ⁶¹And Jonathan's men^p seized about fifty of the men of the country who were leaders in this treachery and killed them.

62 Then Jonathan with his men and Simon withdrew to Bethbasi in the wilderness; he rebuilt the parts of it that had been demolished, and they fortified it. ⁶³When Bacchides learned of this, he assembled all his forces and sent orders to the men of Judea. ⁶⁴Then he came and encamped against Bethbasi; he fought against it for many days and made engines of war.

65 But Jonathan left his brother Simon in the town while he went out into the country, and he went with only a few men. ⁶⁶He struck down Odomera and his kindred and the people of Phasiron in their tents. ⁶⁷Then he^q began to attack and went into battle with his forces, and Simon and his men sallied out from the town and set fire to the engines of war. ⁶⁸They fought with Bacchides, and he was crushed by them. They pressed him very hard, for his plan and his expedition had been in vain. ⁶⁹So he was very angry at the renegades who had counseled him to come into the country, and he killed many of them. Then he decided to go back to his own land. ⁷⁰When Jonathan learned of this, he sent ambassadors to him to make peace with him and obtain release of the captives. ⁷¹He agreed and did as he said, and he swore to Jonathan^r that he would not try to harm him as long as he lived. ⁷²He restored to him the captives whom he had taken previously from the land of Judah; then he turned and went back to his own land and did not come again into their territory. ⁷³Thus the sword ceased from Israel. Jonathan settled in Michmash and began to judge the people, and he destroyed the godless out of Israel.

Revolt of Alexander Epiphanes

10 In the one hundred sixtieth year Alexander Epiphanes, son of Antiochus, landed and occupied Ptolemais. They welcomed him, and there he began to reign. ²When King Demetrius heard of it, he assembled a very large army and marched out to meet him in battle. ³Demetrius sent Jonathan a letter in peaceable words to honor him, ⁴for he said to himself, "Let us act first to make peace with him^s before

---

m 9.48 Gk *they*
n 9.50 Gk *he*
o 9.50 Some authorities omit *and*

p 9.61 Gk *they*
q 9.67 Other ancient authorities read *they*
r 9.71 Gk *him*
s 10.4 Gk *them*

he makes peace with Alexander against us, ⁵for he will remember all the wrongs that we did to him and to his brothers and his nation." ⁶So Demetrius' gave him authority to recruit troops, to equip them with arms, and to become his ally, and he commanded that the hostages in the citadel should be released to him.

7 Then Jonathan came to Jerusalem and read the letter in the hearing of all the people and of those in the citadel. ⁸They were greatly alarmed when they heard that the king had given him authority to recruit troops. ⁹But those in the citadel released the hostages to Jonathan, and he returned them to their parents.

10 And Jonathan took up residence in Jerusalem and began to rebuild and restore the city. ¹¹He directed those who were doing the work to build the walls and encircle Mount Zion with squared stones, for better fortification, and they did so.

12 Then the foreigners who were in the strongholds that Bacchides had built fled; ¹³all of them left their places and went back to their own lands. ¹⁴Only in Beth-zur did some remain who had forsaken the law and the commandments, for it served as a place of refuge.

15 Now King Alexander heard of all the promises that Demetrius had sent to Jonathan, and he heard of the battles that Jonathanᵘ and his brothers had fought, of the brave deeds that they had done, and of the troubles that they had endured. ¹⁶So he said, "Shall we find another such man? Come now, we will make him our friend and ally." ¹⁷And he wrote a letter and sent it to him, in the following words:

Jonathan Becomes High Priest

18 "King Alexander to his brother Jonathan, greetings. ¹⁹We have heard about you, that you are a mighty warrior and worthy to be our friend. ²⁰And so we have appointed you today to be the high priest of your nation; you are to be called the king's Friend, and you are to take our side and keep friendship with us." He also sent him a purple robe and a golden crown.

21 So Jonathan put on the sacred vestments in the seventh month of the one hundred sixtieth year, at the Festival of Booths,ᵛ and he recruited troops and equipped them with arms in abundance. ²²When Demetrius heard of these

things, he was distressed and said, ²³"What is this that we have done? Alexander has gotten ahead of us in forming a friendship with the Jews to strengthen himself. ²⁴I also will write them words of encouragement and promise them honor and gifts, so that I may have their help." ²⁵So he sent a message to them in the following words:

A Letter from Demetrius to Jonathan

"King Demetrius to the nation of the Jews, greetings. ²⁶Since you have kept your agreement with us and have continued your friendship with us and have not sided with our enemies, we have heard of it and rejoiced. ²⁷Now continue still to keep faith with us, and we will repay you with good for what you do for us. ²⁸We will grant you many immunities and give you gifts.

29 "I now free you and exempt all the Jews from payment of tribute and salt tax and crown levies, ³⁰and instead of collecting the third of the grain and the half of the fruit of the trees that I should receive, I release them from this day and henceforth. I will not collect them from the land of Judah or from the three districts added to it from Samaria and Galilee, from this day and for all time. ³¹Jerusalem and its environs, its tithes and its revenues, shall be holy and free from tax. ³²I release also my control of the citadel in Jerusalem and give it to the high priest, so that he may station in it men of his own choice to guard it. ³³And every one of the Jews taken as a captive from the land of Judah into any part of my kingdom, I set free without payment, and let all officials cancel also the taxes on their livestock.

34 "All the festivals and Sabbaths and new moons and appointed days and the three days before a festival and the three after a festival— let them all be days of immunity and release for all the Jews who are in my kingdom. ³⁵No one shall have authority to exact anything from them or trouble any of them about any matter.

36 "Let Jews be enrolled in the king's forces to the number of thirty thousand men, and let the maintenance be given them that is due to all the forces of the king. ³⁷Let some of them be stationed in the great strongholds of the king, and let some of them be put in positions of trust in the kingdom. Let their officers and leaders be of their own number, and let them live by their own laws, just as the king has commanded in the land of Judah.

---

t 10.6 Gk *he*
u 10.15 Gk *he*
v 10.21 Or *Tabernacles*

38 "As for the three districts that have been added to Judea from the country of Samaria, let them be annexed to Judea so that they may be considered to be under one ruler and obey no other authority than the high priest. 39 Ptolemais and the land adjoining it I have given as a gift to the sanctuary in Jerusalem, to meet the necessary expenses of the sanctuary. 40 I also grant fifteen thousand shekels of silver yearly out of the king's revenues from appropriate places. 41 And all the additional funds that the government officials have not paid as they did in the first years,*w* they shall give from now on for the service of the temple.*x* 42 Moreover, the five thousand shekels of silver that my officials*y* have received every year from the income of the services of the temple, this, too, is canceled, because it belongs to the priests who minister there. 43 And all who take refuge at the temple in Jerusalem or in any of its precincts because they owe money to the king or are in debt, let them be released and receive back all their property in my kingdom.

44 "Let the cost of rebuilding and restoring the structures of the sanctuary be paid from the revenues of the king. 45 And let the cost of rebuilding the walls of Jerusalem and fortifying it all around and the cost of rebuilding the walls in Judea also be paid from the revenues of the king."

Death of Demetrius

46 When Jonathan and the people heard these words, they did not believe or accept them, because they remembered the great wrongs that Demetrius*z* had done in Israel and how much he had oppressed them. 47 They favored Alexander because he had been the first to speak peaceable words to them, and they remained his allies all his days.

48 Now King Alexander assembled large forces and encamped opposite Demetrius. 49 The two kings met in battle, and the army of Demetrius fled, and Alexander*a* pursued him and defeated them. 50 He pressed the battle strongly until the sun set, and on that day Demetrius fell.

Treaty of Ptolemy and Alexander

51 Then Alexander sent ambassadors to Ptolemy king of Egypt with the following message: 52 "Since I have returned to my kingdom and have taken my seat on the throne of my ancestors and established my rule—for I crushed Demetrius and gained control of our country; 53 I met him in battle, and he and his army were crushed by us, and we have taken our seat on the throne of his kingdom—54 now therefore let us establish friendship with one another; give me now your daughter as my wife, and I will become your son-in-law and will make gifts to you and to her in keeping with your position."

55 Ptolemy the king replied and said, "Happy was the day on which you returned to the land of your ancestors and took your seat on the throne of their kingdom. 56 And now I will do for you as you wrote, but meet me at Ptolemais, so that we may see one another, and I will become your father-in-law, as you have said."

57 So Ptolemy set out from Egypt, he and his daughter Cleopatra, and came to Ptolemais in the one hundred sixty-second year. 58 King Alexander met him, and Ptolemy*b* gave him his daughter Cleopatra in marriage and celebrated her wedding at Ptolemais with great pomp, as kings do.

59 Then King Alexander wrote to Jonathan to come and meet him. 60 So he went with pomp to Ptolemais and met the two kings; he gave them and their Friends silver and gold and many gifts and found favor with them. 61 A group of malcontents from Israel, renegades, gathered together against him to accuse him, but the king paid no attention to them. 62 The king gave orders to take off Jonathan's garments and to clothe him in purple, and they did so. 63 The king also seated him at his side, and he said to his officers, "Go out with him into the middle of the city and proclaim that no one is to bring charges against him about any matter, and let no one trouble him for any reason." 64 When his accusers saw the honor that was paid him, in accord with the proclamation, and saw him clothed in purple, they all fled. 65 Thus the king honored him and enrolled him among his First Friends and made him general and governor of the province. 66 And Jonathan returned to Jerusalem in peace and gladness.

---

w 10.41 Meaning of Gk uncertain
x 10.41 Gk *house*
y 10.42 Gk *they*
z 10.46 Gk *he*
a 10.49 Other ancient authorities read *Alexander fled, and Demetrius*

---

b 10.58 Gk *he*

Apollonius Is Defeated by Jonathan

67 In the one hundred sixty-fifth year Demetrius son of Demetrius came from Crete to the land of his ancestors. 68 When King Alexander heard of it, he was greatly distressed and returned to Antioch. 69 And Demetrius appointed Apollonius the governor of Coelesyria, and he assembled a large force and encamped against Jamnia. Then he sent the following message to the high priest Jonathan:

70 "You are the only one to rise up against us, and I have fallen into ridicule and disgrace because of you. Why do you assume authority against us in the hill country? 71 If you now have confidence in your forces, come down to the plain to meet us, and let us match strength with each other there, for I have with me the power of the cities. 72 Ask and learn who I am and who the others are who are helping us. People will tell you that you cannot stand before us, for your ancestors were twice put to flight in their own land. 73 And now you will not be able to withstand my cavalry and such an army in the plain, where there is no stone or pebble or place to flee."

74 When Jonathan heard the words of Apollonius, his spirit was aroused. He chose ten thousand men and set out from Jerusalem, and his brother Simon met him to help him. 75 He encamped before Joppa, but the people of the city closed its gates, for Apollonius had a garrison in Joppa. 76 So they fought against it, and the people of the city became afraid and opened the gates, and Jonathan gained possession of Joppa.

77 When Apollonius heard of it, he mustered three thousand cavalry and a large army and went to Azotus as though he were going farther. At the same time he advanced into the plain, for he had a large troop of cavalry and put confidence in it. 78 Jonathan[c] pursued him to Azotus, and the armies engaged in battle. 79 Now Apollonius had secretly left a thousand cavalry behind them. 80 Jonathan learned that there was an ambush behind him, for they surrounded his army and shot arrows at his men from early morning until late afternoon. 81 But his men stood fast, as Jonathan had commanded, and the enemy's[d] horses grew tired. 82 Then Simon brought forward his force and engaged the phalanx in battle (for the cavalry was exhausted); they were overwhelmed by

him and fled, 83 and the cavalry was dispersed in the plain. They fled to Azotus and entered Beth-dagon, the temple of their idol, for safety. 84 But Jonathan burned Azotus and the surrounding towns and plundered them, and the temple of Dagon and those who had taken refuge in it he burned with fire. 85 The number of those who fell by the sword, with those burned alive, came to eight thousand.

86 Then Jonathan left there and encamped against Askalon, and the people of the city came out to meet him with great pomp. 87 He and those with him then returned to Jerusalem with a large amount of plunder. 88 When King Alexander heard of these things, he honored Jonathan still more, 89 and he sent to him a golden buckle, such as it is the custom to give to the King's Kinsmen. He also gave him Ekron and all its environs as his possession.

Ptolemy Invades Syria

11 Then the king of Egypt gathered great forces like the sand by the seashore and many ships, and he tried to get possession of Alexander's kingdom by trickery and add it to his own kingdom. 2 He set out for Syria with peaceable words, and the people of the towns opened their gates to him and went to meet him, for King Alexander had commanded them to meet him, since he was Alexander's[e] father-in-law. 3 But when Ptolemy entered the towns he stationed forces as a garrison in each town.

4 When he[f] approached Azotus, they showed him the burnt-out temple of Dagon, and Azotus and its suburbs destroyed, and the corpses lying about, and the charred bodies of those whom Jonathan[g] had burned in the war, for they had piled them in heaps along his route. 5 They also told the king what Jonathan had done, to throw blame on him, but the king kept silent. 6 Jonathan met the king at Joppa with pomp, and they greeted one another and spent the night there. 7 And Jonathan went with the king as far as the river called Eleutherus; then he returned to Jerusalem.

8 So King Ptolemy gained control of the coastal cities as far as Seleucia by the sea, and he kept devising wicked designs against Alexander. 9 He sent envoys to King Demetrius, saying, "Come, let us make a covenant with

---

c 10.78 Gk *He*
d 10.81 Gk *their*

e 11.2 Gk *his*
f 11.4 Other ancient authorities read *they*
g 11.4 Gk *he*

each other, and I will give you in marriage my daughter who was Alexander's wife, and you shall reign over your father's kingdom. ¹⁰I now regret that I gave him my daughter, for he has tried to kill me." ¹¹He threw blame on Alexander[h] because he coveted his kingdom. ¹²So he took his daughter away from him and gave her to Demetrius. He was estranged from Alexander, and their hostility became apparent.

13 Then Ptolemy entered Antioch and put on the crown of Asia. Thus he put two crowns on his head, the crown of Egypt and that of Asia. ¹⁴Now King Alexander was in Cilicia at that time because the people of that region were in revolt. ¹⁵When Alexander heard of it, he came against him in battle. Ptolemy marched out and met him with a strong force and put him to flight. ¹⁶So Alexander fled into Arabia to find protection there, and King Ptolemy was triumphant. ¹⁷Zabdiel the Arab cut off the head of Alexander and sent it to Ptolemy. ¹⁸But King Ptolemy died three days later, and his troops in the strongholds were killed by the inhabitants of the strongholds. ¹⁹So Demetrius became king in the one hundred sixty-seventh year.

Jonathan's Diplomacy

20 In those days Jonathan assembled the Judeans to attack the citadel in Jerusalem, and he built many engines of war to use against it. ²¹But certain renegades who hated their nation went to the king and reported to him that Jonathan was besieging the citadel. ²²When he heard this he was angry, and as soon as he heard it he set out and came to Ptolemais, and he wrote Jonathan not to continue the siege but to meet him for a conference at Ptolemais as quickly as possible.

23 When Jonathan heard this, he gave orders to continue the siege. He chose some of the elders of Israel and some of the priests and put himself in danger, ²⁴for he went to the king at Ptolemais, taking silver and gold and clothing and numerous other gifts. And he won his favor. ²⁵Although certain renegades of his nation kept making complaints against him, ²⁶the king treated him as his predecessors had treated him; he exalted him in the presence of all his Friends. ²⁷He confirmed him in the high priesthood and in as many other honors as he had formerly had and caused him to be reckoned among his First Friends. ²⁸Then Jonathan asked the king to free

Judea and the three districts and Samaria from tribute and promised him three hundred talents. ²⁹The king consented and wrote a letter to Jonathan about all these things; its contents were as follows:

30 "King Demetrius to his brother Jonathan and to the nation of the Jews, greetings. ³¹This copy of the letter that we wrote concerning you to our kinsman Lasthenes we have written to you also, so that you may know what it says. ³²'King Demetrius to his father Lasthenes, greetings. ³³We have determined to do good to the nation of the Jews, who are our friends and fulfill their obligations to us, because of the goodwill they show toward us. ³⁴We have confirmed as their possession both the territory of Judea and the three districts of Aphairema and Lydda and Ramathaim;[i] the latter, with all the region bordering them, were added to Judea from Samaria. To all those who offer sacrifice in Jerusalem we have granted release from[j] the royal taxes that the king formerly received from them each year, from the crops of the land and the fruit of the trees. ³⁵And the other payments henceforth due to us of the tithes, and the taxes due to us, and the salt pits and the crown taxes due to us—from all these we shall grant them release. ³⁶And not one of these grants shall be canceled from this time on forever. ³⁷Now, therefore, take care to make a copy of this, and let it be given to Jonathan and put up in a conspicuous place on the holy mountain.' "

The Intrigue of Trypho

38 When King Demetrius saw that the land was quiet before him and that there was no opposition to him, he dismissed all his troops, all of them to their own homes, except the foreign troops whom he had recruited from the islands of the nations. So all the troops who had served under his predecessors hated him. ³⁹A certain Trypho had formerly been one of Alexander's supporters; he saw that all the troops were grumbling against Demetrius. So he went to Imalkue the Arab, who was bringing up Antiochus, the young son of Alexander, ⁴⁰and insistently urged him to hand Antiochus[k] over to him, to become king in place of his father. He also reported to Imalkue[l] what Demetrius had

---

i 11.34 Gk *Rathamin*
j 11.34 Or *Samaria, for all those who offer sacrifice in Jerusalem, in place of*
k 11.40 Gk *him*
l 11.40 Gk *him*

h 11.11 Gk *him*

done and told of the hatred that the troops of Demetrius[m] had for him, and he stayed there many days.

41 Now Jonathan sent to King Demetrius the request that he remove the troops of the citadel from Jerusalem and the troops in the strongholds, for they kept fighting against Israel. 42 And Demetrius sent this message back to Jonathan: "Not only will I do these things for you and your nation, but I will confer great honor on you and your nation, if I find an opportunity. 43 Now, then, you will do well to send me men who will help me, for all my troops have revolted." 44 So Jonathan sent three thousand stalwart men to him at Antioch, and when they came to the king, the king rejoiced at their arrival.

45 Then the people of the city assembled within the city, to the number of a hundred and twenty thousand, and they wanted to kill the king. 46 But the king fled into the palace. Then the people of the city seized the main streets of the city and began to fight. 47 So the king called the Jews to his aid, and they all rallied around him and then spread out through the city, and they killed on that day about one hundred thousand. 48 They set fire to the city and seized a large amount of spoil on that day and saved the king. 49 When the people of the city saw that the Jews had gained control of the city as they pleased, their courage failed, and they cried out to the king with this entreaty: 50 "Grant us peace, and make the Jews stop fighting against us and our city." 51 And they threw down their arms and made peace. So the Jews gained glory in the sight of the king and of all the people in his kingdom, and they returned to Jerusalem with a large amount of spoil.

52 So King Demetrius sat on the throne of his kingdom, and the land was quiet before him. 53 But he broke his word about all that he had promised; he became estranged from Jonathan and did not repay the favors that Jonathan[n] had done him but treated him very harshly.

Trypho Seizes Power

54 After this Trypho returned, and with him the young boy Antiochus, who began to reign and put on the crown. 55 All the troops whom Demetrius had discharged gathered around him; they fought against Demetrius,[o] and he fled and was routed. 56 Trypho captured the elephants[p] and gained control of Antioch. 57 Then the young Antiochus wrote to Jonathan, saying, "I confirm you in the high priesthood and set you over the four districts and make you one of the king's Friends." 58 He also sent him gold plates and a table service and granted him the right to drink from gold cups and dress in purple and wear a gold buckle. 59 He appointed Jonathan's[q] brother Simon governor from the Ladder of Tyre to the borders of Egypt.

Campaigns of Jonathan and Simon

60 Then Jonathan set out and traveled beyond the river and among the towns, and all the army of Syria gathered to him as allies. When he came to Askalon, the people of the city met him and paid him honor. 61 From there he went to Gaza, but the people of Gaza shut him out. So he besieged it and burned its suburbs with fire and plundered them. 62 Then the people of Gaza pleaded with Jonathan, and he made peace with them and took the sons of their rulers as hostages and sent them to Jerusalem. And he passed through the country as far as Damascus.

63 Then Jonathan heard that the officers of Demetrius had come to Kadesh in Galilee with a large army, intending to remove him from office. 64 He went to meet them but left his brother Simon in the country. 65 Simon encamped before Beth-zur and fought against it for many days and hemmed it in. 66 Then they asked him to grant them terms of peace, and he did so. He removed them from there, took possession of the town, and set a garrison over it.

67 Jonathan and his army encamped by the waters of Gennesaret. Early in the morning they marched to the plain of Hazor, 68 and there in the plain the army of the foreigners met him; they had set an ambush against him in the mountains, but they themselves met him face to face. 69 Then the men in ambush emerged from their places and joined battle. 70 All the men with Jonathan fled; not one of them was left except Mattathias son of Absalom and Judas son of Chalphi, commanders of the forces of the army. 71 Jonathan tore his clothes, put dust on his head, and prayed. 72 Then he turned back to the battle against the enemy[r] and routed them, and they fled. 73 When his men who were fleeing

---

m 11.40 Gk *his troops*
n 11.53 Gk *he*
o 11.55 Gk *him*

p 11.56 Gk *animals*
q 11.59 Gk *his*
r 11.72 Gk *them*

saw this, they returned to him and joined him in the pursuit as far as Kadesh, to their camp, and there they encamped. 74 As many as three thousand of the foreigners fell that day. And Jonathan returned to Jerusalem.

Alliances with Rome and Sparta

12 Now when Jonathan saw that the time was favorable for him, he chose men and sent them to Rome to confirm and renew the friendship with them. 2 He also sent letters to the same effect to the Spartans and to other places. 3 So they went to Rome and entered the senate chamber and said, "The high priest Jonathan and the Jewish nation have sent us to renew the former friendship and alliance with them." 4 And the Romans^s gave them letters to the people in every place, asking them to provide for the envoys'^t safe conduct to the land of Judah.

5 This is a copy of the letter that Jonathan wrote to the Spartans: 6 "The high priest Jonathan, the council of the nation, the priests, and the rest of the Jewish people to their brothers the Spartans, greetings. 7 Already in time past a letter was sent to the high priest Onias from Arius, who was king among you, stating that you are our brothers, as the appended copy shows. 8 Onias welcomed the envoy with honor and received the letter, which contained a clear declaration of alliance and friendship. 9 Therefore, though we have no need of these things, since we have as encouragement the holy books that are in our hands, 10 we have undertaken to send to renew our family ties and friendship with you, so that we may not become estranged from you, for considerable time has passed since you sent your letter to us. 11 We therefore remember you constantly on every occasion, both at our festivals and on other appropriate days, at the sacrifices that we offer and in our prayers, as it is right and proper to remember brothers. 12 And we rejoice in your glory. 13 But as for ourselves, many trials and many wars have encircled us; the kings around us have waged war against us. 14 We were unwilling to trouble you and our other allies and friends with these wars, 15 for we have the help that comes from heaven for our aid, so we were delivered from our enemies, and our enemies were humbled. 16 We therefore have chosen Numenius son of Antiochus and

Antipater son of Jason and have sent them to Rome to renew our former friendship and alliance with them. 17 We have commanded them to go also to you and greet you and deliver to you this letter from us concerning the renewal of our family ties. 18 And now please send us a reply to this."

19 This is a copy of the letter that they sent to Onias: 20 "King Arius of the Spartans, to the high priest Onias, greetings. 21 It has been found in writing concerning the Spartans and the Jews that they are brothers and are of the family of Abraham. 22 And now that we have learned this, please write us concerning your welfare; 23 we on our part write to you that your livestock and your property belong to us, and ours belong to you. We therefore command that our envoys^u report to you accordingly."

Further Campaigns of Jonathan and Simon

24 Now Jonathan heard that the commanders of Demetrius had returned with a larger force than before to wage war against him. 25 So he marched away from Jerusalem and met them in the region of Hamath, for he gave them no opportunity to invade his own country. 26 He sent spies to their camp, and they returned and reported to him that the enemy^v were being drawn up in formation to attack the Jews^w by night. 27 So when the sun had set, Jonathan commanded his troops to be alert and to keep their arms at hand so as to be ready all night for battle, and he stationed outposts around the camp. 28 When the enemy heard that Jonathan and his troops were prepared for battle, they were afraid and were terrified at heart, so they kindled fires in their camp and withdrew.^x 29 But Jonathan and his troops did not know it until morning, for they saw the fires burning. 30 Then Jonathan pursued them, but he did not overtake them, for they had crossed the Eleutherus River. 31 So Jonathan turned aside against the Arabs who are called Zabadeans, and he crushed them and plundered them. 32 Then he broke camp and went to Damascus and marched through all that region.

33 Simon also went out and marched through the country as far as Askalon and the neighboring strongholds. He turned aside to Joppa and

---

s **12.4** Gk *they*
t **12.4** Gk *them*

u **12.23** Gk *they*
v **12.26** Gk *they*
w **12.26** Gk *them*
x **12.28** Other ancient authorities omit *and withdrew*

took it by surprise, ³⁴for he had heard that they were ready to hand over the stronghold to those whom Demetrius had sent. And he stationed a garrison there to guard it.

³⁵ When Jonathan returned he convened the elders of the people and planned with them to build strongholds in Judea, ³⁶to build the walls of Jerusalem still higher, and to erect a high barrier between the citadel and the city to separate it from the city, in order to isolate it so that its garrison^y could neither buy nor sell. ³⁷So they gathered together to rebuild the city; part of the wall on the valley to the east had fallen, and he repaired the section called Chaphenatha. ³⁸Simon also built Adida in the Shephelah; he fortified it and installed gates with bolts.

Trypho Captures Jonathan

³⁹Then Trypho attempted to become king in Asia and put on the crown and to raise his hand against King Antiochus. ⁴⁰He feared that Jonathan might not permit him to do so but might make war on him, so he kept seeking to seize and kill him, and he marched out and came to Beth-shan. ⁴¹Jonathan went out to meet him with forty thousand picked warriors, and he came to Beth-shan. ⁴²When Trypho saw that he had come with a large army, he was afraid to raise his hand against him. ⁴³So he received him with honor and commended him to all his Friends, and he gave him gifts and commanded his Friends and his troops to obey him as they would himself. ⁴⁴Then he said to Jonathan, "Why have you put all these people to so much trouble when we are not at war? ⁴⁵Dismiss them now to their homes and choose for yourself a few men to stay with you and come with me to Ptolemais. I will hand it over to you, as well as the other strongholds and the remaining troops and all the officials, and will turn around and go home. For that is why I am here."

⁴⁶Jonathan^z trusted him and did as he said; he sent away the troops, and they returned to the land of Judah. ⁴⁷He kept with himself three thousand men, two thousand of whom he left in Galilee, while one thousand accompanied him. ⁴⁸But when Jonathan entered Ptolemais, the people of Ptolemais closed the gates and seized him, and they killed with the sword all who had entered with him.

⁴⁹Then Trypho sent troops and cavalry into Galilee and the Great Plain to destroy all Jonathan's soldiers. ⁵⁰But they realized that Jonathan had been seized and had perished along with his men, and they encouraged one another and kept marching in close formation, ready for battle. ⁵¹When their pursuers saw that they would fight for their lives, they turned back. ⁵²So they all reached the land of Judah safely, and they mourned for Jonathan and his companions and were in great fear, and all Israel mourned deeply. ⁵³All the nations around them tried to destroy them, for they said, "They have no leader or helper. Now, therefore, let us make war on them and blot out the memory of them from humankind."

Simon Takes Command

13 Simon heard that Trypho had assembled a large army to invade the land of Judah and destroy it, ²and he saw that the people were trembling with fear. So he went up to Jerusalem, and gathering the people together ³he encouraged them, saying to them, "You yourselves know what great things my brothers and I and the house of my father have done for the laws and the sanctuary; you know also the wars and the difficulties that my brothers and I have seen. ⁴By reason of this all my brothers have perished for the sake of Israel, and I alone am left. ⁵And now, far be it from me to spare my life in any time of distress, for I am not better than my brothers. ⁶But I will avenge my nation and the sanctuary and your wives and children, for all the nations have gathered together out of hatred to destroy us."

⁷The spirit of the people was rekindled when they heard these words, ⁸and they answered in a loud voice, "You are our leader in place of Judas and your brother Jonathan. ⁹Fight our battles, and all that you say to us we will do." ¹⁰So he assembled all the warriors and hurried to complete the walls of Jerusalem, and he fortified it on every side. ¹¹He sent Jonathan son of Absalom to Joppa and with him a considerable army; he drove out its occupants and remained there.

Deceit and Treachery of Trypho

¹²Then Trypho left Ptolemais with a large army to invade the land of Judah, and Jonathan was with him under guard. ¹³Simon encamped in Adida, facing the plain. ¹⁴Trypho learned that Simon had risen up in place of his brother Jonathan and that he was about to join battle with

---

^y 12.36 Gk *they*
^z 12.46 Gk *He*

him, so he sent envoys to him and said, [15]"It is for the money that your brother Jonathan owed the royal treasury, in connection with the offices he held, that we are detaining him. [16]Send now one hundred talents of silver and two of his sons as hostages, so that when released he will not revolt against us, and we will release him."

[17]Simon knew that they were speaking deceitfully to him, but he sent to get the money and the sons, so that he would not arouse great hostility among the people, who might say, [18]"It was because Simon[a] did not send him the money and the sons that Jonathan[b] perished." [19]So he sent the sons and the hundred talents, but Trypho[c] broke his word and did not release Jonathan.

[20]After this Trypho came to invade the country and destroy it, and he circled around by the way to Adora. But Simon and his army kept marching along opposite him to every place he went. [21]Now the men in the citadel kept sending envoys to Trypho urging him to come to them by way of the wilderness and to send them food. [22]So Trypho got all his cavalry ready to go, but that night a very heavy snow fell, and he did not go because of the snow. He marched off and went into the land of Gilead. [23]When he approached Baskama, he killed Jonathan, and he was buried there. [24]Then Trypho turned and went back to his own land.

Jonathan's Tomb

[25]Simon sent and took the bones of his brother Jonathan and buried him in Modein, the city of his ancestors. [26]All Israel bewailed him with great lamentation and mourned for him many days. [27]And Simon built a monument over the tomb of his father and his brothers; he made it high so that it might be seen, with polished stone at the front and back. [28]He also erected seven pyramids, opposite one another, for his father and mother and four brothers. [29]For the pyramids[d] he devised an elaborate setting, erecting about them great columns, and on the columns he put suits of armor for a permanent memorial, and beside the suits of armor he carved ships, so that they could be seen by all who sail the sea. [30]This is the tomb that he built in Modein; it remains to this day.

Judea Gains Independence

[31]Trypho dealt treacherously with the young King Antiochus; he killed him [32]and became king in his place, putting on the crown of Asia, and he brought great calamity on the land. [33]But Simon built up the strongholds of Judea and walled them all around, with high towers and great walls and gates and bolts, and he stored food in the strongholds. [34]Simon also chose emissaries and sent them to King Demetrius with a request to grant relief to the country, for all that Trypho did was to plunder. [35]King Demetrius sent him a favorable reply to this request and wrote him a letter as follows, [36]"King Demetrius to Simon, the high priest and friend of kings, and to the elders and nation of the Jews, greetings. [37]We have received the gold crown and the palm branch that you sent, and we are ready to make a general peace with you and to write to our officials to grant you release from tribute. [38]All the grants that we have made to you remain valid, and let the strongholds that you have built be your possession. [39]We pardon any errors and offenses committed to this day and cancel the crown tax that you owe, and whatever other tax has been collected in Jerusalem shall be collected no longer. [40]And if any of you are qualified to be enrolled in our bodyguard,[e] let them be enrolled, and let there be peace between us."

[41]In the one hundred seventieth year the yoke of the nations was removed from Israel, [42]and the people began to write in their documents and contracts, "In the first year of Simon the great high priest and commander and leader of the Jews."

The Capture of Gazara by Simon

[43]In those days Simon[f] encamped against Gazara[g] and surrounded it with troops. He made a siege engine, brought it up to the city, and battered and captured one tower. [44]The men in the siege engine leaped out into the city, and a great tumult arose in the city. [45]The men in the city, with their wives and children, went up on the wall with their clothes torn, and they cried out with a loud voice, asking Simon to make peace with them; [46]they said, "Do not treat us according to our wicked acts but according to your mercy." [47]So Simon reached an agreement with

---

a 13.18 Gk *I*
b 13.18 Gk *he*
c 13.19 Gk *he*
d 13.29 Gk *For these*

e 13.40 Or *court*
f 13.43 Gk *he*
g 13.43 Cn: Gk *Gaza*

them and stopped fighting against them. But he expelled them from the city and cleansed the houses in which the idols were located and then entered it with hymns and praise. [48]He removed all uncleanness from it and settled in it those who observed the law. He also strengthened its fortifications and built in it a house for himself.

Simon Regains the Citadel at Jerusalem

[49]Those who were in the citadel at Jerusalem were prevented from going in and out to buy and sell in the country. So they were very hungry, and many of them perished from famine. [50]Then they cried to Simon to make peace with them, and he did so. But he expelled them from there and cleansed the citadel from its pollutions. [51]On the twenty-third day of the second month, in the one hundred seventy-first year, the Jews[h] entered it with praise and palm branches, and with harps and cymbals and stringed instruments, and with hymns and songs, because a great enemy had been crushed and removed from Israel. [52]Simon[i] decreed that every year they should celebrate this day with rejoicing. He strengthened the fortifications of the temple hill alongside the citadel, and he and his men lived there. [53]Simon saw that his son John had reached manhood, so he made him commander of all the forces, and he lived at Gazara.

Capture of Demetrius

14 In the one hundred seventy-second year King Demetrius assembled his forces and marched into Media to obtain help, so that he could make war against Trypho. [2]When King Arsaces of Persia and Media heard that Demetrius had invaded his territory, he sent one of his generals to take him alive. [3]The general[j] went and defeated the army of Demetrius and seized him and took him to Arsaces, who put him under guard.

Eulogy of Simon

[4] The land[k] had rest all the days of Simon.
He sought the good of his nation;
his rule was pleasing to them,
as was the honor shown him all his days.

---

h 13.51 Gk *they*
i 13.52 Gk *He*
j 14.3 Gk *He*
k 14.4 Other ancient authorities add *of Judah*

[5] To crown all his honors he took Joppa for a
harbor
and opened a way to the isles of the sea.
[6] He extended the borders of his nation
and gained full control of the country.
[7] He gathered a host of captives;
he ruled over Gazara and Beth-zur and
the citadel,
and he removed its uncleanness from it,
and there was none to oppose him.
[8] They tilled their land in peace;
the ground gave its increase
and the trees of the plains their fruit.
[9] Old men sat in the streets;
they all talked together of good things,
and the youths put on splendid military
attire.
[10] He supplied the towns with food
and furnished them with the means of
defense,
until his renown spread to the ends of the
earth.
[11] He established peace in the land,
and Israel rejoiced with great joy.
[12] All the people sat under their own vines
and fig trees,
and there was none to make them afraid.
[13] No one was left in the land to fight them,
and the kings were crushed in those days.
[14] He gave help to all the humble among his
people;
he sought out the law
and did away with all the renegades and
outlaws.
[15] He made the sanctuary glorious
and added to the vessels of the sanctuary.

Diplomacy with Rome and Sparta

[16]It was heard in Rome and as far away as Sparta that Jonathan had died, and they were deeply grieved. [17]When they heard that his brother Simon had become high priest in his stead and that he was ruling over the country and the towns in it, [18]they wrote to him on bronze tablets to renew with him the friendship and alliance that they had established with his brothers Judas and Jonathan. [19]And these were read before the assembly in Jerusalem.

[20]This is a copy of the letter that the Spartans sent:

"The rulers and the city of the Spartans to the high priest Simon and to the elders and the priests and the rest of the Jewish people, our brothers, greetings. [21]The envoys who were sent to our people have told us about your glory and honor, and we rejoiced at their coming. ²²We have recorded what they said in our public decrees, as follows, 'Numenius son of Antiochus and Antipater son of Jason, envoys of the Jews, have come to us to renew their friendship with us. ²³It has pleased our people to receive these men with honor and to put a copy of their words in the public archives, so that the people of the Spartans may have a record of them. And they have sent a copy of this to the high priest Simon.' "

24 After this Simon sent Numenius to Rome with a large gold shield weighing one thousand minas to confirm the alliance with the Romans.ˡ

Official Honors for Simon

25 When the people heard these things they said, "How shall we thank Simon and his sons? ²⁶For he and his brothers and the house of his father have stood firm; they have fought and repulsed Israel's enemies and established its freedom." ²⁷So they made a record on bronze tablets and put it on pillars on Mount Zion.

This is a copy of what they wrote: "On the eighteenth day of Elul, in the one hundred seventy-second year, which is the third year of the great high priest Simon, ²⁸in Asaramel, in the great assembly of the priests and the people and the rulers of the nation and the elders of the country, the following was proclaimed to us:

29 "Since wars often occurred in the country, Simon son of Mattathias, of the clan of Joarib, and his brothers, exposed themselves to danger and resisted the enemies of their nation, in order that their sanctuary and the law might be preserved, and they brought great glory to their nation. ³⁰Jonathan rallied theᵐ nation, became their high priest, and was gathered to his people. ³¹When their enemies decided to invade their country and lay hands on their sanctuary, ³²then Simon rose up and fought for his nation. He spent great sums of his own money; he armed the soldiers of his nation and paid them wages. ³³He fortified the towns of Judea, and Beth-zur on the borders of Judea, where formerly the arms of the enemy had been stored, and he placed there a garrison of Jews. ³⁴He also fortified Joppa, which is by the sea, and Gazara, which is on the borders of Azotus, where the enemy formerly lived. He settled Jews there and

provided in those townsⁿ whatever was necessary for their restoration.

35 "The people saw Simon's faithfulnessᵒ and the glory that he had resolved to win for his nation, and they made him their leader and high priest because he had done all these things and because of the justice and loyalty that he had maintained toward his nation. He sought in every way to exalt his people. ³⁶In his days things prospered in his hands, so that the nations were put out of theᵖ country, as were also those in the city of David in Jerusalem, who had built themselves a citadel from which they used to sally forth and defile the environs of the sanctuary, doing great damage to its purity. ³⁷He settled Jews in it and fortified it for the safety of the country and of the city and built the walls of Jerusalem higher.

38 "In view of these things King Demetrius confirmed him in the high priesthood, ³⁹made him one of his Friends, and paid him high honors. ⁴⁰For he had heard that the Jews were addressed by the Romans as friends and allies and brothers and that the Romans�q had received the envoys of Simon with honor.

41 "The Jews and their priests have resolved that Simon should be their leader and high priest forever, until a trustworthy prophet should arise, ⁴²and that he should be governor over them andʳ appoint officials over its tasks and over the country and the weapons and the strongholds, ⁴³and that he should take charge of the sanctuary, and that he should be obeyed by all, and that all contracts in the country should be written in his name, and that he should be clothed in purple and wear gold.

44 "None of the people or priests shall be permitted to nullify any of these decisions or to oppose what he says or to convene an assembly in the country without his permission or to be clothed in purple or put on a gold buckle. ⁴⁵Whoever acts contrary to these decisions or rejects any of them shall be liable to punishment."

46 All the people agreed to grant Simon the right to act in accordance with these decisions. ⁴⁷So Simon accepted and agreed to be high priest, to be commander and ethnarch of the

---

l 14.24 Gk *them*
m 14.30 Gk *their*

n 14.34 Gk *them*
o 14.35 Other ancient authorities read *conduct*
p 14.36 Gk *their*
q 14.40 Gk *they*
r 14.42 Cn: Gk adds *that he should take charge of the sanctuary and*

Jews and priests, and to be protector of them all.[s] 48 And they gave orders to inscribe this decree on bronze tablets, to put them up in a conspicuous place in the precincts of the sanctuary, 49 and to deposit copies of them in the treasury, so that Simon and his sons might have them.

Letter of Antiochus VII

15 Antiochus, son of King Demetrius, sent a letter from the islands of the sea to Simon, the priest and ethnarch of the Jews, and to all the nation; 2 its contents were as follows: "King Antiochus to Simon the high priest and ethnarch and to the nation of the Jews, greetings. 3 Whereas certain scoundrels have gained control of the kingdom of our ancestors, and I intend to lay claim to the kingdom so that I may restore it as it formerly was, and have recruited a host of mercenary troops and have equipped warships, 4 and intend to make a landing in the country so that I may proceed against those who have destroyed our country and those who have devastated many cities in my kingdom, 5 now therefore I confirm to you all the tax remissions that the kings before me have granted you and a release from all the other payments from which they have released you. 6 I permit you to mint your own coinage as money for your country, 7 and I grant freedom to Jerusalem and the sanctuary. All the weapons that you have prepared and the strongholds that you have built and now hold shall remain yours. 8 Every debt you owe to the royal treasury and any such future debts shall be canceled for you from henceforth and for all time. 9 When we gain control of our kingdom, we will bestow great honor on you and your nation and the temple, so that your glory will become manifest in all the earth."

10 In the one hundred seventy-fourth year Antiochus set out and invaded the land of his ancestors. All the troops rallied to him, so that there were only a few with Trypho. 11 Antiochus pursued him, and Trypho[t] came in his flight to Dor, which is by the sea, 12 for he knew that troubles had converged on him, and his troops had deserted him. 13 So Antiochus encamped against Dor, and with him were one hundred twenty thousand warriors and eight thousand cavalry. 14 He surrounded the town, and the ships joined battle from the sea; he pressed the town hard from land and sea and permitted no one to leave or enter it.

Rome Supports the Jews

15 Then Numenius and his companions arrived from Rome, with letters to the kings and countries, in which the following was written: 16 "Lucius, consul of the Romans, to King Ptolemy, greetings. 17 The envoys of the Jews have come to us as our friends and allies to renew our ancient friendship and alliance. They had been sent by the high priest Simon and by the Jewish people 18 and have brought a gold shield weighing one thousand minas. 19 We therefore have decided to write to the kings and countries that they should not seek their harm or make war against them and their cities and their country or make alliance with those who war against them. 20 And it has seemed good to us to accept the shield from them. 21 Therefore if any scoundrels have fled to you from their country, hand them over to the high priest Simon, so that he may punish them according to their law."

22 The consul[u] wrote the same thing to King Demetrius and to Attalus and Ariarathes and Arsaces 23 and to all the countries, and to Sampsames,[v] and to the Spartans, and to Delos, and to Myndos, and to Sicyon, and to Caria, and to Samos, and to Pamphylia, and to Lycia, and to Halicarnassus, and to Rhodes, and to Phaselis, and to Cos, and to Side, and to Aradus and Gortyna and Cnidus and Cyprus and Cyrene. 24 They also sent a copy of these things to the high priest Simon.

Antiochus VII Threatens Simon

25 King Antiochus besieged Dor for the second time, continually throwing his forces against it and making engines of war, and he shut Trypho up and kept him from going out or in. 26 And Simon sent to Antiochus[w] two thousand picked troops, to fight for him, and silver and gold and a large amount of military equipment. 27 But he refused to receive them and broke all the agreements he formerly had made with Simon and became estranged from him. 28 He sent to him Athenobius, one of his Friends, to confer with him, saying, "You hold control of Joppa and Gazara and the citadel in Jerusalem; they are cities of my kingdom. 29 You

---

s **14.47** Or *to preside over them all*
t **15.11** Gk *he*

u **15.22** Gk *He*
v **15.23** The name is uncertain
w **15.26** Gk *him*

have devastated their territory, you have done great damage in the land, and you have taken possession of many places in my kingdom. ³⁰Now, then, hand over the cities that you have seized and the tribute money of the places that you have conquered outside the borders of Judea, ³¹or else pay me five hundred talents of silver for the destruction that you have caused and five hundred talents more for the tribute money of the cities. Otherwise we will come and make war on you."

32 So Athenobius, the king's Friend, came to Jerusalem, and when he saw the splendor of Simon, and the sideboard with its gold and silver plate, and his great magnificence, he was amazed. When he reported to him the king's message, ³³Simon said to him in reply: "We have neither taken foreign land nor seized foreign property, but only the inheritance of our ancestors, which at one time had been unjustly taken by our enemies. ³⁴Now that we have the opportunity, we are firmly holding the inheritance of our ancestors. ³⁵As for Joppa and Gazara, which you demand, they were causing great damage among the people and to our land, for them we will give you one hundred talents."

Athenobius˟ did not answer him a word ³⁶but returned in wrath to the king and reported to him these words and also the splendor of Simon and all that he had seen. And the king was very angry.

Victory over Cendebeus

37 Meanwhile Trypho embarked on a ship and escaped to Orthosia. ³⁸Then the king made Cendebeus commander-in-chief of the coastal country and gave him troops of infantry and cavalry. ³⁹He commanded him to encamp against Judea, to build up Kedron and fortify its gates, and to make war on the people, but the king pursued Trypho. ⁴⁰So Cendebeus came to Jamnia and began to provoke the people and invade Judea and take the people captive and kill them. ⁴¹He built up Kedron and stationed horsemen and troops there, so that they might go out and make raids along the highways of Judea, as the king had ordered him.

16 John went up from Gazara and reported to his father Simon what Cendebeus had done. ²And Simon called in his two eldest sons Judas and John and said to them: "My brothers and I and my father's house have fought the wars of Israel from our youth until this day, and things have prospered in our hands so that we have delivered Israel many times. ³But now I have grown old, and you by heaven's ʸ mercy are mature in years. Take my place and my brother's, and go out and fight for our nation, and may the help that comes from heaven be with you."

4 So John ᶻ chose out of the country twenty thousand warriors and cavalry, and they marched against Cendebeus and camped for the night in Modein. ⁵Early in the morning they started out and marched into the plain, where a large force of infantry and cavalry was coming to meet them, and a wadi lay between them. ⁶Then he and his army lined up against them. He saw that the soldiers were afraid to cross the wadi, so he crossed over first, and when his troops saw him, they crossed over after him. ⁷Then he divided the army and placed the cavalry in the center of the infantry, for the cavalry of the enemy were very numerous. ⁸They sounded the trumpets, and Cendebeus and his army were put to flight; many of them fell wounded, and the rest fled into the stronghold. ⁹At that time Judas the brother of John was wounded, but John pursued them until Cendebeus ᵃ reached Kedron, which he had built. ¹⁰They also fled into the towers that were in the fields of Azotus, and John ᵇ burned it with fire, and about two thousand of them fell. He then returned to Judea safely.

Murder of Simon and His Sons

11 Now Ptolemy son of Abubus had been appointed governor over the plain of Jericho; he had a large store of silver and gold, ¹²for he was son-in-law of the high priest. ¹³His heart was lifted up; he determined to get control of the country and made treacherous plans against Simon and his sons, to do away with them. ¹⁴Now Simon was visiting the towns of the country and attending to their needs, and he went down to Jericho with his sons Mattathias and Judas, in the one hundred seventy-seventh year, in the eleventh month, which is the month of Shebat. ¹⁵The son of Abubus received them treacherously in the little stronghold called Dok, which he had built; he gave them a great banquet and hid men there. ¹⁶When Simon and his sons

---

x 15.35 Gk *He*

y 16.3 Gk *his*

z 16.4 Other ancient authorities read *he*

a 16.9 Gk *he*

b 16.10 Gk *he*

were drunk, Ptolemy and his men rose up, took their weapons, rushed in against Simon in the banquet hall, and killed him and his two sons, as well as some of his servants. ¹⁷So he committed an act of great treachery and returned evil for good.

John Succeeds Simon

18 Then Ptolemy wrote a report about these things and sent it to the king, asking him to send troops to aid him and to turn over to him the towns and the country. ¹⁹He sent other troops to Gazara to do away with John; he sent letters to the captains asking them to come to him so that he might give them silver and gold and gifts, ²⁰and he sent other troops to take possession of Jerusalem and the temple hill. ²¹But someone ran ahead and reported to John at Gazara that his father and brothers had perished and that "he has sent men to kill you also." ²²When he heard this, he was greatly shocked; he seized the men who came to destroy him and killed them, for he had found out that they were seeking to destroy him.

23 The rest of the acts of John and his wars and the brave deeds that he did, and the building of the walls that he completed, and his achievements ²⁴are written in the annals of his high priesthood, from the time that he became high priest after his father.

2 MACCABEES

A Letter to the Jews in Egypt

1 The Jews in Jerusalem and those in the land of Judea,

To their Jewish kindred in Egypt,

Greetings and true peace.

2 May God do good to you, and may he remember his covenant with Abraham and Isaac and Jacob, his faithful servants. 3 May he give you all a heart to worship him and to do his will with a strong heart and a willing spirit. 4 May he open your heart to his law and his commandments, and may he bring peace. 5 May he hear your prayers and be reconciled to you, and may he not forsake you in time of evil. 6 We are now praying for you here.

7 In the reign of Demetrius, in the one hundred sixty-ninth year, we Jews wrote to you, in the critical distress that came upon us in those years after Jason and his company revolted from the holy land and the kingdom 8 and burned the gate and shed innocent blood. We prayed to the Lord and were heard, and we offered sacrifice and grain offering, and we lit the lamps and set out the loaves. 9 And now see that you keep the Festival of Booths*a* in the month of Chislev, in the one hundred eighty-eighth year.

A Letter to Aristobulus

10 The people of Jerusalem and of Judea and the council and Judas,

To Aristobulus, who is of the family of the anointed priests, teacher of King Ptolemy, and to the Jews in Egypt,

Greetings and good health.

11 Having been saved by God out of grave dangers, we thank him greatly for taking our side against the king,*b* 12 for he drove out those who fought against the holy city. 13 When the leader reached Persia with a force that seemed irresistible, they were cut to pieces in the temple of Nanea by a deception employed by the priests of the goddess*c* Nanea. 14 On the pretext of intending to marry her, Antiochus came to the place together with his Friends, to secure most of its treasures as a dowry. 15 When the priests of the temple of Nanea had set out the treasures and Antiochus had come with a few men inside the wall of the sacred precinct, they closed the temple as soon as he entered it. 16 Opening a secret door in the ceiling, they threw stones and struck down the leader and his men; they dismembered them and cut off their heads and threw them to the people outside. 17 Blessed in every way be our God, who has delivered up those who have behaved impiously.

Fire Consumes Nehemiah's Sacrifice

18 Since on the twenty-fifth day of Chislev we shall celebrate the purification of the temple, we thought it necessary to notify you, in order that you also may celebrate the Festival of Booths*d* and the fire given when Nehemiah, who built the temple and the altar, offered sacrifices.

19 For when our ancestors were being led captive to Persia, the pious priests of that time took some of the fire of the altar and secretly hid it in the hollow of a dry cistern, where they took such precautions that the place was unknown to anyone. 20 But after many years had passed, when it pleased God, Nehemiah, having been commissioned by the king of Persia, sent the descendants of the priests who had hidden the fire to get it. And when they reported to us that they had not found fire but only a thick liquid, he ordered them to dip it out and bring it. 21 When the materials for the sacrifices were presented, Nehemiah ordered the priests to sprinkle the liquid on the wood and on the things laid upon it. 22 When this had been done and some time had passed, and when the sun, which had been clouded over, shone out, a great fire blazed

---

a 1.9 Or *Tabernacles*
b 1.11 Cn: Gk *as those who array themselves against a king*

c 1.13 Gk lacks *the goddess*
d 1.18 Or *Tabernacles*

up, so that all marveled. ²³ And while the sacrifice was being consumed, the priests offered prayer—the priests and everyone. Jonathan led, and the rest responded, as did Nehemiah. ²⁴ The prayer was to this effect:

"O Lord, Lord God, Creator of all things, you are awe-inspiring and strong and just and merciful; you alone are king and are kind; ²⁵ you alone are bountiful; you alone are just and almighty and eternal. You rescue Israel from every evil; you chose the ancestors and consecrated them. ²⁶ Accept this sacrifice on behalf of all your people Israel and preserve your portion and make it holy. ²⁷ Gather together our scattered people; set free those who are slaves among the nations; look on those who are rejected and despised; and let the nations know that you are our God. ²⁸ Punish those who oppress and are insolent with pride. ²⁹ Plant your people in your holy place, as Moses promised."

30 Then the priests sang the hymns. ³¹ After the materials of the sacrifice had been consumed, Nehemiah ordered that the liquid that was left should be poured on large stones. ³² When this was done, a flame blazed up, but when the light from the altar shone back, it went out. ³³ When this matter became known and it was reported to the king of the Persians that, in the place where the exiled priests had hidden the fire, the liquid had appeared with which Nehemiah and his associates had burned the materials of the sacrifice, ³⁴ the king investigated the matter and enclosed the place and made it sacred. ³⁵ And with those persons whom the king favored he exchanged many excellent gifts. ³⁶ Nehemiah and his associates called this "nephthar," which means purification, but by most people it is called "naphtha."

Jeremiah Hides the Tent, Ark, and Altar

2 One finds in the records that the prophet Jeremiah ordered those who were being deported to take some of the fire, as has been mentioned, ² and that the prophet, after giving them the law, instructed those who were being deported not to forget the commandments of the Lord or to be led astray in their thoughts on seeing the gold and silver statues and their adornment. ³ And with other similar words he exhorted them that the law should not depart from their hearts.

4 It was also in the same document that the prophet, having received an oracle, ordered that the tent and the ark should follow with him and that he went out to the mountain where Moses had gone up and had seen the inheritance of God. ⁵ Jeremiah came and found a cave dwelling, and he brought there the tent and the ark and the altar of incense; then he sealed up the entrance. ⁶ Some of those who followed him came up intending to mark the way but could not find it. ⁷ When Jeremiah learned of it, he rebuked them and declared, "The place shall remain unknown until God gathers his people together again and shows his mercy. ⁸ Then the Lord will disclose these things, and the glory of the Lord and the cloud will appear, as they were shown in the case of Moses and as Solomon asked that the place should be specially consecrated."

9 It was also made clear that, being possessed of wisdom, Solomon*e* offered sacrifice for the dedication and completion of the temple. ¹⁰ Just as Moses prayed to the Lord and fire came down from heaven and consumed the sacrifices, so also Solomon prayed, and the fire came down and consumed the whole burnt offerings. ¹¹ And Moses said, "They were consumed because the purification offering had not been eaten." ¹² Likewise Solomon also kept the eight days.

13 The same things are reported in the records and in the memoirs of Nehemiah and also that he founded a library and collected the books about the kings and prophets and the writings of David and letters of kings about votive offerings. ¹⁴ In the same way Judas also collected all the books that had been lost on account of the war that had come upon us, and they are in our possession. ¹⁵ So if you have need of them, send people to get them for you.

16 Since, therefore, we are about to celebrate the purification, we write to you. You will do well if you celebrate these days. ¹⁷ It is God who has saved all his people and has returned the inheritance to all and the kingship and the priesthood and the consecration, ¹⁸ as he promised through the law. We have hope in God that he will soon have mercy on us and will gather us from everywhere under heaven into his holy place, for he has rescued us from great evils and has purified the place.

The Compiler's Preface

19 The story of Judas Maccabeus and his brothers, and the purification of the greatest temple, and the dedication of the altar, ²⁰ and

_____
e **2.9** Gk *he*

further the wars against Antiochus Epiphanes and his son Eupator, [21] and the appearances that came from heaven to those who fought bravely for Judaism, so that though few in number they seized the whole land and pursued the barbarian hordes [22] and regained possession of the temple famous throughout the world and liberated the city and reestablished the laws that were about to be abolished, while the Lord with great kindness became gracious to them—[23] all this, which has been set forth by Jason of Cyrene in five volumes, we shall attempt to condense into a single book. [24] For considering the flood of lines written and the difficulty there is for those who wish to enter upon the narratives of history because of the mass of material, [25] we have aimed to please those who wish to read, to make it easy for those who are inclined to memorize, and to profit all readers. [26] For us who have undertaken the toil of abbreviating, it is no light matter but calls for sweat and loss of sleep, [27] just as it is not easy for one who prepares a banquet and seeks the benefit of others. Nevertheless, to secure the gratitude of many we will gladly endure the uncomfortable toil, [28] leaving the responsibility for exact details to the compiler, while devoting our effort to arriving at the outlines of the condensation. [29] For as the master builder of a new house must be concerned with the whole construction, while the one who undertakes its painting and decoration has to consider only what is suitable for its adornment, such in my judgment is the case with us. [30] It is the duty of the original historian to occupy the ground, to discuss matters from every side, and to take trouble with details, [31] but the one who recasts the narrative should be allowed to strive for brevity of expression and to forego exhaustive treatment. [32] At this point, therefore, let us begin our narrative, without adding any more to what has already been said, for it would be foolish to lengthen the preface while cutting short the history itself.

Arrival of Heliodorus in Jerusalem

3 While the holy city was inhabited in unbroken peace and the laws were strictly observed because of the piety of the high priest Onias and his hatred of wickedness, [2] it came about that the kings themselves honored the place and glorified the temple with the finest presents, [3] even to the extent that King Seleucus of Asia defrayed from his own revenues all the expenses connected with the service of the sacrifices.

[4] But a man named Simon, of the tribe of Balgea,[f] who had been made captain of the temple, had a disagreement with the high priest about the administration of the city market. [5] Since he could not prevail over Onias, he went to Apollonius of Tarsus,[g] who at that time was governor of Coelesyria and Phoenicia, [6] and reported to him that the treasury in Jerusalem was full of untold sums of money, so that the amount of the funds could not be reckoned, and that they did not belong to the account of the sacrifices but that it was possible for them to fall under the control of the king. [7] When Apollonius met the king, he told him of the money about which he had been informed. The king[h] chose Heliodorus, who was in charge of his affairs, and sent him with commands to effect the removal of the reported wealth. [8] Heliodorus at once set out on his journey, ostensibly to make a tour of inspection of the cities of Coelesyria and Phoenicia but in fact to carry out the king's purpose.

[9] When he had arrived at Jerusalem and had been kindly welcomed by the high priest of[i] the city, he told about the disclosure that had been made and stated why he had come, and he inquired whether this really was the situation. [10] The high priest explained that there were some deposits belonging to widows and orphans [11] and also some money of Hyrcanus son of Tobias, a man of very prominent position, and that it totaled in all four hundred talents of silver and two hundred of gold. To such an extent the impious Simon had misrepresented the facts. [12] And he said[j] that it was utterly impossible that wrong should be done to those people who had trusted in the holiness of the place and in the sanctity and inviolability of the temple that is honored throughout the whole world.

Heliodorus Plans to Rob the Temple

[13] But Heliodorus,[k] because of the orders he had from the king, said that this money must in any case be confiscated for the king's treasury. [14] So he set a day and went in to direct the inspection of these funds.

There was no little distress throughout the whole city. [15] The priests prostrated themselves before the altar in their priestly vestments and

---

f 3.4 Lat Arm: Gk *Benjamin*
g 3.5 Gk *Tharseas*
h 3.7 Gk *He*
i 3.9 Other ancient authorities read *and*
j 3.12 Gk lacks *And he said*
k 3.13 Gk *the other*

called toward heaven upon him who had given the law about deposits, that he should keep them safe for those who had deposited them. [16]To see the appearance of the high priest was to be wounded at heart, for his face and the change in his color disclosed the anguish of his soul. [17]For terror and bodily trembling had come over the man, which plainly showed to those who looked at him the pain lodged in his heart. [18]People also hurried out of their houses in crowds to make a general supplication because the holy place was about to be brought into dishonor. [19]Women girded with sackcloth under their breasts thronged the streets. Some of the young women who were kept indoors ran together to the gates, and some to the walls, while others peered out of the windows. [20]And holding up their hands to heaven, they all made supplication. [21]There was something pitiable in the prostration of the whole populace and the anxiety of the high priest in his great anguish.

The Lord Protects His Temple

[22]While they were calling upon the Almighty Lord that he would keep what had been entrusted safe and secure for those who had entrusted it, [23]Heliodorus went on with what had been decided. [24]But when he arrived at the treasury with his bodyguard, then and there the Sovereign of spirits and of all authority caused so great a manifestation that all who had been so bold as to accompany him were astounded by the power of God and became faint with terror. [25]For there appeared to them a magnificently adorned horse, with a rider of frightening appearance; it rushed furiously at Heliodorus and struck at him with its front hoofs. Its rider was seen to have armor and weapons of gold. [26]Two young men also appeared to him, remarkably strong, gloriously beautiful and splendidly dressed, who stood on either side of him and flogged him continuously, inflicting many blows on him. [27]When he suddenly fell to the ground and deep darkness came over him, his men took him up, put him on a stretcher, [28]and carried him away—this man who had just entered the aforesaid treasury with a great retinue and all his bodyguard but was now unable to help himself with all his weapons. He recognized clearly the sovereign power of God.

Onias Prays for Heliodorus

[29]While he lay prostrate, speechless because of the divine intervention and deprived of any hope of recovery, [30]they praised the Lord who had acted marvelously for his own place. And the temple, which a little while before was full of fear and disturbance, was filled with joy and gladness, now that the Almighty Lord had appeared.

[31]Some of Heliodorus's friends quickly begged Onias to call upon the Most High to grant life to one who was lying quite at his last breath. [32]So the high priest, fearing that the king might get the notion that some foul play had been perpetrated by the Jews with regard to Heliodorus, offered sacrifice for the man's recovery. [33]While the high priest was making the atonement, the same young men appeared again to Heliodorus dressed in the same clothing, and they stood and said, "Be very grateful to the high priest Onias, since for his sake the Lord has granted you your life. [34]And see that you, who have been flogged by heaven, report to all people the majestic power of God." Having said this, they vanished.

The Conversion of Heliodorus

[35]Then Heliodorus offered sacrifice to the Lord and made very great vows to the Savior of his life, and having bidden Onias farewell, he marched off with his forces to the king. [36]He bore testimony to all concerning the deeds of the supreme God, which he had seen with his own eyes. [37]When the king asked Heliodorus what sort of person would be suitable to send on another mission to Jerusalem, he replied, [38]"If you have any enemy or plotter against your government, send him there, for you will get him back thoroughly flogged, if he survives at all, for there is certainly some power of God about the place. [39]For he who has his dwelling in heaven watches over that place himself and brings it aid, and he strikes and destroys those who come to do it injury." [40]This was the outcome of the episode of Heliodorus and the protection of the treasury.

Simon Accuses Onias

4 The previously mentioned Simon, who had informed about the money against[l] his own country, slandered Onias, saying that it was he who had incited Heliodorus and had been the real cause of the misfortune. [2]He dared to designate as a plotter against the government the man who was the benefactor of the city,

---

l 4.1 Gk *and*

the protector of his compatriots, and a zealot for the laws. [3]When his hatred progressed to such a degree that even murders were committed by one of Simon's approved agents, [4]Onias recognized that the rivalry was serious and that Apollonius son of Menestheus,[m] and governor of Coelesyria and Phoenicia, was intensifying the malice of Simon. [5]So he appealed to the king, not accusing his compatriots but having in view the welfare, both public and private, of all the people. [6]For he saw that, without the king's attention, public affairs could not again reach a peaceful settlement and that Simon would not stop his folly.

Jason's Reforms

[7]When Seleucus died and Antiochus, who was called Epiphanes, succeeded to the kingdom, Jason the brother of Onias obtained the high priesthood by corruption, [8]promising the king through a petition three hundred sixty talents of silver and from another source of revenue eighty talents. [9]In addition to this he promised to pay one hundred fifty more if permission were given to establish by his authority a gymnasium and a body of youth for it and to enroll the people of Jerusalem as the Antiochenes in Jerusalem. [10]When the king assented and Jason[n] came to office, he at once shifted his compatriots over to the Greek way of life.

[11]He set aside the existing royal concessions to the Jews, secured through John the father of Eupolemus, who went on the mission to establish friendship and alliance with the Romans, and he destroyed the lawful ways of living and introduced new customs contrary to the law. [12]He took delight in establishing a gymnasium right under the citadel, and he induced the noblest of the young men to wear the Greek hat. [13]There was such an extreme of Hellenization and increase in the adoption of foreign ways because of the surpassing wickedness of Jason, who was ungodly and no true[o] high priest, [14]that the priests were no longer intent upon their service at the altar. Despising the sanctuary and neglecting the sacrifices, they hurried to take part in the unlawful proceedings in the wrestling arena after the signal for the discus throwing, [15]disdaining the honors prized by their ancestors and putting the highest value

upon Greek forms of prestige. [16]For this reason heavy disaster overtook them, and those whose ways of living they admired and wished to imitate completely became their enemies and punished them. [17]It is no light thing to show irreverence to the divine laws, a fact that later events will make clear.

Jason Introduces Greek Customs

[18]When the quadrennial games were being held at Tyre and the king was present, [19]the vile Jason sent envoys, chosen as being Antiochenes from Jerusalem, to carry three hundred silver drachmas for the sacrifice to Hercules. Those who carried the money, however, thought best not to use it for sacrifice, because that was inappropriate, but to expend it for another purpose. [20]So this money was intended by the sender for the sacrifice to Hercules, but by the decision of its carriers it was applied to the construction of triremes.

[21]When Apollonius son of Menestheus was sent to Egypt for the coronation[p] of Philometor as king, Antiochus learned that Philometor[q] had become hostile to his government, and he took measures for his own security. Therefore upon arriving at Joppa he proceeded to Jerusalem. [22]He was welcomed magnificently by Jason and the city and ushered in with a blaze of torches and with shouts. Then he marched his army into Phoenicia.

Menelaus Becomes High Priest

[23]After a period of three years, Jason sent Menelaus, the brother of the previously mentioned Simon, to carry the money to the king and to complete the records of essential business. [24]But he, when presented to the king, extolled him with an air of authority and secured the high priesthood for himself, outbidding Jason by three hundred talents of silver. [25]After receiving the king's orders, he returned, possessing no qualification for the high priesthood but having the hot temper of a cruel tyrant and the rage of a savage wild beast. [26]So Jason, who after supplanting his own brother was supplanted by another man, was driven as a fugitive into the land of Ammon. [27]Although Menelaus continued to hold the office, he did not pay regularly any of the money promised to the king. [28]When Sostratus the captain of the citadel

---

m 4.4 Vg: Meaning of Gk uncertain
n 4.10 Gk he
o 4.13 Gk lacks true

p 4.21 Meaning of Gk uncertain
q 4.21 Gk he

kept requesting payment—for the collection of the revenue was his responsibility—the two of them were summoned by the king on account of this issue. [29]Menelaus left his own brother Lysimachus as deputy in the high priesthood, while Sostratus left Crates, the commander of the Cyprian troops.

The Murder of Onias

[30]While such was the state of affairs, it happened that the people of Tarsus and of Mallus revolted because their cities had been given as a present to Antiochis, the king's concubine. [31]So the king went hurriedly to settle the trouble, leaving Andronicus, a man of high rank, to act as his deputy. [32]But Menelaus, thinking he had obtained a suitable opportunity, stole some of the gold vessels of the temple and gave them to Andronicus; other vessels, as it happened, he had sold to Tyre and the neighboring cities. [33]When Onias became fully aware of these acts, he publicly exposed them, having first withdrawn to a place of sanctuary at Daphne near Antioch. [34]Therefore Menelaus, taking Andronicus aside, urged him to kill Onias. Andronicus[r] came to Onias and, resorting to treachery, offered him sworn pledges and gave him his right hand; he persuaded him, in spite of his suspicions, to come out from the place of sanctuary; then, with no regard for justice, he immediately put him out of the way.

Andronicus Is Punished

[35]For this reason not only Jews but many also of other nations were grieved and displeased at the unjust murder of the man. [36]When the king returned from the region of Cilicia, the Jews in the city[s] appealed to him with regard to the unreasonable murder of Onias, and the Greeks shared their hatred of the crime. [37]Therefore Antiochus was grieved at heart and filled with pity and wept because of the moderation and good conduct of the deceased. [38]Inflamed with anger, he immediately stripped the purple robe from Andronicus, tore off his clothes, and led him around the whole city to that very place where he had committed the outrage against Onias, and there he dispatched the bloodthirsty fellow. The Lord thus repaid him with the punishment he deserved.

Unpopularity of Lysimachus and Menelaus

[39]When many acts of sacrilege had been committed in the city by Lysimachus with the connivance of Menelaus, and when report of them had spread abroad, the populace gathered against Lysimachus, because many of the gold vessels had already been stolen. [40]Since the crowds were becoming aroused and filled with anger, Lysimachus armed about three thousand men and launched an unjust attack, under the leadership of a certain Auranus, a man advanced in years and no less advanced in folly. [41]But when the Jews[t] became aware that Lysimachus was attacking them, some picked up stones, some blocks of wood, and others took handfuls of the ashes that were lying around and threw them in wild confusion at Lysimachus and his men. [42]As a result, they wounded many of them and killed some and put all the rest to flight; the temple robber himself they killed close by the treasury.

[43]Charges were brought against Menelaus about this incident. [44]When the king came to Tyre, three men sent by the senate presented the case before him. [45]But Menelaus, already as good as beaten, promised a substantial bribe to Ptolemy son of Dorymenes to win over the king. [46]Therefore Ptolemy, taking the king aside into a colonnade as if for refreshment, induced the king to change his mind. [47]Menelaus, the cause of all the trouble, he acquitted of the charges against him, while he sentenced to death those unfortunate men who would have been freed uncondemned if they had pleaded even before Scythians. [48]And so those who had spoken for the city and the villages[u] and the holy vessels quickly suffered the unjust penalty. [49]Therefore even the Tyrians, showing their hatred of the crime, provided magnificently for their funeral. [50]But Menelaus, because of the greed of those in power, remained in office, growing in wickedness, having become the chief plotter against his compatriots.

Jason Tries to Regain Control

5 About this time Antiochus made his second invasion of Egypt. [2]And it happened that, for almost forty days, there appeared over all the city golden-clad cavalry charging through the air, in companies fully armed with lances and drawn swords—[3]troops of cavalry drawn

---

r **4.34** Gk *He*
s **4.36** Or *in each city*

t **4.41** Gk *they*
u **4.48** Other ancient authorities read *the people*

up, attacks and counterattacks made on this side and on that, brandishing of shields, massing of spears, hurling of missiles, the flash of golden trappings, and armor of all kinds. 4 Therefore everyone prayed that the apparition might prove to have been a good omen.

5 When a false rumor arose that Antiochus was dead, Jason took no fewer than a thousand men and suddenly made an assault on the city. When the troops on the wall had been forced back and at last the city was being taken, Menelaus took refuge in the citadel. 6 But Jason kept relentlessly slaughtering his compatriots, not realizing that success at the cost of one's kindred is the greatest misfortune but imagining that he was setting up trophies of victory over enemies and not over compatriots. 7 He did not, however, gain control of the government; in the end, he got only disgrace from his conspiracy and fled again into the country of the Ammonites. 8 Finally, he met a miserable end. Accused[v] before Aretas the ruler of the Arabs, fleeing from city to city, pursued by everyone, hated as a rebel against the laws, and abhorred as the executioner of his country and his compatriots, he was cast ashore in Egypt. 9 There he who had driven many from their own country into exile died in exile, having embarked to go to the Spartans[w] in hope of finding protection because of their kinship. 10 He who had cast out many to lie unburied had no one to mourn for him; he had no funeral of any sort and no place in the tomb of his ancestors.

11 When news of what had happened reached the king, he took it to mean that Judea was in revolt. So, raging inwardly, he left Egypt and took the city by storm. 12 He commanded his soldiers to cut down relentlessly everyone they met and to kill those who went into their houses. 13 Then there was massacre of young and old, destruction of boys, women, and children, and slaughter of young girls and infants. 14 Within the total of three days eighty thousand were destroyed, forty thousand in hand-to-hand fighting, and as many were sold into slavery as were killed.

Pillage of the Temple

15 Not content with this, Antiochus[x] dared to enter the most holy temple in all the world, guided by Menelaus, who had become a traitor both to the laws and to his country. 16 He took the holy vessels with his polluted hands and swept away with profane hands the votive offerings that other kings had made to enhance the glory and honor of the place. 17 Antiochus was elated in spirit and did not perceive that the Lord was angered for a little while because of the sins of those who lived in the city and that this was the reason he was disregarding the holy place. 18 But if it had not happened that they were involved in many sins, this man would have been flogged and turned back from his rash act as soon as he came forward, just as Heliodorus had been, whom King Seleucus sent to inspect the treasury. 19 But the Lord did not choose the nation for the sake of the holy place but the place for the sake of the nation. 20 Therefore the place itself shared in the misfortunes that befell the nation and afterward participated in its benefits, and what was forsaken in the wrath of the Almighty was restored again in all its glory when the great Lord became reconciled.

21 So Antiochus carried off eighteen hundred talents from the temple and hurried away to Antioch, thinking in his arrogance that he could sail on the land and walk on the sea, because his mind was elated. 22 He left governors to oppress the people: at Jerusalem, Philip, by birth a Phrygian and in character more barbarous than the man who appointed him; 23 and at Gerizim, Andronicus; and besides these Menelaus, who lorded it over his compatriots worse than the others did. In his malice toward the Jewish citizens,[y] 24 Antiochus[z] sent Apollonius, the captain of the Mysians, with an army of twenty-two thousand and commanded him to kill all the grown men and to sell the women and boys as slaves. 25 When this man arrived in Jerusalem, he pretended to be peaceably disposed and waited until the holy Sabbath day; then, finding the Jews not at work, he ordered his troops to parade under arms. 26 He put to the sword all those who came out to see them, then rushed into the city with his armed warriors and killed great numbers of people.

27 But Judas Maccabeus, with about nine others, got away to the wilderness and kept himself and his companions alive in the mountains as wild animals do; they continued to live on what grew wild, so that they might not share in the defilement.

---

v 5.8 Cn: Gk *Imprisoned*
w 5.9 Gk *Lacedaemonians*
x 5.15 Gk *he*

y 5.23 Or *worse than the others did in his malice toward
     the Jewish citizens.*
z 5.24 Gk *he*

The Suppression of Judaism

6 Not long after this, the king sent an Athenian[a] senator[b] to compel the Jews to forsake the laws of their ancestors and no longer to live by the laws of God, [2] also to pollute the temple in Jerusalem and to call it the temple of Olympian Zeus and to call the one in Gerizim Zeus-the-Friend-of-Strangers, as the people who live in that place are known.

[3] Harsh and utterly grievous was the onslaught of evil. [4] For the temple was filled with debauchery and reveling by the nations, who dallied with prostitutes and had intercourse with women within the sacred precincts and besides brought in things for sacrifice that were unfit. [5] The altar was covered with abominable offerings that were forbidden by the laws. [6] People could neither keep the Sabbath nor observe the festivals of their ancestors nor so much as confess themselves to be Jews.

[7] On the monthly celebration of the king's birthday, the Jews[c] were taken, under bitter constraint, to partake of the sacrifices, and when a festival of Dionysus was celebrated, they were compelled to wear wreaths of ivy and to walk in the procession in honor of Dionysus. [8] At the suggestion of the people of Ptolemais,[d] a decree was issued to the neighboring Greek cities that they should adopt the same policy toward the Jews and make them partake of the sacrifices [9] and should kill those who did not choose to change over to Greek customs. One could see, therefore, the misery that had come upon them. [10] For example, two women were brought in for having circumcised their children. They publicly paraded them around the city with their babies hanging at their breasts and then hurled them down headlong from the wall. [11] Others who had assembled in the caves nearby in order to observe the seventh day secretly were betrayed to Philip and were all burned together, because their piety kept them from defending themselves, in view of their regard for that most holy day.

Providential Significance of the Persecution

[12] Now I urge those who read this book not to be depressed by such calamities but to recognize that these punishments were designed not to destroy but to discipline our people. [13] In fact, it is a sign of great kindness not to let the impious alone for long but to punish them immediately. [14] For in the case of the other nations the Lord waits patiently to punish them until they have reached the full measure of their sins, but he does not deal in this way with us, [15] in order that he may not take vengeance on us afterward when our sins have reached their height. [16] Therefore he never withdraws his mercy from us. Although he disciplines us with calamities, he does not forsake his own people. [17] Let what we have said serve as a reminder; we must go on briefly with the story.

The Martyrdom of Eleazar

[18] Eleazar, one of the scribes in high position, a man now advanced in age and of noble presence, was being forced to open his mouth to eat pig's flesh. [19] But he, welcoming death with honor rather than life with pollution, went up to the rack of his own accord, [20] spitting it out as all ought to go who have the courage to refuse things that it is not right to taste, even for the natural love of life.

[21] Those who were in charge of that unlawful sacrifice took the man aside because of their long acquaintance with him and privately urged him to bring meat of his own providing, proper for him to use, and to pretend that he was eating the flesh of the sacrificial meal that had been commanded by the king, [22] so that by doing this he might be saved from death and be treated kindly on account of his old friendship with them. [23] But making a high resolve, worthy of his years and the dignity of his old age and the gray hairs that he had reached with distinction and his excellent life even from childhood, and moreover according to the holy God-given law, he declared himself quickly, telling them to send him to Hades.

[24] "Such pretense is not worthy of our time of life," he said, "for many of the young might suppose that Eleazar in his ninetieth year had gone over to a foreign way of life, [25] and through my pretense, for the sake of living a brief moment longer, they would be led astray because of me, while I defile and disgrace my old age. [26] Even if for the present I would avoid the punishment of mortals, yet whether I live or die I will not escape the hands of the Almighty. [27] Therefore, by bravely giving up my life now, I will show myself worthy of my old age [28] and leave to the young a noble example of how to die a good

---

a 6.1 Other ancient authorities read *Antiochian*
b 6.1 Or *Geron an Athenian*
c 6.7 Gk *they*
d 6.8 Or *of Ptolemy*

death willingly and nobly for the revered and holy laws."

When he had said this, he was dragged*e* at once to the rack. 29 Those who a little before had acted toward him with goodwill now changed to ill will, because the words he had uttered were in their opinion sheer madness.*f* 30 When he was about to die under the blows, he groaned aloud and said: "It is clear to the Lord in his holy knowledge that, though I might have been saved from death, I am enduring terrible sufferings in my body under this beating, but in my soul I am glad to suffer these things because I fear him."

31 So in this way he died, leaving in his death an example of nobility and a memorial of courage, not only to the young but to the great body of his nation.

The Martyrdom of Seven Brothers

7 It happened also that seven brothers and their mother were arrested and were being compelled by the king, under torture with whips and straps, to partake of unlawful pig's flesh. 2 One of them, acting as their spokesman, said, "What do you intend to ask and learn from us? For we are ready to die rather than transgress the laws of our ancestors."

3 The king fell into a rage and gave orders to have pans and caldrons heated. 4 These were heated immediately, and he commanded that the tongue of their spokesman be cut out and that they scalp him and cut off his hands and feet, while the rest of the brothers and the mother looked on. 5 When he was utterly helpless, the king*g* ordered them to take him to the fire, still breathing, and to fry him in a pan. The smoke from the pan spread widely, but the brothers*h* and their mother encouraged one another to die nobly, saying, 6 "The Lord God is watching over us and in truth has compassion on us, as Moses declared in his song that bore witness against the people to their faces, when he said, 'And he will have compassion on his servants.' "

7 After the first brother had died in this way, they brought forward the second for their sport. They tore off the skin of his head with the hair and asked him, "Will you eat rather than have

your body punished limb by limb?" 8 He replied in the language of his ancestors and said to them, "No." Therefore he in turn underwent tortures as the first brother had done. 9 And when he was at his last breath, he said, "You accursed wretch, you dismiss us from this present life, but the King of the universe will raise us up to a renewal of everlasting life, because we have died for his laws."

10 After him, the third was the victim of their sport. When it was demanded, he quickly put out his tongue and courageously stretched forth his hands 11 and said nobly, "I got these from heaven, and because of his laws I disdain them, and from him I hope to get them back again." 12 As a result, the king himself and those with him were astonished at the young man's spirit, for he regarded his sufferings as nothing.

13 After he, too, had died, they maltreated and tortured the fourth in the same way. 14 When he was near death, he said, "One cannot but choose to die at the hands of mortals and to cherish the hope God gives of being raised again by him. But for you there will be no resurrection to life!"

15 Next they brought forward the fifth and maltreated him. 16 But he looked at the king*i* and said, "Because you have authority among mortals, though you also are mortal, you do what you please. But do not think that God has forsaken our people. 17 Keep on, and see how his mighty power will torture you and your descendants!"

18 After him they brought forward the sixth. And when he was about to die, he said, "Do not deceive yourself in vain. For we are suffering these things on our own account because of our sins against our own God.*j* 19 But do not think that you will go unpunished for having tried to fight against God!"

20 The mother was especially admirable and worthy of honorable memory. Although she saw her seven sons perish within a single day, she bore it with good courage because of her hope in the Lord. 21 She encouraged each of them in the language of their ancestors. Filled with a noble spirit, she reinforced her woman's reasoning with a man's courage and said to them, 22 "I do not know how you came into being in my womb. It was not I who gave you life and breath nor I who set in order the elements within each of you. 23 Therefore the Creator of

---

e 6.28 Other ancient authorities read *went*
f 6.29 Meaning of Gk uncertain
g 7.5 Gk *he*
h 7.5 Gk *they*

i 7.16 Gk *at him*
j 7.18 Gk adds *Astounding things have happened*

the world, who shaped the beginning of humankind and devised the origin of all things, in his mercy gives life and breath back to you again, since you now forget yourselves for the sake of his laws."

24 Antiochus felt that he was being treated with contempt, and he was suspicious of her reproachful tone. The youngest brother being still alive, Antiochus*k* not only appealed to him in words but promised with oaths that he would make him rich and enviable if he would turn from the ways of his ancestors and that he would take him for his Friend and entrust him with public affairs. 25 Since the young man would not listen to him at all, the king called the mother to him and urged her to advise the youth to save himself. 26 After much urging on his part, she undertook to persuade her son. 27 But, leaning close to him, she spoke in their native language as follows, deriding the cruel tyrant: "My son, have pity on me. I carried you nine months in my womb and nursed you for three years and have reared you and brought you up to this point in your life and have taken care of you. 28 I beg you, my child, to look at the heaven and the earth and see everything that is in them and recognize that God did not make them out of things that existed.*l* And in the same way the human race came into being. 29 Do not fear this butcher but prove worthy of your brothers. Accept death, so that in God's mercy I may get you back again along with your brothers."

30 While she was still speaking, the young man said, "What are you waiting for? I will not obey the king's command, but I obey the command of the law that was given to our ancestors through Moses. 31 But you, who have contrived all sorts of evil against the Hebrews, will certainly not escape the hands of God. 32 For we are suffering because of our own sins. 33 And if our living Lord is angry for a little while, to rebuke and discipline us, he will again be reconciled with his own servants. 34 But you, unholy wretch, you most defiled of all mortals, do not be elated in vain and puffed up by uncertain hopes when you raise your hand against the children of heaven. 35 You have not yet escaped the judgment of the almighty, all-seeing God. 36 For our brothers, after enduring a brief suffering for everlasting life, have fallen under God's covenant, but you, by the judgment of God, will

receive just punishment for your arrogance. 37 I, like my brothers, give up body and life for the laws of our ancestors, appealing to God to show mercy soon to our nation and by trials and plagues to make you confess that he alone is God, 38 and through me and my brothers to bring to an end the wrath of the Almighty that has justly fallen on our whole nation."

39 The king fell into a rage and handled him worse than the others, being exasperated at his scorn. 40 So he died in his integrity, putting his whole trust in the Lord.

41 Last of all, the mother died, after her sons.

42 Let this be enough, then, about the eating of sacrifices and the extreme tortures.

The Revolt of Judas Maccabeus

8 Meanwhile Judas, who was also called Maccabeus, and his companions secretly entered the villages and summoned their kindred and enlisted those who had continued in the Jewish faith, and so they gathered about six thousand. 2 They implored the Lord to look upon the people who were oppressed by all and to have pity on the temple that had been profaned by the godless, 3 to have mercy on the city that was being destroyed and about to be leveled to the ground, to hearken to the blood that cried out to him, 4 to remember also the lawless destruction of the innocent babies and the blasphemies committed against his name, and to show his hatred of evil.

5 As soon as Maccabeus got his army organized, the nations could not withstand him, for the wrath of the Lord had turned to mercy. 6 Coming without warning, he would set fire to towns and villages. He captured strategic positions and put to flight not a few of the enemy. 7 He found the nights most advantageous for such attacks. And talk of his valor spread everywhere.

8 When Philip saw that the man was gaining ground little by little and that he was pushing ahead with more frequent successes, he wrote to Ptolemy, the governor of Coelesyria and Phoenicia, to come to the aid of the king's government. 9 Then Ptolemy*m* promptly appointed Nicanor son of Patroclus, one of the king's First*n* Friends, and sent him, in command of no fewer than twenty thousand men of various nations, to wipe out the entire people of Judea.

---

k 7.24 Gk *he*
l 7.28 Or *God made them out of things that did not exist*

m 8.9 Gk *he*
n 8.9 Gk *one of the first*

He associated with him Gorgias, a general and a man of experience in military service. [10]Nicanor determined to make up for the king the tribute due to the Romans, two thousand talents, by selling the captured Jews into slavery. [11]So he immediately sent to the towns on the seacoast, inviting them to buy Jewish slaves and promising to hand over ninety slaves for a talent, not expecting the judgment from the Almighty that was about to overtake him.

Preparation for Battle

[12]Word came to Judas concerning Nicanor's invasion, and when he told his companions of the arrival of the army, [13]those who were cowardly and distrustful of God's justice ran off and got away. [14]Others sold all their remaining property and at the same time implored the Lord to rescue those who had been sold by the ungodly Nicanor before he ever met them, [15]if not for their own sake, then for the sake of the covenants made with their ancestors and because he had called them by his holy and glorious name. [16]But Maccabeus gathered his forces together, to the number six thousand, and exhorted them not to be frightened by the enemy and not to fear the great multitude of nations who were wickedly coming against them but to fight nobly, [17]keeping before their eyes the lawless outrage that the nations[o] had committed against the holy place and the torture of the derided city, as well as the overthrow of their ancestral way of life. [18]"For they trust to arms and acts of daring," he said, "but we trust in the Almighty God, who is able with a single nod to strike down those who are coming against us, and even, if necessary, the whole world."

[19]Moreover, he told them of the occasions when help came to their ancestors, how, in the time of Sennacherib, when one hundred eighty-five thousand perished, [20]and the time of the battle against the Galatians that took place in Babylonia, when eight thousand Jews[p] fought along with four thousand Macedonians; yet when the Macedonians were hard pressed, the eight thousand, by the help that came to them from heaven, destroyed one hundred twenty thousand Galatians[q] and took a great amount of plunder.

Judas Defeats Nicanor

[21]With these words he filled them with courage and made them ready to die for their laws and their country; then he divided his army into four parts. [22]He appointed his brothers also, Simon and Joseph and Jonathan, each to command a division, putting fifteen hundred men under each. [23]Besides, he appointed Eleazar to read aloud[r] from the holy book and gave the watchword, "The help of God"; then, leading the first division himself, he joined battle with Nicanor.

[24]With the Almighty as their ally, they killed more than nine thousand of the enemy and wounded and disabled most of Nicanor's army and forced them all to flee. [25]They captured the money of those who had come to buy them as slaves. After pursuing them for some distance, they were obliged to return because the hour was late. [26]It was the day before the Sabbath, and for that reason they did not continue their pursuit. [27]When they had collected the arms of the enemy and stripped them of their spoils, they kept the Sabbath, giving great praise and thanks to the Lord, who had preserved them for that day and allotted it to them as the beginning of mercy. [28]After the Sabbath they gave some of the spoils to those who had been tortured and to the widows and orphans and distributed the rest among themselves and their children. [29]When they had done this, they made common supplication and implored the merciful Lord to be wholly reconciled with his servants.

Judas Defeats Timothy and Bacchides

[30]In encounters with the forces of Timothy and Bacchides they killed more than twenty thousand of them and got possession of some exceedingly high strongholds, and they divided a very large amount of plunder, giving to those who had been tortured and to the orphans and widows and also to the aged, shares equal to their own. [31]They collected the arms of the enemy[s] and carefully stored all of them in strategic places; the rest of the spoils they carried to Jerusalem. [32]They killed the commander of Timothy's forces, a most wicked man, and one who had greatly troubled the Jews. [33]While they were celebrating the victory in the city of their ancestors, they burned those who had set fire to the sacred gates, Callisthenes and some others,

---

o **8.17** Gk *they*
p **8.20** Gk lacks *Jews*
q **8.20** Gk lacks *Galatians*

r **8.23** Meaning of Gk uncertain
s **8.31** Gk *their arms*

who had fled into one little house, so these received the proper reward for their impiety.*

34 The thrice-accursed Nicanor, who had brought the thousand merchants to buy the Jews, 35 having been humbled with the help of the Lord by opponents whom he regarded as of the least account, took off his splendid uniform and made his way alone like a runaway slave across the country until he reached Antioch, having succeeded chiefly in the destruction of his own army! 36 So he who had undertaken to secure tribute for the Romans by the capture of the people of Jerusalem proclaimed that the Jews had a Defender and that therefore the Jews were invulnerable because they followed the laws ordained by him.

The Last Campaign of Antiochus Epiphanes

9 About that time, as it happened, Antiochus had retreated in disorder from the region of Persia. 2 He had entered the city called Persepolis and attempted to rob the temples and control the city. Therefore the people rushed to the rescue with arms, and Antiochus and his army were defeated," with the result that Antiochus was put to flight by the inhabitants and beat a shameful retreat. 3 While he was in Ecbatana, news came to him of what had happened to Nicanor and the forces of Timothy. 4 Transported with rage, he conceived the idea of turning upon the Jews the injury done by those who had put him to flight, so he ordered his charioteer to drive without stopping until he completed the journey. But the judgment of heaven rode with him! For in his arrogance he said, "When I get there I will make Jerusalem a cemetery of Jews."

5 But the all-seeing Lord, the God of Israel, struck him with an incurable and invisible blow. As soon as he stopped speaking, he was seized with a pain in his bowels for which there was no relief and with sharp internal tortures—6 and that very justly, for he had tortured the bowels of others with many and strange inflictions. 7 Yet he did not in any way stop his insolence but was even more filled with arrogance, breathing fire in his rage against the Jews and giving orders to drive even faster. And so it came about that he fell out of his chariot as it was rushing along, and the fall was so hard as to torture every limb of his body. 8 Thus, he who only a little while before had thought in his superhuman arrogance

that he could command the waves of the sea and had imagined that he could weigh the high mountains in a balance, was brought down to earth and carried in a litter, making the power of God manifest to all. 9 And so the ungodly man's body swarmed with worms, and while he was still living in anguish and pain, his flesh rotted away, and because of the stench the whole army felt revulsion at his decay. 10 Because of his intolerable stench no one was able to carry the man who a little while before had thought that he could touch the stars of heaven. 11 Then it was that, broken in spirit, he began to lose much of his arrogance and to come to his senses under the scourge of God, for he was tortured with pain every moment. 12 And when he could not endure his own stench, he uttered these words, "It is right to be subject to God; mortals should not think that they are equal to God."v

Antiochus Makes a Promise to God

13 Then the abominable fellow made a vow to the Lord, who would no longer have mercy on him, stating 14 that the holy city, which he was hurrying to level to the ground and to make a cemetery, he was now declaring to be free, 15 and the Jews, whom he had not considered worth burying but had planned to throw out with their children for the wild animals and for the birds to eat, he would make, all of them, equal to citizens of Athens, 16 and the holy sanctuary, which he had formerly plundered, he would adorn with the finest offerings, and all the holy vessels he would give back many times over, and the expenses incurred for the sacrifices he would provide from his own revenues, 17 and in addition to all this he also would become a Jew and would visit every inhabited place to proclaim the power of God. 18 But when his sufferings did not in any way abate, for the judgment of God had justly come upon him, he gave up all hope for himself and wrote to the Jews the following letter, in the form of a supplication. This was its content:

Antiochus's Letter and Death

19 "To his worthy Jewish citizens, Antiochus their king and general sends hearty greetings and good wishes for their health and prosperity. 20 If you and your children are well and your affairs are as you wish, I am glad as my hope is in heaven. 21 Now I was feeling weak, and so I was

---

t **8.33** Meaning of Gk uncertain
u **9.2** Gk *they were defeated*

v **9.12** Or *not think thoughts proper only to God*

remembering with affection your esteem and goodwill. On my way back from the region of Persia I suffered an annoying illness, and I have deemed it necessary to take thought for the general security of all. ²²I do not despair of my condition, for I have good hope of recovering from my illness, ²³but I observed that my father, on the occasions when he made expeditions into the upper country, appointed his successor, ²⁴so that, if anything unexpected happened or any unwelcome news came, the people throughout the realm would not be troubled, for they would know to whom the government was left. ²⁵Moreover, I understand how the princes along the borders and the neighbors of my kingdom keep watching for opportunities and waiting to see what will happen. So I have appointed my son Antiochus to be king, whom I have often entrusted and commended to most of you when I hurried off to the upper provinces, and I have written to him the appended letter. ²⁶I therefore urge and beg you to remember the public and private services rendered to you and to maintain your present goodwill, each of you, toward me and my son. ²⁷For I am sure that he will follow my policy and will treat you with moderation and kindness."

28 So the murderer and blasphemer, having endured the more intense suffering such as he had inflicted on others, came to the end of his life by a most pitiable fate, among the mountains in a strange land. ²⁹And Philip, one of his courtiers, took his body home; then, fearing the son of Antiochus, he withdrew to Ptolemy Philometor in Egypt.

Purification of the Temple

10 Now Maccabeus and his followers, the Lord leading them on, recovered the temple and the city; ²they tore down the altars that had been built in the public square by the foreigners and also destroyed the sacred precincts. ³They purified the sanctuary and made another altar of sacrifice; then, striking fire out of flint, they offered sacrifices, after a lapse of two years, and they offered incense and lighted lamps and set out the bread of the Presence. ⁴When they had done this, they fell prostrate and implored the Lord that they might never again fall into such misfortunes but that, if they should ever sin, they might be disciplined by him with forbearance and not be handed over to blasphemous and barbarous nations. ⁵It happened that on the same day on which the

sanctuary had been profaned by the foreigners, the purification of the sanctuary took place, that is, on the twenty-fifth day of the same month, which was Chislev. ⁶They celebrated it for eight days with rejoicing, in the manner of the Festival of Booths,ʷ remembering how not long before, during the Festival of Booths,ˣ they had been wandering in the mountains and caves like wild animals. ⁷Therefore, carrying ivy-wreathed wands and beautiful branches and also palm fronds, they offered hymns of thanksgiving to him who had given success to the purifying of his own holy place. ⁸They decreed by public edict, ratified by vote, that the whole nation of the Jews should observe these days every year.

9 Such then was the end of Antiochus, who was called Epiphanes.

Accession of Antiochus Eupator

10 Now we will tell what took place under Antiochus Eupator, who was the son of that ungodly man, and will give a brief summary of the principal calamities of the wars. ¹¹This man, when he succeeded to the kingdom, appointed one Lysias to have charge of the government and Protarchos to be governor of Coelesyria and Phoenicia. ¹²Ptolemy, who was called Macron, took the lead in showing justice to the Jews because of the wrong that had been done to them and attempted to maintain peaceful relations with them. ¹³As a result he was accused before Eupator by the king's Friends. He heard himself called a traitor at every turn because he had abandoned Cyprus, which Philometor had entrusted to him, and had gone over to Antiochus Epiphanes. Unable to command the respect due his office,ʸ he took poison and ended his life.

Campaign in Idumea

14 When Gorgias became governor of the region, he maintained a force of mercenaries and at every turn kept attacking the Jews. ¹⁵Besides this, the Idumeans, who had control of important strongholds, were harassing the Jews; they received those who were banished from Jerusalem and endeavored to keep up the war. ¹⁶But Maccabeus and his forces, after making solemn supplication and imploring God to fight on their side, rushed to the strongholds of the

---

w **10.6** Or *Tabernacles*
x **10.6** Or *Tabernacles*
y **10.13** Cn: Meaning of Gk uncertain

Idumeans. [17] Attacking them vigorously, they gained possession of the places and drove back all who fought upon the wall and slaughtered those whom they encountered, killing no fewer than twenty thousand.

[18] When at least nine thousand took refuge in two very strong towers well equipped to withstand a siege, [19] Maccabeus left Simon and Joseph, and also Zacchaeus and his troops, a force sufficient to besiege them, and he himself set off for places where he was more urgently needed. [20] But those with Simon, who were money-hungry, were bribed by some of those who were in the towers and on receiving seventy thousand drachmas let some of them slip away. [21] When word of what had happened came to Maccabeus, he gathered the leaders of the people and accused these men of having sold their kindred for money by setting their enemies free to fight against them. [22] Then he killed these men who had turned traitor and immediately captured the two towers. [23] Having success at arms in everything he undertook, he destroyed more than twenty thousand in the two strongholds.

Judas Defeats Timothy

[24] Now Timothy, who had been defeated by the Jews before, gathered a tremendous force of mercenaries and collected the cavalry from Asia in no small number. He came on, intending to take Judea by storm. [25] As he drew near, Maccabeus and his men sprinkled dust on their heads and girded their loins with sackcloth, in supplication to God. [26] Falling upon the steps before the altar, they implored him to be gracious to them and to be an enemy to their enemies and an adversary to their adversaries, as the law declares. [27] And rising from their prayer they took up their arms and advanced a considerable distance from the city, and when they came near the enemy they halted. [28] Just as dawn was breaking, the two armies joined battle, the one having as pledge of success and victory not only their valor but also their reliance on the Lord, while the other made rage their leader in the fight.

[29] When the battle became fierce, there appeared to the enemy from heaven five resplendent men on horses with golden bridles, and they were leading the Jews. [30] Two of them took Maccabeus between them and, shielding him with their own armor and weapons, they kept him from being wounded. They showered arrows and thunderbolts on the enemy so that, confused and blinded, they were thrown into disorder and cut to pieces. [31] Twenty thousand five hundred were slaughtered, besides six hundred cavalry.

[32] Timothy himself fled to a stronghold called Gazara, especially well garrisoned, where Chaereas was commander. [33] Then Maccabeus and his men were glad, and they besieged the fort for four days. [34] The men within, relying on the strength of the place, kept blaspheming terribly and uttering wicked words. [35] But at dawn of the fifth day, twenty young men in the army of Maccabeus, fired with anger because of the blasphemies, bravely stormed the wall and with savage fury cut down everyone they met. [36] During the distraction, others came up in the same way, wheeled around against the defenders, and set fire to the towers; they kindled fires and burned the blasphemers alive. Others broke open the gates and let in the rest of the force, and they occupied the city. [37] They killed Timothy, who was hiding in a cistern, and his brother Chaereas, and Apollophanes. [38] When they had accomplished these things, with hymns and thanksgivings they blessed the Lord, who shows great kindness to Israel and gives them the victory.

Lysias Besieges Beth-zur

11 Very soon after this, Lysias, the king's guardian and kinsman, who was in charge of the government, being vexed at what had happened, [2] gathered about eighty thousand infantry and all his cavalry and came against the Jews. He intended to make the city a home for Greeks [3] and to levy tribute on the temple as he did on the sacred places of the other nations and to put up the high priesthood for sale every year. [4] He took no account whatever of the power of God but was elated with his ten thousands of infantry and his thousands of cavalry and his eighty elephants. [5] Invading Judea, he approached Beth-zur, which was a fortified place about five schoinoi[z] from Jerusalem, and pressed it hard.

[6] When Maccabeus and his men got word that Lysias[a] was besieging the strongholds, they and all the people, with lamentations and tears, prayed the Lord to send a good angel to save Israel. [7] Maccabeus himself was the first to take

---

z **11.5** A unit for measuring distance
a **11.6** Gk *he*

up arms, and he urged the others to risk their lives with him to aid their kindred. Then they eagerly rushed off together. ⁸And there, while they were still near Jerusalem, a horseman appeared at their head, clothed in white and brandishing weapons of gold. ⁹And together they all praised the merciful God and were strengthened in heart, ready to assail not only humans but the wildest animals or walls of iron. ¹⁰They advanced in battle order, having their heavenly ally, for the Lord had mercy on them. ¹¹They hurled themselves like lions against the enemy and laid low eleven thousand of them and sixteen hundred cavalry and forced all the rest to flee. ¹²Most of them got away wounded and stripped, and Lysias himself escaped by disgraceful flight.

Lysias Makes Peace with the Jews

13 As he was not without intelligence, he pondered over the defeat that had befallen him and realized that the Hebrews were invincible because the mighty God fought on their side. So he sent to them ¹⁴and persuaded them to settle everything on just terms, promising that he would persuade the king, constraining him to be their friend.ᵇ ¹⁵Maccabeus, having regard for the common good, agreed to all that Lysias urged. For the king granted every request in behalf of the Jews that Maccabeus delivered to Lysias in writing.

16 The letter written to the Jews by Lysias was to this effect:

"Lysias to the people of the Jews, greetings. ¹⁷John and Absalom, who were sent by you, have delivered your signed communication and have asked about the matters indicated in it. ¹⁸I have informed the king of everything that needed to be brought before him, and I have agreed to what was possible. ¹⁹If you will maintain your goodwill toward the government, I will endeavor in the future to help promote your welfare. ²⁰And concerning such matters and their details, I have ordered these men and my representatives to confer with you. ²¹Farewell. The one hundred forty-eighth year, Dioscorinthius twenty-fourth."

22 The king's letter ran thus:

"King Antiochus to his brother Lysias, greetings. ²³Now that our father has gone on to the gods, we desire that the subjects of the kingdom be undisturbed in caring for their own affairs.

²⁴We have heard that the Jews do not consent to our father's change to Greek customs but prefer their own way of living and ask that their own customs be allowed them. ²⁵Accordingly, since we choose that this nation also should be free from disturbance, our decision is that their temple be restored to them and that they shall live according to the customs of their ancestors. ²⁶You will do well, therefore, to send word to them and give them pledges of friendship, so that they may know our policy and be of good cheer and go on happily in the conduct of their own affairs."

27 To the nation the king's letter was as follows:

"King Antiochus to the council of the Jews and to the other Jews, greetings. ²⁸If you are well, it is as we desire. We also are in good health. ²⁹Menelaus has informed us that you wish to return home and look after your own affairs. ³⁰Therefore those who go home by the thirtieth of Xanthicus will have our pledge of friendship and full permission ³¹for the Jews to enjoy their own customsᶜ and laws, just as formerly, and none of them shall be molested in any way for what may have been done in ignorance. ³²And I have also sent Menelaus to encourage you. ³³Farewell. The one hundred forty-eighth year, Xanthicus fifteenth."

34 The Romans also sent them a letter, which read thus:

"Quintus Memmius and Titus Manius, envoys of the Romans, to the people of the Jews, greetings. ³⁵With regard to what Lysias the kinsman of the king has granted you, we also give consent. ³⁶But as to the matters that he decided are to be referred to the king, as soon as you have considered them, send someone promptly so that we may make proposals appropriate for you, for we are on our way to Antioch. ³⁷Therefore make haste and send messengers so that we may have your judgment. ³⁸Farewell. The one hundred forty-eighth year, Xanthicus fifteenth."

Incidents at Joppa and Jamnia

12 When this agreement had been reached, Lysias returned to the king, and the Jews went about their farming.

2 But some of the governors in various places, Timothy and Apollonius son of Gennaeus, as well as Hieronymus and Demophon, and in addition to these Nicanor the governor of Cyprus, would not let them live quietly and

---

b 11.14 Meaning of Gk uncertain   *c* 11.31 Cn: Gk *food* in peace. ³And the people of Joppa did so ungodly a deed as this: they invited the Jews who lived among them to embark, with their wives and children, on boats that they had provided, as though there were no ill will to the Jews,ᵈ ⁴and this was done by public vote of the city. When they accepted, because they wished to live peaceably and suspected nothing, the people of Joppaᵉ took them out to sea and drowned them, at least two hundred. ⁵When Judas heard of the cruelty visited on his compatriots, he gave orders to his men ⁶and, calling upon God, the righteous judge, attacked the murderers of his kindred. He set fire to the harbor by night, burned the boats, and massacred those who had taken refuge there. ⁷Then, because the city's gates were closed, he withdrew, intending to come again and root out the whole community of Joppa. ⁸But learning that the people in Jamnia meant in the same way to wipe out the Jews who were living among them, ⁹he attacked the Jamnites by night and set fire to the harbor and the fleet, so that the glow of the light was seen in Jerusalem, thirty milesᶠ distant.

The Campaign in Gilead

10 When they had gone more than a mileᵍ from there on their march against Timothy, at least five thousand Arabs with five hundred cavalry attacked them. ¹¹After a hard fight, Judas and his companions, with God's help, were victorious. The defeated nomads begged Judas to grant them pledges of friendship, promising to give him livestock and to help his peopleʰ in all other ways. ¹²Judas, realizing that they might indeed be useful in many ways, agreed to make peace with them, and after receiving his pledges they went back to their tents.

13 He also attacked a certain town that was strongly fortified with earthworksⁱ and walls and inhabited by all sorts of nations. Its name was Caspin. ¹⁴Those who were within, relying on the strength of the walls and on their supply of provisions, behaved most insolently toward Judas and his men, railing at them and even blaspheming and saying unholy things. ¹⁵But Judas and his men, calling upon the great Sovereign of the world, who without battering

rams or engines of war overthrew Jericho in the days of Joshua, rushed furiously upon the walls. ¹⁶They took the town by the will of God and slaughtered untold numbers, so that the adjoining lake, a quarter of a mileʲ wide, appeared to be running over with blood.

Judas Defeats Timothy's Army

17 When they had gone ninety-five milesᵏ from there, they came to a stockade,ˡ to the Jews who are called Toubiani. ¹⁸They did not find Timothy in that region, for he had by then left there without accomplishing anything, though in one place he had left a very strong garrison. ¹⁹Dositheus and Sosipater, who were captains under Maccabeus, marched out and destroyed those whom Timothy had left in the stronghold, more than ten thousand men. ²⁰But Maccabeus arranged his army in divisions, set menᵐ in command of the divisions, and hurried after Timothy, who had with him one hundred twenty thousand infantry and two thousand five hundred cavalry. ²¹When Timothy learned of the approach of Judas, he sent off the women and the children and also the baggage to a place called Carnaim, for that place was hard to besiege and difficult to access because of the narrowness of all the approaches. ²²But when Judas's first division appeared, terror and fear came over the enemy at the manifestation to them of him who sees all things. In their flight they rushed headlong in every direction, so that often they were injured by their own men and pierced by the points of their own swords. ²³Judas pressed the pursuit with the utmost vigor, putting the sinners to the sword, and destroyed as many as thirty thousand.

24 Timothy himself fell into the hands of Dositheus and Sosipater and their men. With great guile he begged them to let him go in safety, because he held the parents of most of them and the brothers of some, to whom no consideration would be shown. ²⁵And when with many words he had confirmed his solemn promise to restore them unharmed, they let him go, for the sake of saving their kindred.

Judas Wins Other Victories

26 Then Judasⁿ marched against Carnaim and the temple of Atargatis and slaughtered

---

d 12.3 Gk *to them*
e 12.4 Gk *they*
f 12.9 Gk *two hundred forty stadia*
g 12.10 Gk *nine stadia*
h 12.11 Gk *them*
i 12.13 Meaning of Gk uncertain

j 12.16 Gk *two stadia*
k 12.17 Gk *seven hundred fifty stadia*
l 12.17 Or *Charax*
m 12.20 Gk *them*
n 12.26 Gk *he*

twenty-five thousand people. ²⁷After the rout and destruction of these, he marched also against Ephron, a fortified town where Lysias lived with multitudes of people of all nationalities.ᵒ Stalwart young men took their stand before the walls and made a vigorous defense, and great stores of war engines and missiles were there. ²⁸But the Jewsᵖ called upon the Sovereign who with power shatters the might of his enemies, and they got the town into their hands and killed as many as twenty-five thousand of those who were in it.

²⁹Setting out from there, they hastened to Scythopolis, which is seventy-five miles�q from Jerusalem. ³⁰But when the Jews who lived there bore witness to the goodwill that the people of Scythopolis had shown them and their kind treatment of them in times of misfortune, ³¹they thanked them and exhorted them to be well disposed to their race in the future also. Then they went up to Jerusalem, as the Festival of Weeks was close at hand.

Judas Defeats Gorgias

³²After the festival called Pentecost, they hurried against Gorgias, the governor of Idumea, ³³who came out with three thousand infantry and four hundred cavalry. ³⁴When they joined battle, it happened that a few of the Jews fell. ³⁵But a certain Dositheus, one of Bacenor's men,ʳ who was on horseback and was a strong man, caught hold of Gorgias and, grasping his cloak, was dragging him off by main strength, wishing to take the accursed man alive, when one of the Thracian cavalry bore down on him and cut off his arm, so Gorgias escaped and reached Marisa.

³⁶As Esdris and his men had been fighting for a long time and were weary, Judas called upon the Lord to show himself their ally and leader in the battle. ³⁷In the language of their ancestors he raised the battle cry, with hymns; then he charged against Gorgias's troops when they were not expecting it and put them to flight.

Prayers for Those Killed in Battle

³⁸Then Judas assembled his army and went to the city of Adullam. As the seventh day was coming on, they purified themselves according to the custom and kept the Sabbath there.

³⁹On the next day, as had now become necessary, Judas and his men went to take up the bodies of the fallen and to bring them back to lie with their kindred in the tombs of their ancestors. ⁴⁰Then under the tunic of each one of the dead they found sacred tokens of the idols of Jamnia, which the law forbids the Jews to wear. And it became clear to all that this was the reason these men had fallen. ⁴¹So they all blessed the ways of the Lord, the righteous judge, who reveals the things that are hidden, ⁴²and they turned to supplication, praying that the sin that had been committed might be wholly blotted out. The noble Judas exhorted the people to keep themselves free from sin, for they had seen with their own eyes what had happened as the result of the sin of those who had fallen. ⁴³He also took up a collection, man by man, to the amount of two thousand drachmas of silver, and sent it to Jerusalem to provide for a purification offering. In doing this he acted very well and honorably, taking account of the resurrection. ⁴⁴For if he were not expecting that those who had fallen would rise again, it would have been superfluous and foolish to pray for the dead. ⁴⁵But if he was looking to the splendid reward that is laid up for those who fall asleep in godliness, it was a holy and pious thought. Therefore he made atonement for the dead, so that they might be delivered from their sin.

Menelaus Is Put to Death

13 In the one hundred forty-ninth year, word came to Judas and his men that Antiochus Eupator was coming with a great army against Judea, ²and with him Lysias, his guardian, who had charge of the government. Each of them had a Greek force of one hundred ten thousand infantry, five thousand three hundred cavalry, twenty-two elephants, and three hundred chariots armed with scythes.

³Menelaus also joined them and with utter hypocrisy urged Antiochus on, not for the sake of his country's welfare but because he thought that he would be established in office. ⁴But the King of kings aroused the anger of Antiochus against the scoundrel, and when Lysias informed him that this man was to blame for all the trouble, he ordered them to take him to Beroea and to put him to death by the method that is customary in that place. ⁵For there is a tower there, fifty cubits high, full of ashes, and it

---

o 12.27 Meaning of Gk uncertain
p 12.28 Gk *they*
q 12.29 Gk *six hundred stadia*
r 12.35 Other authorities read *the Toubians*

has a rim running around it that on all sides inclines precipitously into the ashes. [6]There they all push to destruction anyone guilty of sacrilege or notorious for other crimes. [7]By such a fate it came about that Menelaus the lawbreaker died, without even burial in the earth. [8]And this was eminently just; because he had committed many sins against the altar whose fire and ashes were holy, he met his death in ashes.

A Battle Near the City of Modein

[9]The king with barbarous arrogance was coming to show the Jews things far worse than those that had been done[s] in his father's time. [10]But when Judas heard of this, he ordered the people to call upon the Lord day and night, now if ever to help those who were on the point of being deprived of the law and their country and the holy temple, [11]and not to let the people who had just begun to revive fall into the hands of the blasphemous nations. [12]When they had all joined in the same petition and had implored the merciful Lord with weeping and fasting and lying prostrate for three days without ceasing, Judas exhorted them and ordered them to stand ready.

[13]After consulting privately with the elders, he determined to march out and decide the matter by the help of God before the king's army could enter Judea and get possession of the city. [14]So, committing the decision to the Creator of the world and exhorting his troops to fight bravely to the death for the laws, temple, city, country, and way of life, he pitched his camp near Modein. [15]He gave his troops the watchword, "God's victory," and with a picked force of the bravest young men, he attacked the king's pavilion at night and killed as many as two thousand men in the camp. He stabbed[t] the leading elephant and its rider. [16]In the end, they filled the camp with terror and confusion and withdrew in triumph. [17]This happened, just as day was dawning, because the Lord's help protected him.

Antiochus Makes a Treaty with the Jews

[18]The king, having had a taste of the daring of the Jews, tried strategy in attacking their positions. [19]He advanced against Beth-zur, a strong fortress of the Jews, was turned back, attacked again,[u] and was defeated. [20]Judas sent in to the garrison whatever was necessary. [21]But

Rhodocus, a man from the ranks of the Jews, gave secret information to the enemy; he was sought for, caught, and put in prison. [22]The king negotiated a second time with the people in Beth-zur, gave pledges, received theirs, withdrew, attacked Judas and his men, was defeated; [23]he got word that Philip, who had been left in charge of the government, had revolted in Antioch; he was dismayed, called in the Jews, yielded and swore to observe all their rights, settled with them and offered sacrifice, honored the sanctuary, and showed generosity to the holy place. [24]He received Maccabeus, left Hegemonides as governor from Ptolemais to Gerar, [25]and went to Ptolemais. The people of Ptolemais were indignant over the treaty; in fact, they were so angry that they wanted to annul its terms.[v] [26]Lysias took the public platform, made the best possible defense, convinced them, appeased them, gained their goodwill, and set out for Antioch. This is how the king's attack and withdrawal turned out.

Alcimus Speaks against Judas

14 Three years later, word came to Judas and his men that Demetrius son of Seleucus had sailed into the harbor of Tripolis with a strong army and a fleet [2]and had taken possession of the country, having made away with Antiochus and his guardian Lysias.

[3]Now a certain Alcimus, who had formerly been high priest but had willfully defiled himself in the days of separation,[w] realized that there was no way for him to be safe or to have access again to the holy altar [4]and went to King Demetrius in about the one hundred fifty-first year, presenting to him a crown of gold and a palm and besides these some of the customary olive branches from the temple. During that day he kept quiet. [5]But he found an opportunity that furthered his mad purpose when he was invited by Demetrius to a meeting of the council and was asked about the attitude and intentions of the Jews. He answered:

[6]"Those of the Jews who are called Hasideans, whose leader is Judas Maccabeus, are keeping up war and stirring up sedition and will not let the kingdom attain tranquility. [7]Therefore I have laid aside my ancestral glory—I mean the high priesthood—and have now come here, [8]first because I am genuinely concerned for the

---

s **13.9** Or *the worst of the things that had been done*
t **13.15** Meaning of Gk uncertain
u **13.19** Or *faltered*

v **13.25** Meaning of Gk uncertain
w **14.3** Other ancient authorities read *of mixing*

interests of the king, and second because I have regard also for my compatriots. For through the folly of those whom I have mentioned our whole nation is now in no small misfortune. ⁹Since you are acquainted, O king, with the details of this matter, may it please you to take thought for our country and our hard-pressed nation with the gracious kindness that you show to all. ¹⁰For as long as Judas lives, it is impossible for the government to find peace." ¹¹When he had said this, the rest of the king's Friends,ˣ who were hostile to Judas, quickly inflamed Demetrius still more. ¹²He immediately chose Nicanor, who had been in command of the elephants, appointed him governor of Judea, and sent him off ¹³with orders to kill Judas and scatter his troops and to install Alcimus as high priest of the greatʸ temple. ¹⁴And the nations throughout Judea, who had fled beforeᶻ Judas, flocked to join Nicanor, thinking that the misfortunes and calamities of the Jews would mean prosperity for themselves.

Nicanor Makes Friends with Judas

¹⁵When the Jewsᵃ heard of Nicanor's coming and the gathering of the nations, they sprinkled dust on their heads and prayed to him who established his own people forever and always upholds his own heritage by manifesting himself. ¹⁶At the command of the leader, theyᵇ set out from there immediately and engaged them in battle at a village called Dessau.ᶜ ¹⁷Simon, the brother of Judas, had encountered Nicanor but had been temporarilyᵈ checked because of the sudden consternation created by the enemy. ¹⁸Nevertheless, Nicanor, hearing of the valor of Judas and his troops and their courage in battle for their country, shrank from deciding the issue by bloodshed. ¹⁹Therefore he sent Posidonius, Theodotus, and Mattathias to give and receive pledges of friendship. ²⁰When the terms had been fully considered and the leader had informed the people and it had appeared that they were of one mind, they agreed to the covenant. ²¹The leadersᵉ set a day on which to meet by themselves. A chariot came forward from each army; seats of honor were set in place; ²²Judas posted armed men in readiness at key places to prevent sudden treachery on the part of the enemy; so they duly held the consultation.

²³Nicanor stayed on in Jerusalem and did nothing out of the way but dismissed the flocks of people who had gathered. ²⁴And he kept Judas always in his presence; he was warmly attached to the man. ²⁵He urged him to marry and have children, so Judasᶠ married, settled down, and shared the common life.

Nicanor Turns against Judas

²⁶But when Alcimus noticed their goodwill for one another, he took the covenant that had been made and went to Demetrius. He told him that Nicanor was disloyal to the government, since he had appointed that conspirator against the kingdom, Judas, to be his successor. ²⁷The king became excited and, provoked by the false accusations of that depraved man, wrote to Nicanor, stating that he was displeased with the covenant and commanding him to send Maccabeus to Antioch as a prisoner without delay.

²⁸When this message came to Nicanor, he was troubled and grieved that he had to annul their agreement when the man had done no wrong. ²⁹Since it was not possible to oppose the king, he watched for an opportunity to accomplish this by a stratagem. ³⁰But Maccabeus, noticing that Nicanor was more austere in his dealings with him and was meeting him more rudely than had been his custom, concluded that this austerity did not spring from the best motives. So he gathered not a few of his men and went into hiding from Nicanor. ³¹When the latter became aware that he had been cleverly outwitted by the man, he went to the greatᵍ and holy temple while the priests were offering the customary sacrifices and commanded them to hand the man over. ³²When they declared on oath that they did not know where the man was whom he wanted, ³³he stretched out his right hand toward the sanctuary and swore this oath: "If you do not hand Judas over to me as a prisoner, I will level this shrine of God to the ground and tear down the altar and build here a splendid temple to Dionysus."

³⁴Having said this, he went away. Then the priests stretched out their hands toward heaven and called upon the constant Defender of our

---

x 14.11 Gk *of the Friends*
y 14.13 Gk *greatest*
z 14.14 Meaning of Gk uncertain
a 14.15 Gk *they*
b 14.16 Gk *he*
c 14.16 Meaning of Gk uncertain
d 14.17 Other ancient authorities read *slowly*
e 14.21 Gk *They*

---

f 14.25 Gk *he*
g 14.31 Gk *greatest*

nation, in these words: 35 "O Lord of all, though you have need of nothing, you were pleased that there should be a temple for your habitation among us, 36 so now, O holy One, Lord of all holiness, keep undefiled forever this house that has been so recently purified."

Razis Dies for His Country

37 A certain Razis, one of the elders of Jerusalem, was denounced to Nicanor as a man who loved his compatriots and was very well thought of and for his goodwill was called father of the Jews. 38 For before the days of separation, he had been accused of Judaism, and he had most zealously risked body and life for Judaism. 39 Nicanor, wishing to exhibit the enmity that he had for the Jews, sent more than five hundred soldiers to arrest him, 40 for he thought that by arresting*h* him he would do them an injury. 41 When the troops were about to capture the tower and were forcing the door of the courtyard, they ordered that fire be brought and the doors burned. Being surrounded, Razis*i* fell upon his own sword, 42 preferring to die nobly rather than to fall into the hands of sinners and suffer outrages unworthy of his noble birth. 43 But in the heat of the struggle he did not hit exactly, and the crowd was now rushing in through the doors. He courageously ran up on the wall and bravely threw himself down into the crowd. 44 But as they quickly drew back, a space opened and he fell in the middle of the empty space. 45 Still alive and aflame with anger, he rose, and though his blood gushed forth and his wounds were severe he ran through the crowd, and standing upon a steep rock, 46 with his blood now completely drained from him, he tore out his entrails, took them in both hands, and hurled them at the crowd, calling upon the Lord of life and spirit to give them back to him again. This was the manner of his death.

Nicanor's Arrogance

15 When Nicanor heard that Judas and his troops were in the region of Samaria, he made plans to attack them with complete safety on the day of rest. 2 When the Jews who were compelled to follow him said, "Do not destroy so savagely and barbarously, but show respect for the day that he who sees all things

has honored and hallowed above other days," 3 the thrice-accursed wretch asked if there were a sovereign in heaven who had commanded the keeping of the Sabbath day. 4 When they declared, "It is the living Lord himself, the Sovereign in heaven, who ordered us to observe the seventh day," 5 he replied, "But I am a sovereign also, on earth, and I command you to take up arms and finish the king's business." Nevertheless, he did not succeed in carrying out his abominable design.

Judas Prepares the Jews for Battle

6 This Nicanor in his utter boastfulness and arrogance had determined to erect a public monument of victory over Judas and his forces. 7 But Maccabeus did not cease to trust with all confidence that he would get help from the Lord. 8 He exhorted his troops not to fear the attack of the nations but to keep in mind the former times when help had come to them from heaven and so to look for the victory that the Almighty would give them. 9 Encouraging them from the Law and the Prophets and reminding them also of the struggles they had won, he made them the more eager. 10 When he had aroused their courage, he issued his orders, at the same time pointing out the treachery of the nations and their violation of oaths. 11 He armed each of them not so much with confidence in shields and spears as with the inspiration of brave words, and he cheered them all by relating a dream, a sort of vision,*j* that was worthy of belief.

12 What he saw was this: Onias, who had been high priest, a noble and good man, of modest bearing and gentle manner, one who spoke fittingly and had been trained from childhood in all that belongs to excellence, was praying with outstretched hands for the whole body of the Jews. 13 Then in the same fashion another appeared, distinguished by his gray hair and dignity, and of marvelous majesty and authority. 14 And Onias spoke, saying, "This is a man who loves the family of Israel and prays much for the people and the holy city: Jeremiah, the prophet of God." 15 Jeremiah stretched out his right hand and gave to Judas a golden sword, and as he gave it he addressed him thus: 16 "Take this holy sword, a gift from God, with which you will strike down your adversaries."

17 Encouraged by the words of Judas, so noble and so effective in arousing valor and

---

h 14.40 Meaning of Gk uncertain
i 14.41 Gk *he*

j 15.11 Meaning of Gk uncertain

awaking courage in the souls of the young, they determined not to carry on a campaign[k] but to attack bravely and to decide the matter by fighting hand to hand with all courage, because the city and the sanctuary and the temple were in danger. [18] Their concern for wives and children and also for brothers and sisters and relatives lay upon them less heavily; their greatest and first fear was for the consecrated sanctuary. [19] And those who had to remain in the city were in no little distress, being anxious over the encounter in the open country.

The Defeat and Death of Nicanor

[20] When all were now looking forward to the coming issue and the enemy was already close at hand with their army drawn up for battle, the elephants[l] strategically stationed and the cavalry deployed on the flanks, [21] Maccabeus, observing the masses that were in front of him and the varied supply of arms and the savagery of the elephants, stretched out his hands toward heaven and called upon the Lord who works wonders, for he knew that it is not by arms but as the Lord[m] decides that he gains the victory for those who deserve it. [22] He called upon him in these words: "O Lord, you sent your angel in the time of King Hezekiah of Judea, and he killed fully one hundred eighty-five thousand in the camp of Sennacherib. [23] So now, O Sovereign of the heavens, send a good angel to spread terror and trembling before us. [24] By the might of your arm may these blasphemers who come against your holy people be struck down." With these words he ended his prayer.

[25] Nicanor and his troops advanced with trumpets and battle songs, [26] but Judas and his troops met the enemy in battle with invocations to God and prayers. [27] So, fighting with their hands and praying to God in their hearts, they laid low at least thirty-five thousand and were greatly gladdened by God's manifestation.

[28] When the action was over and they were returning with joy, they recognized Nicanor, lying dead, in full armor. [29] Then there was shouting and tumult, and they blessed the Sovereign Lord in the language of their ancestors. [30] Then the man who was ever in body and soul the defender of his people, the man who maintained his youthful goodwill toward his compatriots, ordered them to cut off Nicanor's head and arm and carry them to Jerusalem. [31] When he arrived there and had called his compatriots together and stationed the priests before the altar, he sent for those who were in the citadel. [32] He showed them the vile Nicanor's head and that profane man's arm, which had been boastfully stretched out against the holy house of the Almighty. [33] He cut out the tongue of the ungodly Nicanor and said that he would feed it piecemeal to the birds and would hang up these rewards of his folly opposite the sanctuary. [34] And they all, looking to heaven, blessed the Lord who had manifested himself, saying, "Blessed is he who has kept his own place undefiled!" [35] Judas[n] hung Nicanor's head from the citadel, a clear and conspicuous sign to everyone of the help of the Lord. [36] And they all decreed by public vote never to let this day go unobserved but to celebrate the thirteenth day of the twelfth month—which is called Adar in the Aramaic language—the day before Mordecai's day.

[37] This, then, is how matters turned out with Nicanor, and from that time the city has been in the possession of the Hebrews. So I will here end my story.

The Compiler's Epilogue

[38] If it is well told and to the point, that is what I myself desired; if it is poorly done and mediocre, that was the best I could do. [39] For just as it is harmful to drink wine alone or, again, to drink water alone, while wine already mixed with water is delicious and enhances one's enjoyment, so also the style of the story delights the ears of those who read the work. And here will be the end.

---

k 15.17 Or *to remain in camp*
l 15.20 Gk *animals*
m 15.21 Gk *he*

---

n 15.35 Gk *He*

(b) The books from 1 Esdras through 3 Maccabees are recognized as Deuterocanonical Scripture by the Greek and the Russian Orthodox Churches. They are not so recognized by the Roman Catholic Church, but 1 Esdras and the Prayer of Manasseh (together with 2 Esdras) are placed in an appendix to the Latin Vulgate Bible.

1 ESDRAS

Josiah Celebrates the Passover

1 Josiah kept the Passover to his Lord in Jerusalem; he killed the Passover lamb on the fourteenth day of the first month, ²having placed the priests according to their divisions, arrayed in their vestments, in the temple of the Lord. ³He told the Levites, the temple servants of Israel, that they should sanctify themselves to the Lord and put the holy ark of the Lord in the house that King Solomon, son of David, had built, ⁴and he said,ᵃ "You need no longer carry it on your shoulders. Now worship the Lord your God and serve his nation Israel; prepare yourselves by your families and kindred, in accordance with the directions of King David of Israel and the magnificence of his son Solomon. ⁵Stand in order in the templeᵇ according to the groupings of the ancestral houses of you Levites, who minister before your kindred the people of Israel, ⁶and kill the Passover lamb and prepare the sacrifices for your kindred, and keep the Passover according to the commandment of the Lord that was given to Moses."

7 To the people who were present Josiah gave thirty thousand lambs and kids and three thousand calves; these were given from the king's possessions, as he promised, to the people and the priests and Levites. ⁸Hilkiah, Zechariah, and Jehiel, the chief officers of the temple, gave to the priests for the Passover two thousand six hundred sheep and three hundred calves. ⁹And Jeconiah and Shemaiah and his brother Nethanel, and Hashabiah and Ochiel and Joram, captains over thousands, gave the Levites for the Passover five thousand sheep and seven hundred calves.

10 This is what took place. The priests and the Levites, having the unleavened bread, stood in proper order according to kindred and the grouping of the ancestral houses, before the people, to make the offering to the Lord as it is written in the book of Moses; this they did in the morning. ¹¹They roasted the Passover lamb with fire, as required, and they boiled the sacrifices in bronze pots and caldrons, with a pleasing odor, and carried them to all the people. ¹²Afterward they prepared the Passover for themselves and for their kindred the priests, the sons of Aaron, ¹³because the priests were offering the fat until nightfall, so the Levites prepared it for themselves and for their kindred the priests, the sons of Aaron. ¹⁴The temple singers, the sons of Asaph, were in their place according to the arrangement made by David, and also Asaph, Zechariah, and Eddinus, who represented the king. ¹⁵The gatekeepers were at each gate; no one needed to interrupt his daily duties, for their kindred the Levites prepared the Passover for them.

16 So the things that had to do with the sacrifices to the Lord were accomplished that day: the Passover was kept and the sacrifices were offered on the altar of the Lord, according to the command of King Josiah. ¹⁷And the people of Israel who were present at that time kept the Passover and the Festival of Unleavened Bread seven days. ¹⁸No Passover like it had been kept in Israel since the times of the prophet Samuel; ¹⁹none of the kings of Israel had kept such a Passover as was kept by Josiah and the priests and Levites and the people of Judah and all of Israel who were living in Jerusalem. ²⁰In the eighteenth year of the reign of Josiah this Passover was kept.

The End of Josiah's Reign

21 And the deeds of Josiah were upright in the sight of the Lord, for his heart was full of godliness. ²²In ancient times the events of his

---

ᵃ **1.4** Gk lacks *and he said*
ᵇ **1.5** Other ancient authorities read *holy place*

reign have been recorded—concerning those who sinned and acted wickedly toward the Lord beyond any other nation or kingdom and how they grieved the Lord*c* deeply, so that the words of the Lord fell upon Israel.

23 After all these acts of Josiah, it happened that Pharaoh, king of Egypt, went to make war at Carchemish on the Euphrates, and Josiah went out against him. 24 And the king of Egypt sent word to him, saying, "What have we to do with each other, O king of Judea? 25 I was not sent against you by the Lord God, for my war is at the Euphrates. And now the Lord is with me! The Lord is with me, urging me on! Stand aside, and do not oppose the Lord."

26 Josiah, however, did not turn back to his chariot but tried to fight with him and did not heed the words of the prophet Jeremiah from the mouth of the Lord. 27 He joined battle with him in the plain of Megiddo, and the commanders came down against King Josiah. 28 The king said to his servants, "Take me away from the battle, for I am very weak." And immediately his servants took him out of the line of battle. 29 He got into his second chariot, and after he was brought back to Jerusalem he died and was buried in the tomb of his ancestors.

30 In all Judea they mourned for Josiah. The prophet Jeremiah lamented for Josiah, and the principal men, with the women,*d* have made lamentation for him to this day; it was ordained that this should always be done throughout the whole people of Israel. 31 These things are written in the book of the histories of the kings of Judea, and every one of the acts of Josiah and his splendor and his understanding of the law of the Lord and the things that he had done before and these that are now told are recorded in the book of the kings of Israel and Judah.

The Last Kings of Judah

32 The people of the nation took Jeconiah son of Josiah, who was twenty-three years old, and made him king in succession to his father Josiah. 33 He reigned three months in Judah*e* and Jerusalem. Then the king of Egypt deposed him from reigning in Jerusalem 34 and fined the nation one hundred talents of silver and one talent of gold. 35 The king of Egypt made his brother Jehoiakim king of Judea and Jerusalem.

36 Jehoiakim put the nobles in prison and seized his brother Zarius and brought him back from Egypt.

37 Jehoiakim was twenty-five years old when he began to reign in Judea and Jerusalem; he did what was evil in the sight of the Lord. 38 King Nebuchadnezzar of Babylon came up against him; he bound him with a chain of bronze and took him away to Babylon. 39 Nebuchadnezzar also took some holy vessels of the Lord and carried them away and stored them in his temple in Babylon. 40 But the things that are reported about Jehoiakim*f* and his uncleanness and impiety are written in the annals of the kings.

41 His son Jehoiachin became king in his place; when he was made king he was eighteen years old, 42 and he reigned three months and ten days in Jerusalem. He did what was evil in the sight of the Lord. 43 A year later Nebuchadnezzar sent and removed him to Babylon, with the holy vessels of the Lord, 44 and made Zedekiah king of Judea and Jerusalem.

The Fall of Jerusalem

Zedekiah was twenty-one years old, and he reigned eleven years. 45 He also did what was evil in the sight of the Lord and did not heed the words spoken by the prophet Jeremiah from the mouth of the Lord. 46 Although King Nebuchadnezzar had made him swear by the name of the Lord, he broke his oath and rebelled; he stiffened his neck and hardened his heart and transgressed the laws of the Lord, the God of Israel. 47 Even the leaders of the people and of the priests committed many acts of sacrilege and lawlessness beyond all the unclean deeds of all the nations and polluted the temple of the Lord in Jerusalem—the temple that God had made holy. 48 The God of their ancestors sent his messenger to call them back, because he would have spared them and his dwelling place. 49 But they mocked his messengers, and whenever the Lord spoke, they scoffed at his prophets, until God, in his anger against his nation because of their ungodly acts, gave the command to bring the kings of the Chaldeans against them. 50 The Chaldeans killed their young men with the sword around their holy temple and did not spare young man or young woman,*g* elder or child, for he gave them all into their hands. 51 They took all the holy vessels of the Lord, great and

---

c 1.22 Gk *him*
d 1.30 Or *their wives*
e 1.33 Other ancient authorities read *Israel*

f 1.40 Gk *him*
g 1.50 Gk *virgin*

small, the treasure chests of the Lord, and the royal stores and carried them away to Babylon. 52 They burned the house of the Lord, broke down the walls of Jerusalem, burned its towers with fire, 53 and utterly destroyed all its glorious things. Nebuchadnezzar[h] led the survivors away to Babylon with the sword, 54 and they were servants to him and to his sons until the Persians began to reign, in fulfillment of the word of the Lord by the mouth of Jeremiah, 55 saying, "Until the land has enjoyed its Sabbaths, it shall keep Sabbath all the time of its desolation until the completion of seventy years."

Cyrus Permits the Exiles to Return

2 In the first year of Cyrus as king of the Persians, so that the word of the Lord by the mouth of Jeremiah might be accomplished, 2 the Lord stirred up the spirit of King Cyrus of the Persians, and he made a proclamation throughout all his kingdom and also put it in writing:

3 "Thus says Cyrus king of the Persians: The Lord of Israel, the Lord Most High, has made me king of the world, 4 and he has commanded me to build him a house in Jerusalem, which is in Judea. 5 If any of you, therefore, are of his nation, may your Lord be with you;[i] go up to Jerusalem, which is in Judea, and build the house of the Lord of Israel—he is the Lord who dwells in Jerusalem—6 and let each of you, wherever you may live, be helped by your neighbors with gold and silver, with gifts and with horses and cattle, besides the other things added as votive offerings for the temple of the Lord that is in Jerusalem."

7 Then arose the heads of families of the tribes of Judah and Benjamin, and the priests and the Levites, and all whose spirit the Lord had stirred to go up to build the house in Jerusalem for the Lord; 8 their neighbors helped them with everything, with silver and gold, with horses and cattle, and with a very great number of votive offerings from many whose hearts were stirred.

9 King Cyrus also brought out the holy vessels of the Lord that Nebuchadnezzar had carried away from Jerusalem and stored in his temple of idols. 10 When King Cyrus of the Persians brought these out, he gave them to Mithridates, his treasurer, 11 and by him they were given to Sheshbazzar, the governor of Judea.

12 The number of these was: one thousand gold cups, one thousand silver cups, twenty-nine silver censers, thirty gold bowls, two thousand four hundred ten silver bowls, and one thousand other vessels. 13 All the vessels were handed over, gold and silver, five thousand four hundred sixty-nine, 14 and they were carried back by Sheshbazzar with the returning exiles from Babylon to Jerusalem.

Opposition to Rebuilding Jerusalem

15 In the time of King Artaxerxes of the Persians, Bishlam, Mithridates, Tabeel, Rehum, Beltethmus, the scribe Shimshai, and the rest of their associates living in Samaria and other places wrote him the following letter, against those who were living in Judea and Jerusalem:

16 "To King Artaxerxes our lord, your servants the recorder Rehum and the scribe Shimshai and the other members of their council, and the judges in Coelesyria and Phoenicia: 17 Let it now be known to our lord the king that the Jews who came up from you to us have gone to Jerusalem and are building that rebellious and wicked city, repairing its marketplaces and walls and laying the foundations for a temple. 18 Now if this city is built and the walls finished, they will not only refuse to pay tribute but will even resist kings. Since the building of the temple is now going on, we think it best not to neglect such a matter but to speak to our lord the king in order that, if it seems good to you, search may be made in the records of your ancestors. 19 You will find in the annals what has been written about them and will learn that this city was rebellious, troubling both kings and other cities, and that the Jews were rebels and kept setting up blockades in it from of old. That is why this city was laid waste. 20 Therefore we now make known to you, O lord and king, that if this city is built and its walls finished, you will no longer have access to Coelesyria and Phoenicia."

21 Then the king, in reply to the recorder Rehum, Beltethmus, the scribe Shimshai, and the others associated with them and living in Samaria and Syria and Phoenicia, wrote as follows:

22 "I have read the letter that you sent me. So I ordered search to be made, and it has been found that this city from of old has fought against kings, 23 that the people in it were given to rebellion and war, and that mighty and cruel kings ruled in Jerusalem and exacted tribute from Coelesyria and Phoenicia. 24 Therefore I

---

h 1.53 Gk *he*
i 2.5 Gk *him*

have now issued orders to prevent these people from building the city and to take care that nothing more be done and that such wicked proceedings go no further to the annoyance of kings."

25 Then, when the letter from King Artaxerxes was read, Rehum and the scribe Shimshai and their associates went quickly to Jerusalem, with cavalry and a large number of armed troops, and began to hinder the builders. And the building of the temple in Jerusalem stopped until the second year of the reign of King Darius of the Persians.

The Debate of the Three Bodyguards

3 Now King Darius gave a great banquet for all who were under him, all who were born in his house, and all the nobles of Media and Persia, ²and all the satraps and generals and governors who were under him in the hundred twenty-seven satrapies from India to Ethiopia. ³They ate and drank, and when they were satisfied they went away, and King Darius went to his bedroom; he went to sleep but woke up again.

⁴Then the three young men of the bodyguard who kept guard over the person of the king said to one another, ⁵"Let each of us state what one word is strongest, and to the one whose statement seems wisest, King Darius will give rich gifts and great honors of victory. ⁶He shall be clothed in purple and drink from gold cups and sleep on a gold bed^j and have a chariot with gold bridles and a turban of fine linen and a necklace around his neck, ⁷and because of his wisdom he shall sit next to Darius and shall be called Kinsman of Darius."

⁸Then each bodyguard wrote his own statement, and they sealed them and put them under the pillow of King Darius and said, ⁹"When the king wakes, they will give him the writing, and to the one whose statement the king and the three nobles of Persia judge to be wisest the victory shall be given according to what is written." ¹⁰The first wrote, "Wine is strongest." ¹¹The second wrote, "The king is strongest." ¹²The third wrote, "Women are strongest, but above all things truth is victor."^{k}

13 When the king awoke, they took the writing and gave it to him, and he read it. ¹⁴Then he sent and summoned all the nobles of Persia and Media and the satraps and generals and governors and prefects, and he took his seat in the council chamber, and the writing was read in their presence. ¹⁵He said, "Call the young men, and they shall explain their statements." So they were summoned and came in. ¹⁶They said to them, "Explain to us what you have written."

The Speech about Wine

Then the first, who had spoken of the strength of wine, began and said: ¹⁷"Gentlemen, how is wine the strongest? It leads astray the minds of all who drink it. ¹⁸It makes equal the mind of the king and the orphan, of the slave and the free, of the poor and the rich. ¹⁹It turns every thought to feasting and gladness and forgets all sorrow and debt. ²⁰It makes all hearts feel rich, forgets kings and satraps, and makes everyone talk of extravagant sums.^{l} ²¹When people drink they forget to be friendly with friends and kindred, and before long they draw their swords. ²²And when they recover from the wine, they do not remember what they have done. ²³Gentlemen, is not wine the strongest, since it forces people to do these things?" When he had said this, he stopped speaking.

The Speech about the King

4 Then the second, who had spoken of the strength of the king, began to speak: ²"Gentlemen, are not men strongest, who rule over land and sea and all that is in them? ³But the king is stronger; he is their lord and master, and whatever he says to them they obey. ⁴If he tells them to make war on one another, they do it, and if he sends them out against the enemy, they go and conquer mountains, walls, and towers. ⁵They kill and are killed and do not disobey the king's command; if they win the victory, they bring everything to the king—whatever spoil they take and everything else. ⁶Likewise those who do not serve in the army or make war but till the soil; whenever they sow and reap, they bring some to the king, and they compel one another to pay taxes to the king. ⁷And yet he is only one man! If he tells them to kill, they kill; if he tells them to release, they release; ⁸if he tells them to attack, they attack; if he tells them to lay waste, they lay waste; if he tells them to build, they build; ⁹if he tells them to cut down, they cut down; if he tells them to plant, they plant. ¹⁰All his people and his armies obey him.

---

j 3.6 Gk *on gold*
k 3.12 Or *but truth triumphs over all things*

l 3.20 Gk *talents*

Furthermore, he reclines, he eats and drinks and sleeps, [11] but they keep watch around him, and no one may go away to attend to his own affairs, nor do they disobey him. [12] Gentlemen, why is not the king the strongest, since he is to be obeyed in this fashion?" And he stopped speaking.

The Speech about Women

[13] Then the third, who had spoken of women and truth (and this was Zerubbabel), began to speak: [14] "Gentlemen, is not the king great, and are not men many, and is not wine strong? Who is it, then, who rules them or has the mastery over them? Is it not women? [15] Women gave birth to the king and to every people that rules over sea and land. [16] From women they came, and women brought up the very men who plant the vineyards from which comes wine. [17] Women make men's clothes; they bring men glory; men cannot exist without women. [18] If men gather gold and silver or any other beautiful thing and then see a woman lovely in appearance and beauty, [19] they let all those things go and gape at her and with open mouths stare at her, and all prefer her to gold or silver or any other beautiful thing. [20] A man leaves his own father, who brought him up, and his own region and clings to his wife. [21] With his wife he ends his days, with no thought of his father or his mother or his region. [22] Therefore you must realize that women rule over you!

"Do you not labor and toil and bring everything and give it to women? [23] A man takes his sword and goes out to travel and rob and steal and to sail the sea and rivers; [24] he faces lions, and he walks in darkness, and when he steals and robs and plunders, he brings it back to the woman he loves. [25] A man loves his wife more than his father or his mother. [26] Many men have lost their minds because of women and have become slaves because of them. [27] Many have perished or stumbled or sinned because of women. [28] And now do you not believe me?

"Is not the king great in his authority? Do not all lands fear to touch him? [29] Yet I have seen him with Apame, the king's concubine, the daughter of the illustrious Bartacus; she would sit at the king's right hand [30] and take the crown from the king's head and put it on her own and slap the king with her left hand. [31] At this the king would gaze at her with mouth agape. If she smiles at him, he laughs; if she loses her temper with him, he flatters her, so

that she may be reconciled to him. [32] Gentlemen, why are not women strong, since they do such things?"

The Speech about Truth

[33] Then the king and the nobles looked at one another, and he began to speak about truth: [34] "Gentlemen, are not women strong? The earth is vast, and heaven is high, and the sun is swift in its course, for it makes the circuit of the heavens and returns to its place in one day. [35] Is not the one who does these things great? But truth is great and stronger than all things. [36] The whole earth calls upon truth, and heaven blesses it. All the works quake and tremble, and with it[m] there is nothing unrighteous. [37] Wine is unrighteous; the king is unrighteous; women are unrighteous; all humans are unrighteous; all their works are unrighteous and all such things. There is no truth in them, and in their unrighteousness they will perish. [38] But truth endures and is strong forever and lives and prevails forever and ever. [39] With it there is no partiality or preference, but it does what is righteous instead of anything that is unrighteous or wicked. Everyone approves its deeds, [40] and there is nothing unrighteous in its judgment. To it belongs the strength and the kingship and the power and the majesty of all the ages. Blessed be the God of truth!" [41] When he stopped speaking, all the people shouted and said, "Great is truth and strongest of all!"

Zerubbabel's Reward

[42] Then the king said to Zerubbabel,[n] "Ask what you wish, even beyond what is written, and we will give it to you, for you have been found to be the wisest. You shall sit next to me and be called my Kinsman." [43] Then he said to the king, "Remember the vow that you made on the day when you became king, to build Jerusalem [44] and to send back all the vessels that were taken from Jerusalem, which Cyrus set apart when he began[o] to destroy Babylon and vowed to send them back there. [45] You also vowed to build the temple, which the Edomites burned when Judea was laid waste by the Chaldeans. [46] And now, O lord the king, this is what I ask and request of you, and this befits your greatness. I pray, therefore, that you fulfill the vow

---

m 4.36 That is, *heaven*
n 4.42 Gk *him*
o 4.44 Cn: Gk *vowed*

whose fulfillment you vowed to the King of heaven with your own lips."

47 Then King Darius got up and kissed him and wrote letters for him to all the treasurers and governors and generals and satraps, that they should give safe conduct to him and to all who were going up with him to build Jerusalem. 48 And he wrote letters to all the governors in Coelesyria and Phoenicia and to those in Lebanon, to bring cedar timber from Lebanon to Jerusalem and to help him build the city. 49 He wrote in behalf of all the Jews who were going up from his kingdom to Judea, in the interest of their freedom, that no officer or satrap or governor or treasurer should forcibly enter their doors; 50 that all the region that they would occupy should be theirs without tribute; that the Idumeans should give up the villages of the Jews that they held; 51 that twenty talents a year should be given for the building of the temple until it was completed 52 and an additional ten talents a year for burnt offerings to be offered on the altar every day, in accordance with the commandment to make seventeen offerings; 53 and that all who came from Babylonia to build the city should have their freedom, they and their children and all the priests who came. 54 He wrote also concerning their support and the priests' vestments in which they were to minister. 55 He wrote that the support for the Levites should be provided until the day when the temple would be finished and Jerusalem built. 56 He wrote that land and wages should be provided for all who guarded the city. 57 And he sent back from Babylon all the vessels that Cyrus had set apart; everything that Cyrus had ordered to be done, he also commanded to be done and to be sent to Jerusalem.

Zerubbabel's Prayer

58 When the young man went out, he lifted up his face to heaven toward Jerusalem and praised the King of heaven, saying, 59 "From you comes the victory; from you comes wisdom, and yours is the glory. I am your servant. 60 Blessed are you, who have given me wisdom; I give you thanks, O Lord of our ancestors."

61 So he took the letters and went to Babylon and told this to all his kindred. 62 And they praised the God of their ancestors because he had given them freedom and permission 63 to go up and build Jerusalem and the temple that is called by his name, and they feasted, with music and rejoicing, for seven days.

List of the Returning Exiles

5 After this the heads of ancestral houses were chosen to go up, according to their tribes, with their wives and sons and daughters and their male and female servants and their livestock. 2 And Darius sent with them a thousand cavalry to take them back to Jerusalem in safety, with the music of drums and flutes; 3 all their kindred were making merry. And he made them go up with them.

4 These are the names of the men who went up, according to their ancestral houses in the tribes, over their groups: 5 the priests, the descendants of Phinehas son of Aaron; Jeshua son of Jozadak son of Seraiah and Joakim son of Zerubbabel son of Shealtiel, of the house of David, of the lineage of Phares, of the tribe of Judah, 6 who spoke wise words before King Darius of the Persians, in the second year of his reign, in the month of Nisan, the first month.

7 These are the Judeans who came up out of their sojourn in exile, whom King Nebuchadnezzar of Babylon had carried away to Babylon 8 and who returned to Jerusalem and the rest of Judea, each to his own town. They came with Zerubbabel and Jeshua, Nehemiah, Seraiah, Resaiah, Eneneus, Mordecai, Beelsarus, Aspharasus, Borolias, Rehum, and Baanah, their leaders.

9 The number of those of the nation and their leaders: the descendants of Parosh, two thousand one hundred seventy-two. The descendants of Shephatiah, four hundred seventy-two. 10 The descendants of Arah, seven hundred fifty-six. 11 The descendants of Pahath-moab, of the descendants of Jeshua and Joab, two thousand eight hundred twelve. 12 The descendants of Elam, one thousand two hundred fifty-four. The descendants of Zattu, nine hundred forty-five. The descendants of Chorbe, seven hundred five. The descendants of Bani, six hundred forty-eight. 13 The descendants of Bebai, six hundred twenty-three. The descendants of Azgad, one thousand three hundred twenty-two. 14 The descendants of Adonikam, six hundred sixty-seven. The descendants of Bigvai, two thousand sixty-six. The descendants of Adin, four hundred fifty-four. 15 The descendants of Ater, namely, of Hezekiah, ninety-two. The descendants of Kilan and Azetas, sixty-seven. The descendants of Azaru, four hundred thirty-two. 16 The descendants of Annias, one hundred one. The descendants of Arom. The descendants of Bezai, three hundred twenty-three. The descendants of Arsiphurith, one hundred twelve.

¹⁷The descendants of Baiterus, three thousand five. The descendants of Bethlomon, one hundred twenty-three. ¹⁸Those from Netophah, fifty-five. Those from Anathoth, one hundred fifty-eight. Those from Bethasmoth, forty-two. ¹⁹Those from Kiriatharim, twenty-five. Those from Chephirah and Beeroth, seven hundred forty-three. ²⁰The Chadiasans and Ammidians, four hundred twenty-two. Those from Kirama and Geba, six hundred twenty-one. ²¹Those from Macalon, one hundred twenty-two. Those from Betolio, fifty-two. The descendants of Niphish, one hundred fifty-six. ²²The descendants of the other Calamolalus and Ono, seven hundred twenty-five. The descendants of Jerechus, three hundred forty-five. ²³The descendants of Senaah, three thousand three hundred thirty.

24 The priests: the descendants of Jedaiah son of Jeshua, of the descendants of Anasib, nine hundred seventy-two. The descendants of Immer, one thousand and fifty-two. ²⁵The descendants of Pashhur, one thousand two hundred forty-seven. The descendants of Charme, one thousand seventeen.

26 The Levites: the descendants of Jeshua and Kadmiel and Bannas and Sudias, seventy-four. ²⁷The temple singers: the descendants of Asaph, one hundred twenty-eight. ²⁸The gatekeepers: the descendants of Shallum, the descendants of Ater, the descendants of Talmon, the descendants of Akkub, the descendants of Hatita, the descendants of Shobai, in all one hundred thirty-nine.

29 The temple servants: the descendants of Esau, the descendants of Hasupha, the descendants of Tabbaoth, the descendants of Keros, the descendants of Sua, the descendants of Padon, the descendants of Lebanah, the descendants of Hagabah, ³⁰the descendants of Akkub, the descendants of Uthai, the descendants of Ketab, the descendants of Hagab, the descendants of Subai, the descendants of Hana, the descendants of Cathua, the descendants of Geddur, ³¹the descendants of Jairus, the descendants of Daisan, the descendants of Noeba, the descendants of Chezib, the descendants of Gazera, the descendants of Uzza, the descendants of Phinoe, the descendants of Hasrah, the descendants of Basthai, the descendants of Asnah, the descendants of Maani, the descendants of Nephisim, the descendants of Acuph, the descendants of Hakupha, the descendants of Asur, the descendants of Pharakim, the descendants of Bazluth, ³²the descendants of Mehida, the descendants

of Cutha, the descendants of Charea, the descendants of Barkos, the descendants of Serar, the descendants of Temah, the descendants of Neziah, the descendants of Hatipha.

33 The descendants of Solomon's servants: the descendants of Assaphioth, the descendants of Peruda, the descendants of Jaalah, the descendants of Lozon, the descendants of Isdael, the descendants of Shephatiah, ³⁴the descendants of Agia, the descendants of Pochereth-hazzebaim, the descendants of Sarothie, the descendants of Masiah, the descendants of Gas, the descendants of Addus, the descendants of Subas, the descendants of Apherra, the descendants of Barodis, the descendants of Shaphat, the descendants of Allon.

35 All the temple servants and the descendants of Solomon's servants were three hundred seventy-two.

36 The following are those who came up from Tel-melah and Tel-harsha, under the leadership of Cherub, Addan, and Immer, ³⁷though they could not prove by their ancestral houses or lineage that they belonged to Israel: the descendants of Delaiah son of Tobiah, and the descendants of Nekoda, six hundred fifty-two.

38 Of the priests the following had assumed the priesthood but were not found registered: the descendants of Habaiah, the descendants of Hakkoz, and the descendants of Jaddus who had married Agia, one of the daughters of Barzillai, and was called by his name. ³⁹When a search was made in the register and the genealogy of these men was not found, they were excluded from serving as priests. ⁴⁰And Nehemiah and Attharias[p] told them not to share in the holy things until a high priest[q] should appear wearing Urim and Thummim.[r]

41 All those of Israel, twelve or more years of age, besides male and female servants, were forty-two thousand three hundred sixty; their male and female servants were seven thousand three hundred thirty-seven; there were two hundred forty-five musicians and singers. ⁴²There were four hundred thirty-five camels, seven thousand thirty-six horses, two hundred forty-five mules, and five thousand five hundred twenty-five donkeys.

43 Some of the heads of families, when they came to the temple of God that is in Jerusalem,

---

p **5.40** Or *the governor*
q **5.40** Other ancient authorities read *priest*
r **5.40** Gk *Manifestation and Truth*

vowed that, to the best of their ability, they would erect the house on its site [44]and that they would give to the sacred treasury for the work a thousand minas of gold, five thousand minas of silver, and one hundred priests' vestments.

[45]The priests, the Levites, and some of the people[s] settled in Jerusalem and its region and the temple singers, the gatekeepers, and all Israel in their towns.

Worship Begins Again

[46]When the seventh month came and the Israelites were all in their own homes, they gathered with a single purpose in the square before the first gate toward the east. [47]Then Jeshua son of Jozadak, with his fellow priests, and Zerubbabel son of Shealtiel, with his kinsmen, took their places and prepared the altar of the God of Israel, [48]to offer burnt offerings upon it, in accordance with the directions in the book of Moses the man of God. [49]And some joined them from the other nations of the land. And they erected the altar in its place, for all the peoples of the land were hostile to them and were stronger than they, and they offered sacrifices at the proper times and burnt offerings to the Lord morning and evening. [50]They kept the Festival of Booths,[t] as it is commanded in the law, and offered the proper sacrifices every day [51]and thereafter the regular offerings and sacrifices on Sabbaths and at new moons and at all the consecrated feasts. [52]And all who had made any vow to God began to offer sacrifices to God, from the new moon of the seventh month, though the temple of God was not yet built. [53]They gave money to the masons and the carpenters and food and drink and carts[u] to the Sidonians and the Tyrians to bring cedar logs from Lebanon and convey them in rafts to the harbor of Joppa, according to the decree that they had in writing from King Cyrus of the Persians.

The Foundations of the Temple Laid

[54]In the second year after their coming to the temple of God in Jerusalem, in the second month, Zerubbabel son of Shealtiel and Jeshua son of Jozadak made a beginning, together with their kindred and the Levitical priests and all who had come back to Jerusalem from exile, [55]and they laid the foundation of the temple of

God on the new moon of the second month in the second year after they came to Judea and Jerusalem. [56]They appointed the Levites who were twenty or more years of age to have charge of the work of the Lord. And Jeshua arose and his sons and kindred and his brother Kadmiel and the sons of Jeshua Emadabun and the sons of Joda son of Iliadun, with their sons and kindred, all the Levites, pressing forward the work on the house of God with a single purpose.

So the builders built the temple of the Lord. [57]And the priests stood arrayed in their vestments, with musical instruments and trumpets, and the Levites, the sons of Asaph, with cymbals, praising the Lord and blessing him, according to the directions of King David of Israel; [58]they sang hymns, giving thanks to the Lord, "For his goodness and his glory are forever upon all Israel." [59]And all the people sounded trumpets and shouted with a great shout, praising the Lord for the erection of the house of the Lord. [60]Some of the Levitical priests and heads of ancestral houses, old men who had seen the former house, came to the building of this one with outcries and loud weeping, [61]while many came with trumpets and a joyful noise, [62]so that the people could not hear the trumpets because of the weeping of the people.

For the multitude sounded the trumpets loudly, so that the sound was heard far away, [63]and when the enemies of the tribe of Judah and Benjamin heard it, they came to find out what the sound of the trumpets meant. [64]They learned that those who had returned from exile were building the temple for the Lord God of Israel. [65]So they approached Zerubbabel and Jeshua and the heads of the ancestral houses and said to them, "We will build with you. [66]For we obey your Lord just as you do, and we have been sacrificing to him ever since the days of King Esar-haddon of the Assyrians, who brought us here." [67]But Zerubbabel and Jeshua and the heads of the ancestral houses in Israel said to them, "You have nothing to do with us in building the house for the Lord our God, [68]for we alone will build it for the Lord of Israel, as Cyrus, the king of the Persians, has commanded us." [69]But the nations of the land besieged[v] those in Judea, cut off their supplies, and hindered their building, [70]and by plots and demagoguery and uprisings they prevented the completion of the building as long as King Cyrus lived. They

---

s 5.45 Or *those who were of the people*
t 5.50 Or *Tabernacles*
u 5.53 Meaning of Gk uncertain

v 5.69 Meaning of Gk uncertain

were kept from building for two years, until the reign of Darius.

Work on the Temple Begins Again

6 Now in the second year of the reign of Darius, the prophets Haggai and Zechariah son of Iddo prophesied to the Jews who were in Judea and Jerusalem; they prophesied to them in the name of the Lord God of Israel. ²Then Zerubbabel son of Shealtiel and Jeshua son of Jozadak began to build the house of the Lord that is in Jerusalem, with the help of the prophets of the Lord who were with them.

3 At the same time Sisinnes the governor of Syria and Phoenicia and Sathrabuzanes and their associates came to them and said, ⁴"By whose order are you building this house and this roof and finishing all the other things? And who are the builders who are finishing these things?" ⁵Yet the elders of the Jews were dealt with kindly, for the providence of the Lord was over the captives; ⁶they were not prevented from building until word could be sent to Darius concerning them and a report made.

7 A copy of the letter that Sisinnes the governor of Syria and Phoenicia and Sathrabuzanes and their associates the local rulers in Syria and Phoenicia wrote and sent to Darius:

"To King Darius, greetings. ⁸Let it be fully known to our lord the king that, when we went to the region of Judea and entered the city of Jerusalem, we found the elders of the Jews, who had been in exile, building in the city of Jerusalem a great new house for the Lord, of hewn stone, with costly timber laid in the walls. ⁹These operations are going on rapidly, and the work is prospering in their hands and being completed with all splendor and care. ¹⁰Then we asked these elders, 'At whose command are you building this house and laying the foundations of this structure?' ¹¹In order that we might inform you in writing who the leaders are, we questioned them and asked them for a list of the names of those who are instigating the disturbance. ¹²They answered us, 'We are the servants of the Lord who created the heaven and the earth. ¹³The house was built many years ago by a king of Israel who was great and strong, and it was finished. ¹⁴But when our ancestors sinned against the Lord of Israel who is in heaven and provoked him, he gave them over into the hands of King Nebuchadnezzar of Babylon, king of the Chaldeans, ¹⁵and they pulled down the house and burned it and carried the people

away captive to Babylon. ¹⁶But in the first year that Cyrus reigned over the region of Babylonia, King Cyrus wrote that this house should be rebuilt. ¹⁷And the holy vessels of gold and of silver that Nebuchadnezzar had taken out of the house in Jerusalem and stored in his own temple, these King Cyrus took out again from the temple in Babylon, and they were delivered to Zerubbabel and Sheshbazzar the governor ¹⁸with the command that he should take all these vessels back and put them in the temple at Jerusalem and that this temple of the Lord should be rebuilt on its site. ¹⁹Then this Sheshbazzar, after coming here, laid the foundations of the house of the Lord that is in Jerusalem. Although it has been in process of construction from that time until now, it has not yet reached completion.' ²⁰Now therefore, O king, if it seems wise to do so, let search be made in the royal archives of our lordʷ the king that are in Babylon; ²¹if it is found that the building of the house of the Lord in Jerusalem was done with the consent of King Cyrus, and if it is approved by our lord the king, let him send us directions concerning these things."

Official Permission Granted

22 Then Darius commanded that search be made in the royal archives that were deposited in Babylon. And in Ecbatana, the fortress that is in the region of Media, a scrollˣ was found in which this was recorded: ²³"In the first year of the reign of King Cyrus, he ordered the building of the house of the Lord in Jerusalem, where they sacrifice with fire continuously: ²⁴its height sixty cubits and its width sixty cubits, with three courses of hewn stone and one course of new native timber; the cost to be paid from the treasury of King Cyrus; ²⁵and the holy vessels of the house of the Lord, both of gold and of silver, that Nebuchadnezzar took out of the house in Jerusalem and carried away to Babylon to be restored to the house in Jerusalem, to be placed where they had been."

26 So Dariusʸ commanded Sisinnes the governor of Syria and Phoenicia and Sathrabuzanes and their associates and those who were appointed as local rulers in Syria and Phoenicia to keep away from the place and to permit Zerubbabel, the servant of the Lord and governor of

---

w **6.20** Other ancient authorities read *of Cyrus*
x **6.22** Other authorities read *passage*
y **6.26** Gk *he*

Judea, and the elders of the Jews to build this house of the Lord on its site. 27 "And I command that it be built completely and that full effort be made to help those who have returned from the exile of Judea until the house of the Lord is finished 28 and that out of the tribute of Coelesyria and Phoenicia a portion be scrupulously given to these men, that is, to Zerubbabel the governor, for sacrifices to the Lord, for bulls and rams and lambs, 29 and likewise wheat and salt and wine and oil, regularly every year, without quibbling, for daily use as the priests in Jerusalem may indicate, 30 in order that libations may be made to the Most High God for the king and his children and prayers be offered for their lives."

31 He commanded that if anyone should transgress or nullify any of the things herein written,[z] a beam should be taken out of the house of the perpetrator, who then should be impaled upon it and all property forfeited to the king.

32 "Therefore may the Lord, whose name is there called upon, destroy every king and nation that shall stretch out their hands to hinder or damage that house of the Lord in Jerusalem.

33 "I, King Darius, have decreed that it be done with all diligence as here prescribed."

The Temple Is Dedicated

7 Then Sisinnes the governor of Coelesyria and Phoenicia and Sathrabuzanes and their associates, following the orders of King Darius, 2 supervised the holy work with very great care, assisting the elders of the Jews and the chief officers of the temple. 3 The holy work prospered, while the prophets Haggai and Zechariah prophesied, 4 and they completed it by the command of the Lord God of Israel. So with the consent of Cyrus and Darius and Artaxerxes, kings of the Persians, 5 the holy house was finished by the twenty-third day of the month of Adar, in the sixth year of King Darius. 6 And the people of Israel, the priests, the Levites, and the rest of those who returned from exile who joined them did according to what was written in the book of Moses. 7 They offered at the dedication of the temple of the Lord one hundred bulls, two hundred rams, four hundred lambs, 8 and twelve male goats for the sin of all Israel, according to the number of the twelve leaders of the tribes of Israel,

9 and the priests and the Levites stood arrayed in their vestments, according to divisions, for the services of the Lord God of Israel in accordance with the book of Moses, and the gatekeepers were at each gate.

The Passover

10 The people of Israel who came from exile kept the Passover on the fourteenth day of the first month, after the priests and the Levites were purified together. 11 Not all of the returned captives were purified, but the Levites were all purified together,[a] 12 and they sacrificed the Passover lamb for all the returned captives and for their kindred the priests and for themselves. 13 The people of Israel who had returned from exile ate it, all those who had separated themselves from the abominations of the nations of the land and sought the Lord. 14 They also kept the Festival of Unleavened Bread seven days, rejoicing before the Lord, 15 because he had changed the will of the king of the Assyrians concerning them, to strengthen their hands for the service of the Lord God of Israel.

Ezra Arrives in Jerusalem

8 After these things, when Artaxerxes, the king of the Persians, was reigning, Ezra came, the son of Seraiah, son of Azariah, son of Hilkiah, son of Shallum, 2 son of Zadok, son of Ahitub, son of Amariah, son of Uzzi, son of Bukki, son of Abishua, son of Phineas, son of Eleazar, son of Aaron the high[b] priest. 3 This Ezra came up from Babylon as a scribe skilled in the law of Moses, which was given by the God of Israel, 4 and the king showed him honor, for he found favor before the king[c] in all his requests. 5 There came up with him to Jerusalem some of the people of Israel and some of the priests and Levites and temple singers and gatekeepers and temple servants, 6 in the seventh year of the reign of Artaxerxes, in the fifth month (this was the king's seventh year), for they left Babylon on the new moon of the first month and arrived in Jerusalem on the new moon of the fifth month, by the successful journey that the Lord gave them. 7 For Ezra possessed great knowledge, so that he omitted nothing from the law of the Lord or the commandments but taught all Israel all the ordinances and judgments.

---

z 6.31 Other authorities read *stated above* or *added in writing*

a 7.11 Meaning of Gk uncertain
b 8.2 Gk *the first*
c 8.4 Gk *him*

The King's Mandate

8 The following is a copy of the written decree from King Artaxerxes that was delivered to Ezra the priest and reader of the law of the Lord: 9 "King Artaxerxes to Ezra the priest and reader of the law of the Lord, greeting. 10 In accordance with my gracious decision, I have given orders that those of the Jewish nation and of the priests and Levites and others in our realm, those who freely choose to do so, may go with you to Jerusalem. 11 Let as many as are so disposed, therefore, leave with you, just as I and the seven Friends who are my counselors have decided, 12 in order to look into matters in Judea and Jerusalem, in accordance with what is in the law of the Lord, 13 and to carry to Jerusalem the gifts for the Lord of Israel that I and my Friends have vowed, and to collect for the Lord in Jerusalem all the gold and silver that may be found in the region of Babylonia, together with what is given by the nation for the temple of their Lord that is in Jerusalem, 14 both gold and silver for bulls and rams and lambs and what goes with them, 15 so as to offer sacrifices on the altar of their Lord that is in Jerusalem. 16 Whatever you and your kindred wish to do with the gold and silver, perform it in accordance with the will of your God; 17 deliver the holy vessels of the Lord that are given you for the use of the temple of your God that is in Jerusalem. And whatever else occurs to you as necessary for the temple of your God, 18 you may provide out of the royal treasury.

19 "I, King Artaxerxes, have commanded the treasurers of Syria and Phoenicia that whatever Ezra the priest and reader of the law of the Most High God sends for, they shall take care to give him, up to a hundred talents of silver, 20 and likewise up to a hundred cors of wheat, a hundred baths of wine, and salt in abundance. 21 Let all things prescribed in the law of God be scrupulously fulfilled for the Most High God, so that wrath may not come upon the kingdom of the king and his sons. 22 You are also informed that no tribute or any other tax is to be laid on any of the priests or Levites or temple singers or gatekeepers or temple servants or persons employed in this temple and that no one has authority to impose any tax on them. 23 "And you, Ezra, according to the wisdom of God, appoint judges and justices to judge all those who know the law of your God throughout all Syria and Phoenicia, and you shall teach it to those who do not know it. 24 All who

transgress the law of your God or the law of the kingdom shall be strictly punished, whether by death or some other punishment, either fine or imprisonment."

Ezra Praises God

25 Then Ezra the scribe said,[d] "Blessed be the Lord alone, who put this into the heart of the king, to glorify his house that is in Jerusalem, 26 and who honored me in the sight of the king and his counselors and all his Friends and nobles. 27 I was encouraged by the help of the Lord my God, and I gathered men from Israel to go up with me."

The Leaders Who Returned

28 These are the leaders, according to their ancestral houses and their groups, who went up with me from Babylon, in the reign of King Artaxerxes: 29 Of the descendants of Phineas, Gershom. Of the descendants of Ithamar, Gamael. Of the descendants of David, Hattush son of Shecaniah. 30 Of the descendants of Parosh, Zechariah and with him a hundred fifty men enrolled. 31 Of the descendants of Pahath-moab, Eliehoenai son of Zerahiah and with him two hundred men. 32 Of the descendants of Zattu, Shecaniah son of Jahaziel and with him three hundred men. Of the descendants of Adin, Obed son of Jonathan and with him two hundred fifty men. 33 Of the descendants of Elam, Jeshaiah son of Gotholiah and with him seventy men. 34 Of the descendants of Shephatiah, Zeraiah son of Michael and with him seventy men. 35 Of the descendants of Joab, Obadiah son of Jehiel and with him two hundred twelve men. 36 Of the descendants of Bani, Shelomith son of Josiphiah and with him a hundred sixty men. 37 Of the descendants of Bebai, Zechariah son of Bebai and with him twenty-eight men. 38 Of the descendants of Azgad, Johanan son of Hakkatan and with him a hundred ten men. 39 Of the descendants of Adonikam, the last ones, their names being Eliphelet, Jeuel, and Shemaiah, and with them seventy men. 40 Of the descendants of Bigvai, Uthai son of Istalcurus and with him seventy men.

41 I assembled them at the river called Theras, and we encamped there three days, and I inspected them. 42 When I found there none of the descendants of the priests or of the Levites, 43 I

---

d 8.25 Other ancient authorities lack *Then Ezra the scribe said* sent word to Eleazar, Iduel, Maasmas, Elnathan, Shemaiah, Jarib, Nathan, Elnathan, Zechariah, and Meshullam, who were leaders and men of understanding; 44 I told them to go to Iddo, who was the leading man at the place of the treasury, 45 and ordered them to tell Iddo and his kindred and the treasurers at that place to send us men to serve as priests in the house of our Lord. 46 And by the mighty hand of our Lord they brought us competent men of the descendants of Mahli son of Levi, son of Israel, namely, Sherebiah with his descendants and kinsmen, eighteen; 47 also Hashabiah and Annunus and his brother Jeshaiah, of the descendants of Hananiah, and their descendants, twenty men; 48 and of the temple servants whom David and the leaders had given for the service of the Levites, two hundred twenty temple servants; the list of all their names was reported.

Ezra Proclaims a Fast

49 There I proclaimed a fast for the young men before our Lord, 50 to seek from him a successful journey for ourselves and for our children and the livestock with us. 51 For I was ashamed to ask the king for infantry and cavalry and an escort to keep us safe from our adversaries, 52 for we had said to the king, "The power of our Lord will be with those who seek him and will support them in every way." 53 And again we prayed to our Lord about these things, and we found him very merciful.

The Gifts for the Temple

54 Then I set apart twelve of the leaders of the priests, Sherebiah and Hashabiah and ten of their kinsmen with them, 55 and I weighed out to them the silver and the gold and the holy vessels of the house of our Lord that the king himself and his counselors and the nobles and all Israel had given. 56 I weighed and gave to them six hundred fifty talents of silver, and silver vessels worth a hundred talents, and a hundred talents of gold, and twenty golden bowls, and twelve bronze vessels of fine bronze that glittered like gold. 57 And I said to them, "You are holy to the Lord, and the vessels are holy, and the silver and the gold are vowed to the Lord, the Lord of our ancestors. 58 Be watchful and on guard until you deliver them to the leaders of the priests and the Levites and to the heads of the ancestral houses of Israel, in Jerusalem, in the chambers of the house of our Lord." 59 So the priests and the Levites who took the silver and the gold and the

vessels that had been in Jerusalem carried them to the temple of the Lord.

The Return to Jerusalem

60 We left the River Theras on the twelfth day of the first month, and we arrived in Jerusalem by the mighty hand of our Lord, which was upon us; he delivered us from every enemy on the way, and so we came to Jerusalem. 61 When we had been there three days, the silver and the gold were weighed and delivered in the house of our Lord to the priest Meremoth son of Uriah; 62 with him was Eleazar son of Phinehas, and with them were Jozabad son of Jeshua and Moeth son of Binnui, the Levites. The whole was counted and weighed, and the weight of everything was recorded at that very time. 63 And those who had returned from exile offered sacrifices to the Lord, the God of Israel, twelve bulls for all Israel, ninety-six rams, seventy-two lambs, and as a thank offering twelve male goats—all as a sacrifice to the Lord. 64 They delivered the king's orders to the royal stewards and to the governors of Coelesyria and Phoenicia, and these officials* honored the nation and the temple of the Lord.

Ezra's Prayer

65 After these things had been done, the leaders came to me and said, 66 "The nation of Israel and the rulers and the priests and the Levites have not separated themselves from the foreign nations of the land and their pollutions, the Canaanites, the Hittites, the Perizzites, the Jebusites, the Moabites, the Egyptians, and the Edomites. 67 For they and their sons have married the daughters of these people,f and the holy seed has been mixed with the foreign nations of the land, and from the beginning of this matter the leaders and the nobles have been sharing in this iniquity."

68 As soon as I heard these things, I tore my garments and my holy vestments and pulled out hair from my head and beard and sat down in anxiety and grief. 69 And all who were ever moved atg the word of the Lord of Israel gathered around me, as I mourned over this iniquity, and I sat grief-stricken until the evening sacrifice. 70 Then I rose from my fast, with my garments and my holy vestments torn, and

---

e 8.64 Gk *they*
f 8.67 Gk *their daughters*
g 8.69 Or *zealous for*

kneeling down and stretching out my hands to the Lord I said,

71 "O Lord, I am ashamed and dishonored before your face. 72 For our sins have risen higher than our heads, and our mistakes have mounted up to heaven 73 from the times of our ancestors, and we are in great sin to this day. 74 Because of our sins and the sins of our ancestors, we with our kindred and our kings and our priests were given over to the kings of the earth, to the sword and exile and plundering, in shame until this day. 75 And now in some measure mercy has come to us from you, O Lord, to leave to us a root and a name in your holy place 76 and to uncover a light for us in the house of the Lord our God and to give us food in the time of our servitude. Even in our bondage we were not forsaken by our Lord, 77 but he brought us into favor with the kings of the Persians, so that they have given us food 78 and glorified the temple of our Lord and raised Zion from desolation, to give us a stronghold in Judea and Jerusalem.

79 "And now, O Lord, what shall we say when we have these things? For we have transgressed your commandments that you gave by your servants the prophets, saying, 80 'The land that you are entering to possess is a land polluted with the pollution of the foreigners of the land, and they have filled it with their uncleanness. 81 Therefore do not give your daughters in marriage to their sons, and do not take their daughters for your sons; 82 do not seek ever to have peace with them, so that you may be strong and eat the good things of the land and leave it for an inheritance to your children forever.' 83 And all that has happened to us has come about because of our evil deeds and our great sins. For you, O Lord, lifted the burden of our sins 84 and gave us such a root as this, but we turned back again to transgress your law by mixing with the uncleanness of the nations of the land. 85 Were you not angry enough with us to destroy us without leaving a root or seed or name? 86 O Lord of Israel, you are faithful, for we are left as a root to this day. 87 See, we are now before you in our iniquities, for we can no longer stand in your presence because of these things."

The Plan for Ending Mixed Marriages

88 While Ezra was praying and making his confession, weeping and lying on the ground before the temple, there gathered around him a very great crowd of men and women and youths

from Jerusalem, for there was great weeping among the multitude. 89 Then Shecaniah son of Jehiel, one of the men of Israel, called out and said to Ezra, "We have sinned against the Lord and have married foreign women from the nations of the land, but even now there is hope for Israel. 90 Let us take an oath to the Lord about this, that we will put away all our foreign wives with their children, as seems good to you and to all who obey the law of the Lord. 91 Rise up[h] and take action, for it is your task, and we are with you to take strong measures." 92 Then Ezra rose up and made the leaders of the priests and Levites of all Israel swear that they would do this. And they swore to it.

The Expulsion of Foreign Wives

9 Then Ezra set out and went from the court of the temple to the chamber of Jehohanan son of Eliashib 2 and spent the night there, and he did not eat bread or drink water, for he was mourning over the great iniquities of the multitude. 3 And a proclamation was made throughout Judea and Jerusalem to all who had returned from exile that they should assemble at Jerusalem 4 and that if any did not meet there within two or three days, in accordance with the decision of the ruling elders, their livestock would be seized for sacrifice and the men themselves[i] expelled from the multitude of those who had returned from the captivity.

5 Then the men of the tribe of Judah and Benjamin assembled at Jerusalem within three days; this was the ninth month, on the twentieth day of the month. 6 All the multitude sat in the open square before the temple, shivering because of the bad weather that prevailed. 7 Then Ezra stood up and said to them, "You have broken the law and married foreign women and so have increased the sin of Israel. 8 Now, then, make confession and give glory to the Lord the God of our ancestors 9 and do his will; separate yourselves from the nations of the land and from your foreign wives."

10 Then all the multitude shouted and said with a loud voice, "We will do as you have said. 11 But the multitude is great, and it is winter, and we are not able to stand in the open air. This is not a work we can do in one day or two, for

---

h **8.91** Other ancient authorities read *as seems good to you." And all who obeyed the law of the Lord rose and said to Ezra,* 95 "Rise up
i **9.4** Gk *he himself*

we have sinned too much in these things. [12] So let the leaders of the multitude stay, and let all those in our settlements who have foreign wives come at the time appointed [13] with the elders and judges of each place, until we are freed from the wrath of the Lord over this matter."

[14] Jonathan son of Asahel and Jahzeiah son of Tikvah undertook the matter on these terms, and Meshullam and Levi and Shabbethai served with them as judges. [15] And those who had returned from exile acted in accordance with all this.

[16] Ezra the priest chose for himself the leading men of their ancestral houses, all of them by name, and on the new moon of the tenth month they began their sessions to investigate the matter. [17] And the cases of the men who had foreign wives were brought to an end by the new moon of the first month.

[18] Of the priests, those who were brought in and found to have foreign wives were: [19] of the descendants of Jeshua son of Jozadak and his kindred, Maaseiah, Eliezar, Jarib, and Jodan. [20] They pledged themselves to put away their wives and to offer rams in expiation of their error. [21] Of the descendants of Immer: Hanani and Zebadiah and Maaseiah and Shemaiah and Jehiel and Azariah. [22] Of the descendants of Pashhur: Elioenai, Maaseiah, Ishmael, and Nathanael, and Gedaliah, and Salthas.

[23] And of the Levites: Jozabad and Shimei and Kelaiah, who was Kelita, and Pethahiah and Judah and Jonah. [24] Of the temple singers: Eliashib and Zaccur. [25] Of the gatekeepers: Shallum and Telem.

[26] Of Israel: of the descendants of Parosh: Ramiah, Izziah, Malchijah, Mijamin, and Eleazar, and Asibias, and Benaiah. [27] Of the descendants of Elam: Mattaniah and Zechariah, Jezrielus and Abdi, and Jeremoth and Elijah. [28] Of the descendants of Zamoth: Eliadas, Eliashib, Othoniah, Jeremoth, and Zabad and Zerdaiah. [29] Of the descendants of Bebai: Jehohanan and Hananiah and Zabbai and Emathis. [30] Of the descendants of Mani: Olamus, Mamuchus, Adaiah, Jashub, and Sheal and Jeremoth. [31] Of the descendants of Addi: Naathus and Moossias, Laccunus and Naidus, and Bescaspasmys and Sesthel, and Belnuus and Manasseas. [32] Of the descendants of Annan, Elionas and Asaias and Melchias and Sabbaias and Simon Chosamaeus. [33] Of the descendants of Hashum: Mattenai and Mattattah and Zabad and Eliphelet and Manasseh and Shimei. [34] Of the descendants of Bani: Jeremai,

Momdius, Maerus, Joel, Mamdai and Bedeiah and Vaniah, Carabasion and Eliashib and Mamitanemus, Eliasis, Binnui, Elialis, Shimei, Shelemiah, Nethaniah. Of the descendants of Ezora: Shashai, Azarel, Azael, Samatus, Zambris, Joseph. [35] Of the descendants of Nooma: Mazitias, Zabad, Iddo, Joel, Benaiah. [36] All these had married foreign women, and they put them away together with their children.

Ezra Reads the Law to the People

[37] The priests and the Levites and the Israelites settled in Jerusalem and in the region. On the new moon of the seventh month, when the people of Israel were in their settlements, [38] the whole multitude gathered with one accord in the open square before the east gate of the temple; [39] they told Ezra the chief priest and reader to bring the law of Moses that had been given by the Lord God of Israel. [40] So Ezra the chief priest brought the law, for all the multitude, men and women, and all the priests to hear the law, on the new moon of the seventh month. [41] He read aloud in the open square before the gate of the temple from early morning until midday, in the presence of both men and women, and all the multitude gave attention to the law. [42] Ezra the priest and reader of the law stood on the wooden platform that had been prepared, [43] and beside him stood Mattathiah, Shema, Ananias, Azariah, Uriah, Hezekiah, and Baalsamus on his right, [44] and on his left Pedaiah, Mishael, Malchijah, Lothasubus, Nabariah, and Zechariah. [45] Then Ezra took up the book of the law in the sight of the multitude, for he had the place of honor in the presence of all. [46] When he opened the law, they all stood erect. And Ezra blessed the Lord God Most High, the God of hosts, the Almighty, [47] and the multitude answered, "Amen." They lifted up their hands and fell to the ground and worshiped God.[j] [48] Jeshua and Anniuth and Sherebiah, Jadinus, Akkub, Shabbethai, Hodiah, Maiannas and Kelita, Azariah and Jozabad, Hanan, Pelaiah, the Levites, taught the law of the Lord,[k] at the same time explaining what was read.

[49] Then Attharates[l] said to Ezra the chief priest[m] and reader and to the Levites who were

j **9.47** Other ancient authorities read *the Lord*
k **9.48** Other ancient authorities add *and read the law of the Lord to the multitude*
l **9.49** Or *the governor*
m **9.49** Other ancient authorities read *priest*

teaching the multitude and to all, [50] "This day is holy to the Lord"—now they were all weeping as they heard the law—[51] "so go your way, eat the fat and drink the sweet, and send portions to those who have none, [52] for the day is holy to the Lord, and do not be sorrowful, for the Lord will exalt you." [53] The Levites commanded all the people, saying, "This day is holy; do not be sorrowful." [54] Then they all went their way, to eat and drink and enjoy themselves and to give portions to those who had none and to make great rejoicing, [55] because they were inspired by the words which they had been taught. And they came together."

---

n **9.55** The Greek text ends abruptly

THE PRAYER OF MANASSEH

Ascription of Praise

1 O Lord Almighty,
   God of our ancestors,
   of Abraham and Isaac and Jacob
   and of their righteous offspring,
2 you who made heaven and earth
   with all their order,
3 who shackled the sea by your word of
      command,
   who confined the deep
   and sealed it with your terrible and glorious
      name,
4 at whom all things shudder
   and tremble before your power,
5 for your glorious splendor cannot be borne,
   and the wrath of your threat to sinners is
      unendurable;
6 yet immeasurable and unsearchable
   is your promised mercy,
7 for you are the Lord Most High,
   of great compassion, long-suffering, and
      very merciful,
   and you relent at human suffering.
   O Lord, according to your great goodness
   you have promised repentance and
      forgiveness
   to those who have sinned against you,
   and in the multitude of your mercies
   you have appointed repentance for sinners,
   so that they may be saved.*a*
8 Therefore you, O Lord, God of the
      righteous,
   have not appointed repentance for the
      righteous,
   for Abraham and Isaac and Jacob, who did
      not sin against you,
   but you have appointed repentance for me,
      who am a sinner.

Confession of Sins

9 For the sins I have committed are more in
      number than the sand of the sea;
   my transgressions are multiplied, O Lord,
      they are multiplied!
   I am not worthy to look up and see the
      height of heaven
   because of the multitude of my iniquities.
10 I am weighted down with many an iron
      fetter,
   so that I am rejected*b* because of my sins,
   and I have no relief,
   for I have provoked your wrath
   and have done what is evil in your sight,
   setting up abominations and multiplying
      offenses.

Supplication for Pardon

11 And now I bend the knee of my heart,
   imploring you for your kindness.
12 I have sinned, O Lord, I have sinned,
   and I acknowledge my transgressions.
13 I earnestly implore you,
   forgive me, O Lord, forgive me!
   Do not destroy me with my transgressions!
   Do not be angry with me forever or store
      up evil for me;
   do not condemn me to the depths of the
      earth.
   For you, O Lord, are the God of those who
      repent,
14 and in me you will manifest your goodness,
   for, unworthy as I am, you will save me
      according to your great mercy,
15 and I will praise you continually all the
      days of my life.
   For all the host of heaven sings your praise,
   and yours is the glory forever. Amen.

---

a 7 Other ancient authorities lack *O Lord, according . . .*
   be saved

b 10 Other ancient authorities read *so that I cannot lift*
   up my head

PSALM 151

This psalm is ascribed to David as his own composition (though it is outside the number*a*), after he had fought in single combat with Goliath.

1 I was small among my brothers
and the youngest in my father's house;
I tended my father's sheep.

2 My hands made a harp;
my fingers fashioned a lyre.

3 And who will tell my Lord?
The Lord himself; it is he who hears.*b*

4 It was he who sent his messenger*c*
and took me from my father's sheep
and anointed me with his anointing oil.

5 My brothers were handsome and tall,
but the Lord was not pleased with
them.

6 I went out to meet the foreigner,*d*
and he cursed me by his idols.

7 But I drew his own sword;
I beheaded him and removed disgrace
from the people of Israel.

---

a **151.1** Other ancient authorities add *of the one hundred fifty* (psalms)
b **151.3** Other ancient authorities add *everything*; others add *me*; others read *who will hear me*

c **151.4** Gk: Q ms *prophet*
d **151.6** Gk: Q ms *Philistine*

3 MACCABEES

The Battle of Raphia

1 When Philopator learned from those who returned that the regions that he had controlled had been seized by Antiochus, he gave orders to all his forces, both infantry and cavalry, took with him his sister Arsinoë, and marched out to the region near Raphia, where the army of Antiochus was encamped. ² But a certain Theodotus, determined to carry out the plot he had devised, took with him the best of the Ptolemaic arms that had been previously issued to him*ᵃ* and crossed over by night to the tent of Ptolemy, intending single-handedly to kill him and thereby end the war. ³ But Dositheus, known as the son of Drimylus, a Jew by birth who later changed his customs and abandoned the ancestral traditions, had led the king away and arranged that a certain insignificant man should sleep in the tent, and so it turned out that this man incurred the punishment meant for the king.*ᵇ* ⁴ A fierce battle ensued, and when matters were turning out rather in favor of Antiochus, Arsinoë went to the troops with wailing and tears, her locks all disheveled, and exhorted them to defend themselves and their children and wives bravely, promising to give them each two minas of gold if they won the battle. ⁵ And so it came about that the enemy was routed in the action, and many captives also were taken. ⁶ Now that he had foiled the plot, Ptolemy*ᶜ* decided to visit the neighboring cities and encourage them. ⁷ By doing this and by endowing their sacred enclosures with gifts, he strengthened the morale of his subjects.

Philopator Attempts to Enter the Temple

₈ Since the Jews had sent some of their council and elders to greet him, to bring him gifts of welcome, and to congratulate him on what had happened, he was all the more eager to visit them as soon as possible. ⁹ After he had arrived in Jerusalem, he offered sacrifice to the supreme God and made thank offerings and did what was fitting for the place. Then, upon entering the place and being impressed by its excellence and its beauty, ¹⁰ he marveled at the good order of the temple and conceived a desire to enter the sanctuary. ¹¹ When they said that this was not permitted because not even members of their own nation were allowed to enter, not even all of the priests, but only the high priest who was preeminent over all—and he only once a year—the king was by no means persuaded. ¹² Even after the law had been read to him, he did not cease to maintain that he ought to enter, saying, "Even if those men are deprived of this honor, I ought not to be." ¹³ And he inquired why, when he entered every other temple,*ᵈ* no one there had stopped him. ¹⁴ And someone answered thoughtlessly that it was wrong to place any significance in that.*ᵉ* ¹⁵ "But since this has happened," the king*ᶠ* said, "why should not I at least enter, whether they wish it or not?"

Jewish Resistance to Ptolemy

₁₆ Then the priests in all their vestments prostrated themselves and entreated the supreme God to aid in the present situation and to avert the violence of this evil design, and they filled the temple with cries and tears; ¹⁷ those who remained behind in the city were agitated and hurried out, supposing that something mysterious was occurring. ¹⁸ Young women who had been secluded in their chambers rushed out with their mothers, sprinkled their hair with dust,*ᵍ* and filled the streets with groans and lamentations. ¹⁹ Those women who had recently been arrayed for marriage abandoned the

---

a 1.2 Or *the best of the Ptolemaic soldiers previously put under his command*
b 1.3 Gk *that one*
c 1.6 Gk *he*

d 1.13 Or *entered the temple precincts*
e 1.14 Gk *take that as a portent*
f 1.15 Gk *he*
g 1.18 Other ancient authorities add *and ashes*

bridal chambers[h] prepared for wedded union and, neglecting proper modesty, in a disorderly rush flocked together in the city. [20]Mothers and nurses abandoned even newborn children here and there, some in houses and some in the streets, and without a backward look they crowded together at the most high temple. [21]Various were the supplications of those gathered there because of what the king was profanely plotting. [22]In addition, the bolder of the citizens would not tolerate the completion of his plans or the fulfillment of his intended purpose. [23]They shouted to their compatriots to take arms and die courageously for the ancestral law and created a considerable disturbance in the place, and, being barely restrained by the old men and the elders,[i] they resorted to the same posture of supplication as the others. [24]Meanwhile, the crowd, as before, was engaged in prayer, [25]while the elders near the king tried in various ways to change his arrogant mind from the plan that he had conceived. [26]But he, in his arrogance, took heed of nothing and began now to approach, determined to bring the aforesaid plan to a conclusion. [27]When those who were around him observed this, they turned, together with our people, to call upon him who has all power to defend them in the present trouble and not to overlook this unlawful and haughty deed. [28]The continuous, vehement, and concerted cry of the crowds[j] resulted in an immense uproar, [29]for it seemed that not only the people but also the walls and the whole earth around echoed, because indeed all at that time[k] preferred death to the profanation of the place.

The Prayer of the High Priest Simon

2 [[Then the high priest Simon, facing the sanctuary, bending his knees, and extending his hands with calm dignity, prayed as follows:]][l] [2]"Lord, Lord, king of the heavens and sovereign of all creation, holy among the holy ones, the only ruler, almighty, give attention to us who are suffering grievously from an impious and profane man, puffed up in his audacity and power. [3]For you, the creator of all things and the governor of all, are a just ruler, and you judge those who have done anything in insolence and arrogance. [4]You destroyed those who in the past committed injustice, among whom were even giants who trusted in their strength and boldness, whom you destroyed by bringing on them a boundless flood. [5]You consumed with fire and sulfur the people of Sodom who acted arrogantly, who were notorious for their vices,[m] and you made them an example to those who should come afterward. [6]By inflicting many and varied punishments on the audacious pharaoh who had enslaved your holy people Israel, you made known your sovereignty; thus you made known your great strength. [7]And when he pursued them with chariots and a mass of troops, you overwhelmed him in the depths of the sea but carried through safely those who had put their confidence in you, the Ruler over the whole creation. [8]And when they had seen the works of your hand, they praised you, the Almighty. [9]You, O King, when you had created the boundless and immeasurable earth, chose this city and sanctified this place for your name, though you have no need of anything, and when you had glorified it by your magnificent manifestation, you made it a firm foundation for the glory of your great and honored name. [10]And because you love the house of Israel, you promised that, if we should have reverses and tribulation should overtake us, you would listen to our petition when we come to this place and pray. [11]And indeed you are faithful and true. [12]And because oftentimes when our fathers were oppressed you helped them in their humiliation and rescued them from great evils, [13]see now, O holy King, that because of our many and great sins we are crushed with suffering, subjected to our enemies, and overtaken by helplessness. [14]In our downfall this audacious and profane man undertakes to violate the holy place on earth dedicated to your glorious name. [15]For your dwelling is the heaven of heavens, unapproachable by human beings. [16]But because you were pleased that your glory should dwell among your people Israel, you sanctified this place. [17]Do not punish us for the defilement committed by these men or call us to account for this profanation; otherwise the transgressors will boast in their wrath and exult in the arrogance of their tongue, saying, [18]'We have trampled down the house of holiness as the houses of the abominations are trampled down.' [19]Wipe

---

h 1.19 Or *the canopies*
i 1.23 Other ancient authorities read *priests*
j 1.28 Other ancient authorities read *vehement cry of the assembled crowds*
k 1.29 Other ancient authorities lack *at that time*
l 2.1 Many ancient authorities lack 2.1

---

m 2.5 Other ancient authorities read *secret in their vices* away our sins and disperse our errors and reveal your mercy at this hour. [20] Speedily let your mercies overtake us, put praises in the mouths of those who are downcast and broken in spirit, and give us peace."

God's Punishment of Ptolemy

[21] Thereupon God, who oversees all things, the first Father of all, holy among the holy ones, having heard the lawful supplication, scourged him who had exalted himself in insolence and audacity. [22] He shook him on this side and that as a reed is shaken by the wind, so that he lay helpless on the ground and, besides being paralyzed in his limbs, was unable even to speak, since he was ensnared by a righteous judgment. [23] Then both Friends and bodyguards, seeing the severe punishment that had overtaken him and fearing that he would lose his life, quickly dragged him out, panic-stricken in their exceedingly great fear. [24] After a while he recovered, and though he had been punished, he by no means repented but went away uttering bitter threats.

Hostile Measures against the Jews

[25] When he arrived in Egypt, he increased in his deeds of malice, abetted by the previously mentioned drinking companions and comrades who were strangers to everything just. [26] He was not content with his uncounted licentious deeds but even continued with such audacity that he established an evil reputation in the various localities, and many of his Friends, intently observing the king's purpose, themselves also followed his will. [27] He proposed to inflict public disgrace on the nation, and he set up a stone on the tower in the courtyard with this inscription: [28] "None of those who do not sacrifice shall enter their sanctuaries, and all Jews shall be subjected to a registration involving poll tax and to the status of slaves. Those who object to this are to be taken by force and put to death; [29] those who are registered are also to be branded on their bodies by fire with the ivy-leaf symbol of Dionysus, and they shall also be reduced to their former limited status." [30] In order that he might not appear to be an enemy of all, he inscribed below: "But if any of them prefer to join those who have been initiated into the mysteries, they shall have equal citizenship with the Alexandrians."

[31] Now some, with an obvious abhorrence of the price to be exacted for maintaining the piety of their city,[n] readily gave themselves up, since they expected to enhance their reputation by their future association with the king. [32] But the majority acted firmly with a courageous spirit and did not abandon their piety, and by paying money in exchange for life they boldly attempted to save themselves from the registration. [33] They remained resolutely hopeful of obtaining help, and they abhorred those who separated themselves from them, considering them to be enemies of the nation and depriving them of common fellowship and mutual help.

The Jews and Their Neighbors

3 When the impious king comprehended this situation, he became so infuriated that not only was he enraged against those Jews who lived in Alexandria but was still more bitterly hostile toward those in the countryside, and he ordered that all should promptly be gathered into one place and put to death by the most cruel means. [2] While these matters were being arranged, a hostile rumor was circulated against the people by some who conspired to do them ill, a pretext being given by a report that they hindered others[o] from the observance of their customs. [3] The Jews, however, continued to maintain goodwill and unswerving loyalty toward the dynasty, [4] but because they worshiped God and conducted themselves by his law, they kept their separateness with respect to foods. For this reason they appeared hateful to some, [5] but since they adorned their style of life with the good deeds of upright people, they were established in good repute with everyone. [6] Nevertheless, foreigners paid no heed to the good conduct of the people, which was common talk among all; [7] instead, they gossiped about the differences in worship and foods, alleging that these people were loyal neither to the king nor to his authorities but were hostile and greatly opposed to his government. So it was no ordinary reproach that they attached to them.

[8] The Greeks in the city, though wronged in no way, when they saw an unexpected tumult around these people and the crowds that suddenly were forming, were not strong enough to help them, for they lived under tyranny. They did try to console them, being grieved at the situation, and expected that matters would

---

n 2.31 Meaning of Gk uncertain
o 3.2 Gk *them*

change, ⁹for such a great community ought not be left to its fate when it had committed no offense. ¹⁰And already some of their neighbors and friends and business associates had taken some of them aside privately and were pledging to protect them and to do everything in their power to help.

Ptolemy's Decree That All Jews Be Arrested

¹¹Then the king, boastful of his present good fortune and not considering the might of the supreme God, but assuming that he would persevere constantly in his same purpose, wrote this letter against them:

¹²"King Ptolemy Philopator to his generals and soldiers in Egypt and all its districts, greetings and good health:

¹³"I myself and our government are faring well. ¹⁴When our expedition took place in Asia, as you yourselves know, it was brought to conclusion, according to plan, by the gods' deliberate alliance with us in battle, ¹⁵and we considered that we should not rule the nations inhabiting Coelesyria and Phoenicia by the power of the spear but should cherish them with clemency and great benevolence, gladly treating them well. ¹⁶And when we had granted very great revenues to the temples in the cities, we came on to Jerusalem also and went up to honor the temple of those wicked people, who never cease from their folly. ¹⁷They accepted our presence by word but insincerely by deed, because when we proposed to enter their inner temple and honor it with magnificent and most beautiful offerings, ¹⁸they were carried away by their traditional arrogance and excluded us from entering, but they were spared the exercise of our power because of the benevolence that we have toward all. ¹⁹By maintaining their manifest ill-will toward us, they become the only people among all nations who hold their heads high in defiance of kings and their own benefactors and are unwilling to regard any action as sincere.

²⁰"But we, when we arrived in Egypt victorious, accommodated ourselves to their folly and did as was proper, since we treat all nations with benevolence. ²¹Among other things, we made known to all our amnesty toward their compatriots here, both because of their alliance with us and the myriad affairs liberally entrusted to them from the beginning, and we ventured to make a change, by deciding both to deem them worthy of Alexandrian citizenship and to make them participants in our regular religious rites.^p ²²But in their innate malice they took this in a contrary spirit and disdained what is good. Since they incline constantly to evil, ²³they not only spurn the priceless citizenship, but also both by speech and by silence they abhor those few among them who are sincerely disposed toward us; in every situation, in accordance with their infamous way of life, they secretly suspect that we may soon alter our policy. ²⁴Therefore, fully convinced by these indications that they are ill-disposed toward us in every way, we have taken precautions so that, if a sudden disorder later arises against us, we shall not have these impious people behind our backs as traitors and barbarous enemies. ²⁵Therefore we have given orders that, as soon as this letter arrives, you are to send to us those who live among you, together with their wives and children, with insulting and harsh treatment and bound securely with iron fetters, to suffer the sure and shameful death that befits enemies. ²⁶For when all of these have been punished, we are sure that for the remaining time the government will be established for ourselves in good order and in the best state. ²⁷But those who shelter any of the Jews, whether old people or children or even infants, will be tortured to death with the most hateful torments, together with their families. ²⁸Any who are willing to give information will receive the property of those who incur the punishment, and also two thousand drachmas from the royal treasury, and will be awarded their freedom.^q ²⁹Every place detected sheltering a Jew is to be made unapproachable and burned with fire and shall become useless for all time to any mortal creature." ³⁰The letter was written in the above form.

The Jews Deported to Alexandria

4 In every place, then, where this decree arrived, a feast at public expense was arranged for the nations with shouts and gladness, for the inveterate enmity that had long ago been in their minds was now made evident and outspoken. ²But among the Jews there was indescribable mourning, lamentation, and tearful cries and groans; everywhere their hearts were burning, and they groaned because of the unexpected destruction that

---

p **3.21** Other ancient authorities read *partners of our regular priests*

q **3.28** Gk *crowned with freedom*

had suddenly been decreed for them. ³What district or city, or what habitable place at all, or what streets were not filled with mourning and wailing for them? ⁴For with such a harsh and ruthless spirit were they being sent off, all together, by the generals in every city that at the sight of their unusual punishments even some of their enemies, perceiving the common object of pity before their eyes, reflected on the uncertainty of life and shed tears at the most miserable expulsion of these people. ⁵For a multitude of gray-headed old men, sluggish and bent with age, was being led away, forced to march at a swift pace by the violence with which they were driven in such a shameful manner. ⁶And young women who had just entered the bridal chamber*r* to share married life exchanged joy for wailing, their myrrh-perfumed hair sprinkled with ashes, and were carried away unveiled, all together raising a lament instead of a wedding song, as they were torn by the harsh treatment of foreign nations. ⁷In bonds and in public view they were violently dragged along as far as the place of embarkation. ⁸Their husbands, in the prime of youth, their necks encircled with ropes instead of garlands, spent the remaining days of their marriage festival in lamentations instead of feasting and youthful revelry, seeing Hades already lying at their feet. ⁹They were brought on board like wild animals, driven under the constraint of iron bonds; some were fastened by the neck to the benches of the boats; others had their feet secured by unbreakable fetters, ¹⁰and in addition they were confined under a solid deck, so that, with their eyes in total darkness, they would undergo treatment befitting traitors during the whole voyage.

The Jews Imprisoned at Schedia

¹¹When these people had been brought to the place called Schedia and the voyage was concluded as the king had decreed, he commanded that they should be enclosed in the hippodrome that had been built with an immense perimeter wall in front of the city and that was well suited to make them an obvious spectacle to all coming back into the city and to those from the city*s* going out into the country, so that they could neither communicate with the king's forces nor in any way claim to be

inside the circuit of the city.*t* ¹²And when this had happened, the king, hearing that the Jews' compatriots from the city frequently went out in secret to lament bitterly the ignoble misfortune of their kindred, ¹³ordered in his rage that these people be dealt with in precisely the same fashion as the others, not omitting any detail of their punishment. ¹⁴The entire people was to be registered individually, not for the hard labor that has been briefly mentioned before but to be tortured with the outrages that he had ordered and at the end to be destroyed in the space of a single day. ¹⁵The registration of these people was therefore conducted with bitter haste and zealous intensity from the rising of the sun until its setting, coming to an end after forty days but still not completed.

16 The king was greatly and continually filled with joy, organizing banquets in honor of all his idols, with a mind alienated from truth and with a profane mouth, praising speechless things that are not able even to communicate or to come to one's help and uttering improper words against the supreme God. ¹⁷But after the previously mentioned interval of time the scribes declared to the king that they were no longer able to take the census of the Jews because of their immense number, ¹⁸though most of them were still in the country, some still residing in their homes, and some at the place;*u* the task was impossible for all the generals in Egypt. ¹⁹After he had threatened them severely, charging that they had been bribed to contrive a means of escape, he was clearly convinced about the matter ²⁰when they said and proved that both the papyrus and the reeds they used for writing had already given out. ²¹But this was an act of the invincible providence of him who was aiding the Jews from heaven.

Execution of the Jews Is Twice Thwarted

5 Then the king, completely inflexible, was filled with overpowering anger and wrath, so he summoned Hermon, keeper of the elephants, ²and ordered him on the following day to drug all the elephants—five hundred in number—with large handfuls of frankincense and plenty of unmixed wine and to drive them in, maddened by the lavish abundance of

---

r 4.6 Or *the canopy*
s 4.11 Gk *those of them*

t 4.11 Or *claim protection of the walls*; meaning of Gk uncertain
u 4.18 Other ancient authorities read *on the way*

drink, so that the Jews might meet their doom. [3] When he had given these orders he returned to his feasting, together with those of his Friends and of the army who were especially hostile toward the Jews. [4] And Hermon, keeper of the elephants, proceeded faithfully to carry out the orders. [5] The officials in charge of the Jews[v] went out in the evening and bound the hands of the wretched people and arranged for their continued custody through the night, convinced that the whole people would experience its final destruction. [6] For to the nations it appeared that the Jews were left without any aid, because in their bonds they were forcibly confined on every side. [7] But with tears and a voice hard to silence they all called upon the Almighty Lord and Ruler of all power, their merciful God and Father, praying [8] that he avert the evil plot against them and in a glorious manifestation rescue them from the fate now prepared for them. [9] So their entreaty ascended fervently to heaven.

[10] Hermon, however, when he had drugged the pitiless elephants until they had been filled with a great abundance of wine and satiated with frankincense, presented himself at court early in the morning to report to the king about these preparations. [11] But the Lord[w] sent upon the king a portion of sleep, that beneficence that from the beginning, night and day, is bestowed by him who grants it to whomever he wishes. [12] And by the action of the Lord he was overcome by so pleasant and deep a sleep[x] that he quite failed in his lawless purpose and was completely frustrated in his inflexible plan. [13] Then the Jews, since they had escaped the appointed hour, praised their holy God and again implored him who is easily reconciled to show the might of his all-powerful hand to the arrogant nations.

[14] But now, since it was nearly the middle of the tenth hour, the person in charge of the invitations, seeing that the guests were assembled, approached the king and nudged him. [15] And when he had with difficulty roused him, he pointed out that the hour of the banquet was already slipping by, and he gave him an account of the situation. [16] The king, after considering this, returned to his drinking and ordered those present for the banquet to recline opposite him. [17] When this was done he urged them to give themselves over to feasting and to make the present portion of the banquet joyful by celebrating all the more. [18] After the party had been going on for some time, the king summoned Hermon and with bitter threats demanded to know why the Jews had been allowed to remain alive through the present day. [19] But when he, with the corroboration of the king's[y] Friends, pointed out that while it was still night he had carried out completely the order given him, [20] the king,[z] possessed by a savagery worse than that of Phalaris, said that the Jews[a] were benefited by today's sleep, "but," he added, "tomorrow without delay prepare the elephants in the same way for the destruction of the lawless Jews!" [21] When the king had spoken, all those present readily and joyfully with one accord gave their approval, and all went to their own homes. [22] But they did not so much spend the duration of the night in sleep as in devising all sorts of insults for those they thought to be doomed.

[23] Then, as soon as the cock had crowed in the early morning, Hermon, having equipped[b] the animals, began to move them along in the great colonnade. [24] The crowds of the city had been assembled for this most pitiful spectacle and were eagerly waiting for daybreak. [25] But the Jews, being at that very moment at their last gasp, stretched their hands toward heaven and with most tearful supplication and mournful dirges implored the supreme God to help them again at once. [26] The rays of the sun were not yet shed abroad, and while the king was receiving his Friends, Hermon arrived and invited him to come out, indicating that what the king desired was ready for action. [27] But he, on receiving the report and being struck by the unusual invitation to come out—since he had been completely overcome by incomprehension—inquired what the matter was for which this had been so zealously completed for him. [28] This was the act of God who rules over all things, for he had implanted in the king's mind a forgetfulness of the things he had previously devised. [29] Then Hermon and all the king's Friends[c] pointed out that the animals and the armed forces were ready,

---

v 5.5 Gk *them*
w 5.11 Gk *he*
x 5.12 Other ancient authorities add *from evening until the ninth hour*

y 5.19 Gk *his*
z 5.20 Gk *he*
a 5.20 Gk *they*
b 5.23 Or *armed*
c 5.29 Gk *all the Friends*

"O king, according to your eager purpose."[d] [30]But at these words he was filled with an overpowering wrath because by the providence of God his whole mind had been deranged concerning these matters, and with a threatening look he said, [31]"If your parents or children were present, I would have prepared them to be a rich feast for the savage animals instead of the Jews, who give me no ground for complaint and have exhibited to an extraordinary degree a full and firm loyalty to my ancestors. [32]In fact, you would have been deprived of life instead of these, were it not for the affection arising from our common upbringing and lifelong association." [33]So Hermon suffered an unexpected and dangerous threat, and his eyes wavered and his face fell. [34]The Friends one by one sullenly slipped away and dismissed the assembled people to their own occupations. [35]Then the Jews, on hearing what the king had said, praised the manifest Lord God, King of kings, since this also was his aid that they had received.

[36]The king, however, reconvened the banquet in the same manner and urged the guests to return to their celebrating. [37]After summoning Hermon he said in a threatening tone, "How many times, you wretched man, must I give you orders about these things? [38]Equip[e] the elephants now once more for the destruction of the Jews tomorrow!" [39]But the Kinsmen who were at table with him, wondering at his instability of mind, remonstrated as follows: [40]"O king, how long will you put us to the test, as though we are idiots, ordering now for a third time that they be destroyed and again revoking your decree in the matter?[f] [41]As a result the city is in a tumult because of its expectation; it is crowded with mobs of people and also in constant danger of being plundered."

[42]At this the king, a Phalaris in everything and filled with madness, took no account of the changes of mind that had come about within him for the protection of the Jews, and he firmly swore an irrevocable oath that he would send them to Hades without delay, mangled by the knees and feet of the animals, [43]and would also march against Judea and rapidly level it to the ground with fire and spear, and by burning to the ground the temple inaccessible to him[g] would quickly render it forever empty of those who offered sacrifices there. [44]Then the Friends and Kinsmen departed with great joy, and they confidently posted the armed forces at the places in the city most favorable for keeping guard.

[45]Now when the animals had been brought virtually to a state of madness, so to speak, by the very fragrant draughts of wine mixed with frankincense and had been equipped with frightful devices, the elephant keeper [46]entered the court around dawn—the city now being filled with countless masses of people crowding their way into the hippodrome—and urged the king on to the matter at hand. [47]So he, when he had filled his impious mind with a deep rage, rushed out in full force along with the animals, wishing to witness, with invulnerable heart and with his own eyes, the grievous and pitiful destruction of the aforementioned people.

[48]When the Jews saw the dust raised by the elephants going out at the gate and by the following armed forces, as well as by the trampling of the crowd, and heard the loud and tumultuous noise, [49]they thought that this was their last moment of life, the end of their most miserable suspense, and giving way to lamentation and groans they kissed each other, embracing relatives and falling into one another's arms[h]—parents and children, mothers and daughters, and others with babies at their breasts who were drawing their last milk. [50]Nevertheless, when they considered the help that they had received before from heaven, they prostrated themselves with one accord on the ground, removing the babies from their breasts, [51]and cried out in a very loud voice, imploring the Ruler over every power to manifest himself and be merciful to them, as they stood now at the gates of Hades.

The Prayer of Eleazar

6 Then a certain Eleazar, famous among the priests of the country, who had attained a ripe old age and throughout his life had been adorned with every virtue, directed the elders around him to stop calling upon the holy God, and he prayed as follows: [2]"King of great power, Almighty God Most High, governing all creation with mercy, [3]look upon the descendants of Abraham, O Father, upon the

---

d **5.29** Other ancient authorities read *pointed to the beasts and the armed forces, saying, "They are ready, O king, according to your eager purpose."*

e **5.38** Or *Arm*

f **5.40** Other ancient authorities read *when the matter is in hand*

---

g **5.43** Gk *us*

h **5.49** Gk *falling upon their necks*

children of the consecrated Jacob, a people of your consecrated inheritance who are perishing as foreigners in a foreign land. ⁴Pharaoh with his abundance of chariots, the former ruler of this Egypt, exalted with lawless insolence and boastful tongue, you destroyed together with his arrogant army by drowning them in the sea, manifesting the light of your mercy on the people of Israel. ⁵Sennacherib exulting in his countless forces, oppressive king of the Assyrians, who had already gained control of the whole world by the spear and was lifted up against your holy city, speaking grievous words with boasting and insolence, you, O Lord, broke in pieces, showing your power to many nations. ⁶The three companions in Babylon who had voluntarily surrendered their lives to the flames so as not to serve vain things, you rescued unharmed, even to a hair, moistening the fiery furnace with dew and turning the flame against all their enemies. ⁷Daniel, who through envious slanders was thrown down into the ground to lions as food for wild animals, you brought up to the light unharmed. ⁸And Jonah, wasting away in the belly of a huge, sea-born monster, you, Father, watched over and restored*ⁱ* unharmed to all his family. ⁹And now, you who hate insolence, all-merciful and protector of all, reveal yourself quickly to those of the people of Israel*ʲ* who are being outrageously treated by the abominable and lawless nations.

10 "Even if our lives have become entangled in impieties in our exile, rescue us from the hand of the enemy and destroy us, Lord, by whatever fate you choose. ¹¹Let not the vainminded praise their vanities*ᵏ* at the destruction of your beloved ones, saying, 'Not even their god rescued them.' ¹²But you, O Eternal One, who have all might and all power, watch over us now and have mercy on us who by the senseless insolence of the lawless are being deprived of life in the manner of traitors. ¹³And let the nations cower today in fear of your invincible might, O honored One, who have power to save the people of Jacob. ¹⁴The whole throng of infants and their parents entreat you with tears. ¹⁵Let it be shown to all the nations that you are with us, O Lord, and have not turned your face from us, but just as you said, 'Not even when

they were in the land of their enemies did I neglect them,' so accomplish it, O Lord."

Two Angels Rescue the Jews

16 Just as Eleazar was ending his prayer, the king arrived at the hippodrome with the animals and all the arrogance of his forces. ¹⁷And when the Jews observed this they raised great cries to heaven so that even the nearby valleys resounded with them and brought an uncontrollable terror upon the entire army. ¹⁸Then the most glorious, almighty, and true God revealed his holy face and opened the heavenly gates, from which two glorious angels of fearful aspect descended, visible to all but the Jews. ¹⁹They opposed the forces of the enemy and filled them with confusion and terror, binding them with immovable shackles. ²⁰Even the body of the king began to shudder, and he forgot his sullen insolence. ²¹The animals turned back upon the armed forces following them and began trampling and destroying them.

22 Then the king's anger was turned to pity and tears because of the things that he had devised earlier. ²³For when he heard the shouting and saw them all lying prostrate for destruction, he wept and angrily threatened his Friends, saying, ²⁴"You are committing treason and surpassing tyrants in cruelty, and even me, your benefactor, you are now attempting to deprive of dominion and life by secretly devising acts of no advantage to the kingdom. ²⁵Who has driven from their homes those who faithfully kept our country's fortresses and contrary to reason has gathered every one of them here? ²⁶Who is it that has so lawlessly encompassed with outrageous treatment those who from the beginning in every way surpassed all nations in their goodwill toward us and often have accepted willingly the worst of human dangers? ²⁷Loose and untie their unjust bonds! Send them back to their homes in peace, begging pardon for your former actions!*ˡ* ²⁸Release the children of the almighty and living God of heaven, who from the time of our ancestors until now has granted uninterrupted stability and glory to our government." ²⁹These then were the things he said, and the Jews, immediately released, praised their holy God and Savior, since they now had escaped death.

---

i **6.8** Other ancient authorities read *rescued and restored*; others, *mercifully restored*

j **6.9** Other ancient authorities read *to the holy ones of Israel*

k **6.11** Or *bless their vain gods*

l **6.27** Other ancient authorities read *revoking your former commands*

The Jews Celebrate Their Deliverance

30 Then the king, when he had returned to the city, summoned the official in charge of the revenues and ordered him to provide to the Jews both wines and everything else needed for a festival of seven days, deciding that they should celebrate a festival of deliverance with all joyfulness in that same place in which they had expected to meet their destruction. 31 Accordingly, those disgracefully treated and near to Hades, or rather, who stood at its gates, arranged for a banquet of deliverance instead of a bitter and lamentable death, and full of joy they apportioned to groups of revelers the place that had been prepared for their destruction and burial. 32 They stopped their chanting of dirges and took up the song of their ancestors, praising God, their Savior and worker of wonders.*m* Putting an end to all mourning and wailing, they formed choruses*n* as a sign of peaceful joy. 33 Likewise also the king, after convening a lavish banquet to celebrate these events, gave thanks to heaven unceasingly and lavishly for the unexpected rescue that he*o* had experienced. 34 Those who had previously believed that the Jews would be destroyed and become food for birds and had joyfully registered them groaned as they themselves were overcome by disgrace and their fire-breathing boldness was ignominiously*p* quenched.

35 The Jews, as we have said before, arranged the aforementioned choral group*q* and passed the time in feasting to the accompaniment of joyous thanksgiving and psalms. 36 And when they had ordained a public rite for these things for their whole community for generations to come, they instituted the observance of the aforesaid days as a festival, not for drinking and gluttony but because of the deliverance that had come to them through God. 37 Then they petitioned the king, asking for dismissal to their homes. 38 So their registration was carried out from the twenty-fifth of Pachon to the fourth of Epeiph, for forty days, and their destruction was set for the fifth to the seventh of Epeiph, the three days 39 on which the Lord of all most gloriously revealed his mercy and rescued them

all together and unharmed. 40 Then they feasted, being provided with everything by the king, until the fourteenth day, on which also they made the petition for their dismissal. 41 The king granted their request and wrote the following letter for them to the generals in the cities, magnanimously expressing his concern:

Ptolemy's Letter on Behalf of the Jews

7 "King Ptolemy Philopator to the generals in Egypt and all in authority in his government, greetings and good health:

2 "We ourselves and our children are faring well, the great God guiding our affairs according to our desire. 3 Certain of our Friends, frequently urging us with malicious intent, persuaded us to gather together the Jews of the kingdom in a body and to punish them with extraordinary penalties as traitors, 4 for they declared that our government would never be firmly established until this was accomplished because of the ill-will that these people had toward all nations. 5 They also led them out with harsh treatment as slaves, or rather as traitors, and, girding themselves with a cruelty more savage than that of Scythian custom, they tried without any inquiry or examination to put them to death. 6 But we very severely threatened them for these acts, and in accordance with the clemency that we have toward all people we barely spared their lives. Since we have come to realize that the God of heaven surely defends the Jews, always taking their part as a father does for his children, 7 and since we have taken into account the friendly and firm goodwill that they have shown toward us and our ancestors, we justly have acquitted them of every charge of whatever kind. 8 We also have ordered all people to return to their own homes, with no one in any place*r* doing them harm at all or reproaching them for the irrational things that have happened. 9 For you should know that, if we devise any evil against them or cause them any grief at all, we always shall have not a mortal but the Ruler over every power, the Most High God, in everything and inescapably as an antagonist to avenge such acts. Farewell."

The Jews Return Home with Joy

10 On receiving this letter the Jews*s* did not immediately hurry to make their departure,

---

m 6.32 Other ancient authorities read *praising Israel and the wonder-working God*; or *praising Israel's Savior, the wonder-working God*

n 6.32 Or *dances*

o 6.33 Other ancient authorities read *they*

p 6.34 Other ancient authorities read *completely*

q 6.35 Or *dance*

---

r 7.8 Other ancient authorities read *way*

s 7.10 Gk *they*

but they requested of the king that at their own hands those of the Jewish people who had willfully transgressed against the holy God and the law of God should receive the punishment they deserved. [11] They declared that those who for the belly's sake had transgressed the divine commandments would never be favorably disposed toward the king's government. [12] The king[t] then, admitting and approving the truth of what they said, granted them a general license so that freely and without royal authority or supervision they might destroy those everywhere in his kingdom who had transgressed the law of God. [13] When they had applauded him in fitting manner, their priests and the whole multitude shouted the Hallelujah and joyfully departed. [14] And so on their way they punished and put to a public and shameful death any whom they met of their compatriots who had become defiled. [15] In that day they put to death more than three hundred men, and they kept the day as a joyful festival, since they had destroyed the profaners. [16] But those who had held fast to God even to death and had received the full enjoyment of deliverance began their departure from the city crowned with all sorts of very fragrant flowers, joyfully and loudly giving thanks to the God of their ancestors, the eternal Savior[u]

of Israel, in words of praise and all kinds of melodious songs.

[17] When they had arrived at Ptolemais, called "rose-bearing" because of its characteristic feature, the fleet waited for them, in accordance with the common desire, for seven days. [18] There they celebrated their deliverance,[v] for the king had generously provided all things to them for their journey until all of them arrived at their own houses. [19] And when they had all landed in peace with appropriate thanksgiving, there also in like manner they decided to observe these days as a joyous festival during the time of their stay. [20] Then, after inscribing them as holy on a pillar and dedicating a place of prayer at the site of the banquet, they departed unharmed, free, and overjoyed, since at the king's command they had all of them been brought safely by land and sea and river to their own homes. [21] They also possessed greater prestige among their enemies, being held in honor and awe, and they were not subject at all to confiscation of their belongings by anyone. [22] Besides, they all recovered all of their property, in accordance with the registration, so that those who held any of it restored it to them with extreme fear.[w] So the supreme God perfectly performed great deeds for their deliverance. [23] Blessed be the Deliverer of Israel through all times! Amen.

---

t 7.12 Gk *He*
u 7.16 Other ancient authorities read *the holy Savior*, others, *the holy one*

v 7.18 Gk *they made a cup of deliverance*
w 7.22 Other ancient authorities read *with a very large supplement*

2 ESDRAS

Comprising what is sometimes called
5 Ezra (chapters 1–2), 4 Ezra (chapters
3–14), and 6 Ezra (chapters 15–16)

The Genealogy of Ezra

1 The book*a* of the prophet Ezra son of Seraiah, son of Azariah, son of Hilkiah, son of Shallum, son of Zadok, son of Ahitub, ²son of Ahijah, son of Phinehas, son of Eli, son of Amariah, son of Azariah, son of Meraimoth, son of Arna, son of Uzzi, son of Borith, son of Abishua, son of Phinehas, son of Eleazar, ³son of Aaron, of the tribe of Levi, who was a captive in the country of the Medes in the reign of Artaxerxes, king of the Persians.

Ezra's Prophetic Call

⁴The word of the Lord came to me, saying, ⁵"Go, declare to my people their evil deeds and to their children the iniquities that they have committed against me, so that they may tell their children's children ⁶that the sins of their parents have increased in them, for they have forgotten me and have offered sacrifices to strange gods. ⁷Was it not I who brought them out of the land of Egypt, out of the house of bondage? But they have angered me and despised my counsels. ⁸Now you, pull out the hair of your head and hurl*b* all evils upon them, for they have not obeyed my law—they are a rebellious people. ⁹How long shall I endure them, on whom I have bestowed such great benefits? ¹⁰For their sake I have overthrown many kings; I struck down Pharaoh with his servants and all his army. ¹¹I destroyed all nations before them and scattered in the east the peoples of two provinces,*c* Tyre and Sidon; I killed all their enemies.

God's Mercies to Israel

¹²"But speak to them and say: Thus says the Lord: ¹³Surely it was I who brought you through the sea and made safe highways for you where there was no road; I gave you Moses as leader and Aaron as priest; ¹⁴I provided light for you from a pillar of fire and did great wonders among you. Yet you have forgotten me, says the Lord.

¹⁵"Thus says the Lord Almighty:*d* The quails were a sign to you; I gave you camps for your protection, and in them you complained. ¹⁶You have not exulted in my name at the destruction of your enemies, but to this day you still complain.*e* ¹⁷Where are the benefits that I bestowed on you? When you were hungry and thirsty in the wilderness, did you not cry out to me, ¹⁸saying, 'Why have you led us into this wilderness to kill us? It would have been better for us to serve the Egyptians than to die in this wilderness.' ¹⁹I pitied your groanings and gave you manna for food; you ate the bread of angels. ²⁰When you were thirsty, did I not split the rock so that waters flowed in abundance? Because of the heat I clothed you with the leaves of trees.*f* ²¹I divided fertile lands among you; I drove out the Canaanites,*g* the Perizzites, and the Philistines*h* before you. What more can I do for you? says the Lord. ²²Thus says the Lord Almighty:*i* When you were in the wilderness, at the bitter stream, thirsty and blaspheming my name, ²³I did not send fire on you for your blasphemies

---

a 1.1 Other ancient authorities read *The second book*
b 1.8 Other ancient authorities read *and shake out*
c 1.11 Other ancient authorities read *Did I not destroy the city of Bethsaida because of you and to the south burn two cities . . . ?*

d 1.15 Other ancient authorities lack *Almighty*
e 1.16 Other ancient authorities read *I sank your pursuer with his army in the sea, but still the people complain about their own destruction.*
f 1.20 Other ancient authorities read *I made for you trees with leaves*
g 1.21 Other ancient authorities add *the Hittites*
h 1.21 Other ancient authorities read *and their children*
i 1.22 Other ancient authorities lack *Almighty*

but threw a tree into the water and made the stream sweet.

Israel's Disobedience and Rejection

24 "What shall I do to you, O Jacob? You, Judah, would not obey me. I will turn to other nations and will give them my name, so that they may keep my statutes. 25 Because you have forsaken me, I also will forsake you. When you beg mercy of me, I will show you no mercy. 26 When you call to me, I will not listen to you, for you have defiled your hands with blood, and your feet are swift to commit murder. 27 It is not as though you had forsaken me; you have forsaken yourselves, says the Lord.

28 "Thus says the Lord Almighty: Have I not entreated you as a father entreats his sons or a mother her daughters or a nurse her children, 29 so that you should be my people and I should be your God and that you should be my children and I should be your father? 30 I gathered you as a hen gathers her chicks under her wings. But now, what shall I do to you? I will cast you out from my presence. 31 When you offer oblations to me, I will turn my face from you, for I have rejected your*j* festal days and new moons and circumcisions of the flesh.*k* 32 I sent you my servants the prophets, but you have taken and killed them and torn their bodies*l* in pieces; I will require their blood of you, says the Lord.

33 "Thus says the Lord Almighty: Your house is desolate; I will drive you out as the wind drives straw, 34 and your sons will have no children, because with you*m* they have neglected my commandment and have done what is evil in my sight. 35 I will give your houses to a people that will come, who without having heard me will believe. Those to whom I have shown no signs will do what I have commanded. 36 They have seen no prophets, yet will recall their former state.*n* 37 I call to witness the gratitude of the people that is to come, whose children rejoice with gladness;*o* though they do not see me with bodily eyes, yet with the spirit they will believe the things I have said.

38 "And now, father,*p* look with pride and see the people coming from the east; 39 to them I will give as leaders Abraham, Isaac, and Jacob, and Hosea and Amos and Micah and Joel and Obadiah and Jonah 40 and Nahum and Habakkuk, Zephaniah, Haggai, Zechariah, and Malachi, who is also called the messenger of the Lord.*q*

God's Judgment on Israel

2 "Thus says the Lord: I brought this people out of bondage, and I gave them commandments through my servants the prophets, but they would not listen to them and made my counsels void. 2 The mother who bore them says to them, 'Go, my children, because I am a widow and forsaken. 3 I brought you up with gladness, but with mourning and sorrow I have lost you, because you have sinned before the Lord God and have done what is evil in my sight.*r* 4 But now what can I do for you? For I am a widow and forsaken. Go, my children, and ask for mercy from the Lord.' 5 Now I call upon you, father, as a witness in addition to the mother of the children, because they would not keep my covenant, 6 so that you may bring confusion on them and bring their mother to ruin, so that they may have no offspring. 7 Let them be scattered among the nations; let their names be blotted out from the earth, because they have despised my covenant.

8 "Woe to you, Assyria, who conceal the unrighteous within you! O wicked nation, remember what I did to Sodom and Gomorrah, 9 whose land lies in lumps of pitch and heaps of ashes.*s* That is what I will do to those who have not listened to me, says the Lord Almighty."

10 Thus says the Lord to Ezra: "Tell my people that I*t* will give them the kingdom of Jerusalem, which I was going to give to Israel. 11 Moreover, I will take back to myself their glory and will give to them the everlasting habitations, which I had prepared for Israel. 12 The tree of life shall give them fragrant perfume, and they shall neither toil nor

---

j 1.31 Other ancient authorities read *I did not command for you*

k 1.31 Other ancient authorities lack *of the flesh*

l 1.32 Other ancient authorities read *the bodies of the apostles*

m 1.34 Other ancient authorities lack *with you*

n 1.36 Other ancient authorities read *their iniquities*

o 1.37 Other ancient authorities read *The apostles bear witness to the coming people with joy*

p 1.38 Other ancient authorities read *brother*

q 1.40 Other ancient authorities read *and Jacob, Elijah and Enoch, Zechariah and Hosea, Amos, Joel, Micah, Obadiah, Zephaniah, 40Nahum, Jonah, Mattia (or Mattathias), Habakkuk, and twelve angels with flowers*

r 2.3 Other ancient authorities read *in his sight*

s 2.9 Other ancient authorities read *whose land descends to hell*

t 2.10 Other ancient authorities add *have prepared for them to eat, and I* become weary. [13]Go[u] and you will receive; pray that your days may be few, that they may be shortened. The kingdom is already prepared for you; be on the watch! [14]Call, O call heaven and earth to witness: I set aside evil and created good, for I am the Living One, says the Lord.

Exhortation to Good Works

[15]"Mother, embrace your children; bring them up with gladness, as does a dove; strengthen their feet, because I have chosen you, says the Lord. [16]And I will raise up the dead from their places and bring them out from their tombs, because I recognize my name in them. [17]Do not fear, mother of children, for I have chosen you, says the Lord. [18]I will send you help: my servants Isaiah and Jeremiah. According to their counsel I have consecrated and prepared for you twelve trees loaded with various fruits [19]and the same number of springs flowing with milk and honey and seven mighty mountains on which roses and lilies grow; by these I will fill your children with joy.

[20]"Guard the rights of the widow, secure justice for the ward, give to the needy, defend the orphan, clothe the naked, [21]care for the injured and the weak, do not ridicule the lame, protect the maimed, and let the blind have a vision of my splendor. [22]Protect the old and the young within your walls.[v] [23]When you find any who are dead, commit them to the grave and mark it,[w] and I will give you the first place in my resurrection. [24]Pause and be quiet, my people, because your rest will come.

[25]"Good nurse, nourish your children; strengthen their feet. [26]Not one of the servants whom I have given you will perish, for I will require them from among your number. [27]Do not be anxious, for when the day of tribulation and anguish comes, others shall weep and be sorrowful, but you shall rejoice and have abundance. [28]The nations shall envy you, but they shall not be able to do anything against you, says the Lord. [29]My power will protect[x] you, so that your children may not see Gehenna.[y]

[30]"Rejoice, O mother, with your children, because I will deliver you, says the Lord. [31]Remember your children who sleep, because I will bring them out of the hiding places of the earth and will show mercy to them, for I am merciful, says the Lord Almighty. [32]Embrace your children until I come, and proclaim mercy to them, because my springs run over, and my grace will not fail."

Ezra on Mount Horeb

[33]I, Ezra, received a command from the Lord on Mount Horeb to go to Israel. When I came to them, they rejected me and refused the Lord's commandment. [34]Therefore I say to you, O nations that hear and understand, "Wait for your shepherd; he will give you everlasting rest, because he who will come at the end of the age is close at hand. [35]Be ready for the rewards of the kingdom, because perpetual light will shine on you forevermore. [36]Flee from the shadow of this age; receive the joy of your glory; I publicly call on my savior to witness.[z] [37]Receive what the Lord has entrusted to you and be joyful, giving thanks to him who has called you to the celestial kingdoms. [38]Rise, stand erect, and see the number of those who have been sealed at the feast of the Lord. [39]Those who have departed from the shadow of this age have received glorious garments from the Lord. [40]Take again your full number, O Zion, and close the list of your people who are clothed in white, who have fulfilled the law of the Lord. [41]The number of your children, whom you desired, is now complete; implore the Lord's authority that your people, who have been called from the beginning, may be made holy."

Ezra Sees the Son of God

[42]I, Ezra, saw on Mount Zion a great multitude that I could not number, and they all were praising the Lord with songs. [43]In their midst was a young man of great stature, taller than any of the others, and on the head of each of them he placed a crown, but he was more exalted than they. And I was held spellbound. [44]Then I asked an angel, "Who are these, my lord?" [45]He answered and said to me, "These are they who have put off mortal clothing and have put on the immortal and have confessed the name of God. Now they are being crowned

---

u 2.13 Other ancient authorities read *Seek*

v 2.22 Other ancient authorities add *Watch over your infants. Let enslaved and free alike be joyful, and your whole company will be happy*

w 2.23 Other ancient authorities read *When I find your dead, I will raise them; I will watch for signs*

x 2.29 Lat *hands will cover*

y 2.29 Other ancient authorities read *All tremble because of me; my eyes see Gehenna*

z 2.36 Other ancient authorities read *I testify that my savior has been commissioned by the Lord* and receive palms." [46] Then I said to the angel, "Who is that young man who is placing crowns on them and putting palms in their hands?" [47] He answered and said to me, "He is the Son of God, whom they confessed in the world." So I began to praise those who had stood valiantly for the name of the Lord.[a] [48] Then the angel said to me, "Go, tell my people how great and how many are the wonders of the Lord God that you have seen."

Ezra's Prayer of Complaint

3 In the thirtieth year after the destruction of the city, I was in Babylon—I, Salathiel, who am also called Ezra. I was troubled as I lay on my bed, and my thoughts welled up in my heart [2] because I saw the desolation of Zion and the wealth of those who lived in Babylon. [3] My spirit was greatly agitated, and I began to speak anxious words to the Most High and said, [4] "O sovereign Lord, did you not speak at the beginning when you planted[b] the earth—and that without help—and commanded the dust[c] [5] and it gave you Adam, a lifeless body? Yet he was the creation of your hands, and you breathed into him the breath of life, and he was made alive in your presence. [6] And you led him into the garden that your right hand had planted before the earth appeared. [7] And you laid upon him one commandment of yours, but he transgressed it, and immediately you appointed death for him and for his descendants. From him there sprang nations and tribes, peoples and clans without number. [8] And every nation walked after its own will; they did ungodly things in your sight and rejected your commands, and you did not hinder them. [9] But again, in its time you brought the flood upon the inhabitants of the world and destroyed them. [10] And the same fate befell all of them: just as death came upon Adam, so the flood upon them. [11] But you left one of them, Noah with his household, and all the righteous who have descended from him.

[12] "When those who lived on earth began to multiply, they produced children and peoples and many nations, and again they began to be more ungodly than were their ancestors. [13] And when they were committing iniquity in your sight, you chose for yourself one of them, whose name was Abraham; [14] you loved him, and to him alone you revealed the end of the times, secretly by night. [15] You made an everlasting covenant with him and promised him that you would never forsake his descendants, and you gave him Isaac, and to Isaac you gave Jacob and Esau. [16] You set apart Jacob for yourself, but Esau you rejected, and Jacob became a great multitude. [17] And when you led his descendants out of Egypt, you brought them to Mount Sinai. [18] You bent down the heavens and shook[d] the earth and moved the world and caused the depths to tremble and troubled the times. [19] Your glory passed through the four gates of fire and earthquake and wind and ice, to give the law to the descendants of Jacob and your commandment to the posterity of Israel.

[20] "Yet you did not take away their evil heart from them, so that your law might produce fruit in them. [21] For the first Adam, burdened with an evil heart, transgressed and was overcome, as were also all who were descended from him. [22] Thus the disease became permanent; the law was in the hearts of the people along with the evil root, but what was good departed, and the evil remained. [23] So the times passed and the years were completed, and you raised up for yourself a servant named David. [24] You commanded him to build a city for your name and there to offer you oblations from what is yours. [25] This was done for many years, but the inhabitants of the city transgressed, [26] in everything doing just as Adam and all his descendants had done, for they also had the evil heart. [27] So you handed over your city to your enemies.

Babylon Compared with Zion

[28] "Then I said in my heart, Are the deeds of those who inhabit Babylon any better? Is that why it has gained dominion over Zion? [29] For when I came here I saw ungodly deeds without number, and my soul has seen many sinners during these thirty years.[e] And my heart failed me [30] because I have seen how you endure those who sin and have spared those who act wickedly and have destroyed your people and have protected your enemies [31] and have not shown to anyone how your way may

---

a **2.47** Other ancient authorities read *to praise and glorify the Lord*
b **3.4** Other ancient authorities read *formed*
c **3.4** Syr Ethiop Georg: Lat *people* or *world*

d **3.18** Syr Ethiop Arab 1 Georg: Lat *set fast*
e **3.29** Ethiop Arab 1 Arm: Lat Syr *in this thirtieth year*

be comprehended.*f* Are the deeds of Babylon better than those of Zion? 32 Or has another nation known you besides Israel? Or what tribes have so believed the covenants as these tribes of Jacob? 33 Yet their reward has not appeared, and their labor has borne no fruit. For I have traveled widely among the nations and have seen that they abound in wealth, though they are unmindful of your commandments. 34 Now therefore weigh in a balance our iniquities and those of the inhabitants of the world, and it will be found which way the arrow of the scale tips. 35 When have the inhabitants of the earth not sinned in your sight? Or what nation has kept your commandments so well? 36 You may indeed find individuals who have kept your commandments, but nations you will not find."

Limitations of the Human Mind

4 Then the angel that had been sent to me, whose name was Uriel, answered 2 and said to me, "Your understanding has utterly failed regarding this world, and do you think you can comprehend the way of the Most High?" 3 Then I said, "Yes, my lord." And he replied to me, "I have been sent to show you three ways and to put before you three problems. 4 If you can solve one of them for me, then I will show you the way you desire to see and will teach you why the heart is evil."

5 I said, "Speak, my lord."

And he said to me, "Go, weigh for me the weight of fire, or measure for me a blast*g* of wind, or call back for me the day that is past."

6 I answered and said, "Who of those that have been born can do that, that you should ask me about such things?"

7 And he said to me, "If I had asked you, 'How many dwellings are in the heart of the sea, or how many streams are at the source of the deep, or how many streams are above the firmament, or which are the exits of Hades, or which are the entrances*h* of paradise?' 8 perhaps you would have said to me, 'I never went down into the deep, nor as yet into Hades, neither did I ever ascend into heaven.' 9 But now I have asked you only about fire and wind and the day, things that you have experienced and from which you cannot be separated, and you have given me no

answer about them." 10 He said to me, "You cannot understand the things with which you have grown up; 11 how, then, can your mind comprehend the way of the Most High?*i* And how can one who is already worn out by the corrupt world understand incorruption?"*j* When I heard this, I fell on my face*k* 12 and said to him, "It would have been better for us not to be here than to come here and live in ungodliness and to suffer and not understand why."

Parable of the Forest and the Sea

13 He answered me and said, "I went into a forest of trees of the plain, and they made a plan 14 and said, 'Come, let us go and make war against the sea, so that it may recede before us and so that we may make for ourselves more forests.' 15 In like manner the waves of the sea also made a plan and said, 'Come, let us go up and subdue the forest of the plain so that there also we may gain more territory for ourselves.' 16 But the plan of the forest was in vain, for the fire came and consumed it; 17 likewise also the plan of the waves of the sea was in vain,*l* for the sand stood firm and blocked it. 18 If now you were a judge between them, which would you undertake to justify and which to condemn?"

19 I answered and said, "Each made a foolish plan, for the land has been assigned to the forest and the locale of the sea a place to carry its waves."

20 He answered me and said, "You have judged rightly, but why have you not judged so in your own case? 21 For as the land has been assigned to the forest and the sea to its waves, so also those who inhabit the earth can understand only what is on the earth, and he who is*m* above the heavens can understand what is above the height of the heavens."

The New Age Will Make All Things Clear

22 Then I answered and said, "I implore you, my lord, why*n* have I been endowed with the power of understanding? 23 For I did not wish to inquire about the ways above but about those things that we daily experience: why Israel has been given over to the nations in disgrace; why

---

f **3.31** Syr; compare Ethiop: Lat *how this way should be forsaken*

g **4.5** Syr Ethiop Arab 1 Arab 2 Georg *a measure*

h **4.7** Syr Compare Ethiop Arab 2 Arm: Lat lacks *of Hades, or which are the entrances*

i **4.11** Syr Ethiop add *For the way of the Most High is created immeasurable*

j **4.11** Syr Ethiop *the way of the incorruptible?*

k **4.11** Syr Ethiop Arab 1: Meaning of Lat uncertain

l **4.17** Lat lacks *was in vain*

m **4.21** Arab 2 Arm Georg *those who are*

n **4.22** Syr Ethiop Arm Georg: Meaning of Lat uncertain

the people whom you loved has been given over to godless tribes and the law of our ancestors has been brought to destruction and the written covenants no longer exist. 24 We pass from the world like locusts, and our life is like a mist,^{o} and we are not worthy to obtain mercy. 25 But what will he do for his^p name that is invoked over us? It is about these things that I have asked."

26 He answered me and said, "If you are alive, you will see, and if you live long,^{q} you will often marvel, because the age is hurrying swiftly to its end. 27 It will not be able to bring the things that have been promised to the righteous in their appointed times, because this age is full of sadness and infirmities. 28 For the evil about which you ask me has been sown, but the harvest of it has not yet come. 29 If therefore that which has been sown is not reaped, and if the place where the evil has been sown does not pass away, the field where the good has been sown will not come. 30 For a grain of evil seed was sown in Adam's heart from the beginning, and how much ungodliness it has produced until now—and will produce until the time of threshing comes! 31 Consider now for yourself how much fruit of ungodliness a grain of evil seed has produced. 32 When heads of grain without number are sown, how great a threshing floor they will fill!"

When Will the New Age Come?

33 Then I answered and said, "How long?^{r} When will these things be? Why are our years few and evil?" 34 He answered me and said, "Do not be in a greater hurry than the Most High. You, indeed, are in a hurry for yourself,^{s} but the Highest is in a hurry on behalf of many. 35 Did not the souls of the righteous in their chambers ask about these matters, saying, 'How long are we to remain here?'^{t} And when will the harvest of our reward come?' 36 And the archangel Jeremiel answered and said, 'When the number of those like yourselves^u is completed, for he has weighed the age in the balance, 37 and measured the times by measure, and numbered the times by number, and he will not move or arouse them until that measure is fulfilled.' "

38 Then I answered and said, "But, O sovereign Lord, all of us also are full of ungodliness. 39 It is perhaps on account of us that the time of threshing is delayed for the righteous—on account of the sins of those who inhabit the earth."

40 He answered me and said, "Go and ask a pregnant woman whether, when her nine months have been completed, her womb can keep the fetus within her any longer."

41 And I said, "No, lord, it cannot."

He said to me, "In Hades the chambers of the souls are like the womb. 42 For just as a woman who is in labor makes haste to escape the pangs of birth, so also do these places hasten to give back those things who were committed to them from the beginning. 43 Then the things that you desire to see will be disclosed to you."

How Much Time Remains?

44 I answered and said, "If I have found favor in your sight, and if it is possible, and if I am worthy, 45 show me this also: whether more time is to come than has passed or whether for us the greater part has gone by. 46 For I know what has gone by, but I do not know what is to come."

47 And he said to me, "Stand at my right side, and I will show you the interpretation of a parable."

48 So I stood and looked, and a flaming furnace passed by before me, and when the flame had gone by I looked, and the smoke remained. 49 And after this a cloud full of water passed before me and poured down a heavy and violent rain, and when the violent rainstorm had passed, drops still remained in it.

50 He said to me, "Consider it for yourself, for just as the rain is more than the drops and the fire is greater than the smoke, so the quantity that passed was far greater, but drops and smoke remained."

51 Then I prayed and said, "Do you think that I shall live until those days? Or who will be alive in those days?"

52 He answered me and said, "Concerning the signs about which you ask me, I can tell you in part, but I was not sent to tell you concerning your life, for I do not know.

Signs of the End

5 "Now concerning the signs: behold, the days are coming when those who inhabit the earth shall be seized with great terror,^{v} and

---

o 4.24 Lat mss Syr Ethiop Arab 1 Georg: Lat *terror*
p 4.25 Ethiop adds *holy*
q 4.26 Syr: Lat *live*
r 4.33 Syr Ethiop: Meaning of Lat uncertain
s 4.34 Syr Ethiop Arab Arm: Meaning of Lat uncertain
t 4.35 Syr Ethiop Arab 2 Georg: Lat *How long do I hope thus?*
u 4.36 Syr Ethiop Arab 2: Lat *number of seeds*

---

v 5.1 Syr Georg Ethiop: Meaning of Lat uncertain

the way of truth shall be hidden, and the land shall be barren of faith. ²Unrighteousness shall be increased beyond what you yourself see and beyond what you heard of formerly. ³And the land that you now see ruling shall be a trackless waste, and people shall see it desolate. ⁴But if the Most High grants that you live, you shall see it thrown into confusion after the third period,ʷ
and the sun shall suddenly begin to shine
    at night
    and the moon during the day.
⁵ Blood shall drip from wood,
    and the stone shall utter its voice;
    the peoples shall be troubled,
    and the skies shall be changed.ˣ
⁶"And one shall reign whom those who inhabit the earth do not expect, and the birds shall fly away together, ⁷and the sea of Sodom shall cast up fish, and one whom the many do not know shall make his voice heard by night, and all shall hear his voice.ʸ ⁸There shall be chaos also in many places, fire shall often break out, the wild animals shall roam beyond their haunts, and menstruous women shall bring forth monsters. ⁹Salt waters shall be found in the sweet, and all friends shall conquer one another; then shall reason hide itself, and wisdom shall withdraw into its chamber, ¹⁰and it shall be sought by many but shall not be found, and unrighteousness and unrestraint shall increase on earth. ¹¹One country shall ask its neighbor, 'Has righteousness or anyone who does right passed through you?' And it will answer, 'No.' ¹²At that time people shall hope but not obtain; they shall labor, but their ways shall not prosper. ¹³These are the signs that I am permitted to tell you, and if you pray again and weep as you do now and fast for seven days, you shall hear yet greater things than these."

Conclusion of the Vision

14 Then I woke up, and my body shuddered violently, and my soul was so troubled that it fainted. ¹⁵But the angel who had come and talked with me held me and strengthened me and set me on my feet.

16 Now on the second night Phaltiel, a chief of the people, came to me and said, "Where have you been? And why is your face sad? ¹⁷Or do you not know that Israel has been entrusted to you in the land of their exile? ¹⁸Rise therefore and eat some bread, and do not forsake us like a shepherd who leaves the flock in the power of savage wolves."

19 Then I said to him, "Go away from me and do not come near me for seven days; then you may come to me."

He heard what I said and left me. ²⁰So I fasted seven days, mourning and weeping, as the angel Uriel had commanded me.

Ezra's Second Prayer of Complaint

21 After seven days the thoughts of my heart were very grievous to me again. ²²Then my soul recovered the spirit of understanding, and I began once more to speak words in the presence of the Most High. ²³I said, "O sovereign Lord, from every forest of the earth, and from all its trees you have chosen one vine, ²⁴and from all the lands of the world you have chosen for yourself one region,ᶻ and from all the flowers of the world you have chosen for yourself one lily, ²⁵and from all the depths of the sea you have filled for yourself one river, and from all the cities that have been built you have consecrated Zion for yourself, ²⁶and from all the birds that have been created you have named for yourself one dove, and from all the flocks that have been made you have provided for yourself one sheep, ²⁷and from all the multitude of peoples you have gotten for yourself one people, and to this people, whom you have loved, you have given the law that is approved by all. ²⁸And now, O Lord, why have you handed the one over to the many and dishonoredᵃ the one root beyond the others and scattered your only one among the many? ²⁹And those who opposed your promises have trampled on those who believed your covenants. ³⁰If you really hate your people, they should be punished at your own hands."

Response to Ezra's Complaints

31 When I had spoken these words, the angel who had come to me on a previous night was sent to me. ³²He said to me, "Listen to me, and I will instruct you; pay attention to me, and I will tell you more."

---

w 5.4 Ethiop *three months*; Arm *the third vision*; Georg *the third day*; Arab 1 *three signs*
x 5.5 Syr Georg Arab 1 Arab 2 Arm; Ethiop *and the stars shall fall*: Meaning of Lat uncertain
y 5.7 Cn: Lat *fish, and it shall make its voice heard by night, which the many have not known, but all shall hear its voice.*

z 5.24 Syr: Lat *pit*
a 5.28 Syr Ethiop Arab: Lat *prepared*

33 Then I said, "Speak, my lord." And he said to me, "Are you greatly disturbed in mind over Israel? Or do you love him more than his Maker does?"

34 I said, "No, my lord, but because of my grief I have spoken, for every hour I suffer agonies of heart while I strive to understand the way of the Most High and to search out some part of his judgment."

35 He said to me, "You cannot." And I said, "Why not, my lord? Why, then, was I born? Or why did not my mother's womb become my grave, so that I would not see the travail of Jacob and the exhaustion of the people of Israel?"

36 He said to me, "Count up for me those who have not yet come, and gather for me the scattered raindrops, and make the withered flowers bloom again for me; 37 open for me the closed chambers, and bring out for me the winds shut up in them, or show me the picture of a voice, and then I will explain to you the travail that you ask to see."

38 I said, "O sovereign Lord, who is able to know these things except him whose dwelling is not with mortals? 39 As for me, I am without wisdom, and how can I speak concerning the things that you have asked me?"

40 He said to me, "Just as you cannot do one of the things that were mentioned, so you cannot discover my judgment or the goal of the love that I have promised to my people."

Why Successive Generations Have Been Created

41 I said, "Yet, O Lord, you have charge of those who are alive at the end, but what will those do who lived before me, or we ourselves, or those who come after us?"

42 He said to me, "I shall liken my judgment to a circle;[b] just as for those who are last there is no slowness, so for those who are first there is no haste."

43 Then I answered and said, "Could you not have created at one time those who have been and those who are and those who will be, so that you might show your judgment the sooner?"

44 He replied to me and said, "The creation cannot move faster than the Creator, nor can the world hold at one time those who have been created in it."

45 I said, "How have you said to your servant that you[c] will certainly give life at one time to

your creation? If therefore all creatures will live at one time[d] and the creation will sustain them, it might even now be able to support all of them present at one time."

46 He said to me, "Ask a woman's womb, and say to it, 'If you bear ten children, why one after another?' Request it therefore to produce ten at one time."

47 I said, "Of course it cannot, but only each in its own time."

48 He said to me, "Even so I have given the womb of the earth to those who from time to time are sown in it. 49 For as an infant does not bring forth, and a woman who has become old does not bring forth any longer, so I have made the same rule for the world that I created."

When and How Will the End Come?

50 Then I inquired and said, "Since you have now given me the opportunity, let me speak before you. Is our mother, of whom you have told me, still young, or is she now approaching old age?"

51 He replied to me, "Ask a woman who bears children, and she will tell you. 52 Say to her, 'Why are those whom you have borne recently not like those whom you bore before, but smaller in stature?' 53 And she herself will answer you, 'Those born in the strength of youth are different from those born during the time of old age, when the womb is failing.' 54 Therefore you also should consider that you and your contemporaries are smaller in stature than those who were before you, 55 and those who come after you will be smaller than you, as born of a creation that already is aging and passing the strength of youth."

56 I said, "I implore you, O Lord, if I have found favor in your sight, show your servant through whom you will visit your creation."

6 He said to me, "At the beginning of the circle of the earth, before[e] the portals of the world were in place, and before the assembled winds blew, 2 and before the rumblings of thunder sounded, and before the flashes of lightning shone, and before the foundations of paradise

---

b 5.42 Or *crown*

c 5.45 Syr Ethiop Arab 1: Meaning of Lat uncertain

d 5.45 Syr: Lat lacks *If . . . one time*

e 6.1 Meaning of Lat uncertain: Compare Syr *The beginning is by the hand of humankind, but the end is by my own hands. For as before the land of the world existed there, and before;* Ethiop: *At first by the Son of Man, and afterwards I myself. For before the earth and the lands were created, and before* were laid, ³and before the beautiful flowers were seen, and before the powers of movements*f* were established, and before the innumerable hosts of angels were gathered together, ⁴and before the heights of the air were lifted up, and before the measures of the firmaments were named, and before the footstool of Zion was established, ⁵and before the present years were reckoned, and before the imaginations of those who now sin were estranged, and before those who stored up treasures of faith were sealed—⁶then I planned these things, and they were made through me alone and not through another, just as the end shall come through me alone and not through another."

The Dividing of the Times

7 I answered and said, "What will be the dividing of the times, or when will be the end of the first age and the beginning of the age that follows?"

8 He said to me, "From Abraham to Isaac,*g* because from him were born Jacob and Esau, for Jacob's hand held Esau's heel from the beginning. ⁹Now Esau is the end of this age, and Jacob is the beginning of the age that follows. ¹⁰The beginning of a person is the hand, and the end of a person is the heel;*h* seek for nothing else, Ezra, between the heel and the hand, Ezra!"

More Signs of the End

11 I answered and said, "O sovereign Lord, if I have found favor in your sight, ¹²show your servant the last of your signs of which you showed me a part on a previous night."

13 He answered and said to me, "Rise to your feet, and you will hear a full, resounding voice. ¹⁴And if the place where you are standing is greatly shaken ¹⁵while the voice is speaking, do not be terrified, because the word concerns the end, and the foundations of the earth will understand ¹⁶that the speech concerns them. They will tremble and be shaken, for they know that their end must be changed."

17 When I heard this, I got to my feet and listened; a voice was speaking, and its sound was like the sound of mighty*i* waters. ¹⁸It said, "The days are coming when I draw near to visit the inhabitants of the earth, ¹⁹and when I require

from the doers of iniquity the penalty of their iniquity, and when the humiliation of Zion is complete. ²⁰When the seal is placed upon the age that is about to pass away, then I will show these signs: the books shall be opened before the face of the firmament, and all shall see my judgment*j* together. ²¹Children a year old shall speak with their voices, and pregnant women shall give birth to premature children at three and four months, and these shall live and leap about. ²²Sown places shall suddenly appear unsown, and full storehouses shall suddenly be found to be empty; ²³the trumpet shall sound aloud, and when all hear it they shall suddenly be terrified. ²⁴At that time friends shall make war on friends like enemies, the earth and those who inhabit it shall be terrified, and the springs of the fountains shall stand still, so that for three hours they shall not flow.

25 "It shall be that whoever remains after all that I have foretold to you shall be saved and shall see my salvation and the end of my world. ²⁶And they shall see those who were taken up, who from their birth have not tasted death, and the heart of the earth's*k* inhabitants shall be changed and converted to a different spirit. ²⁷For evil shall be blotted out, and deceit shall be quenched; ²⁸faithfulness shall flourish, and corruption shall be overcome, and the truth, which has been so long without fruit, shall be revealed."

Conclusion of the Second Vision

29 While he spoke to me, little by little the place where I was standing began to rock to and fro. ³⁰And he said to me, "I have come to show you these things this night.*l* ³¹If therefore you will pray again and fast again for seven days, I will again declare to you greater things than these,*m* ³²because your voice has surely been heard by the Most High, for the Mighty One has seen your uprightness and has also observed the purity that you have maintained from your youth. ³³Therefore he sent me to show you all these things and to say to you: 'Believe and do not be afraid! ³⁴Do not be quick to think vain thoughts concerning the former times; then you will not act hastily in the last times.' "

---

f 6.3 Or *earthquakes*
g 6.8 Syr: Lat *to Abraham*
h 6.10 Syr: Meaning of Lat uncertain
i 6.17 Lat *many*

j 6.20 Syr: Lat lacks *my judgment*
k 6.26 Syr Compare Ethiop Arab 1 Arm: Lat lacks *earth's*
l 6.30 Syr Compare Ethiop: Meaning of Lat uncertain
m 6.31 Syr Ethiop Arab 1 Arm: Lat adds *by day*

The Third Vision

35 Now after this I wept again and fasted seven days in the same way as before, in order to complete the three weeks that had been prescribed for me. 36 Then on the eighth night my heart was troubled within me again, and I began to speak in the presence of the Most High. 37 My spirit was greatly aroused, and my soul was in distress.

God's Work in Creation

38 I said, "O Lord, you spoke at the beginning of creation and said on the first day, 'Let heaven and earth be made,' and your word accomplished the work. 39 Then the spirit was blowing, and darkness and silence embraced everything; the sound of human voices was not yet there." 40 Then you commanded a ray of light to be brought out from your storehouses, so that your works could be seen.

41 "Again, on the second day, you created the spirit of the firmament and commanded it to divide and separate the waters, so that one part might move upward and the other part remain beneath.

42 "On the third day you commanded the waters to be gathered together in a seventh part of the earth; six parts you dried up and kept so that some of them might be planted and cultivated and be of service before you. 43 For your word went forth, and at once the work was done. 44 Immediately fruit came forth in endless abundance and of varied appeal to the taste, and flowers of inimitable color, and odors of inexpressible fragrance. These were made on the third day.

45 "On the fourth day you commanded the brightness of the sun, the light of the moon, and the arrangement of the stars to come into being, 46 and you commanded them to serve the human who was about to be formed.

47 "On the fifth day you commanded the seventh part, where the water had been gathered together, to bring forth living creatures, birds, and fishes, and so it was done. 48 The dumb and lifeless water produced living creatures, as it was commanded, so that therefore the nations might declare your wondrous works.

49 "Then you kept in existence two living creatures that you created;° the one you called Behemoth^p and the name of the other Leviathan.

50 And you separated one from the other, for the seventh part where the water had been gathered together could not hold them both. 51 And you gave Behemoth^q one of the parts that had been dried up on the third day, to live in it, where there are a thousand mountains, 52 but to Leviathan you gave the seventh part, the watery part, and you have kept them to be eaten by whom you wish and when you wish.

53 "On the sixth day you commanded the earth to bring forth before you cattle, wild animals, and creeping things, 54 and over these you placed Adam, as ruler over all the works that you had made, and from him we have all come, the people whom you have chosen.

Why Do God's People Suffer?

55 "All this I have spoken before you, O Lord, because you have said that it was for us that you created this world.^r 56 As for the other nations that have descended from Adam, you have said that they are nothing and that they are like spittle, and you have compared their abundance to a drop from a bucket. 57 And now, O Lord, these nations, which are reputed to be as nothing, domineer over us and devour us. 58 But we your people, whom you have called your firstborn, only begotten, zealous for you,^s and most dear, have been given into their hands. 59 If the world has indeed been created for us, why do we not possess our world as an inheritance? How long will this be so?"

Response to Ezra's Questions

7 When I had finished speaking these words, the angel who had been sent to me on the former nights was sent to me again. 2 He said to me, "Rise, Ezra, and listen to the words that I have come to speak to you."

3 I said, "Speak, my lord." And he said to me, "There is a sea set in a wide expanse so that it is deep and vast, 4 but it has an entrance set in a narrow place, so that it is like a river. 5 If there are those who wish to reach the sea, to look at it or to navigate it, how can they come to the broad part unless they pass through the narrow part? 6 Another example: There is a city built and set on a plain, and it is full of all good things, 7 but the entrance to it is narrow and set in a precipitous place, so that there is fire on the

---

n 6.39 Syr Ethiop: Lat *was not yet from you*
o 6.49 Syr Ethiop: Lat lacks *that you created*
p 6.49 Other Lat authorities read *Enoch*

q 6.51 Other Lat authorities read *Enoch*
r 6.55 Syr Ethiop Arab 2: Lat *the firstborn world*
s 6.58 Lat lacks *for you*

right hand and deep water on the left. ⁸There is only one path lying between them, that is, between the fire and the water, so that only one person can walk on the path. ⁹If now the city is given to someone as an inheritance, how will the heir receive the inheritance unless by passing through the appointed danger?"

¹⁰I said, "That is right, lord." He said to me, "So also is Israel's portion. ¹¹For I made the world for their sake, and when Adam transgressed my statutes, what had been made was judged. ¹²And so the entrances of this world were made narrow and sorrowful and toilsome; they are few and evil, full of dangers and involved in great hardships. ¹³But the entrances of the greater world are broad and safe and yield the fruit of immortality. ¹⁴Therefore unless the living pass through the difficult and futile experiences, they can never receive those things that have been reserved for them. ¹⁵Now, therefore, why are you disturbed, seeing that you are to perish? Why are you moved, seeing that you are mortal? ¹⁶Why have you not considered in your mind what is to come rather than what is now present?"

The Fate of the Ungodly

17Then I answered and said, "O sovereign Lord, you have ordained in your law that the righteous shall inherit these things but that the ungodly shall perish. ¹⁸The righteous, therefore, can endure difficult circumstances while hoping for easier ones, but those who have done wickedly have suffered the difficult circumstances and will never see the easier ones."

19He said to me, "You are not a better judge than the Lord*t* or wiser than the Most High! ²⁰Let many perish who are now living rather than that the law of God that is set before them be disregarded! ²¹For the Lord*u* strictly commanded those who came into the world, when they came, what they should do to live and what they should observe to avoid punishment. ²²Nevertheless, they were not obedient and spoke against him;
they devised for themselves vain thoughts
23   and proposed to themselves wicked frauds;
they even declared that the Most High does not exist,
and they ignored his ways.

²⁴ They scorned his law
and denied his covenants;
they have been unfaithful to his statutes
and have not performed his works.
²⁵"That is the reason, Ezra, that empty things are for the empty and full things are for the full.

The Temporary Messianic Kingdom

26"For indeed the time will come when the signs that I have foretold to you will come to pass, that the city that now is not seen shall appear*v* and the land that now is hidden shall be disclosed. ²⁷Everyone who has been delivered from the evils that I have foretold shall see my wonders. ²⁸For my son the Messiah*w* shall be revealed with those who are with him, and those who remain shall rejoice four hundred years. ²⁹After those years my son the Messiah shall die, and all who draw human breath.*x* ³⁰Then the world shall be turned back to primeval silence for seven days, as it was at the first beginnings, so that no one shall be left. ³¹After seven days the world that is not yet awake shall be roused, and that which is corruptible shall perish. ³²The earth shall give up those who are asleep in it and the dust those who rest there in silence, and the chambers shall give up the souls that have been committed to them. ³³The Most High shall be revealed on the seat of judgment, and compassion shall pass away, and patience shall be withdrawn.*y* ³⁴Only judgment shall remain, truth shall stand, and faithfulness shall grow strong. ³⁵Recompense shall follow, and the reward shall be manifested; righteous deeds shall awake, and unrighteous deeds shall not sleep. ³⁶The pit*z* of torment shall appear, and opposite it shall be the place of rest, and the furnace of Gehenna shall be disclosed, and opposite it the paradise of delight. ³⁷Then the Most High will say to the nations that have been raised from the dead, 'Look now, and understand whom you have denied, whom you have not served, whose commandments you have despised. ³⁸Look on this side and on that; here are delight and rest, and there are fire and torments.' Thus he will

---

t 7.19 Other ancient authorities read *God*; Ethiop Georg *the only One*

u 7.21 Other ancient authorities read *God*

v 7.26 Arm: Lat Syr *that the bride shall appear, even the city appearing*

w 7.28 Syr Arab 1: Ethiop *my Messiah*; Arab 2 *the Messiah*; Arm *the Messiah of God*; Lat *my son Jesus*

x 7.29 Arm *all who have continued in faith and in patience*

y 7.33 Lat *shall gather together*

z 7.36 Syr Ethiop: Lat *place*

speak to them on the day of judgment, [39]a day that has no sun or moon or stars, [40]or cloud or thunder or lightning, or wind or water or air, or darkness or evening or morning, [41]or summer or spring or heat or winter*a* or frost or cold, or hail or rain or dew, [42]or noon or night, or dawn or shining or brightness or light, but only the splendor of the glory of the Most High, by which all shall see what has been destined. [43]It will last as though for a week of years. [44]This is my judgment and its prescribed order, and to you alone I have shown these things."

Only a Few Will Be Saved

[45]I answered and said, "O sovereign Lord, I said then and*b* I say now: Blessed are those who are alive and keep your commandments! [46]But what of those for whom I prayed? For who among the living is there who has not sinned, or who is there among mortals who has not transgressed your covenant? [47]And now I see that the world to come will bring delight to few but torments to many. [48]For an evil heart has grown up in us that has alienated us from these and has brought us into corruption and the ways of death and has shown us the paths of perdition and removed us far from life—and that not merely for a few but for almost all who have been created."

[49]He answered me and said, "Listen to me, Ezra,*c* and I will instruct you and will admonish you once more. [50]For this reason the Most High has made not one world but two. [51]Inasmuch as you have said that the righteous are not many but few, while the ungodly abound, hear the explanation for this.

[52]"If you have just a few precious stones, will you add to them lead and clay?"*d* [53]I said, "Lord, how could that be?" [54]And he said to me, "Not only that, but ask the earth, and she will tell you; defer to her, and she will declare it to you. [55]Say to her, 'You produce gold and silver and bronze and also iron and lead and clay, [56]but silver is more abundant than gold, and bronze than silver, and iron than bronze, and lead than iron, and clay than lead.' [57]Judge therefore which things are precious and desirable, those that are abundant or those that are rare?"

[58]I said, "O sovereign Lord, what is plentiful is of less worth, for what is more rare is more precious."

[59]He answered me and said, "Consider within yourself what you have thought, for the person who has what is hard to get rejoices more than the person who has what is plentiful. [60]So also will be the judgment*e* that I have promised, for I will rejoice over the few who shall be saved because it is they who have made my glory to prevail now, and through them my name has now been honored. [61]I will not grieve over the great number of those who perish, for it is they who are now like a mist and are similar to a flame and smoke—they are set on fire and burn hotly and are extinguished."

Lamentation of Ezra, with Response

[62]I replied and said, "O earth, what have you brought forth, if the mind is made out of the dust like the other created things? [63]For it would have been better if the dust itself had not been born, so that the mind might not have been made from it. [64]But now the mind grows with us, and therefore we are tormented, because we perish and we know it. [65]Let the human race lament, but let the wild animals of the field be glad; let all who have been born lament, but let the cattle and the flocks rejoice. [66]It is much better with them than with us, for they do not look for a judgment, and they do not know of any torment or salvation promised to them after death. [67]What does it profit us that we shall be preserved alive but cruelly tormented? [68]For all who have been born are entangled in*f* iniquities and are full of sins and burdened with transgressions. [69]And if after death we were not to come into judgment, perhaps it would have been better for us."

[70]He answered me and said, "When the Most High made the world and Adam and all who have come from him, he first prepared the judgment and the things that pertain to the judgment. [71]But now, understand from your own words, for you have said that the mind grows with us. [72]For this reason, therefore, those who live on earth shall be tormented, because though they had understanding they committed iniquity, and though they received the commandments they did not keep them, and though they obtained the law they dealt

---

a **7.41** Or *storm*
b **7.45** Syr: Lat *And I answered, "I said then, O Lord, and*
c **7.49** Syr Arab 1 Georg: Lat Ethiop lack *Ezra*
d **7.52** Arab 1: Meaning of Lat Syr Ethiop uncertain

e **7.60** Syr Arab 1: Lat *creation*
f **7.68** Syr *defiled with*

unfaithfully with what they received. 73 What, then, will they have to say in the judgment, or how will they answer in the last times? 74 How long the Most High has been patient with those who inhabit the world!—and not for their sake but because of the times that he has foreordained."

State of the Dead before Judgment

75 I answered and said, "If I have found favor in your sight, O Lord, show this also to your servant: whether after death, as soon as everyone of us yields up the soul, we shall be kept in rest until those times come when you will renew the creation, or whether we shall be tormented at once?"

76 He answered me and said, "I will show you that also, but do not include yourself with those who have shown scorn, or number yourself among those who are tormented. 77 For you have a treasure of works stored up with the Most High, but it will not be shown to you until the last times. 78 Now concerning death, the teaching is: When the decisive decree has gone out from the Most High that a person shall die, as the spirit leaves the body to return again to him who gave it, first of all it adores the glory of the Most High. 79 If it is one of those who have shown scorn and have not kept the way of the Most High, who have despised his law and hated those who fear God, 80 such spirits shall not enter into habitations but shall immediately wander about in torments, always grieving and sad, in seven ways. 81 The first way: because they have scorned the law of the Most High. 82 The second way: because they cannot now make a good repentance so that they may live. 83 The third way: they shall see the reward laid up for those who have trusted the covenants of the Most High. 84 The fourth way: they shall consider the torment laid up for themselves in the last days. 85 The fifth way: they shall see how the habitations of the others are guarded by angels in profound quiet. 86 The sixth way: they shall see how some of them will cross over*g* into torments. 87 The seventh way, which is worse than all the ways that have been mentioned: because they shall utterly waste away in confusion and be consumed with shame*h* and shall wither with fear at seeing the glory of the Most High in whose presence they sinned while they

were alive and in whose presence they are to be judged in the last times.

88 "Now this is the order of those who have kept the ways of the Most High, when they shall be separated from their mortal body.*i* 89 During the time that they lived in it,*j* they laboriously served the Most High and withstood danger every hour so that they might keep the law of the Lawgiver perfectly. 90 Therefore this is the teaching concerning them: 91 First of all, they shall see with great joy the glory of him who receives them, for they shall have rest in seven orders. 92 The first order: because they have striven with great effort to overcome the evil thought that was formed with them, so that it might not lead them astray from life into death. 93 The second order: because they see the perplexity in which the souls of the ungodly wander and the punishment that awaits them. 94 The third order: they see the witness that he who formed them bears concerning them, that throughout their life they kept the law with which they were entrusted. 95 The fourth order: they understand the rest that they now enjoy, being gathered into their chambers and guarded by angels in profound quiet and the glory waiting for them in the last days. 96 The fifth order: they rejoice that they have now escaped what is corruptible and shall inherit what is to come; moreover, they see the straits and toil from which they have been delivered and the spacious liberty that they are to receive and enjoy in immortality. 97 The sixth order: when it is shown them how their face is to shine like the sun and how they are to be made like the light of the stars, being incorruptible from then on. 98 The seventh order, which is greater than all that have been mentioned: because they shall rejoice with boldness and shall be confident without confusion and shall be glad without fear, for they press forward to see the face of him whom they served in life and from whom they are to receive their reward when glorified. 99 This is the order of the souls of the righteous, as henceforth is announced,*k* and the previously mentioned are the ways of torment that those who would not give heed shall suffer hereafter."

100 Then I answered and said, "Will time therefore be given to the souls, after they have been separated from the bodies, to see what you have described to me?"

---

g 7.86 Cn: Meaning of Lat uncertain
h 7.87 Syr Ethiop: Meaning of Lat uncertain

i 7.88 Lat *the corruptible vessel*
j 7.89 Syr Ethiop: Meaning of Lat uncertain
k 7.99 Syr: Meaning of Lat uncertain

101 He said to me, "They shall have freedom for seven days, so that during these seven days they may see the things of which you have been told, and afterward they shall be gathered in their habitations."

No Intercession for the Ungodly

102 I answered and said, "If I have found favor in your sight, show further to me, your servant, whether on the day of judgment the righteous will be able to intercede for the ungodly or to entreat the Most High for them—103 fathers for sons or sons for parents, brothers for brothers, relatives for their kindred, or friends for those who are most dear."

104 He answered me and said, "Since you have found favor in my sight, I will show you this also. The day of judgment is decisive[^l] and displays to all the seal of truth. Just as now a father does not send his son, or a son his father, or a master his servant, or a friend his dearest friend, to be ill[^m] or sleep or eat or be healed in his place, 105 so no one shall ever pray for another on that day, neither shall anyone lay a burden on another,[^n] for then all shall bear their own righteousness and unrighteousness."

106 I answered and said, "How, then, do we find that first Abraham prayed for the people of Sodom, and Moses for our ancestors who sinned in the desert, 107 and Joshua after him for Israel in the days of Achan, 108 and Samuel in the days of Saul,[^o] and David for the plague, and Solomon for those at the dedication, 109 and Elijah for those who received the rain and for the one who was dead, that he might live, 110 and Hezekiah for the people in the days of Sennacherib, and many others prayed for many? 111 So if now, when corruption has increased and unrighteousness has multiplied, the righteous have prayed for the ungodly, why will it not be so then as well?"

112 He answered me and said, "This present world is not the end; the glory of God[^p] does not[^q] remain in it; therefore those who were strong prayed for the weak. 113 But the day of judgment will be the end of this age and the beginning[^r]

of the immortal age to come, in which corruption has passed away, 114 sinful indulgence has come to an end, unbelief has been cut off, and righteousness has increased, and truth has appeared. 115 Therefore no one will then be able to have mercy on someone who has been condemned in the judgment or to harm[^s] someone who is victorious."

Lamentation over the Fate of Most People

116 I answered and said, "This is my first and last comment: it would have been better if the earth had not produced Adam or else, when it had produced him, had restrained him from sinning. 117 For what good is it to all that they live in sorrow now and expect punishment after death? 118 O Adam, what have you done? For though it was you who sinned, the fall was not yours alone but ours also who are your descendants. 119 For what good is it to us, if an immortal time has been promised to us, but we have done deeds that bring death? 120 And what good is it that an everlasting hope has been promised to us, but we have miserably failed? 121 Or that safe and healthful habitations have been reserved for us, but we have lived wickedly? 122 Or that the glory of the Most High will defend those who have led a pure life, but we have walked in the most wicked ways? 123 Or that a paradise shall be revealed, whose fruit remains unspoiled and in which are abundance and healing, but we shall not enter it 124 because we have lived in perverse places? 125 Or that the faces of those who practiced self-control shall shine more than the stars, but our faces shall be blacker than darkness? 126 For while we lived and committed iniquity we did not consider what we should suffer after death."

127 He answered and said, "This is the significance of the contest that all who are born on earth shall wage: 128 if they are defeated they shall suffer what you have said, but if they are victorious they shall receive what I have said.[^t] 129 For this is the way of which Moses, while he was alive, spoke to the people, saying, 'Choose life for yourself, so that you may live!' 130 But they did not believe him or the prophets after him or even myself who have spoken to them. 131 Therefore there shall not be[^u] grief at their destruction so much as joy over those to whom salvation is assured."

[^l]: 7.104 Lat *bold*
[^m]: 7.104 Syr Ethiop Arm: Lat *to understand*
[^n]: 7.105 Syr Ethiop: Lat lacks *on that . . . another*
[^o]: 7.108 Syr Ethiop Arab 1: Lat Arab 2 Arm lack *in the days of Saul*
[^p]: 7.112 Syr Ethiop Georg: Lat lacks *of God*
[^q]: 7.112 Syr: Lat lacks *not*
[^r]: 7.113 Syr Ethiop: Lat lacks *the beginning*
[^s]: 7.115 Syr Ethiop: Lat *overwhelm*
[^t]: 7.128 Syr Ethiop Arab 1: Lat *what I say*
[^u]: 7.131 Syr: Lat *there was not*

Ezra Appeals to God's Mercy

132 I answered and said, "I know, O Lord, that the Most High is now called merciful because he has mercy on those who have not yet come into the world; 133 and gracious because he is gracious to those who turn in repentance to his law; 134 and patient because he shows patience toward those who have sinned, since they are his own creatures; 135 and bountiful because he would rather give than take away;[v] 136 and abundant in compassion because he makes his compassions abound more and more to those now living and to those who are gone and to those yet to come—137 for if he did not make them abound, the world with those who inhabit it would not have life—138 and he is called the giver because if he did not give out of his goodness so that those who have committed iniquities might be relieved of them, not one ten-thousandth of humankind could have life; 139 and the judge because if he did not pardon those who were created by his word and blot out the multitude of their sins,[w] 140 there would probably be left only very few of the innumerable multitude."

8 He answered me and said, "The Most High made this world for the sake of many but the world to come for the sake of only a few. 2 But I tell you a parable, Ezra. Just as, when you ask the earth, it will tell you that it provides a large amount of clay from which earthenware is made but only a little dust from which gold comes, so is the course of the present world. 3 Many have been created, but only a few shall be saved."

Ezra Again Appeals to God's Mercy

4 I answered and said, "Then drink your fill of[x] understanding, O my soul, and drink wisdom, O my heart. 5 For not of your own will did you come into the world,[y] and against your will you depart, for you have been given only a short time to live. 6 O Lord above us, grant to your servant that we may pray before you, and give us a seed for our heart and cultivation of our understanding so that fruit may be produced, by which every mortal who bears the likeness[z] of a human may be able to live. 7 For you alone exist, and we are a work of your hands, as you have declared. 8 And because you give life to the body that is now fashioned in the womb and furnish it with members, what you have created is preserved amid fire and water, and for nine months the womb[a] endures your creature that has been created in it. 9 But that which keeps and that which is kept shall both be kept by your keeping. And when the womb gives up again what has been created in it, 10 you have commanded that from the members themselves (that is, from the breasts) milk, the fruit of the breasts, should be supplied, 11 so that what has been fashioned may be nourished for a time, and afterward you will still guide it in your mercy. 12 You have nurtured it in your righteousness and instructed it in your law and reproved it in your wisdom. 13 You put it to death as your creation and make it live as your work. 14 If then you will suddenly and quickly[b] destroy what with so great labor was fashioned by your command, to what purpose was it made? 15 And now I will speak out: About all humankind you know best, but I will speak about your people, for whom I am grieved, 16 and about your inheritance, for whom I lament, and about Israel, for whom I am sad, and about the seed of Jacob, for whom I am troubled. 17 Therefore I will pray before you for myself and for them, for I see the failings of us who inhabit the earth, 18 and now also[c] I have heard of the swiftness of the judgment that is to come. 19 Therefore hear my voice and understand my words, and I will speak before you."

Ezra's Prayer

The beginning of the words of Ezra's prayer,[d] before he was taken up. He said: 20 "O Lord, you who inhabit eternity,[e] whose eyes[f] are exalted and whose upper chambers are in the air, 21 whose throne is beyond measure and whose glory is beyond comprehension, before whom the hosts of angels stand trembling 22 and at whose command they are changed to wind and fire,[g] whose word is sure and whose utterances are certain, whose command is strong and whose ordinance is terrible, 23 whose look dries up the depths and whose indignation makes

---

v 7.135 Or *he is ready to give according to requests*
w 7.139 Lat *contempts*
x 8.4 Syr: Lat *release*
y 8.5 Syr: Meaning of Lat uncertain
z 8.6 Syr: Lat *place*
a 8.8 Lat *what you have formed*
b 8.14 Syr: Lat *will with a light command*
c 8.18 Syr: Lat *but*
d 8.19 Syr Ethiop: Lat *beginning of Ezra's words*
e 8.20 Or *you who abide forever*
f 8.20 Another Lat text reads *heavens*
g 8.22 Syr: Lat *they whose service takes the form of wind and fire*

the mountains melt away, and whose truth is established[h] forever—24hear, O Lord, the prayer of your servant, and give ear to the petition of your creature; attend to my words. 25For as long as I live I will speak, and as long as I have understanding I will answer. 26O do not look on the sins of your people but on those who serve you in truth. 27Do not take note of the endeavors of those who act wickedly but of the endeavors of those who have kept your covenants amid afflictions. 28Do not think of those who have lived wickedly in your sight, but remember those who have willingly acknowledged that you are to be feared. 29Do not will the destruction of those who have the ways of cattle, but regard those who have gloriously taught your law.[i] 30Do not be angry with those who are deemed worse than wild animals, but love those who have always put their trust in your glory. 31For we and our ancestors have passed our lives in ways that bring death,[j] but it is because of us sinners that you are called merciful. 32For if you have desired to have pity on us, who have no works of righteousness, then you will be called merciful. 33For the righteous, who have many works laid up with you, shall receive their reward in consequence of their own deeds. 34But what are mortals that you are angry with them, or what is a corruptible race that you are so bitter against it? 35For in truth there is no one among those who have been born who has not acted wickedly; among those who have existed there is no one who has not done wrong. 36For in this, O Lord, your righteousness and goodness will be declared: when you are merciful to those who have no store of good works."

Response to Ezra's Prayer

37He answered me and said, "Some things you have spoken rightly, and it will turn out according to your words. 38For indeed I will not concern myself about the fashioning of those who have sinned or about their death, their judgment, or their destruction, 39but I will rejoice over the creation of the righteous, over their pilgrimage also, and their salvation, and their receiving their reward. 40As I have spoken, therefore, so it shall be.

41"For just as the farmer sows many seeds in the ground and plants a multitude of seedlings and yet not all that have been sown will come up[k] in due season and not all that were planted will take root, so also those who have been sown in the world will not all be saved."

42I answered and said, "If I have found favor in your sight, let me speak. 43If the farmer's seed does not come up because it has not received your rain in due season or if it has been ruined by too much rain, it perishes.[l] 44But people, who have been formed by your hands and are called your own image because they are made like you and for whose sake you have formed all things, have you also made them like the farmer's seed? 45Surely not, O Lord[m] above! But spare your people and have mercy on your inheritance, for you have mercy on your own creation."

Ezra's Final Appeal for Mercy

46He answered me and said, "Things that are present are for those who live now, and things that are future are for those who will live hereafter. 47For you come far short of being able to love my creation more than I love it. But you have often compared yourself[n] to the unrighteous. Never do so! 48But even in this respect you will be praiseworthy before the Most High, 49because you have humbled yourself, as is becoming for you, and have not considered yourself to be among the righteous. You will receive the greatest glory, 50for many miseries will affect those who inhabit the world in the last times because they have walked in great pride. 51But think of your own case, and inquire concerning the glory of those who are like yourself, 52because it is for you that paradise is opened, the tree of life is planted, the age to come is prepared, plenty is provided, a city is built, rest is appointed,[o] goodness is established, and wisdom is perfected beforehand. 53The root of evil[p] is sealed up from you, illness is banished from you, and death[q] is hidden; Hades has fled, and corruption has been forgotten;[r] 54sorrows have passed away, and in the end the treasure

---

k **8.41** Syr Ethiop *will live*; Lat *will be saved*
l **8.43** Cn: Compare Syr Arab 1 Arm Georg 2: Meaning of Lat uncertain
m **8.45** Ethiop Arab Compare Syr: Lat lacks *O Lord*
n **8.47** Syr Ethiop: Lat *brought yourself near*
o **8.52** Syr Ethiop: Lat *allowed*
p **8.53** Lat lacks *of evil*
q **8.53** Syr Ethiop Arm: Lat lacks *death*
r **8.53** Syr: Lat *Hades and corruption have fled into oblivion*; or *corruption has fled into Hades to be forgotten*

---

h **8.23** Arab 2: Lat *truth bears witness*
i **8.29** Syr *have received the brightness of your law*
j **8.31** Syr Ethiop: Meaning of Lat uncertain

of immortality is made manifest. ⁵⁵Therefore do not ask any more questions about the great number of those who perish. ⁵⁶For when they had opportunity to choose, they despised the Most High and were contemptuous of his law and abandoned his ways. ⁵⁷Moreover, they have even trampled on his righteous ones ⁵⁸and said in their hearts that there is no God—though they knew well that they must die. ⁵⁹For just as the things that I have predicted await^s you, so the thirst and torment that are prepared await them. For the Most High did not intend that anyone should be destroyed, ⁶⁰but those who were created have themselves defiled the name of him who made them and have been ungrateful to him who prepared life for them now. ⁶¹Therefore my judgment is now drawing near; ⁶²I have not shown this to all people but only to you and a few like you."

Then I answered and said, ⁶³"O Lord, you have already shown me a great number of the signs that you will do in the last times, but you have not shown me when you will do them."

More about the Signs of the End

9 He answered me and said, "Measure carefully in your mind, and when you see that some of the predicted signs have occurred, ²then you will know that it is the very time when the Most High is about to visit the world that he has made. ³So when there shall appear in the world earthquakes, tumult of peoples, intrigues of nations, wavering of leaders, confusion of princes, ⁴then you will know that it was of these that the Most High spoke from the days that were of old, from the beginning. ⁵For just as with everything that has occurred in the world, the beginning is evident^t and the end manifest; ⁶so also are the times of the Most High: the beginnings are manifest in wonders and mighty works and the end in penalties^u and in signs.

⁷"It shall be that all who will be saved and will be able to escape on account of their works or on account of the faith by which they have believed ⁸will survive the dangers that have been predicted and will see my salvation in my land and within my borders, which I have sanctified for myself from the beginning. ⁹Then

those who have now abused my ways shall be amazed, and those who have rejected them with contempt shall live in torments. ¹⁰For as many as did not acknowledge me in their lifetime, though they received my benefits, ¹¹and as many as scorned my law while they still had freedom ¹²and did not understand but despised it while an opportunity of repentance was still open to them, these must in torment acknowledge it^v after death. ¹³Therefore, do not continue to be curious about how the ungodly will be punished, but inquire how the righteous will be saved, those to whom the age belongs and for whose sake the age was made."^w

The Argument Recapitulated

14I answered and said, ¹⁵"I said before, and I say now and will say it again: there are more who perish than those who will be saved, ¹⁶as a wave is greater than a drop of water."

17He answered me and said, "As is the field, so is the seed, and as are the flowers, so are the colors, and as is the work, so is the product, and as is the farmer, so is the threshing floor. ¹⁸For there was a time in this age when I was preparing for those who now exist, before the world was made for them to live in, and no one opposed me then, for no one existed, ¹⁹but now those who have been created in this world, which is supplied both with an unfailing table and an inexhaustible pasture,^x have become corrupt in their ways. ²⁰So I considered my world and saw that it was lost. I saw that my earth was in peril because of the devices of those who^y had come into it. ²¹And I saw and spared some^z with great difficulty and saved for myself one grape out of a cluster and one plant out of a great forest.^a ²²So let the multitude perish that has been born in vain, but let my grape and my plant be saved, because with much labor I have perfected them.

23"Now, if you will let seven days more pass—do not, however, fast during them, ²⁴but go into a field of flowers where no house has been built, and eat only of the flowers of the field, and taste no meat and drink no wine but

---

s **8.59** Syr: Lat *will receive*
t **9.5** Syr: Ethiop *is in the word*; meaning of Lat uncertain
u **9.6** Syr: Lat Ethiop *in effects*

v **9.12** Or *me*
w **9.13** Syr: Lat *saved, and whose is the age and for whose sake the age was made and when*
x **9.19** Cn: Lat *law*
y **9.20** Cn: Lat *devices that*
z **9.21** Lat *them*
a **9.21** Syr Ethiop Arab 1: Lat *tribe*

eat only flowers—²⁵and pray to the Most High continually, then I will come and talk with you."

The Abiding Glory of the Mosaic Law

26 So I went, as he directed me, into the field that is called Ardat;*ᵇ* there I sat among the flowers and ate of the plants of the field, and the nourishment they afforded satisfied me. ²⁷After seven days, while I lay on the grass, my heart was troubled again as it was before. ²⁸Then my mouth was opened, and I began to speak before the Most High and said, ²⁹"O Lord, you showed yourself among us to our ancestors in the wilderness when they came out from Egypt and when they came into the untrodden and unfruitful wilderness, ³⁰and you said, 'Hear me, O Israel, and give heed to my words, O descendants of Jacob. ³¹For I sow my law in you, and it shall bring forth fruit in you, and you shall be glorified through it forever.' ³²But though our ancestors received the law, they did not keep it and did not observe the*ᶜ* statutes, yet the fruit of the law did not perish, for it could not, because it was yours. ³³Yet those who received it perished because they did not keep what had been sown in them. ³⁴Now this is the general rule, that when the ground has received seed or the sea a ship or any dish food or drink, and when it comes about that what was sown or what was launched or what was put in is destroyed, ³⁵they are destroyed, but the things that held them remain, yet with us it has not been so. ³⁶For we who have received the law and sinned will perish, as well as our hearts that received it; ³⁷the law, however, does not perish but survives in its glory."

The Vision of a Weeping Woman

38 When I said these things in my heart, I looked around,*ᵈ* and on my right I saw a woman; she was mourning and weeping with a loud voice and was deeply grieved at heart; her clothes were torn, and there were ashes on her head. ³⁹Then I dismissed the thoughts with which I had been engaged and turned to her ⁴⁰and said to her, "Why are you weeping, and why are you grieved at heart?"

41 She said to me, "Let me alone, my lord, so that I may weep for myself and continue to mourn, for I am greatly embittered in spirit and deeply distressed."

42 I said to her, "What has happened to you? Tell me."

43 And she said to me, "Your servant was barren and had no child, though I lived with my husband for thirty years. ⁴⁴Every hour and every day during those thirty years I prayed to the Most High, night and day. ⁴⁵And after thirty years God heard your servant and looked upon my low estate and considered my distress and gave me a son. I rejoiced greatly over him, I and my husband and all my neighbors,*ᵉ* and we gave great glory to the Mighty One. ⁴⁶And I brought him up with much care. ⁴⁷So when he grew up and I came to take a wife for him, I set a day for the marriage feast.

10 "But it happened that, when my son entered his wedding chamber, he fell down and died. ²So all of us put out our lamps, and all my neighbors*ᶠ* attempted to console me; I remained quiet until the evening of the second day. ³But when all of them had stopped consoling me, encouraging me to be quiet, I got up in the night and fled, and I came to this field, as you see. ⁴And now I intend not to return to the town but to stay here; I will neither eat nor drink but will mourn and fast continually until I die."

5 Then I broke off the reflections with which I was still engaged and answered her in anger and said, ⁶"You most foolish of women, do you not see our mourning and what has happened to us? ⁷For Zion, the mother of us all, is in deep grief and great distress. ⁸It is most appropriate to mourn now, because we are all mourning, and to be sorrowful, because we are all sorrowing; you are sorrowing for one son.*ᵍ* ⁹Now ask the earth, and she will tell you that it is she who ought to mourn over so many who have come into being upon her. ¹⁰From the beginning all have been born of her, and others will come, and, behold, almost all walk to perdition, and a multitude of them will come to doom. ¹¹Who, then, ought to mourn the more: she who lost so great a multitude or you who are grieving for one alone? ¹²But if you say to me, 'My lamentation is not like the earth's, for I have lost the fruit of my womb, which I brought forth in pain and bore in sorrow, ¹³but it is with the earth

---

ᵇ **9.26** Syr Ethiop *Arpad*; Arm *Ardab*
ᶜ **9.32** Lat *my*
ᵈ **9.38** Syr Arab Arm: Lat *I looked about me with my eyes*

ᵉ **9.45** Lat *all my fellow citizens*
ᶠ **10.2** Lat *all my fellow citizens*
ᵍ **10.8** Syr adds *but we, the whole world, for our mother*

according to the way of the earth: the multitude that is now in it goes as it came,' [14] then I say to you, 'Just as you brought forth in sorrow, so the earth also has from the beginning given her fruit, that is, humankind, to him who made her.' [15] Now, therefore, keep your sorrow to yourself, and bear bravely the troubles that have come upon you. [16] For if you acknowledge the decree of God to be just, you will receive your son back in due time and will be praised among women. [17] Therefore go into the town to your husband."

[18] She said to me, "I will not do so; I will not go into the city, but I will die here."

[19] So I spoke again to her and said, [20] "Do not do that, but let yourself be persuaded—for how many are the adversities of Zion?—and be consoled because of the sorrow of Jerusalem. [21] For you see how our sanctuary has been laid waste, our altar thrown down, our temple destroyed; [22] our harp has been laid low, our song has been silenced, and our rejoicing has been ended; the light of our lampstand has been put out, the ark of our covenant has been plundered, our holy things have been polluted, and the name by which we are called has been almost profaned; our children[h] have suffered abuse, our priests have been burned to death, our Levites have gone into exile, our virgins have been defiled, and our wives have been ravished; our righteous men[i] have been carried off, our little ones have been cast out, our young men have been enslaved and our strong men made powerless. [23] And, worst of all, the seal of Zion has been deprived of its glory and given over into the hands of those who hate us. [24] Therefore shake off your great sadness and lay aside your many sorrows, so that the Mighty One may be merciful to you again and the Most High may give you rest, a respite from your troubles."

[25] While I was talking to her, her face suddenly began to shine exceedingly; her countenance flashed like lightning, so that I was too frightened to approach her, and my heart was terrified. While[j] I was wondering what this meant, [26] she suddenly uttered a loud and fearful cry so that the earth shook at the sound. [27] When I looked up, the woman was no longer visible to me, but a city was being built,[k] and a place of huge foundations showed itself. I was afraid and cried with a loud voice and said, [28] "Where is the angel Uriel, who came to me at first? For it was he who brought me into this overpowering bewilderment; my end has become corruption and my prayer a reproach."

Uriel's Interpretation of the Vision

[29] While I was speaking these words, the angel who had come to me at first came to me, and when he saw me [30] lying there like a corpse, deprived of my understanding, he grasped my right hand and strengthened me and set me on my feet and said to me, [31] "What is the matter with you? And why are you troubled? And why are your understanding and the thoughts of your mind troubled?"

[32] I said, "It was because you abandoned me. I did as you directed and went out into the field, and behold, what I have seen and can still see, I am unable to explain."

[33] He said to me, "Stand up like a man, and I will instruct you."

[34] I said, "Speak, my lord; only do not forsake me, so that I may not die before my time.[l] [35] For I have seen what I did not know, and I hear[m] what I do not understand [36] —or is my mind deceived and my soul dreaming? [37] Now therefore I beg you to give your servant an explanation of this bewildering vision."

[38] He answered me and said, "Listen to me, and I will teach you and tell you about the things that you fear, for the Most High has revealed many secrets to you. [39] He has seen your righteous conduct and that you have sorrowed continually for your people and mourned greatly over Zion. [40] This therefore is the meaning of the vision. [41] The woman who appeared to you a little while ago, whom you saw mourning and whom you began to console [42] (you do not now see the form of a woman, but there appeared to you a city being built)[n] [43] and who told you about the misfortune of her son—this is the interpretation: [44] The woman whom you saw is Zion, which you now behold as a city being built.[o] [45] And as for her telling you that she was barren for thirty years, the reason is that there were three thousand[p] years in the world before

---

h 10.22 Ethiop *free men*
i 10.22 Syr *our seers*
j 10.25 Syr Ethiop Arab 1: Lat lacks *I was too . . . terrified. While*
k 10.27 Lat: Syr Ethiop Arab 1 Arab 2 Arm *but there was an established city*

l 10.34 Syr Ethiop Arab: Lat *die to no purpose*
m 10.35 Other ancient authorities read *have heard*
n 10.42 Lat: Syr Ethiop Arab 1 Arab 2 Arm *an established city*
o 10.44 Cn: Lat *an established city*
p 10.45 Syr Ethiop Arab 1 Arab 2: Most Lat mss read *three*

any offering was offered in it.*q* *46*And after three thousand*r* years Solomon built the city and offered offerings; then it was that the barren woman bore a son. *47*And as for her telling you that she brought him up with much care, that was the period of residence in Jerusalem. *48*And as for her saying to you, 'My son died as he entered his wedding chamber,' and that misfortune had overtaken her,*s* this was the destruction that befell Jerusalem. *49*So you saw her likeness, how she mourned for her son, and you began to console her for what had happened.*t* *50*For now the Most High, seeing that you are sincerely grieved and profoundly distressed for her, has shown you the brilliance of her glory and the loveliness of her beauty. *51*Therefore I told you to remain in the field where no house had been built, *52*for I knew that the Most High would reveal these things to you. *53*Therefore I told you to go into the field where there was no foundation of any building, *54*because no work of human construction could endure in a place where the city of the Most High was to be revealed.

55 "Therefore do not be afraid, and do not let your heart be terrified, but go in and see the splendor or*u* the vastness of the building, as far as it is possible for your eyes to see it, *56*and afterward you will hear as much as your ears can hear. *57*For you are more blessed than many, and you have been called to be with*v* the Most High as few have been. *58*But tomorrow night you shall remain here, *59*and the Most High will show you in those dream visions what the Most High will do to those who inhabit the earth in the last days."

So I slept that night and the following one, as he had told me.

The Vision of the Eagle

11 On the second night I had a dream: I saw rising from the sea an eagle that had twelve feathered wings and three heads. *2*I saw it spread its wings over*w* the whole earth, and all the winds of heaven blew upon it, and the clouds were gathered around it.*x* *3*I saw that out of its wings there grew opposing wings, but they became little, puny wings. *4*But its heads were at rest; the middle head was larger than the other heads, but it, too, was at rest with them. *5*Then I saw that the eagle flew with its wings, and it reigned over the earth and over those who inhabit it. *6*And I saw how all things under heaven were subjected to it, and no one spoke against it—not a single creature that was on the earth. *7*Then I saw the eagle rise upon its talons, and it uttered a cry to its wings, saying, *8*"Do not all watch at the same time; let each sleep in its own place, and watch in its turn, *9*but let the heads be reserved for the last."

*10*I looked again and saw that the voice did not come from its heads but from the middle of its body. *11*I counted its rival wings, and there were eight of them. *12*As I watched, one wing on the right side rose up, and it reigned over all the earth. *13*And after a time its reign came to an end, and it disappeared, so that even its place was no longer visible. Then the next wing rose up and reigned, and it continued to reign a long time. *14*While it was reigning its end came also, so that it disappeared like the first. *15*And a voice sounded, saying to it, *16*"Listen to me, you who have ruled the earth all this time; I announce this to you before you disappear. *17*After you no one shall rule as long as you have ruled, not even half as long."

*18*Then the third wing raised itself up and held the rule as the earlier ones had done, and it also disappeared. *19*And so it went with all the wings; they wielded power one after another and then were never seen again. *20*I kept looking, and in due time the wings that followed*y* also rose up on the right*z* side, in order to rule. There were some of them that ruled, yet disappeared suddenly, *21*and others of them rose up but did not hold the rule.

*22*And after this I looked and saw that the twelve wings and the two little wings had disappeared, *23*and nothing remained on the eagle's body except the three heads that were at rest and six little wings.

*24*As I kept looking I saw that two little wings separated from the six and remained under the head that was on the right side, but four remained in their place. *25*Then I saw that these little wings*a* planned to set themselves up and

---

q 10.45 Cn: Lat Syr Arab Arm *her*
r 10.46 Syr Ethiop Arab 1 Arm: Lat *three*
s 10.48 Or *him*
t 10.49 Lat mss Syr Ethiop Arab 1: Most Lat mss add *These were the things to be opened to you*
u 10.55 Other ancient authorities read *and*
v 10.57 Or *been named by*
w 11.2 Arab 2 Arm: Lat Syr Ethiop *in*
x 11.2 Syr: Compare Ethiop Arab: Lat lacks *the clouds* and *around it*

y 11.20 Syr Arab 2 *the little wings*
z 11.20 Some Ethiop mss read *left*
a 11.25 Syr: Lat *underwings*

hold the rule. [26] As I kept looking, one was set up but suddenly disappeared; [27] a second also, and this disappeared more quickly than the first. [28] While I continued to look, the two that remained were planning between themselves to reign together; [29] and while they were planning, one of the heads at rest (the one that was in the middle) suddenly awoke; it was greater than the other two heads. [30] And I saw how it allied the two heads with itself [31] and how the head turned with those that were with it and devoured the two little wings*b* that were planning to reign. [32] Moreover, this head gained control of the whole earth and with much oppression dominated its inhabitants; it had greater power over the world than all the wings that had gone before.

[33] After this I looked again and saw the head in the middle suddenly disappear, just as the wings had done. [34] But the two heads remained, which also in like manner ruled over the earth and its inhabitants. [35] And while I looked, I saw the head on the right side devour the one on the left.

A Lion Roused from the Forest

[36] Then I heard a voice saying to me, "Look in front of you and consider what you see." [37] When I looked, I saw what seemed to be a lion roused from the forest, roaring, and I heard how it uttered a human voice to the eagle and spoke, saying, [38] "Listen, and I will speak to you. The Most High says to you, [39] 'Are you not the one that remains of the four beasts that I had made to reign in my world, so that the end of my times might come through them? [40] You, the fourth that has come, have conquered all the beasts that have gone before, and you have held sway over the world with great terror and over all the earth with grievous oppression, and for so long you have lived on the earth with deceit.*c* [41] You have judged the earth but not with truth, [42] for you have oppressed the meek and injured the peaceable; you have hated those who tell the truth and have loved liars; you have destroyed the homes of those who brought forth fruit and have laid low the walls of those who did you no harm. [43] Your insolence has come up before the Most High and your pride to the Mighty

One. [44] The Most High has looked at his times; now they have ended, and his ages have reached completion. [45] Therefore you, eagle, will surely disappear, you and your terrifying wings, your most evil little wings, your malicious heads, your most evil talons, and your whole worthless body, [46] so that the whole earth, freed from your violence, may be refreshed and relieved and may hope for the judgment and mercy of him who made it.' "

12 While the lion was saying these words to the eagle, I looked [2] and saw that the remaining head had disappeared. The two wings that had gone over to it rose up and*d* set themselves up to reign, and their reign was brief and full of tumult. [3] When I looked again, they were already vanishing. The whole body of the eagle was burned, and the earth was exceedingly terrified.

Then I woke up in great perplexity of mind and great fear, and I said to my spirit, [4] "You have brought this upon me because you search out the ways of the Most High. [5] I am still weary in mind and very weak in my spirit, and not even a little strength is left in me because of the great fear with which I have been terrified tonight. [6] Therefore I will now entreat the Most High that he may strengthen me to the end."

The Interpretation of the Vision

[7] Then I said, "O sovereign Lord, if I have found favor in your sight, and if I have been accounted righteous before you beyond many others, and if my prayer has indeed come up before your face, [8] strengthen me and show me, your servant, the interpretation and meaning of this terrifying vision so that you may fully comfort my soul. [9] For you have judged me worthy to be shown the end of the times and the last events of the times."

[10] He said to me, "This is the interpretation of this vision that you have seen: [11] The eagle that you saw coming up from the sea is the fourth kingdom that appeared in a vision to your brother Daniel. [12] But it was not explained to him as I now explain to you or have explained it. [13] The days are coming when a kingdom shall rise on earth, and it shall be more terrifying than all the kingdoms that have been before it. [14] And twelve kings shall reign in it, one after another. [15] But the second that is to reign shall hold sway for a longer time than any other one

---

b 11.31 Syr: Lat *underwings*

c 11.40 Syr Arab Arm: Lat Ethiop *The fourth came, however, and conquered . . . and held sway . . . and for so long lived*

d 12.2 Ethiop: Lat lacks *rose up and*

of the twelve. ¹⁶ This is the interpretation of the twelve wings that you saw.

¹⁷ "As for your hearing a voice that spoke, coming not from the eagle's*e* heads but from the midst of its body, ¹⁸ this is the interpretation: In the midst of*f* the time of that kingdom great struggles shall arise, and it shall be in danger of falling; nevertheless, it shall not fall then but shall regain its former power.*g* ¹⁹ As for your seeing eight little wings*h* clinging to its wings, this is the interpretation: ²⁰ Eight kings shall arise in it whose times shall be short and their years swift; ²¹ two of them shall perish when the middle of its time draws near, and four shall be kept for the time when its end approaches, but two shall be kept until the end.

²² "As for your seeing three heads at rest, this is the interpretation: ²³ In its last days the Most High will raise up three kings,*i* and they*j* shall renew many things in it and shall rule the earth ²⁴ and its inhabitants more oppressively than all who were before them. Therefore they are called the heads of the eagle, ²⁵ because it is they who shall sum up his wickedness and perform his last actions. ²⁶ As for your seeing that the large head disappeared, one of the kings*k* shall die in his bed but in agonies. ²⁷ But as for the two who remained, the sword shall devour them. ²⁸ For the sword of one shall devour him who was with him, but he also shall fall by the sword in the last days.

²⁹ "As for your seeing two little wings*l* passing over to*m* the head that was on the right side, ³⁰ this is the interpretation: It is these whom the Most High has kept for the eagle's*n* end; this was the reign that was brief and full of tumult, as you have seen.

³¹ "And as for the lion whom you saw rousing up out of the forest and roaring and speaking to the eagle and reproving him for his unrighteousness, and as for all his words that you have heard, ³² this is the Messiah whom the Most High has kept until the end of days, who will arise from the offspring of David and will come

and speak*o* with them. He will denounce them for their ungodliness and for their wickedness and will display before them their contemptuous dealings. ³³ For first he will bring them alive before his judgment seat, and when he has reproved them, then he will destroy them. ³⁴ But in mercy he will set free the remnant of my people, those who have been saved throughout my borders, and he will make them joyful until the end comes, the day of judgment, of which I spoke to you at the beginning. ³⁵ This is the dream that you saw, and this is its interpretation. ³⁶ And you alone were worthy to learn this secret of the Most High. ³⁷ Therefore write all these things that you have seen in a book, put it*p* in a hidden place, ³⁸ and you shall teach them to the wise among your people, whose hearts you know are able to comprehend and keep these secrets. ³⁹ But as for you, wait here seven days more, so that you may be shown whatever it pleases the Most High to show you." Then he left me.

The People Come to Ezra

⁴⁰ When all the people heard that the seven days were past and I had not returned to the city, they all gathered together, from the least to the greatest, and came to me and spoke to me, saying, ⁴¹ "How have we offended you, and what harm have we done you, that you have forsaken us and sit in this place? ⁴² For of all the prophets you alone are left to us, like a cluster of grapes from the vintage and like a lamp in a dark place and like a haven for a ship saved from a storm. ⁴³ Are not the disasters that have befallen us enough? ⁴⁴ Therefore if you forsake us, how much better it would have been for us if we also had been consumed in the burning of Zion. ⁴⁵ For we are no better than those who died there." And they wept with a loud voice.

Then I answered them and said, ⁴⁶ "Take courage, O Israel, and do not be sorrowful, O house of Jacob, ⁴⁷ for the Most High has you in remembrance, and the Mighty One has not forgotten you in your struggle. ⁴⁸ As for me, I have neither forsaken you nor withdrawn from you, but I have come to this place to pray on account of the desolation of Zion and to seek mercy on account of the humiliation of our*q* sanctuary. ⁴⁹ Now go to your homes, every one

---

e 12.17 Lat *his*

f 12.18 Syr Arm: Lat *After*

g 12.18 Ethiop Arab 1 Arm: Lat Syr *its beginning*

h 12.19 Syr: Lat *underwings*

i 12.23 Syr Ethiop Arab Arm: Lat *kingdoms*

j 12.23 Syr Ethiop Arm: Lat *he*

k 12.26 Lat *them*

l 12.29 Arab 1: Lat *underwings*

m 12.29 Syr Ethiop: Lat lacks *to*

n 12.30 Lat *his*

---

o 12.32 Syr: Lat lacks *of days . . . and speak*

p 12.37 Ethiop Arab 1 Arab 2 Arm: Lat Syr *them*

q 12.48 Syr Ethiop: Lat *your*

of you, and after these days I will come to you." ⁵⁰So the people went into the city, as I told them to do. ⁵¹But I sat in the field seven days, as the angel^r had commanded me, and I ate only of the flowers of the field, and plants were my food plants during those days.

The Man from the Sea

13 After seven days I dreamed a dream in the night. ²And behold, a wind arose from the sea and stirred up^s all its waves. ³As I kept looking the wind made something like the figure of a man come up out of the heart of the sea. And I saw^t that this man flew^u with the clouds of heaven, and wherever he turned his face to look, everything under his gaze trembled, ⁴and whenever his voice issued from his mouth, all who heard his voice melted as wax melts when it feels the fire.

⁵After this I looked and saw that an innumerable multitude of people were gathered together from the four winds of heaven to make war against the man who came up out of the sea. ⁶And I looked and saw that he carved out for himself a great mountain and flew up on to it. ⁷And I tried to see the region or place from which the mountain was carved, but I could not.

⁸After this I looked and saw that all who had gathered together against him to wage war with him were filled with fear, yet they dared to fight. ⁹When he saw the onrush of the approaching multitude, he neither lifted his hand nor held a spear or any weapon of war, ¹⁰but I saw only how he sent forth from his mouth something like a stream of fire and from his lips a flaming breath and from his tongue he shot forth a storm of sparks. All these were mingled together, the stream of fire and the flaming breath and the great storm, ¹¹and fell on the onrushing multitude that was prepared to fight and burned up all of them, so that suddenly nothing was seen of the innumerable multitude but only the dust of ashes and the smell of smoke. When I saw it, I was amazed.

¹²After this I saw the same man come down from the mountain and call to himself another multitude that was peaceable. ¹³Then the forms of many people appeared to him, some of whom

were joyful and some sorrowful; some of them were bound, and some were bringing others as offerings.

The Interpretation of the Vision

Then I woke up in great terror and prayed to the Most High and said, ¹⁴"From the beginning you have shown your servant these wonders and have deemed me worthy to have my prayer heard by you; ¹⁵now show me the interpretation of this dream also. ¹⁶For as I consider it in my mind, alas for those who will be left in those days! And still more, alas for those who are not left! ¹⁷For those who are not left will be sad ¹⁸because they understand the things that are reserved for the last days but cannot attain them. ¹⁹But alas for those also who are left and for that very reason! For they shall see great dangers and much distress, as these dreams show. ²⁰Yet it is better^v to come into these things,^w though incurring peril, than to pass from the world like a cloud and not to see what will happen in the last days."

He answered me and said, ²¹"I will tell you the interpretation of the vision, and I will also explain to you the things that you have mentioned. ²²As for what you said about those who survive, and concerning those who do not survive,^x this is the interpretation: ²³The one who brings the peril at that time will protect those who fall into peril, who have works and faith toward the Almighty. ²⁴Understand, therefore, that those who are left are more blessed than those who have died.

²⁵"This is the interpretation of the vision: As for your seeing a man come up from the heart of the sea, ²⁶this is he whom the Most High has been keeping for many ages, who will himself deliver his creation, and he will direct those who are left. ²⁷And as for your seeing wind and fire and a storm coming out of his mouth ²⁸and as for his not holding a spear or weapon of war, yet destroying the onrushing multitude that came to conquer him, this is the interpretation: ²⁹The days are coming when the Most High will deliver those who are on the earth. ³⁰And bewilderment of mind shall come over those who inhabit the earth. ³¹They shall plan to make war against one another, city against city, place against place, people against people, and

---

r 12.51 Lat *he*

s 13.2 Other ancient authorities read *I saw a wind arise from the sea and stir up*

t 13.3 Syr: Lat lacks *the wind . . . I saw*

u 13.3 Syr Ethiop Arab Arm: Lat *grew strong*

---

v 13.20 Ethiop Compare Arab 2: Lat *easier*

w 13.20 Syr: Lat *this*

x 13.22 Syr Arab 1: Lat lacks *and . . . not survive*

kingdom against kingdom. ³²When these things take place and the signs occur that I showed you before, then my Son will be revealed, whom you saw as a man coming up from the sea.*y*

33 "Then, when all the nations hear his voice, all the nations shall leave their own lands and the warfare that they have against one another, ³⁴and an innumerable multitude shall be gathered together, as you saw, wishing to come and conquer him. ³⁵But he shall stand on the top of Mount Zion. ³⁶And Zion shall come and be made manifest to all people, prepared and built, as you saw the mountain carved out without hands. ³⁷Then he, my Son, will reprove the assembled nations for their ungodliness (this was symbolized by the storm) ³⁸and will reproach them to their face with their evil thoughts and the torments with which they are to be tortured (which were symbolized by the flames) and will destroy them without effort by means of the law*z* (which was symbolized by the fire).

39 "And as for your seeing him gather to himself another multitude that was peaceable, ⁴⁰these are the nine*a* tribes that were taken away from their own land into exile in the days of King Hoshea, whom Shalmaneser, king of the Assyrians, made captives; he took them across the river, and they were taken into another land. ⁴¹But they formed this plan for themselves, that they would leave the multitude of the nations and go to a more distant region where no humans had ever lived, ⁴²so that there at least they might keep their statutes that they had not kept in their own land. ⁴³And they went in by the narrow passages of the River Euphrates. ⁴⁴For at that time the Most High performed signs for them and stopped the channels of the river until they had crossed over. ⁴⁵Through that region there was a long way to go, a journey of a year and a half, and that country is called Arzareth.

46 "Then they lived there until the last times, and now, when they are about to come again, ⁴⁷the Most High will stop*b* the channels of the river again, so that they may be able to cross over. Therefore you saw the multitude gathered together in peace. ⁴⁸But those who are left of your people, who are found within my holy borders, shall be saved.*c* ⁴⁹Therefore when he

destroys the multitude of the nations that are gathered together, he will defend the people who remain. ⁵⁰And then he will show them very many wonders."

51 I said, "O sovereign Lord, explain this to me: Why did I see the man coming up from the heart of the sea?"

52 He said to me, "Just as no one can explore or know what is in the depths of the sea, so no one on earth can see my Son or those who are with him, except in the time of his day.*d* ⁵³This is the interpretation of the dream that you saw. And you alone have been enlightened about this, ⁵⁴because you have forsaken your own ways and have applied yourself to mine and have searched out my law, ⁵⁵for you have devoted your life to wisdom and called understanding your mother. ⁵⁶Therefore I have shown you these things, for there is a reward laid up with the Most High. For it will be that after three more days I will tell you other things and explain weighty and wondrous matters to you."

57 Then I got up and walked in the field, giving great glory and praise to the Most High for the wonders that he did from time to time ⁵⁸and because he governs the times and whatever things come to pass in their seasons. And I stayed there three days.

The Lord Commissions Ezra

14 On the third day, while I was sitting under an oak, suddenly a voice came out of a bush opposite me and said, "Ezra, Ezra!" ²And I answered, "Here I am, Lord," and I rose to my feet. ³Then he said to me, "I revealed myself in a bush and spoke to Moses when my people were in bondage in Egypt, ⁴and I sent him and led*e* my people out of Egypt, and I led him up on Mount Sinai, where I kept him with me many days. ⁵I told him many wondrous things and showed him the secrets of the times and declared to him*f* the end of the times. Then I commanded him, saying, ⁶'These words you shall publish openly, and these you shall keep secret.' ⁷And now I say to you: ⁸Lay up in your heart the signs that I have shown you, the dreams that you have seen, and the interpretations that you have heard, ⁹for you shall be taken up from among humankind,

---

y 13.32 Syr and most Lat mss lack *from the sea*

z 13.38 Syr: Lat *effort and the law*

a 13.40 Other Lat mss *ten*; Syr Ethiop Arab 1 Arm *nine and a half*

b 13.47 Syr: Lat *stops*

c 13.48 Syr: Lat lacks *shall be saved*

d 13.52 Syr: Ethiop *except when his time and his day have come*; Lat lacks *his*

e 14.4 Syr Arab 1 Arab 2 *he led*

f 14.5 Syr Ethiop Arab Arm: Lat lacks *declared to him*

and henceforth you shall live with my Son and with those who are like you, until the times are ended. [10] The age has lost its youth, and the times begin to grow old. [11] For the age is divided into twelve parts, and nine[g] of its parts have already passed, [12] as well as half of the tenth part; so two of its parts remain, besides half of the tenth part.[h] [13] Now, therefore, set your house in order, and reprove your people; comfort the lowly among them, and instruct those who are wise.[i] And now renounce the life that is corruptible, [14] and put away from you mortal thoughts; cast away from you the burdens of humankind, and divest yourself now of your weak nature; [15] lay to one side the thoughts that are most grievous to you, and hurry to escape from these times. [16] For evils worse than those that you have now seen happen shall take place hereafter. [17] For the weaker the world becomes through old age, the more shall evils be increased upon its inhabitants. [18] Truth shall go farther away, and falsehood shall come near. For the eagle[j] that you saw in the vision is already hurrying to come."

Ezra's Concern to Restore the Scriptures

[19] Then I answered and said, "Let me speak[k] in your presence, Lord. [20] For I will go, as you have commanded me, and I will reprove the people who are now living, but who will warn those who will be born hereafter? For the world lies in darkness, and its inhabitants are without light. [21] For your law has been burned, so no one knows the things that have been done or will be done by you. [22] If then I have found favor with you, send the holy spirit into me, and I will write everything that has happened in the world from the beginning, the things that were written in your law, so that people may be able to find the path and that those who want to live in the last days may do so."

[23] He answered me and said, "Go and gather the people, and tell them not to seek you for forty days. [24] But prepare for yourself many writing tablets, and take with you Sarea, Dabria, Selemia, Ethanus, and Asiel—these five, who are trained to write rapidly, [25] and you

shall come here, and I will light in your heart the lamp of understanding, which shall not be put out until what you are about to write is finished. [26] And when you have finished, some things you shall make public, and some you shall deliver in secret to the wise; tomorrow at this hour you shall begin to write."

Ezra's Last Words to the People

[27] Then I went as he commanded me, and I gathered all the people together and said, [28] "Hear these words, O Israel. [29] At first our ancestors lived as aliens in Egypt, and they were liberated from there [30] and received the law of life, which they did not keep, which you also have transgressed after them. [31] Then land was given to you for a possession in the land of Zion, but you and your ancestors committed iniquity and did not keep the ways that the Most High commanded you. [32] And since he is a righteous judge, in due time he took from you what he had given. [33] And now you are here, and your people[l] are farther in the interior.[m] [34] If you, then, will rule over your minds and discipline your hearts, you shall be kept alive, and after death you shall obtain mercy. [35] For after death the judgment will come, when we shall live again, and then the names of the righteous shall become manifest, and the deeds of the ungodly shall be disclosed. [36] But let no one come to me now, and let no one seek me for forty days."

The Restoration of the Scriptures

[37] So I took the five men, as he had commanded me, and we proceeded to the field and remained there. [38] And on the next day a voice called me, saying, "Ezra, open your mouth and drink what I give you to drink." [39] So I opened my mouth, and a full cup was offered to me; it was full of something like water, but its color was like fire. [40] I took it and drank, and when I had drunk it, my heart poured forth understanding, and wisdom increased in my breast, for my spirit retained its memory, [41] and my mouth was opened and was no longer closed. [42] Moreover, the Most High gave understanding to the five men, and by turns they wrote what was dictated, using characters that they did not know.[n] They sat forty days; they wrote during

---

g 14.11 Cn: Lat Ethiop *ten*
h 14.12 Syr lacks 14.11, 12: Ethiop *For the world is divided into ten parts, and has come to the tenth, and half of the tenth remains. Now . . .*
i 14.13 Lat lacks *and . . . wise*
j 14.18 Syr Ethiop Arab Arm: Meaning of Lat uncertain
k 14.19 Most Lat mss lack *Let me speak*

l 14.33 Lat *brothers*
m 14.33 Syr Ethiop Arm: Lat *are among you*
n 14.42 Syr Compare Ethiop Arab 2 Arm: Meaning of Lat uncertain

the daytime and ate their bread at night. [43]But as for me, I spoke in the daytime and was not silent at night. [44]So during the forty days, ninety-four[o] books were written. [45]And when the forty days were ended, the Most High spoke to me, saying, "Make public the twenty-four[p] books that you wrote first, and let the worthy and the unworthy read them, [46]but keep the seventy that were written last, in order to give them to the wise among your people. [47]For in them is the spring of understanding, the fountain of wisdom, and the river of knowledge." [48]And I did so.[q]

Vengeance on the Wicked

15[r] Speak in the ears of my people the words of the prophecy that I will put in your mouth, says the Lord, [2]and cause them to be written on paper, for they are trustworthy and true. [3]Do not fear the plots against you, and do not be troubled by the unbelief of those who oppose you. [4]For all unbelievers shall die in their unbelief.[s]

[5]Beware, says the Lord, I am bringing evils upon the world, the sword and famine, death and destruction, [6]because iniquity has spread throughout every land, and their harmful doings have reached their limit. [7]Therefore, says the Lord, [8]I will be silent no longer concerning their ungodly acts that they impiously commit, neither will I tolerate their wicked practices. Innocent and righteous blood cries out to me, and the souls of the righteous cry out continually. [9]I will surely avenge them, says the Lord, and will receive to myself all the innocent blood from among them. [10]See, my people are being led like a flock to the slaughter; I will not allow them to live any longer in the land of Egypt, [11]but I will bring them out with a mighty hand and with an uplifted arm and

will strike Egypt with plagues, as before, and will destroy all its land.

[12]Let Egypt mourn and its foundations, because of the plague of chastisement and castigation that the Lord will bring upon it. [13]Let the farmers that who the ground mourn because their seed shall fail to grow[t] and their trees shall be ruined by blight and hail and by a terrible tempest. [14]Alas for the world and for those who live in it! [15]For the sword and misery draw near them, and nation shall rise up to fight against nation, with swords in their hands. [16]For there shall be unrest among people; growing strong against one another, they shall in their might have no respect for their king or the chief of their leaders. [17]For a person will desire to go into a city and shall not be able to do so. [18]Because of their pride the cities shall be in confusion, the houses shall be destroyed, and people shall be afraid. [19]People shall have no pity for their neighbors but shall make an assault upon[u] their houses with the sword and plunder their goods because of hunger for bread and because of great tribulation.

[20]See how I am calling together all the kings of the earth to turn to me, says God, from the rising sun and from the south, from the east and from Lebanon, to turn and repay what they have given them. [21]Just as they have done to my elect until this day, so I will do and will pay it back into their laps. Thus says the Lord God: [22]My right hand will not spare the sinners, and my sword will not cease from those who shed innocent blood on earth. [23]And a fire went forth from his wrath and consumed the foundations of the earth and the sinners, like burnt straw. [24]Alas for those who sin and do not observe my commandments, says the Lord;[v] [25]I will not spare them. Depart, you faithless children! Do not pollute my sanctuary. [26]For God[w] knows all who sin against him; therefore he will hand them over to death and slaughter. [27]Already calamities have come upon the whole earth, and you shall remain in them; God[x] will not deliver you, because you have sinned against him.

A Terrifying Vision of Warfare

[28]What a terrifying sight, appearing from the east! [29]The nations of the dragons of Arabia

---

o 14.44 Syr Ethiop Arab 1 Arm: Meaning of Lat uncertain

p 14.45 Syr Arab 1: Lat lacks *twenty-four*

q 14.48 Syr adds *in the seventh year of the sixth week, five thousand years and three months and twelve days after creation. At that time Ezra was caught up, and taken to the place of those who are like him, after he had written all these things. And he was called the scribe of the knowledge of the Most High for ever and ever.* Ethiop Arab 1 Arm have a similar ending

r 15.1 Chapters 15 and 16 (except 15.57–59, which has been found in Greek) are extant only in Lat

s 15.4 Other ancient authorities add *and all who believe shall be saved by their faith*

t 15.13 Lat lacks *to grow*

u 15.19 Cn: Lat *shall empty*

v 15.24 Other ancient authorities read *God*

w 15.26 Other ancient authorities read *the Lord*

x 15.27 Other ancient authorities read *the Lord*

shall come out with many chariots, and from the day that they set out their hissing shall spread over the earth, so that all who hear them will fear and tremble. ³⁰Also the Carmonians, raging in wrath, shall go forth like wild boars^y from the forest, and with great power they shall come and engage them in battle, and with their tusks they shall devastate a portion of the land of the Assyrians with their teeth. ³¹And then the dragons,^z remembering their origin, shall become still stronger, and if they combine in great power and turn to pursue them, ³²then these shall be disorganized and silenced by their power and shall turn and flee.^a ³³And from the land of the Assyrians an enemy in ambush shall attack them and destroy one of them, and fear and trembling shall come upon their army and indecision upon their kings.

Judgment on Babylon

34 See the clouds from the east and from the north to the south! Their appearance is exceedingly threatening, full of wrath and storm. ³⁵They shall clash against one another and shall pour out a heavy tempest on the earth and their own tempest,^b and there shall be blood from the sword as high as a horse's belly ³⁶and a man's thigh and a camel's hock. ³⁷And there shall be fear and great trembling on the earth; those who see that wrath shall be horror-stricken, and they shall be seized with trembling. ³⁸After that, heavy storm clouds shall be stirred up from the south and from the north and another part from the west. ³⁹But the winds from the east shall prevail over the cloud that was^c raised in wrath and shall dispel it, and the tempest^d that was to cause destruction by the east wind shall be driven violently toward the south and west. ⁴⁰Great and mighty clouds full of wrath and tempest^e shall rise and destroy all the earth and its inhabitants and shall pour out upon every high and lofty place^f a terrible tempest,^g ⁴¹fire and hail and flying swords and floods of water, so that all the fields and all the streams shall

be filled with the abundance of those waters. ⁴²They shall destroy cities and walls, mountains and hills, trees of the forests, and grass of the meadows and their grain. ⁴³They shall go on steadily to Babylon and blot it out. ⁴⁴They shall come to it and surround it; they shall pour out on it the tempest^h and all its fury;ⁱ then the dust and smoke shall reach the sky, and all who are around it shall mourn for it. ⁴⁵And those who survive shall serve those who have destroyed it.

Judgment on Asia

46 And you, Asia, who share in the splendor of Babylon and the glory of her person, ⁴⁷woe to you, miserable wretch! For you have made yourself like her; you have decked out your daughters for prostitution to please and glory in your lovers, who have always lusted after you. ⁴⁸You have imitated that hateful one in all her deeds and devices.^j Therefore, God^k says, ⁴⁹I will send evils upon you: widowhood, poverty, famine, sword, and pestilence, bringing ruin to your houses, bringing destruction and death. ⁵⁰And the glory of your strength shall wither like a flower when the heat shall rise that is sent upon you. ⁵¹You shall be weakened like a wretched woman who is beaten and wounded, so that you cannot receive your mighty lovers. ⁵²Would I have dealt with you so violently, says the Lord, ⁵³if you had not killed my chosen people continually, exulting and clapping your hands and talking about their death when you were drunk?

54 Beautify your face! ⁵⁵The reward of a prostitute is in your lap; therefore you shall receive your recompense. ⁵⁶As you will do to my chosen people, says the Lord, so God will do to you and will hand you over to adversities. ⁵⁷Your children shall die of hunger, and you shall fall by the sword; your cities shall be wiped out, and all your people who are in the open country shall fall by the sword. ⁵⁸Those who are in the mountains and highlands^l shall perish of hunger, and they shall eat their own flesh in hunger for bread and drink their own blood in thirst for water. ⁵⁹Unhappy above all others, you shall

---

y 15.30 Other ancient authorities lack *like wild boars*
z 15.31 Cn: Lat *dragon*
a 15.32 Other ancient authorities read *turn their face to the north*
b 15.35 Meaning of Lat uncertain
c 15.39 Lat *that he*
d 15.39 Lat *star*
e 15.40 Lat *star*
f 15.40 Or *eminent person*
g 15.40 Lat *star*

h 15.44 Lat *star*
i 15.44 Other ancient authorities add *until they destroy it to its foundations*
j 15.48 Other ancient authorities read *devices, and you have followed after that one about to gratify her magnates and leaders so that you may be made proud and be pleased by her fornications*
k 15.48 Other ancient authorities read *the Lord*
l 15.58 Gk: Lat omits *and highlands*

come and suffer fresh miseries. ⁶⁰As they pass by they shall crush the hateful*ᵐ* city and shall destroy a part of your land and abolish a portion of your glory, when they return from devastated Babylon. ⁶¹You shall be broken down by them like stubble,*ⁿ* and they shall be like fire to you. ⁶²They shall devour you and your cities, your land and your mountains; they shall burn with fire all your forests and your fruitful trees. ⁶³They shall carry your children away captive, plunder your wealth, and mar the glory of your face.

Further Denunciations

16 Woe to you, Babylon and Asia! Woe to you, Egypt and Syria! ²Bind on sackcloth and cloth of goats' hair,*ᵒ* and wail for your children, and lament for them, for your destruction is at hand. ³The sword has been sent upon you, and who is there to turn it back? ⁴A fire has been sent upon you, and who is there to quench it? ⁵Calamities have been sent upon you, and who is there to drive them away? ⁶Can one drive off a hungry lion in the forest or quench a fire in the stubble once it has started to burn?*ᵖ* ⁷Can one turn back an arrow shot by a strong archer? ⁸The Lord God sends calamities, and who will drive them away? ⁹Fire will go forth from his wrath, and who is there to quench it? ¹⁰He will flash lightning, and who will not be afraid? He will thunder, and who will not be terrified? ¹¹The Lord will threaten, and who will not be utterly shattered at his presence? ¹²The earth and its foundations quake, the sea is churned up from the depths, and its waves and the fish with them shall be troubled at the presence of the Lord and the glory of his power. ¹³For his right hand that bends the bow is strong, and his arrows that he shoots are sharp, and when they are shot to the ends of the world they will not miss once. ¹⁴Calamities are sent forth and shall not return until they come over the earth. ¹⁵The fire is kindled and shall not be put out until it consumes the foundations of the earth. ¹⁶Just as an arrow shot by a mighty archer does not return, so the calamities that are sent upon the earth shall not return. ¹⁷Alas for me! Alas for me! Who will deliver me in those days?

The Horror of the Last Days

¹⁸The beginning of sorrows, when there shall be much lamentation; the beginning of famine, when many shall perish; the beginning of wars, when the powers shall be terrified; the beginning of calamities, when all shall tremble. ¹⁹What shall they do when the calamities come? ²⁰Famine and plague, tribulation and anguish are sent as scourges for the correction of humankind. ²¹Yet for all this they will not turn from their iniquities or ever be mindful of the scourges. ²²Indeed, provisions will be so cheap upon earth that people will imagine that peace is assured for them, and then calamities shall spring up on the earth—the sword, famine, and great confusion. ²³For many of those who live on the earth shall perish by famine, and those who survive the famine shall die by the sword. ²⁴And the dead shall be thrown out like dung, and there shall be no one to console them, for the earth shall be left desolate, and its cities shall be demolished. ²⁵No one shall be left to cultivate the earth or to sow it. ²⁶The trees shall bear fruit, but who will gather it? ²⁷The grapes shall ripen, but who will tread them? For in all places there shall be great solitude; ²⁸a person will long to see another human or even to hear a human voice. ²⁹For ten shall be left out of a city, and two out of the field, those who have hidden themselves in thick groves and clefts in the rocks. ³⁰Just as in an olive orchard three or four olives may be left on every tree, ³¹or just as, when a vineyard is gathered, some clusters may be left*q* by those who search carefully through the vineyard, ³²so in those days three or four shall be left by those who search their houses with the sword. ³³The earth shall be left desolate, and its fields shall be plowed up,*ʳ* and its roads and all its paths shall bring forth thorns, because no sheep will go along them. ³⁴Virgins shall mourn because they have no bridegrooms; women shall mourn because they have no husbands; their daughters shall mourn because they have no help. ³⁵Their bridegrooms shall be killed in war, and their husbands shall perish of famine.

God's People Must Prepare for the End

³⁶Listen now to these things, and understand them, you who are servants of the Lord.

---

m **15.60** Other ancient authorities read *idle* or *tranquil*
n **15.61** Other ancient authorities read *like dry straw*
o **16.2** Other ancient authorities lack *cloth of goats' hair*
p **16.6** Other ancient authorities read *fire when dry straw has been set on fire*

q **16.31** Other ancient authorities read *a cluster may remain exposed*
r **16.33** Other ancient authorities read *be for briers*

37 This is the word of the Lord; receive it and do not disbelieve what the Lord says.[s] 38 The calamities draw near and are not delayed. 39 Just as a pregnant woman, in the ninth month when the time of her delivery draws near, has great pains around her womb for two or three hours beforehand, but when the child comes forth from the womb, there will not be a moment's delay, 40 so the calamities will not delay in coming upon the earth, and the world will groan, and pains will seize it on every side.

41 Hear my words, O my people; prepare for battle, and in the midst of the calamities be like strangers on the earth. 42 Let the one who sells be like one who will flee; let the one who buys be like one who will lose; 43 let the one who does business be like one who will not make a profit; and let the one who builds a house be like one who will not live in it; 44 let the one who sows be like one who will not reap; so also the one who prunes the vines, like one who will not gather the grapes; 45 those who marry, like those who will have no children; and those who do not marry, like those who are widowed. 46 Because of this, those who labor, labor in vain, 47 for strangers shall gather their fruits and plunder their goods, overthrow their houses, and take their children captive, for in captivity and famine they will produce their children.[t] 48 Those who conduct business do so only to have it plundered; the more they adorn their cities, their houses and possessions, and their persons, 49 the more angry I will be with them for their sins, says the Lord. 50 Just as a respectable and virtuous woman abhors a prostitute, 51 so righteousness shall abhor iniquity when she decks herself out and shall accuse her to her face when he comes to defend the one who searches out every sin on earth.

The Power and Wisdom of God

52 Therefore do not be like her or her works. 53 For in a very short time iniquity will be removed from the earth, and righteousness will reign over us. 54 Sinners must not say that they have not sinned,[u] for coals of fire will burn on the head of everyone who says, "I have not

sinned before God and his glory." 55 The Lord[v] certainly knows everything that people do; he knows their imaginations and their thoughts and their hearts. 56 He said, "Let the earth be made," and it was made, and "Let the heaven be made," and it was made. 57 At his word the stars were fixed in their places, and he knows the number of the stars. 58 He searches the abyss and its treasures; he has measured the sea and its contents; 59 he has confined the sea in the midst of the waters;[w] and by his word he has suspended the earth over the water. 60 He has spread out the heaven like a dome and made it secure upon the waters; 61 he has put springs of water in the desert and pools on the tops of the mountains, so as to send rivers from the heights to water the earth. 62 He formed humans and put a heart in the midst of each body and gave each person breath and life and understanding 63 and the spirit[x] of Almighty God,[y] who surely made all things and searches out hidden things in hidden places. 64 He knows your imaginations and what you think in your hearts! Woe to those who sin and want to hide their sins! 65 The Lord will strictly examine all their works and will make a public spectacle of all of you. 66 You shall be put to shame when your sins come out before others, and your own iniquities shall stand as your accusers on that day. 67 What will you do? Or how will you hide your sins before the Lord and his glory? 68 Indeed, God[z] is the judge; fear him! Cease from your sins and forget your iniquities, never to commit them again, so God[a] will lead you forth and deliver you from all tribulation.

Impending Persecution of God's People

69 The burning wrath of a great multitude is kindled over you; they shall drag some of you away and force you to eat what was sacrificed to idols. 70 And those who consent to eat shall be held in derision and contempt and shall be trampled under foot. 71 For in many places[b] and in neighboring cities there shall be a great uprising against those who fear the Lord. 72 They

---

s 16.37 Cn: Lat *do not believe the gods of whom the Lord speaks*

t 16.47 Other ancient authorities read *therefore those who are married may know that they will produce children for captivity and famine*

u 16.54 Other ancient authorities add *or the unjust done injustice*

v 16.55 Other ancient authorities read *Lord God*

w 16.59 Other ancient authorities read *confined the world between the waters and the waters*

x 16.63 Or *breath*

y 16.63 Other ancient authorities read *of the Lord Almighty*

z 16.68 Other ancient authorities read *the Lord*

a 16.68 Other ancient authorities read *the Lord*

b 16.71 Meaning of Lat uncertain

shall*c* be like maniacs, sparing no one, but plundering and destroying those who continue to fear the Lord.*d* ⁷³For they shall destroy and plunder their goods and drive them out of house and home. ⁷⁴Then the tested quality of my elect shall be manifest, like gold that is tested by fire.

Promise of Divine Deliverance

75 Listen, my elect ones, says the Lord; the days of tribulation are at hand, but I will deliver you from them. ⁷⁶Do not fear or doubt, for God*e* is your guide. ⁷⁷You who keep my commandments and precepts, says the Lord God, must not let your sins weigh you down or your iniquities prevail over you. ⁷⁸Woe to those who are choked by their sins and overwhelmed by their iniquities! They are like a field choked with underbrush and its path*f* overwhelmed with thorns, so that no one can pass through. It is shut off and given up to be consumed by fire.

---

c **16.72** Other ancient authorities read *For people, because of their misfortunes, shall*

d **16.72** Other ancient authorities read *fear God*

e **16.76** Other ancient authorities read *the Lord*

f **16.78** Other ancient authorities read *seed*

4 MACCABEES

The Author's Definition of His Task

1 The subject that I am about to discuss is most philosophical, that is, whether pious reason is sovereign over the passions. So it is right for me to advise you to pay earnest attention to philosophy. ²For the subject is essential to everyone who is seeking knowledge, and in addition it includes the praise of the highest virtue—I mean, of course, rational judgment. ³If, then, it is evident that reason rules over those passions that hinder self-control, namely, gluttony and lust, ⁴it is also clear that it masters the passions that hinder one from justice, such as malice, and those that stand in the way of courage, namely, anger, fear, and pain. ⁵Some might perhaps ask, "If reason rules the passions, why is it not sovereign over forgetfulness and ignorance?" Their attempt at argument is ridiculous! ⁶For reason does not rule its own passions but those that are opposed to justice, courage, and self-control,[a] and it is not for the purpose of destroying them but so that one may not give way to them.

7 I could prove to you from many and various examples that reason[b] is absolute ruler over the passions, ⁸but I can demonstrate it best from the noble bravery of those who died for the sake of virtue: Eleazar and the seven brothers and their mother. ⁹All of these, by despising sufferings that bring death, demonstrated that reason controls the passions. ¹⁰On the anniversary of these events it is fitting for me to praise for their virtues those who, with their mother, died for the sake of nobility and goodness, and I would also call them blessed for the honor in which they are held. ¹¹All people, even their torturers, marveled at their courage and endurance, and they became the cause of the downfall of tyranny over their nation. By their endurance they conquered the tyrant, and thus their native land was purified through them. ¹²I shall shortly have an opportunity to speak of this, but, as my custom is, I shall begin by stating my main principle, and then I shall turn to their story, giving glory to the all-wise God.

The Supremacy of Reason

13 Our inquiry, accordingly, is whether reason is sovereign over the passions. ¹⁴We shall decide just what reason is and what passion is, how many kinds of passions there are, and whether reason rules over all these. ¹⁵Now reason is the mind that with sound logic prefers the life of wisdom. ¹⁶Wisdom, next, is the knowledge of divine and human matters and the causes of these. ¹⁷This, in turn, is education in the law, by which we learn divine matters reverently and human affairs to our advantage. ¹⁸Now the kinds of wisdom are rational judgment, justice, courage, and self-control. ¹⁹Rational judgment is supreme over all of these, since by means of it reason rules over the passions. ²⁰The two most comprehensive types of the passions are pleasure and pain, and each of these is by nature concerned with both body and soul. ²¹There are many sequences of passions with both pleasure and pain. ²²Thus desire precedes pleasure, and delight follows it. ²³Fear precedes pain, and sorrow comes after. ²⁴Anger, as a person will see by reflecting on this experience, is a passion embracing pleasure and pain. ²⁵In pleasure there exists even a malevolent tendency, which is the most complex of all the passions. ²⁶In the soul it is boastfulness, love of money, thirst for honor, rivalry, and malice; ²⁷in the body, indiscriminate eating, gluttony, and eating alone.

28 Just as pleasure and pain are two plants growing from the body and the soul, so there are many offshoots of these plants,[c] ²⁹each of

---

a **1.6** Other ancient authorities add *and rational judgment*

b **1.7** Other ancient authorities read *devout reason*

---

c **1.28** Another reading is *these passions*

which the master cultivator, reason, weeds and prunes and ties up and waters and thoroughly irrigates and so tames the jungle of habits and passions. [30] For reason is the guide of the virtues, but over the passions it is sovereign.

Observe now, first of all, that rational judgment is sovereign over the passions by virtue of the restraining power of self-control. [31] Self-control, then, is dominance over the desires. [32] Some desires belong to the soul, others to the body, and reason obviously rules over both. [33] Otherwise, how is it that when we are attracted to forbidden foods we abstain from the pleasure to be had from them? Is it not because reason is able to rule over appetites? I for one think so. [34] Therefore when we crave seafood and fowl and animals and all sorts of foods that are forbidden to us by the law, we abstain because of domination by reason. [35] For the passions of the appetites are restrained, checked by the temperate mind, and all the impulses of the body are bridled by reason.

Compatibility of the Law with Reason

2 And why is it amazing that the desires of the soul for the enjoyment of beauty are rendered powerless? [2] It is for this reason, certainly, that the temperate Joseph is praised, because by mental effort[d] he overcame the prospect of pleasure. [3] For when he was young and in his prime for intercourse, by reason he nullified the frenzy[e] of the passions. [4] Reason is proved to rule not only over the frenzied urge of sexual desire but also over every desire.[f] [5] Thus the law says, "You shall not covet your neighbor's wife or anything that is your neighbor's." [6] In fact, since the law has told us not to covet, I could prove to you all the more that reason is able to control desires.

Just so it is with the passions that hinder one from justice. [7] Otherwise how could it be that someone who is habitually a solitary eater, a glutton, or even a drunkard can learn a better way, unless reason is clearly lord of the passions? [8] Thus, as soon as one adopts a way of life in accordance with the law, even though a lover of money, one is forced to act contrary to natural ways and to lend without interest to those who plead for assistance and to cancel the debt when the seventh year arrives. [9] If one is greedy,

one is ruled by the law through reason so that one neither gleans the harvest nor gathers the last grapes from the vineyard.

In other matters we can recognize that reason rules the passions. [10] For the law prevails even over affection for parents, so that virtue is not abandoned for their sakes. [11] It overrules love for one's wife so that one rebukes her when she breaks the law. [12] It overrules love for children so that one punishes them for misdeeds. [13] It is sovereign over the relationship of friends so that one rebukes friends when they act wickedly. [14] Do not consider it paradoxical when reason, through the law, can prevail even over enmity. The fruit trees of the enemy are not cut down, but one preserves the property of enemies from marauders and helps raise up what has fallen.[g]

[15] It is evident that reason rules even[h] the more violent passions: lust for power, vanity, boasting, arrogance, and malice. [16] For the temperate mind repels all these malicious passions, just as it repels anger—for it is sovereign over even this. [17] When Moses was angry with Dathan and Abiram, he did nothing against them in anger but controlled his anger by reason. [18] For, as I have said, the temperate mind is able to get the better of the passions, to correct some and to render others powerless. [19] Why else did Jacob, our most wise father, censure the households of Simeon and Levi for their irrational slaughter of the entire tribe of the Shechemites, saying, "Cursed be their anger"? [20] For if reason could not control anger, he would not have spoken thus. [21] Now when God fashioned humans, he planted in them passions and inclinations, [22] but at the same time he enthroned the mind among the senses as a sacred governor over them all. [23] To the mind he gave the law, and one who lives subject to this will rule a kingdom that is temperate, just, good, and courageous.

[24] How is it then, one might say, that if reason is master of the passions, it does not control **3** forgetfulness and ignorance? [1] But this argument is entirely ridiculous, for it is evident that reason rules not over its own passions but over those of the body. [2] No one of us can eradicate that kind of desire, but reason can provide a way for us not to be enslaved by desire. [3] No one of you can eradicate anger from the mind, but reason can help to deal with anger. [4] No one of us can eradicate malice, but reason can fight at

---

d **2.2** Another ancient authority adds *in reasoning*

e **2.3** Gk *he swatted the gadfly*

f **2.4** Or *all covetousness*

g **2.14** Or *the beasts that have fallen*

h **2.15** Other ancient authorities read *through*

our side so that we are not overcome by malice. [5] For reason does not uproot the passions but is their antagonist.

King David's Thirst

[6] Now this can be explained more clearly by the story of King David's thirst. [7] David had been attacking the Philistines all day long and together with the soldiers of his nation had killed many of them. [8] Then when evening fell, he[i] came, sweating and quite exhausted, to the royal tent, around which the whole army of our ancestors had encamped. [9] Now all the rest were at dinner, [10] but the king was extremely thirsty, and though springs were plentiful there, he could not satisfy his thirst from them. [11] But a certain irrational desire for the water in the enemy's territory tormented and inflamed him, undid and consumed him. [12] When his guards complained bitterly because of the king's craving, two staunch young soldiers, respecting[j] the king's desire, armed themselves fully and taking a pitcher climbed over the enemy's ramparts. [13] Eluding the sentinels at the gates, they went searching throughout the enemy camp [14] and found the spring and from it boldly brought the king a drink. [15] But David,[k] though he was burning with thirst, considered it an altogether fearful danger to his soul to drink what was regarded as equivalent to blood. [16] Therefore, opposing reason to desire, he poured out the drink as an offering to God. [17] For the temperate mind can conquer the drives of the passions and quench the flames of frenzied desires; [18] it can overthrow bodily agonies even when they are extreme and by nobility of reason spurn all domination by the passions.

An Attempt on the Temple Treasury

[19] The present occasion now invites us to a narrative demonstration of temperate reason.

[20] At a time when our ancestors were enjoying profound peace because of their observance of the law and were prospering, so that even Seleucus Nicanor, king of Asia, had both appropriated money to them for the temple service and recognized their way of life—[21] just at that time certain persons attempted a revolution against the public harmony and caused many and various disasters.

4 Now there was a certain Simon, a political opponent of the noble and good man Onias, who then held the high priesthood for life. When, despite bringing charges against him on behalf of the nation, he was unable to injure Onias, he fled the country with the purpose of betraying it. [2] So he came to Apollonius, governor of Syria, Phoenicia, and Cilicia, and said, [3] "I have come here because I am loyal to the king's government, to report that in the Jerusalem treasuries there are deposited tens of thousands in private funds that are not the property of the temple but belong to King Seleucus." [4] When Apollonius learned the details of these things, he praised Simon for his service to the king and went up to Seleucus to inform him of the rich treasure. [5] On receiving authority to deal with this matter, he proceeded quickly to our country accompanied by the accursed Simon and a very strong military force. [6] He said that he had come with the king's authority to seize the private funds in the treasury. [7] The people indignantly protested his words, considering it outrageous that those who had committed deposits to the sacred treasury should be deprived of them, and did all that they could to prevent it. [8] But, uttering threats, Apollonius went on to the temple. [9] While the priests together with women and children were imploring God in the temple to shield the holy place that was being treated so contemptuously, [10] and while Apollonius was going up with his armed forces to seize the money, angels on horseback with lightning flashing from their weapons appeared from heaven, instilling in them great fear and trembling. [11] Then Apollonius fell down half-dead in the temple area that was open to all, stretched out his hands toward heaven, and with tears begged the Hebrews to pray for him and propitiate the wrath of the heavenly army. [12] For he said that he had committed a sin deserving of death and that if he were spared he would praise the blessedness of the holy place before all people. [13] Moved by these words, although otherwise cautious lest King Seleucus suppose that Apollonius had been overcome by human treachery and not by divine justice, the high priest Onias prayed for him. [14] So Apollonius,[l] having been saved beyond all expectations, went away to report to the king what had happened to him.

---

i **3.8** Other ancient authorities read *he hurried and*
j **3.12** Or *embarrassed because of*
k **3.15** Gk *he*

l **4.14** Gk *he*

Antiochus's Persecution of the Jews

15 When King Seleucus died, his son Antiochus Epiphanes succeeded to the throne, an arrogant and terrible man 16 who removed Onias from the priesthood and appointed Onias's*m* brother Jason as high priest. 17 Jason*n* agreed that if the office were conferred on him he would pay the king three thousand six hundred sixty talents annually. 18 So the king appointed him high priest and ruler of the nation. 19 Jason*o* changed the nation's customs and altered its form of government in complete violation of the law, 20 so that he not only constructed a gymnasium at the very citadel*p* of our native land but also abolished the temple service. 21 The divine justice was angered by these acts and caused Antiochus himself to make war on them. 22 For when he was warring against Ptolemy in Egypt, he heard that a rumor of his death had spread and that the people of Jerusalem had rejoiced greatly. He speedily marched against them, 23 and after he had ravaged them he issued a decree that if any of them were found observing the ancestral law they should die. 24 When, by means of his decrees, he had not been able in any way to put an end to the people's observance of the law but saw that all his threats and punishments were being disregarded, 25 even to the extent that women, because they had circumcised their sons, were thrown headlong from heights along with their infants, though they had known beforehand that they would suffer this, 26 when, I say, his decrees were despised by the people, he himself tried through torture to compel everyone in the nation to renounce Judaism by eating defiling foods.

Antiochus's Encounter with Eleazar

5 The tyrant Antiochus, sitting in state with his counselors on a certain high place and with his armed soldiers standing around him, 2 ordered the guards to seize each and every Hebrew and to compel them to eat pork and food sacrificed to idols. 3 If any were not willing to eat defiling food, they were to be broken on the wheel and killed. 4 When many persons had been rounded up, one*q* man, Eleazar by name, leader of the flock, was brought*r* before the king.

He was a man of priestly family, learned in the law, advanced in age, and known to many in the tyrant's court because of his long career.

5 When Antiochus saw him he said, 6 "Before I begin to torture you, old man, I would advise you to save yourself by eating pork, 7 for I respect your age and your gray hairs. Although you have had them for so long a time, it does not seem to me that you are a philosopher when you observe the religion of the Jews. 8 When nature has granted it to us, why should you abhor eating the very excellent meat of this animal? 9 It is senseless not to enjoy delicious things that are not shameful and wrong to spurn the gifts of nature. 10 It seems to me that you will do something even more senseless if, by holding a vain opinion concerning the truth, you continue to despise me to your own hurt. 11 Will you not awaken from your foolish philosophy, dispel the emptiness of your reasonings, adopt a mind appropriate to your years, philosophize according to the truth of what is beneficial, 12 and have compassion on your old age by honoring my humane advice? 13 For consider this: if there is some power watching over this religion of yours, it will excuse you from any transgression that arises out of compulsion."

14 When the tyrant urged him in this fashion to eat meat unlawfully, Eleazar asked to have a word. 15 When he had received permission to speak, he began to address the people as follows: 16 "We, O Antiochus, who have been persuaded to govern our lives by the divine law think that there is no compulsion more powerful than our obedience to the law. 17 Therefore we consider that we should not transgress it in any respect. 18 Even if, as you suppose, our law were not truly divine and we had wrongly held it to be divine, not even so would it be right for us to invalidate our reputation for piety. 19 Therefore do not suppose that it would be a petty sin if we were to eat defiling food; 20 to transgress the law in matters either small or great is of equal seriousness, 21 for in either case the law is equally despised. 22 You scoff at our philosophy as though living by it were irrational, 23 but it teaches us self-control, so that we master all pleasures and desires, and it also trains us in courage, so that we endure any suffering willingly; 24 it instructs us in justice, so that in all our dealings we give what is due;*s* and it teaches us piety, so that with

_____

m 4.16 Gk *his*
n 4.17 Gk *He*
o 4.19 Gk *He*
p 4.20 Or *high place*
q 5.4 Other ancient authorities add *Hebrew*
r 5.4 Or *was the first of the flock to be brought*

_____

s 5.24 Or *so that we hold in balance all our habitual inclinations* proper reverence we worship the only living God.

25 "Therefore we do not eat defiling food, for since we believe that the law was established by God, we know that the Creator of the world in giving us the law has shown sympathy toward us in accordance with nature. 26 He has permitted us to eat what will be most suitable for our lives,[t] but he has forbidden us to eat meats that would be contrary to this. 27 It would be tyrannical for you to compel us not only to transgress the law but also to eat in such a way that you may deride us for eating defiling foods, which are most hateful to us. 28 But you shall have no such occasion to laugh at me, 29 nor will I transgress the sacred oaths of my ancestors concerning the keeping of the law, 30 not even if you gouge out my eyes and burn my entrails. 31 I am not so old and cowardly as not to be young in reason on behalf of piety. 32 Therefore get your torture wheels ready and fan the fire more vehemently! 33 I do not so pity my old age as to overthrow the ancestral law by my own act. 34 I will not play false to you, O law that trained me, nor will I renounce you, beloved self-control. 35 I will not put you to shame, philosophical reason, nor will I reject you, honored priesthood and knowledge of the law. 36 You, O king,[u] shall not defile the honorable mouth of my old age nor my long life lived lawfully. 37 My ancestors will receive me as pure, as one who does not fear your violence even to death. 38 You will tyrannize the ungodly, but you shall not dominate my reasonings on behalf of piety, either by words or through deeds."

Martyrdom of Eleazar

6 When Eleazar in this manner had made eloquent response to the exhortations of the tyrant, the guards who were standing by dragged him violently to the instruments of torture. 2 First they stripped the old man, though he remained adorned with the gracefulness of his piety. 3 After they had tied his arms behind him, they flogged him from both sides, 4 while a herald who faced him cried out, "Obey the king's commands!" 5 But the courageous and noble man, like a true Eleazar,[v] was unmoved, as though being tortured in a dream, 6 yet while the old man's eyes were raised to heaven, his flesh was being torn by scourges, his blood flowing, and his sides were being cut to pieces. 7 Although he fell to the ground because his body could not endure the agonies, he kept his reason upright and unswerving. 8 One of the cruel guards rushed at him and began to kick him in the side to make him get up again after he fell. 9 But he bore the pains and scorned the punishment and endured the tortures. 10 Like a noble athlete the old man, while being beaten, was victorious over his torturers; 11 in fact, with his face bathed in sweat and gasping heavily for breath, he amazed even his torturers by his courageous spirit.

12 At that point, partly out of pity for his old age, 13 partly out of sympathy from their acquaintance with him, partly out of admiration for his endurance, some of the king's retinue came to him and said, 14 "Eleazar, why are you so irrationally destroying yourself through these evil things? 15 We will set before you some cooked meat; save yourself by pretending to eat pork."

16 But Eleazar, as though more bitterly tormented by this counsel, cried out, 17 "Never may we, the children of Abraham, think so basely that out of cowardice we feign a role unbecoming to us! 18 For it would be irrational if, having lived in accordance with truth up to old age and having guarded the reputation of a life lived lawfully, we should now change our course 19 and ourselves become a pattern of impiety to the young by setting them an example in the eating of defiling food. 20 It would be shameful if we should survive for a little while and during that time be a laughingstock to all for our cowardice 21 and be despised by the tyrant as unmanly by not contending even to death for our divine law. 22 Therefore, O children of Abraham, die nobly for the sake of piety! 23 And you, guards of the tyrant, why do you delay?"

24 When they saw that he was so courageous in the face of the afflictions and that he had not been changed by their compassion, the guards brought him to the fire. 25 There they burned him with maliciously contrived instruments, threw him down, and poured stinking liquids into his nostrils. 26 When he was now burned to his very bones and about to expire, he lifted up his eyes to God and said, 27 "You know, O God, that, though I might have saved myself, I am dying in burning torments for the sake of the law. 28 Be merciful to your people, and let our punishment suffice for them. 29 Make my blood

---

t 5.26 Or *souls*

u 5.36 Gk lacks *O king*

v 6.5 *Eleazar* means *God helps*

their purification, and take my life in exchange for theirs." ³⁰After he said this, the holy man died nobly in his tortures; even in the tortures of death he resisted, by virtue of reason, for the sake of the law.

31 Admittedly, then, pious reason is sovereign over the passions. ³²For if the passions had prevailed over reason, we would have testified to their domination. ³³But now that reason has conquered the passions, we properly attribute to it the power to govern. ³⁴It is right for us to acknowledge the dominance of reason when it masters even external agonies. It would be ridiculous to deny it.ʷ ³⁵I have proved not only that reason has mastered agonies but also that it masters pleasures and in no respect yields to them.

An Encomium on Eleazar

7 For like a most skillful pilot, the reason of our father Eleazar steered the ship of piety over the sea of the passions, ²and though buffeted by the stormings of the tyrant and overwhelmed by the mighty waves of tortures, ³in no way did he turn the rudder of piety until he sailed into the haven of immortal victory. ⁴No city besieged with many ingenious war machines has ever held out as did that most holy man. Although his sacred life was consumed by tortures and racks, he conquered the besiegers because reason was shielding his piety. ⁵For in setting his mind firm like a jutting cliff, our father Eleazar broke the maddening waves of the passions. ⁶O priest, worthy of the priesthood, you neither defiled your sacred teeth nor profaned your stomach, which had room only for reverence and purity, by eating defiling foods. ⁷O man in harmony with the law and philosopher of divine life! ⁸Such should be those who are administrators of the law, shielding it with their own blood and noble sweat in sufferings even to death. ⁹You, father, validated our obedience to the law through your endurance unto glory, and you did not abandon the holiness that you praised, but by your deeds you made your words of divineˣ philosophy credible. ¹⁰O aged man, more powerful than tortures; O elder, fiercer than fire; O supreme king over the passions, Eleazar! ¹¹For just as our father Aaron, armed with the censer, ran through the multitude of the people and conquered the fiery angel, ¹²so the descendant of Aaron, Eleazar, though being consumed by the fire, remained unmoved in his reason. ¹³Most amazing, indeed, though he was an old man, his body no longer tense and firm,ʸ his muscles flabby, his sinews feeble, he became young again ¹⁴in spirit through reason, and by reason like that of Isaac he rendered the many-headed rack ineffective. ¹⁵O man of blessed age and of venerable gray hair and of law-abiding life, whom the faithful seal of death has perfected!

16 If, therefore, because of piety an aged man despised tortures even to death, most certainly pious reason is governor of the passions. ¹⁷Some perhaps might say, "Not all have full command of their passions, because not all have prudent reason." ¹⁸But as many as attend to piety with a whole heart, these alone are able to control the passions of the flesh, ¹⁹since they believe that they, like our patriarchs Abraham and Isaac and Jacob, do not die to God but live to God. ²⁰No contradiction therefore arises when some persons appear to be dominated by their passions because of the weakness of their reason. ²¹What person who livesᶻ as a philosopher by the whole rule of philosophy and trusts in God ²²and knows that it is blessed to endure any suffering for the sake of virtue would not be able to overcome the passions through godliness? ²³For only the wiseᵃ and courageous are masters of their passions.

Seven Brothers Defy the Tyrant

8 For this is why even the very young, by following a philosophy in accordance with pious reason, have prevailed over the most painful instruments of torture. ²For when the tyrant was conspicuously defeated in his first attempt, being unable to compel an aged man to eat defiling foods, then in violent rage he commanded that others of the Hebrew captives be brought and that any who ate defiling food would be freed after eating, but if any were to refuse, they would be tortured even more cruelly.

3 When the tyrant had given these orders, seven brothers—handsome, modest, noble, and accomplished in every way—were brought before him along with their aged mother. ⁴When the tyrant saw them, grouped about their mother as though a chorus, he was pleased with

---

w 6.34 Syr: Meaning of Gk uncertain

x 7.9 Other ancient authorities lack *divine*

y 7.13 Gk *the tautness of the body already loosed*

z 7.21 Another ancient authority adds *piously*

a 7.23 Another ancient authority adds *prudent*

them. And struck by their appearance and nobility, he smiled at them and summoned them nearer and said, 5 "Young men, with favorable feelings I admire each and every one of you and greatly respect the beauty and the number of such brothers. Not only do I advise you not to display the same madness as that of the old man who has just been tortured, but I also exhort you to yield to me and enjoy my friendship. 6 Just as I am able to punish those who disobey my orders, so I can be a benefactor to those who are disposed to obey me. 7 Trust me, then, and you will receive positions of authority in my government if you will renounce the ancestral tradition of your national life. 8 Enjoy your youth by adopting the Greek way of life and by changing your manner of living. 9 But if by disobedience you rouse my anger, you will compel me to destroy each and every one of you with dreadful punishments through tortures. 10 Therefore take pity on yourselves. Even I, your enemy, have compassion for your youth and handsome appearance. 11 Will you not consider this, that if you disobey, nothing remains for you but to die on the rack?"

12 When he had said these things, he ordered the instruments of torture to be brought forward so as to persuade them out of fear to eat the defiling food. 13 When the guards had placed before them wheels and joint-dislocators, rack and hooks[b] and catapults and caldrons, braziers and thumbscrews and iron claws and wedges and bellows, the tyrant resumed speaking: 14 "Be afraid, young fellows; whatever justice you revere will be merciful to you when you transgress under compulsion."

15 But when they had heard the inducements and saw the dreadful devices, not only were they not afraid, but they also opposed the tyrant with their own philosophy and by their right reasoning nullified his tyranny. 16 Let us consider, on the other hand, what arguments might have been used if some of them had been cowardly and unmanly. Would they not have been the following? 17 "O wretches that we are and so senseless! Since the king has summoned and exhorted us to accept kind treatment if we obey him, 18 why do we take pleasure in vain resolves and venture upon a disobedience that brings death? 19 O men and brothers, should we not fear the instruments of torture and consider the threats of torments and give up this vanity

and this arrogance that threatens to destroy us? 20 Let us take pity on our youth and have compassion on our mother's age, 21 and let us seriously consider that if we disobey we are dead! 22 Also, divine justice will excuse us for fearing the king when we are under compulsion. 23 Why do we banish ourselves from this most pleasant life and deprive ourselves of this delightful world? 24 Let us not struggle against compulsion[c] or take hollow pride in being put to the rack. 25 Not even the law itself would consent to put us to death for fearing the instruments of torture. 26 Why does such contentiousness excite us and such a fatal stubbornness please us, when we can live in peace if we obey the king?"

27 But the youths, though about to be tortured, neither said any of these things nor even seriously considered them. 28 For they were contemptuous of the passions and sovereign over agonies, 29 so that as soon as the tyrant had ceased counseling them to eat defiling food, all with one voice together, as from one mind, said:

9 "Why do you delay, O tyrant? For we are ready to die rather than transgress our ancestral commandments; 2 we are obviously putting our forebears to shame unless we should practice ready obedience to the law and to Moses[d] our counselor. 3 Tyrant and counselor of lawlessness, in your hatred for us do not pity us more than we pity ourselves.[e] 4 For we consider this pity of yours, which ensures our safety through transgression of the law, to be more grievous than death itself. 5 You are trying to terrify us by threatening us with death by torture, as though a short time ago you learned nothing from Eleazar. 6 And if, on account of piety, the aged men of the Hebrews fulfilled their pious duty while enduring torture, it would be even more fitting that we young men should die despising your coercive tortures, which our aged instructor also overcame. 7 Therefore, tyrant, put us to the test, and if you take our lives because of our piety, do not suppose that you can injure us by torturing us. 8 For we, through this severe suffering and endurance, shall have the prizes of virtue and shall be with God, on whose account we suffer; 9 but you, because of your bloodthirstiness toward us, will deservedly undergo from the divine justice eternal torment by fire."

---

b 8.13 Meaning of Gk uncertain

c 8.24 Or *fate*
d 9.2 Other ancient authorities read *knowledge*
e 9.3 Meaning of Gk uncertain

The Torture of the First and Second Brothers

10 When they had said these things, the tyrant was not only indignant, as at those who are disobedient, but also infuriated, as at those who are ungrateful. 11 Then at his command the guards brought forward the eldest, and having torn off his tunic, they bound his hands and arms with straps on each side. 12 When they had worn themselves out beating him with scourges, without accomplishing anything, they placed him upon the wheel. 13 When the noble youth was stretched out around this, his limbs were dislocated, 14 and with every member disjointed he denounced the tyrant, saying, 15 "Most abominable tyrant, enemy of heavenly justice, savage of mind, you are mangling me in this manner not because I am a murderer or as one who acts impiously but because I protect the divine law." 16 And when the guards said, "Agree to eat so that you may be released from the tortures," 17 he replied, "You abominable lackeys, your wheel is not so powerful as to strangle my reason. Cut my limbs, burn my flesh, and twist my joints; 18 through all these tortures I will convince you that children of the Hebrews alone are invincible when virtue is at stake." 19 While he was saying these things, they spread fire under him, and while fanning the flames*f* they tightened the wheel further. 20 The wheel was completely smeared with blood, and the heap of coals was being quenched by the drippings of gore, and pieces of flesh were falling off the axles of the machine. 21 Although the ligaments joining his bones were already severed, the courageous youth, worthy of Abraham, did not groan, 22 but as though transformed by fire into immortality he nobly endured the rackings. 23 "Imitate me, brothers," he said. "Do not leave your post in my struggle*g* or renounce our courageous family ties. 24 Fight the sacred and noble battle for piety. Thereby the just Providence of our ancestors may become merciful to our nation and take vengeance on the accursed tyrant." 25 When he had said this, the devout youth broke the thread of life.

26 While all were marveling at his courageous spirit, the guards brought forward the next eldest, and after fitting themselves with iron gauntlets having sharp hooks, they bound him to the torture machine and catapult. 27 Before torturing him, they inquired if he were willing to eat, and they heard his noble decision. 28 These leopard-like beasts tore out his sinews with the iron hands, flayed all his flesh up to his chin, and tore away his scalp. But he steadfastly endured this agony and said, 29 "How sweet is any kind of death for our ancestral piety!" 30 To the tyrant he said, "Do you not think, you most savage tyrant, that you are being tortured more than I, as you see the arrogant design of your tyranny being defeated by our endurance for the sake of piety? 31 I lighten my pain by the joys that come from virtue, 32 but you suffer torture by the threats that come from impiety. You will not escape, you most abominable tyrant, the penalties of the divine wrath."

The Torture of the Third and Fourth Brothers

10 When he, too, had endured a glorious death, the third was brought forward, and many repeatedly urged him to save himself by tasting the meat. 2 But he shouted, "Do you not know that the same father begot me as well as those who died and the same mother bore me and that I was brought up on the same teachings? 3 I do not renounce the noble kinship that binds me to my brothers."*h* 5 Enraged by the man's boldness, they disjointed his hands and feet with their instruments, dismembering him by prying his limbs from their sockets, 6 and breaking his fingers and arms and legs and elbows. 7 Since they were unable in any way to break his spirit,*i* they abandoned the instruments*j* and scalped him with their fingernails in a Scythian fashion. 8 They immediately brought him to the wheel, and while his vertebrae were being dislocated by this, he saw his own flesh torn all around and drops of blood flowing from his entrails. 9 When he was about to die, he said, 10 "We, most abominable tyrant, are suffering because of our godly training and virtue, 11 but you, because of your impiety and bloodthirstiness, will undergo unceasing torments."

12 When he, too, had died in a manner worthy of his brothers, they dragged forward the fourth, saying, 13 "As for you, do not give way to the same insanity as your brothers, but obey the king and save yourself." 14 But he said to them,

---

f **9.19** Meaning of Gk uncertain

g **9.23** Other ancient authorities read *post forever*

h **10.3** Other ancient authorities add 10.4, *So if you have any instrument of torture, apply it to my body; for you cannot touch my soul, even if you wish."*

i **10.7** Gk *to strangle him*

j **10.7** Other ancient authorities read *they tore off his skin*

"You do not have a fire hot enough to make me play the coward. [15]No, by the blessed death of my brothers, by the eternal destruction of the tyrant, and by the everlasting[k] life of the pious, I will not renounce our noble family ties. [16]Contrive tortures, tyrant, so that you may learn from them that I am a brother to those who have just now been tortured." [17]When he heard this, the bloodthirsty, murderous, and utterly abominable Antiochus gave orders to cut out his tongue. [18]But he said, "Even if you remove my organ of speech, God hears also those who are mute. [19]See, here is my tongue; cut it off, for in spite of this you will not make our reason speechless. [20]Gladly, for the sake of God, we let our bodily members be mutilated. [21]God will visit you swiftly, for you are cutting out a tongue that has been melodious with divine hymns."

The Torture of the Fifth and Sixth Brothers

11 When he, too, died, after being cruelly tortured, the fifth leaped up, saying, [2]"I will not refuse, tyrant, to be tortured for the sake of virtue. [3]I have come of my own accord so that by murdering me you will incur punishment from the heavenly justice for even more crimes. [4]Hater of virtue, hater of humankind, for what act of ours are you destroying us in this way? [5]Is it because[l] we revere the Creator of all things and live according to his virtuous law? [6]But these deeds deserve honors, not tortures."[m] [9]While he was saying these things, the guards bound him and dragged him to the catapult; [10]they tied him to it on his knees, and fitting iron clamps on them, they twisted his back[n] around the wedge on the wheel,[o] so that he was completely curled back like a scorpion, and all his members were disjointed. [11]In this condition, gasping for breath and in anguish of body, [12]he said, "Tyrant, they are splendid favors that you grant us against your will, because through these noble sufferings you give us an opportunity to show our endurance for the law."

[13]When he, too, had died, the sixth, a mere boy, was led forward. When the tyrant inquired whether he was willing to eat and be released, he said, [14]"I am younger in age than my brothers, but I am their equal in mind. [15]Since to this end we were born and bred, we ought likewise to die for the same principles. [16]So if you intend to torture me for not eating defiling foods, go on torturing!" [17]When he had said this, they led him to the wheel. [18]He was carefully stretched tight upon it, his back was broken, and he was roasted from underneath. [19]To his back they applied sharp spits that had been heated in the fire and pierced his ribs so that his entrails were burned through. [20]While being tortured he said, "O contest befitting holiness, in which so many of us brothers have been summoned to an arena of sufferings for the sake of piety and in which we have not been defeated! [21]For pious knowledge, O tyrant, is invincible. [22]I also, equipped with nobility, will die with my brothers, [23]and I myself will bring a great avenger upon you, you inventor of tortures and enemy of those who are truly pious. [24]We six boys have overthrown your tyranny. [25]Since you have not been able to persuade us to change our mind or to force us to eat defiling foods, is not this your downfall? [26]Your fire is cold to us, and the catapults painless, and your violence powerless. [27]For it is not the guards of the tyrant but those of the divine law that are set over us; therefore we hold fast to invincible reason."

The Torture of the Seventh Brother

12 When he, too, thrown into the caldron, had died a blessed death, the seventh and youngest of all came forward. [2]Even though the tyrant had been vehemently reproached by the brothers, he felt strong compassion for this child when he saw that he was already in fetters. He summoned him to come nearer and tried to persuade him, saying, [3]"You see the result of your brothers' stupidity, for they died in torments because of their disobedience. [4]You, too, if you do not obey, will be miserably tortured and die before your time, [5]but if you yield to persuasion you will be my friend and a leader in the government of the kingdom." [6]When he had thus appealed to him, he sent for the boy's mother to show compassion on her who had been bereaved of so many sons and to influence her to persuade the surviving son to obey and save himself. [7]But after his mother had exhorted him in the Hebrew language, as we shall tell a

---

k 10.15 Another ancient authority reads *celebrated*

l 11.5 Other ancient authorities read *Or does it seem evil to you that*

m 11.6 Other authorities add 11.7 and 8, [7]*If you but understood human feelings and had hope of salvation from God—*[8]*but, as it is, you are a stranger to God and make war against those who serve him.*

n 11.10 Gk *loins*

o 11.10 Meaning of Gk uncertain

little later, [8]he said, "Let me loose, let me speak to the king and to all his Friends who are with him." [9]Extremely pleased by the boy's declaration, they freed him at once. [10]Running to the nearest of the braziers, [11]he said, "You profane tyrant, most impious of all the wicked, since you have received good things and also your kingdom from God, were you not ashamed to murder his servants and torture on the wheel the athletes of piety? [12]Because of this, justice[p] has laid up for you a more intense and eternal fire and tortures, and these throughout all time will never let you go. [13]As a man, were you not ashamed, you most savage beast, to cut out the tongues of people who have feelings like yours and are made of the same elements as you and to maltreat and torture them in this way? [14]Surely they by dying nobly fulfilled their pious duty to God, but you will wail bitterly for having killed without cause the contestants for virtue." [15]Then because he, too, was about to die, he said, [16]"I do not desert the excellent example[q] of my brothers, [17]and I call on the God of our ancestors to be merciful to our nation,[r] [18]but on you he will take vengeance both in this present life and when you are dead." [19]After he had uttered these imprecations, he flung himself into the braziers and so ended his life.[s]

Reason's Sovereignty in the Seven

13 Since, then, the seven brothers despised sufferings even unto death, everyone must concede that pious reason is sovereign over the passions. [2]For if they had been slaves to their passions and had eaten defiling food, we would say that they had been conquered by these passions. [3]But in fact it was not so. Instead, by reason, which is praised before God, they prevailed over their passions. [4]The supremacy of the mind over these cannot be overlooked, for the brothers[t] mastered both passions and pains. [5]How, then, can one fail to confess the sovereignty of right reason over passion in those who were not turned back by fiery agonies? [6]For just as towers jutting out over harbors hold back the threatening waves and make it calm for those who sail into the inner basin, [7]so the seven-towered right reason of the youths, by fortifying the harbor of

piety, conquered the tempest of the passions. [8]For they constituted a holy chorus of piety and emboldened one another, saying, [9]"Brothers, let us die like brothers for the sake of the law; let us imitate the three youths in Assyria who despised the same ordeal[u] of the furnace. [10]Let us not be cowardly in the demonstration of our piety." [11]While one said, "Courage, brother," another said, "Bear up nobly," [12]and another reminded them, "Remember whence you came, and the father by whose hand Isaac would have submitted to being slain for the sake of piety." [13]Each of them and all of them together looking at one another, cheerful and undaunted, said, "Let us with all our hearts consecrate ourselves to God, who gave us our lives,[v] and let us use our bodies as a bulwark for the law. [14]Let us not fear him who thinks he is killing us, [15]for great is the soul's contest and the danger of eternal torment lying before those who transgress the commandment of God. [16]Therefore let us put on the full armor of mastery of the passions that divine reason provides. [17]For if we so die,[w] Abraham and Isaac and Jacob will welcome us, and all the fathers will praise us." [18]Those who were left behind said to each of the brothers who were being dragged away, "Do not put us to shame, brother, or betray the brothers who have died before us."

[19]You are not ignorant of the affection of family ties, which the divine and all-wise Providence has bequeathed through the fathers to their descendants and which was implanted in the mother's womb. [20]There the brothers spent the same length of time and were shaped during the same period of time, and growing from the same blood and through the same life, they were brought to the light of day. [21]When they were born after an equal time of gestation, they drank milk from the same fountains. From such embraces brotherly loving souls are nourished, [22]and they grow stronger from this common nurture and daily companionship and from both general education and our discipline in the law of God.

[23]Therefore, when sympathy and brotherly affection had been so established, the seven brothers were the more sympathetic to one another. [24]Since they had been educated by the same law and trained in the same virtues and

---

p 12.12 Another ancient authority reads *divine justice*
q 12.16 Other ancient authorities read *the witness*
r 12.17 Other ancient authorities read *my people*
s 12.19 Gk *and so gave up*
t 13.4 Gk *they*

---

u 13.9 Cn: Gk *citizen rights*
v 13.13 Or *souls*
w 13.17 Other ancient authorities read *suffer*

brought up together in right living, they loved one another all the more. 25 A common zeal for nobility strengthened their goodwill toward one another and their concord, 26 because they could make their brotherly love more fervent with the aid of piety. 27 But although nature and companionship and virtuous habits had augmented the affection of family ties, those who were left endured for the sake of piety, watching their brothers being maltreated and tortured to death.

14 Furthermore, they encouraged them to face the torture so that they not only despised their agonies but also mastered the passions of brotherly love.

2 O reason,[x] more royal than kings and freer than the free! 3 O sacred harmony of the seven brothers, well-tuned in regard to piety! 4 None of the seven youths proved coward or shrank from death, 5 but all of them, as though running the course toward immortality, hastened to death by torture. 6 Just as the hands and feet are moved in harmony with the guidance of the mind, so those holy youths, as though moved by an immortal spirit of piety, agreed to go to death for its sake. 7 O most holy seven, brothers in harmony! For just as the seven days of creation move in choral dance around piety, 8 so these youths, forming a chorus of seven,[y] encircled the fear of tortures and dissolved it. 9 Even now, we ourselves shudder as we hear of the suffering of these young men; they not only saw what was happening, not only heard the direct word of threat, but also bore the sufferings steadfastly, and in agonies of fire at that. 10 What could be more excruciatingly painful than this? For the power of fire is intense and swift, and it consumed their bodies quickly.

An Encomium on the Mother of the Seven

11 Do not consider it amazing that reason had full command over these men in their tortures, since even the mind of woman despised more diverse agonies, 12 for the mother of the seven young men bore up under the rackings of each one of her children.

13 Observe how complex is a mother's love for her children, which draws everything toward a sympathy felt in her inmost parts. 14 Even unreasoning animals, as well as humans, have a sympathy and parental love for their offspring.

15 For example, among birds, the ones that are tame protect their young by building on the housetops, 16 and the others, by building at the tops of mountains and the depths of chasms, in holes of trees, and on treetops, hatch the nestlings and ward off the intruder. 17 If they are not able to keep the intruder[z] away, they do what they can to help their young by flying in circles around them in the anguish of love, warning them with their own calls. 18 And why is it necessary to demonstrate sympathy for children by the example of unreasoning animals, 19 since even bees at the time for making honeycombs defend themselves against intruders and, as though with an iron dart, sting those who approach their hive and defend it even to the death? 20 But sympathy for her children did not sway the mother of the young men; she was of the same mind as Abraham.

15 O reason of the children, tyrant over the passions! O piety, more desirable to the mother than her children! 2 Two courses were open to this mother, that of piety and that of preserving her seven sons for a time, as the tyrant had promised. 3 She loved piety more, the piety that preserves them for eternal life according to God's promise.[a] 4 In what manner might I express the passions of parents who love their children? We impress upon the character of a small child a wondrous likeness both of mind and of form. Especially is this true of mothers, who because of their birth pangs have a deeper sympathy toward their offspring than do the fathers. 5 For to the extent that mothers are of tender spirit and bear more children, so much the more attached are they to their children. 6 The mother of the seven boys, more than any other mother, loved her children. In seven pregnancies she had implanted in herself tender love toward them, 7 and because of the many pains she suffered with each of them she had sympathy for them, 8 yet because of the fear of God she disdained the temporary safety of her children. 9 Not only so, but also because of the nobility of her sons and their ready obedience to the law, she felt a greater tenderness toward them. 10 For they were just and self-controlled and courageous and magnanimous and loved their brothers and their mother so that they obeyed her even to death in keeping the ordinances.

---

x 14.2 Or *O minds*
y 14.8 Meaning of Gk uncertain

z 14.17 Gk *it*
a 15.3 Gk *according to God*

11 Nevertheless, though so many factors influenced the mother to suffer with them out of love for her children, in the case of none of them were the various tortures strong enough to pervert her reason. 12 But each child separately and all of them together the mother urged on to death for piety's sake. 13 O sacred nature, parental affection, tender love toward offspring, nursing, and indomitable maternal passions! 14 This mother, who saw them tortured and burned one by one, for piety's sake did not change her attitude. 15 She watched the flesh of her children being consumed by fire, their toes and fingers scattered[b] on the ground, and the flesh of the head to the chin exposed like masks.

16 O mother, tried now by more bitter pains than even the birth pangs you suffered for them! 17 O woman, who alone gave birth to such perfect piety! 18 Neither when the firstborn breathed his last, it did not turn you aside, nor when the second in torments looked at you piteously nor when the third expired, 19 nor did you weep when you looked at the eyes of each one in his tortures gazing boldly at the same agonies and saw in their nostrils the signs of the approach of death. 20 When you saw the flesh of children burned[c] upon the flesh of other children, severed hands upon hands, scalped heads upon heads, and corpses fallen on other corpses, and when you saw the place filled with many spectators because of the children's torments, you did not shed tears. 21 Neither the melodies of sirens nor the songs of swans attract the attention of their hearers as did the voices of the children in torture calling to their mother. 22 How great and how many torments the mother then suffered as her sons were tortured on the wheel and with the hot irons! 23 But pious reason, giving her heart a man's courage in the very midst of her passions, strengthened her to disregard, for the time, her parental love.

24 Although she witnessed the destruction of seven children and the ingenious and various rackings, this noble mother disregarded all these[d] because of faith in God. 25 For as in the council chamber of her own soul she saw mighty advocates—nature, family, parental love, and the instruments of torture awaiting her children—26 this mother held two ballots, one bearing death and the other deliverance for her children. 27 She did not approve the deliverance that would preserve the seven sons for a short time, 28 but as the daughter of God-fearing Abraham she remembered his fortitude.

29 O mother of the nation, vindicator of the law, and defender of piety who carried away the prize of the contest in your heart! 30 O more noble than males in steadfastness and more courageous than men in endurance! 31 Just as Noah's ark, carrying the world in the universal flood, stoutly endured the waves, 32 so you, O guardian of the law, overwhelmed from every side by the flood of your passions and the violent winds—the torture of your sons—endured nobly and withstood the wintry storms raging on piety's account.

16 If, then, a woman advanced in years and mother of seven sons endured seeing her children tortured to death, it must be admitted that pious reason is sovereign over the passions. 2 Thus I have demonstrated not only that men have ruled over the passions but also that a woman has despised the fiercest tortures. 3 The lions surrounding Daniel were not so savage nor was the raging fiery furnace of Mishael so intensely hot as was her innate parental love consuming her as she saw her seven sons tortured in such varied ways. 4 But the mother quenched so many and such great passions by pious reason.

5 Consider this also: If this woman, though a mother, had been fainthearted, she would have mourned over them and perhaps spoken as follows: 6 "O how wretched am I and thrice-wretched over and over! After bearing seven children, I am now the mother of none! 7 O seven childbirths all in vain, seven profitless pregnancies, fruitless nurturings and wretched nursings! 8 In vain, my sons, I endured many birth pangs for you and the more grievous anxieties of your upbringing. 9 Alas for my children, some unmarried, others married and without offspring.[e] I shall not see your children or have the happiness of being called grandmother. 10 Alas, I who had so many and beautiful children am a widow and alone, with many sorrows.[f] 11 And when I die, I shall have none of my sons to bury me."

12 Yet that holy and God-fearing mother did not wail with such a lament for any of them,

---

b 15.15 Or *quivering*

c 15.20 Other ancient authorities read *the amputated flesh of children*

d 15.24 Other ancient authorities read *having bidden them farewell, surrendered them*

e 16.9 Gk *without benefit*

f 16.10 Or *much to be pitied*

nor did she dissuade any of them from dying, nor did she grieve as they were dying. [13]On the contrary, as though having a mind like adamant and giving rebirth for immortality to the whole number of her sons, she implored them and urged them on to death for the sake of piety. [14]O mother, soldier of God in the cause of piety, elder and woman! By steadfastness you have conquered even a tyrant, and in word and deed you have proved more powerful than a man. [15]For when you and your sons were arrested together, you stood and watched Eleazar being tortured and said to your sons in the Hebrew language, [16]"My sons, noble is the contest to which you are called to bear witness for the nation. Fight zealously for our ancestral law. [17]For it would be shameful if, while an aged man endures such agonies for the sake of piety, you young men were to be terrified by tortures. [18]Remember that it is through God that you have had a share in the world and have enjoyed life, [19]and therefore you ought to endure every suffering for the sake of God. [20]For his sake also our father Abraham was zealous to sacrifice his son Isaac, the ancestor of our nation, and when Isaac saw his father's hand wielding a knife[g] and descending upon him, he did not cower. [21]Daniel the righteous was thrown to the lions, and Hananiah, Azariah, and Mishael were hurled into the fiery furnace and endured it for the sake of God. [22]You, too, must show the same faithfulness toward God and not be grieved. [23]It is unreasonable for people who have knowledge of piety not to withstand pain."

[24]By these words the mother of the seven encouraged and persuaded each of her sons to die rather than violate God's commandment. [25]They knew also that those who die for the sake of God live to God, as do Abraham and Isaac and Jacob and all the patriarchs.

17 Some of the guards said that when she also was about to be seized and put to death she threw herself into the flames so that no one might touch her body.

[2]O mother, who with your seven sons nullified the violence of the tyrant, frustrated his evil designs, and showed the nobility of your faith! [3]Nobly set like a roof on the pillars of your sons, you held firm and unswerving against the earthquake of the tortures. [4]Take courage, therefore, O holy-minded mother, maintaining firm an enduring hope in God. [5]The moon in heaven with the stars is not so majestic as you, who, after lighting the way of your star-like seven sons to piety, stand in honor before God and are firmly set in heaven with them. [6]For your children were true descendants of father Abraham.[h]

The Effect of the Martyrdoms

[7]If it were possible for us to paint the history of your piety as an artist might, would not those who beheld it shudder as they saw the mother of the seven children enduring their varied tortures to death for the sake of piety? [8]Indeed, it would be proper to inscribe on their tomb these words as a reminder to the people of our nation:[i]

[9]"Here lie buried an aged priest and an aged woman and seven children because of the violence of the tyrant who wished to destroy the way of life of the Hebrews. [10]They vindicated their nation, looking to God and enduring torture even to death."

[11]Truly the contest in which they were engaged was divine, [12]for on that day virtue gave the awards and tested them for their endurance. The prize was immortality in endless life. [13]Eleazar was the first contestant, the mother of the seven sons entered the competition, and the brothers contended. [14]The tyrant was the antagonist, and the world and the human race were the spectators. [15]Reverence for God was victor and gave the crown to its own athletes. [16]Who did not admire the athletes of the divine[j] legislation? Who were not amazed?

[17]The tyrant himself and all his council marveled at their endurance, [18]because of which they now stand before the divine throne and live the life of eternal blessedness. [19]For Moses says, "All who are consecrated are under your hands." [20]These, then, who have been consecrated for the sake of God are honored not only with this honor but also by the fact that because of them our enemies did not rule over our nation, [21]the tyrant was punished, and the homeland purified—they having become, as it were, a ransom for the sin of our nation. [22]And through the blood of those pious ones and their death as an atoning sacrifice, divine

---

g 16.20 Gk *sword*

h 17.6 Gk *For your childbearing was from Abraham the father*; other ancient authorities read *For . . . Abraham the servant*

i 17.8 Or *as a memorial to the heroes of our people*

j 17.16 Other ancient authorities read *true*

Providence preserved Israel that previously had been mistreated.

23 For the tyrant Antiochus, when he saw the courage of their virtue and their endurance under the tortures, proclaimed their endurance to his soldiers as an example, 24 and this made them high-minded and courageous for infantry battle and siege, and he ravaged and conquered all his enemies.

18 O Israelite children, offspring of the seed of Abraham, obey this law and exercise piety in every way, 2 knowing that pious reason is master of the passions, not only of sufferings from within but also of those from without.

3 Therefore those who gave over their bodies in suffering for the sake of piety were not only admired by mortals but also were deemed worthy to share in a divine inheritance. 4 Because of them the nation gained peace, and by reviving observance of the law in the homeland they ravaged the enemy. 5 The tyrant Antiochus was both punished on earth and is being chastised after his death. Since in no way whatever was he able to compel the Israelites to adopt foreign ways and to abandon their ancestral customs, he left Jerusalem and marched against the Persians.

The Mother's Address to Her Children

6 The mother of seven sons expressed also these principles to her children: 7 "I was a pure virgin and did not go outside my father's house, but I guarded the rib from which woman was made.[k] 8 No seducer corrupted me on a desert plain, nor did the destroyer, the deceitful serpent, defile the purity of my virginity. 9 In the time of my maturity I remained with my husband, and when these sons had grown up their father died. A fortunate man was he, who lived out his life with good children and did not have the grief of bereavement. 10 While he was still with you, he taught you the Law and the Prophets. 11 He read to you about Abel slain by Cain and Isaac who was offered as a burnt offering and about Joseph in prison. 12 He told you of the zeal of Phinehas, and he taught you about Hananiah, Azariah, and Mishael in the fire. 13 He praised Daniel in the den of the lions and blessed him. 14 He reminded you of the scripture of Isaiah, which says, 'Even though you go through the fire, the flame shall not consume you.' 15 He sang to you songs of the psalmist David, who said, 'Many are the afflictions of the righteous.' 16 He recounted to you Solomon's proverb, 'There[l] is a tree of life for those who do his will.' 17 He confirmed the query of Ezekiel, 'Shall these dry bones live?' 18 For he did not forget to teach you the song that Moses taught, which says, 19 'I kill, and I make alive; this is your life and the length of your days.' "

20 O bitter was that day—and yet not bitter—when that bitter tyrant of the Greeks quenched fire with fire in his cruel caldrons and in his burning rage brought those seven sons of the daughter of Abraham to the catapult and back again to more[m] tortures, 21 pierced the pupils of their eyes and cut out their tongues, and put them to death with various tortures. 22 For these crimes divine justice pursued and will pursue the accursed tyrant. 23 But the sons of Abraham with their victorious mother are gathered together into the chorus of the fathers and have received pure and immortal souls from God, 24 to whom be glory forever and ever. Amen.

---
k **18.7** Gk *the rib that was built*

l **18.16** Or *He*

m **18.20** Other ancient authorities read *to all his*

ABBREVIATIONS

The Apocryphal/Deuterocanonical Book Abbreviations:

Tobit	Tob	Bel and the Dragon	Bel
Judith	Jdt	1 Maccabees	1 Macc
Esther (Greek)	Add Esth	2 Maccabees	2 Macc
Wisdom of Solomon	Wis	1 Esdras	1 Esd
Sirach	Sir	Prayer of Manasseh	Pr Man
Baruch	Bar	Psalm 151	Ps 151
Letter of Jeremiah	Let Jer	3 Maccabees	3 Macc
Azariah and the Three Jews	Song of Thr	2 Esdras	2 Esd
Susanna	Sus	4 Maccabees	4 Macc

The following abbreviations are used in the NRSVue *text notes.*

Arab	Arabic
Arm	Armenian
Cn	Correction; provides the most probable reconstruction of the original text where the text has suffered in transmission and the versions provide no satisfactory restoration
Ethiop	Ethiopic
Georg	Georgian
Gk	Greek
Heb	Hebrew
Jerome	Jerome's Latin translation of Psalms based on the Hebrew
Lat	Latin
ms(s)	manuscript(s)
OL	Old Latin
Q	Qumran
S	Codex Sinaiticus
Syr	Syriac Version of the Old Testament
Vg	Vulgate